0   ¼   ½   ¾   1 mile

GRASSMERE 287 acres

BEL AIR MILLS

EVENINGSIDE

MORNINGSIDE

O. Benedict

J. E. Merrill

T. Allen MAPLEHURST

E. H. Kellogg

P. Toohey SCHOOL
T. Sullivan

Wm Murphy
R.R. Co.

H. Noble
A. Rice
A. C. Morse
A. Rice
H. C. Ha

F. C. Peck

MORNINGSIDE

M. Killian

KUNKAMET ST.

Burn
Pierce

PITTSFIELD P.O.

Mrs. Stearns
J. H. Mooney
P. Manen

G. Fuller
Mrs. Burlingham
Bryant
F. Hubbard
F. C. Peck
J. Herrick
Nash

S. A. Goodell

SILVER LAKE

BEAVER ST.

J. Morgan

GOODRICH POND

C. A. Read
C. Read
E. Davis
J. Ryder
W. Martin
J. Bartlett
J. Coe

BERKSHIRE
PLEASURE
PARK

Mrs. W. Pollock

Fius
Pen
C. A. Read
T. Parker
G. Parker
R. Pomeroy Foe

J. Foote

R. Davis

M. C. Tracy
SCHOOL

W. R. Spra
H. Eldridge

Mr.
A. W.
M. K.

Cole

J. Bernard

H. Herrick

E. Learned
W. C. Backus
E. Learned

T. E. Johnson

C. Barrett
E. Spencer

J. S. Barrett
C. Strong
G. W. Spragu
wet

J. N. Dunham

S. Warren
Mrs. Hamilton

S. Sprague
Wm. Sprague
J. H. Wright

Res.

J. H. Noble

D. Sprague

J. Chency
C. Miller

Sacketts Br.
J.

NIC

C. H. Wakefield
W. Warren
S. Warren
H. Dellwood
J. R. Morewood

HOUSATONIC

RIVER

G. Willis
SCHOOL

R. Pomeroy
J. Kernochan

Mrs. E. C. Warner

J. Carver
C. G. Leslie

SOUTH ST.

MELVILLE LAKE

Mrs. D. D. Booth

J. Foote

R.R.

Mrs. M. Coe

A. B. Sikes
Br.

Sykes
SCHOOL
J. Picket

G. Brown

E. Hubbard
S. Clarke

H. B. Sikes

A. R. Sikes

Luce
Carey

Melville Est.
R. Lathers

Res.

J. C. Gaylord
R. Lathers

J. C. McL

B. S. Sh
arry

E. J. Humphrey

E. J. Parker
R. Lathers

M. E

*

THE MELVILLE LOG

*

JAY LEYDA

THE MELVILLE LOG

A Documentary Life of Herman Melville

1819-1891

VOLUME TWO

HARCOURT, BRACE AND COMPANY, NEW YORK

PS
2386
.L4
v. 2

Contents

[v]

List of Plates

[*vii*]

PLATES

ALLAN MELVILL, a portrait by Ezra Ames, ca. 1820

[PLATE I]

Maria Melvill, a portrait by Ezra Ames, ca. 1820

[PLATE II]

[PLATE III]

GANSEVOORT MELVILLE,
a miniature by an
unknown Albany artist,
painted 13 June 1836

"TOBY"—
RICHARD TOBIAS GREENE,
a daguerreotype taken
in Buffalo, 1846

The *Acushnet* passing Gay-Head

[PLATE IV] Water-color drawings made by HENRY M. JOHNSON, boat-steerer, on the second voyage of the *Acushnet*, before his death on 24 December 1847.

The boats of the *Acushnet* chasing whales

[PLATE V]

LEMUEL SHAW, Chief Justice
of Massachusetts,
a daguerreotype by
Southworth & Hawes,
Boston, 1851

ELIZABETH SHAW MELVILLE, &
MALCOLM,
a daguerreotype, 1849

[PLATE VI]

HERMAN MELVILLE,
a painting by Asa W. Twitchell, Albany, ca. 1847

[PLATE VII]

ALLAN MELVILLE

SOPHIA THURSTON MELVILLE

daguerreotypes
taken in New York,
1847

[PLATE VIII] The Melville Sisters in Later Years

HELEN MARIA GRIGGS

AUGUSTA MELVILLE, a photograph by Winslow, New York, 1864

CATHERINE HOADLEY

FRANCES PRISCILLA MELVILLE, a photograph by Notman, Albany, 1879

Arrowhead: a drawing by Melville while on board the *Meteor*, September 1860

[PLATE IX]

Arrowhead: the house & buildings photographed from the north field, ca. 1862

[PLATE X]

NATHANIEL HAWTHORNE,
an engraving by T. Phillibrown
(after the portrait
by C. G. Thompson)
presented to Melville
by Sophia Hawthorne, 1851

Nathaniel Hawthorne

JOHN C. HOADLEY,
a photograph, ca. 1855

[PLATE XI]

MARIA MELVILLE,
a photograph by Hall, Lawrence,
ca. 1865

HERMAN & THOMAS MELVILLE,
an ambrotype by Davis, Boston,
May 1860

The MELVILLE children,
photographed ca. 1860:
STANWIX, FRANCES (Fanny),
MALCOLM, ELIZABETH (Bessie)

LIEUTENANT HENRY SANFORD GANSEVOORT *(seated second from left)* with his fellow officers of the Thirteenth New York Cavalry, at Vienna, Virginia, 1864, a photograph by Alexander Gardner

[PLATE XII]

The Gansevoort family on the steps to their garden, Albany, ca. 1862; *on steps:* CATHERINE GANSEVOORT, ANNA LANSING; *in chairs:* PETER & SUSAN GANSEVOORT, MRS. LANSING; *standing:* her son, ABRAHAM LANSING

[PLATE XIII]

HERMAN MELVILLE

Above, photograph by Rodney Dewey, Pittsfield, 1861

Right, photograph, New York, ca. 1868

[PLATE XIV]

HERMAN MELVILLE

Above, painting by J. O. Eaton,
New York, May 1870

Left, two tintypes,
New York, ca. 1870

[PLATE XV]

ELIZABETH & HERMAN MELVILLE,
photographs by Rockwood, New York, October 1885

Above, FRANCES MELVILLE & her fiancé,
HENRY B. THOMAS,
photographed at Overlook Mountain House,
Catskills, 1879

Right, above, ELIZABETH (Bessie) MELVILLE,
a photograph, ca. 1880

Right, STANWIX MELVILLE,
a photograph by Cramer, San Francisco, ca. 1880

THE MELVILLE LOG

1855 **VI** 1859

1855: *Mar, Melville's second daughter, Frances, is born &* Israel Potter *is published as a book in the U. S. (English issue in May); Summer, at the request of the family Dr. O. W. Holmes examines Melville; Fall, Melville begins his ninth novel & proposes the collection of his Putnam stories in a volume*

1856: *Spring, publication in U. S. & England of* The Piazza Tales; *Summer, completion of* The Confidence-Man *& submission to Dix & Edwards; Oct 11, with money borrowed from his father-in-law Melville sails for Europe to restore his health; he goes through Scotland & England to Liverpool where he sees the countryside with Hawthorne & sails for the Mediterranean & Asia Minor on Nov 18: Malta, Syra, Salonica, Constantinople, Alexandria, Cairo*

1857: *Jan, a month's tour of Palestine; Feb, Greece, Sicily – Naples, Rome; Mar, Florence, Pisa, Padua; Apr,* The Confidence-Man *is published in U. S. & England; Melville sees Venice, Milan, Turin, Genoa – Switzerland, Germany, Netherlands, England; the family seek a post for him at the New York Custom House; May 5, leaves Liverpool & Hawthorne for New York; in the panic of this year the plates for Melville's last three books are auctioned; Fall, Melville accepts engagements for a lecture tour*

1858: *Jan-Feb, the lecture tour takes him as far South as Tennessee & up by riverboat through Ohio; Mar, Melville is ill at his mother's home in Gansevoort; Sept, Melville accompanies George Duyckinck on a Berkshire excursion; Winter, Melville's second lecture season*

1859: *Jan-Feb, the lecture tour extends as far as Baltimore & Milwaukee; Summer, Melville works on poems; Fall, the third & last lecture season*

*

1 8 5 5

*

NEW YORK January [1] Putnam's Monthly Magazine *publishes the seventh installment of* Israel Potter, *for which M is paid $44 (8¾ pages).*

PITTSFIELD January 23 *M drives into town to pay his Town, County & State Taxes for 1854: a Total Tax of $33.24.*

NEW YORK January? *Publication of* Putnam Portraits [*by J. E. Tuel*], *including verses on M:*

>Next in order comes Herman — a child of the seas,
>Who spreads his broad pennant 'tween tempest and breeze . . .
>He has quitted old Neptune, and ta'en to the land,
>And with letters of gold he strews jewels with sand . . .
>He has left the dead sea, and now upon land
>His works rise to life, and before our gaze stand —
>Paul Jones at his quarters — the sage and the sailor —
>For harpooning the British and manning a whaler . . .
>A fierce pen engagement on this *quarter* deck,
>Finds his brains scattered o'er, and his head from his neck.

February [1] Putnam's Monthly Magazine *publishes the eighth installment of* Israel Potter:

[Ethan] Allen seems to have been a curious combination of a Hercules, a Joe Miller, a Bayard, and a Tom Hyer; had a person like the Belgian giants; mountain music in him like a Swiss; a heart plump as Cœur de Lion's. Though born in New England, he exhibited no trace of her character. He was frank; bluff; companionable as a Pagan; convivial; a Roman; hearty as a harvest. His spirit was essentially western; and herein is his peculiar Americanism; for the western spirit is, or will yet be (for no other is, or can be) the true American one. (XXII)

For thirteen weary weeks, lorded over by the taskmasters, Israel toiled in his pit . . . The yard was encamped, with all its endless rows of tented sheds, and kilns, and mills, upon a wild waste moor, belted round by bogs and fens. The blank horizon, like a rope, coiled round the whole.

Sometimes the air was harsh and bleak; the ridged and mottled sky looked scourged; or cramping fogs set in from sea, for leagues around, ferreting out each rheumatic human bone, and racking it; the sciatic limpers shivered; their aguish rags sponged up the mists. No shelter, though it hailed. The sheds were for the bricks. Unless, indeed according to the phrase, each man was a "brick," which, in sober scripture, was the case; brick is no bad name for any son of Adam; Eden was but a brick-yard; what is a mortal but a few luckless shovelfuls of clay, moulded in a mould, laid out on a sheet to dry, and ere long quickened into his queer caprices by the sun? Are not men built into communities just like bricks into a wall? . . . As man serves bricks, so God him; building him up by billions into the edifices of his purposes. Man attains not to the nobility of a brick, unless taken in the aggregate. Yet is there a difference in brick, whether quick or dead . . . (XXIII)

PITTSFIELD February 1 *An item in* The Pittsfield Sun:
New Work by Melville. — G. P. Putnam & Co. of New York announce that "Herman Melville's new Book, *Israel Potter*, will be ready March 1st."

NEW YORK After February 1 Putnam's *pays M $35 for the eighth installment (5 pages) of* Israel Potter.

SANDUSKY February 12 *The Sandusky* Register *announces a lecture by Richard Tobias Greene: "Typee; or Life in the South Pacific."*

PITTSFIELD February 15 *Priscilla Melvill inserts a running advertisement in* The Pittsfield Sun:
☞ Miss Melville will devote herself to EMBROIDERY and the making of the nicer articles pertaining to Ladies,' Gentlemen's, or Children's wardrobes — at her room, opposite the Methodist Church in Fenn Street, up stairs.

FREMONT February 16 [Malcolm's 6th birthday] *Richard Tobias Greene reads his "Typee" lecture.*

TOLEDO February 17 *"Toby" repeats his lecture here.*

PITTSFIELD February *Elizabeth Melville's memoir of M:*
In Feb 1855 he had his first attack of severe rheumatism in his back — so that he was helpless . . .

NEW YORK March [1] Putnam's Monthly Magazine *publishes the final installment of* Israel Potter:
All night long, men sat before the mouth of the kilns, feeding them with fuel. A dull smoke — a smoke of their torments — went up from their tops . . . When, at last, the fires would be extinguished, the bricks being duly baked, Israel often took a peep into the low vaulted ways at the base, where the flaming faggots had crackled. The bricks immediately lining the vaults would be all burnt to useless scrolls, black as charcoal, and twisted into shapes the most grotesque; the next tier would be a little less withered, but hardly fit for service; and gradually, as you went higher and higher along the successive layers of the kiln, you came to the midmost ones, sound, square, and perfect bricks, bringing the highest prices; from these the contents of the kiln gradually deteriorated in the opposite direction, upward. But the topmost layers, though inferior to the best, by no means presented the distorted look of the furnace-bricks. The furnace-bricks were haggard, with the immediate blister-

ing of the fire — the midmost ones were ruddy with a genial and tempered glow — the summit ones were pale with the languor of too exclusive an exemption from the burden of the blaze. (xxiv)

After March 1   Putnam's *pays M $32.50 for the final installment* (6½ *pages*) *of* Israel Potter.

PITTSFIELD March 2   *Elizabeth Melville gives birth to her fourth & last child* [*Frances*].

ELYRIA March 6   *"Toby" gives his "Typee" lecture here.*
The lecture, last evening, by R. T. Greene, Esq., was one of deep and thrilling interest. Mr. Greene is an easy speaker, and has evidently traveled to some purpose — his lecture evinces that he has improved the opportunities for observation, which his travels have placed in his way. (*Lorain Argus*, Mar 7)

BOSTON March 7   *The March number of* Putnam's Monthly *is noticed in the* Boston Daily Advertiser:
Israel Potter is brought to a conclusion, satisfactory doubtless, to those who have kept the run of it.

BATH March 8   *Amos Nourse writes to Lemuel Shaw:*
We had not heard before of Elizabeth's confinement — another girl equalizes matters, which is very pleasant always — If it grows up to be as fine a child as the rest, she can have nothing more to desire —

SANDUSKY March 9   *A note in the Sandusky* Register:
"Toby" is now gone East on a lecturing tour.

NEW YORK March 9   *G. W. Curtis writes to William Douglas O'Connor:*
Now I am going to tell you some secrets, which will come out by & by.
Putnam has sold his magazine to Dix & Edwards, or J. H. Dix & Co . . .
They have offered me the exclusive Editorship upon terms the most flattering & advantageous, and I, for reasons which I will tell you, when we meet, have declined. But I remain the friend of the Mag. and shall help with my advice & pen as much as possible . . .
. . . Putnam, under the new regime will pay better, nearly twice as well as before.

March 10   *Deposited in the Clerk's Office of the Southern District of New-York:*
ISRAEL POTTER: | *His Fifty Years of Exile.* | BY | HERMAN MELVILLE, | AUTHOR OF "TYPEE," "OMOO," ETC. | *New York:* | G. P. PUTNAM & CO., 10 PARK PLACE. | 1855.

BOSTON March 15   Israel Potter *is reviewed in the* Boston Post:

. . . It is now published as the work of Herman Melville, whose earlier productions placed him high among our writers of fiction, but whose late works have been unsatisfactory, not to say ridiculous . . . Mr Melville has made an interesting book from the facts at his command — a book, not great, not rema[r]kable for any particular in it, but of a curt, manly, independent tone, dealing with truth honestly, and telling it feelingly. Its *Paul Jones* and *Benjamin Franklin,* to be sure, are not without a spice of Melville's former "humors," as they used to be called; but upon the whole, its style, sentiment and construction are so far above those of "Pierre" and some of its predecessors, that we dislike to say one word against it . . . We trust its successor will be quite as sensible, but be of wider scope and a larger subject.

PITTSFIELD March *Howard Townsend presents to his friend, Augusta Melville,* The Complete Works of Lord Byron.

NEW YORK April [1] *Publication of [M's sketch] "Paradise of Bachelors and Tartarus of Maids" in* Harpers New Monthly Magazine.

BOSTON April 5 *The* Boston Post *reviews Kingsley's* Westward Ho!:
It is somewhat singular that Melville in America, and Kingsley in England, should almost simultaneously have written "Israel Potter" and "Amyas Leigh." For each of these books is an oddity in itself, and yet each is wonderfully like the other. Both are modern imitations of by-gone styles of writing and talking — both are supposed biographies of real personages, and are actually based upon more or less of undoubted fact. Of "Israel Potter" we have heretofore spoken [March 15] . . . we must think that the American book, after making every proper deduction, is more truth-like, pithy, vigorous and readable than the English. But on the other hand, "Amyas Leigh" is far superior to "Israel Potter," in scope, in brilliancy, in tone and in character.

PITTSFIELD Early April? *M submits the manuscript of* Benito Cereno *to* Putnam's Monthly Magazine.

April 12 *M renews his subscription to* Harpers Magazine *for 3 years.*

PROVIDENCE Mid-April? *G. W. Curtis writes to J. H. Dix:*
Send along the *MSS.* I can manage them.
I should decline any novel from Melville that is not extremely good.

April 17 *G. W. Curtis writes to J. H. Dix:*
I am anxious to see Melville's story [*Benito Cereno*], which is in his best style of subject.

PITTSFIELD April 19 *M sends a copy of* Israel Potter *to his uncle, Herman Gansevoort.*

PROVIDENCE April 19 *G. W. Curtis writes to J. H. Dix:*
Melville's story [*Benito Cereno*] is very good. It is a great pity he did not work it up as a connected tale instead of putting in the dreary docu-

ments at the end. — They should have made part of the substance of the story. It is a little spun out, — but it is very striking & well done: and I agree with Mr Law that it ought not to be lost.

April 20   *G. W. Curtis writes to J. H. Dix:*
I return Melville's story to day. — I wrote you yesterday about what I thought of it. He does everything too hurriedly now.

ALBANY? April 30   Israel Potter *is reviewed in* [?]:
. . . Melville often, with a few words, selected with marvelous aptness, gives us a finer and more life-like description than most men create out of long chapters and thick books . . .
& Catherine Gansevoort sends the clipping to M.

NEW YORK   May [1]   Israel Potter *is reviewed in* Putnam's Monthly:
It has sometimes been inquired whether Mr. MELVILLE's *Israel Potter* is a romance or an authentic narrative . . .
The original [pamphlet], however, is not so rare as Mr. Melville seems to think. At any rate, we have a copy before us, as we write . . .
Mr. Melville departs considerably from his original. He makes Israel born in Berkshire, Mass., and brings him acquainted with Paul Jones, as he was not. How far he is justified in the historical liberties he has taken, would be a curious case of literary casuistry.

Israel Potter *is reviewed in* The National Magazine:
. . . a story of the revolutionary times, written in a half-comic, half-patriotic vein, yet withal exceedingly attractive, and not a little instructive, both in vividly recalling many of the scenes of that stirring period, and by the pithy moralisms strangely interspersed amid its almost burlesque companions . . . A tinge of obscure sarcasm pervades the book, most apparent in its dedication to the Bunker Hill Monument!

LONDON   May 5   Israel Potter *is reviewed in* The Leader.

BOSTON   May 12   *The* Meteor *sails for San Francisco & the East Indies; Samuel W. Pike in command, Thomas Melville as first mate.*

LAWRENCE   May 30   *To John & Catherine Hoadley is born a daughter* [*Maria Gansevoort*].

PITTSFIELD   May?   *M submits the manuscript of "The Bell-Tower" to* Putnam's Monthly Magazine.

LONDON   June 2   Israel Potter *is reviewed in* The Athenæum:
Mr. Melville tries for power and commands rhetoric, — but he becomes wilder and wilder, and more and more turgid in each successive book . . . Mr. Melville, to conclude, does not improve as an artist, — yet his book, with all its faults, is not a bad shilling's worth for any railway reader, who does not object to small type and a style the glories of which are nebulous.

LENOX June 16 *The Melvilles visit Catherine Gansevoort at Mrs Elizabeth Sedgwick's School.* (Fanny Augusta Herman & the children came to see me to day they are all well. — *Catherine Gansevoort's diary*)

PROVIDENCE June 18 *G. W. Curtis writes to J. H. Dix:*
[P.S.] Melville [*The Bell-Tower*] & Cozzens have *not* passed muster. I'll send them tomorrow with Clark's Birds.with reasons.

June 19 *G. W. Curtis writes to J. H. Dix:*
"The Bell Tower" is, after all, too good to lose. — It is picturesque & of a profound morality. It is rich in treatment, not unlike the quaint carving of the bell.

I meant to say no, — and so wrote you; but looking again, I am converted, and, making some erasures, we cannot afford to lose it.

To many the style will seem painfully artificial and pompously self-conscious. But it seems to me well suited to the theme. — The story has the touch of genius in it — and so — spite of the style — it should be accepted . . .

In reading "The Bell Tower" you must remember that the style is *consistently* picturesque. It isn't Addisonian nor is it Johnsonese. — Neither is Malmsey wine, Springwater.

PITTSFIELD June 30-31 *Catherine Gansevoort spends the week-end at Arrowhead.* (If convenient to yourself & pleasing to Mrs Sedgwick, we will drive over for you on Saturday — if pleasant — as soon after breakfast as possible, & will promise to see you safely home again on Sunday evening. — *Augusta Melville to Catherine Gansevoort, June 25;* spent last Saturday at Cousin Herman's . . . — *Catherine Gansevoort's diary, entry of July 4*)

June *Elizabeth Melville's memoir of M:*
. . . and in the following June an attack of Sciatica. Our neighbor in Pittsfield Dr O. W. Holmes attended & prescribed for him.

. . . when at one time Mr. Melville was seriously ill, Dr. Holmes visited him with fraternal tenderness, incidentally of course giving him his best medical advice, without — that also, of course — intruding upon the province of the local practitioner. (Smith, *Evening Journal*, Dec 16, 1891)

At length it came to pass that a master-mason — a rough sort of architect — one Mr. Scribe, was summoned to a conference. I formally introduced him to my chimney. A previous introduction from my wife had introduced him to myself. He had been not a little employed by that lady, in preparing plans and estimates for some of her extensive operations in drainage. Having, with much ado, extorted from my spouse the promise that she would leave us to an unmolested survey, I began by leading Mr. Scribe down to the root of the matter, in the cellar. Lamp in hand, I descended; for though up stairs it was noon, below it was night.

We seemed in the pyramids; and I, with one hand holding my lamp over head, and with the other pointing out, in the obscurity, the hoar mass of the chimney, seemed some Arab guide, showing the cobwebbed mausoleum of the great god Apis.

"This is a most remarkable structure, sir," said the master mason, after long contemplating it in silence, "a most remarkable structure, sir."

"Yes," said I, complacently, "every one says so." ("I and My Chimney," *Putnam's Monthly*, Mar 1856)

Dr Holmes makes his report to M.

New Petra, April 1st.

Sir: — During my last examination of your chimney, possibly you may have noted that I frequently applied my rule to it in a manner apparently unnecessary. Possibly also, at the same time, you might have observed in me more or less of perplexity, to which, however, I refrained from giving any verbal expression.

I now feel it obligatory upon me to inform you of what was then but a dim suspicion, and as such would have been unwise to give utterance to, but which now, from various subsequent calculations assuming no little probability, it may be important that you should not remain in further ignorance of.

It is my solemn duty to warn you, sir, that there is architectural cause to conjecture that somewhere concealed in your chimney is a reserved space, hermetically closed, in short, a secret chamber, or rather closet. How long it has been there, it is for me impossible to say. What it contains is hid, with itself, in darkness. But probably a secret closet would not have been contrived except for some extraordinary object, whether for the concealment of treasure, or what other purpose, may be left to those better acquainted with the history of the house to guess.

But enough: in making this disclosure, sir, my conscience is eased. Whatever step you choose to take upon it is, of course, a matter of indifference to me; though, I confess, as respects the character of the closet, I cannot but share in a natural curiosity.

Trusting that you may be guided aright, in determining whether it is Christian-like knowingly to reside in a house, hidden in which is a secret closet,

I remain, With much respect,

Yours very humbly,

HIRAM SCRIBE . . .

"Sir," said I, "really I am much obliged to you for this survey. It has quite set my mind at rest. And no doubt you, too, Mr. Scribe, must feel much relieved. Sir," I added, "you have made three visits to the chimney. With a business man, time is money. Here are fifty dollars, Mr. Scribe. Nay, take it. You have earned it. Your opinion is worth it. And by the way" — as he modestly received the money — "have you any objections to give me a — a — little certificate — something, say, like a steamboat certificate, certifying that you, a competent surveyor, have surveyed my chimney, and found no reason to believe any unsoundness; in short, any — any secret closet in it. Would you be so kind, Mr. Scribe?" . . .

That evening I had the certificate framed and hung over the dining-room fireplace, trusting that the continual sight of it would forever put at rest at once the dreams and stratagems of my household. ("I and My Chimney")

Who in the rainbow can draw the line where the violet tint ends and the orange tint begins? . . . So with sanity and insanity . . . in some supposed cases, in various degrees supposedly less pronounced, to draw the exact line of demarkation few will undertake, though for a fee some professional experts will. There is nothing nameable but that some men will undertake to do it for pay. In other words, there are instances where it is next to impossible to determine whether a man is in his mind or beginning to be otherwise. (*Billy Budd*, XXII)

But seeing that, despite all, I and my chimney still smoke our pipes, my wife re-occupies the ground of the secret closet, enlarging upon what wonders are there, and what a shame it is, not to seek it out and explore it.
  "Wife," said I, upon one of these occasions, "why speak more of that secret closet, when there before you hangs contrary testimony of a master-mason, elected by yourself to decide. Besides, even if there were a secret closet, secret it should remain, and secret it shall. Yes, wife, here for once I must say my say. Infinite sad mischief has resulted from the profane bursting open of secret recesses . . ." ("I and My Chimney")

Mid-July? *M submits a sketch to* Putnam's, *"I and My Chimney."*

NEWPORT July 31   *G. W. Curtis writes to J. H. Dix:*
  The *mss* [including "I and My Chimney"] came safely . . .
  Why, if you don't want to begin *Owlcopse*, don't you take up *Benito Cereno* of Melville. You have paid for it. I should alter all the dreadful statistics at the end. Oh! dear, why can't Americans write good stories. They tell good lies enough, & plenty of 'em.

PARIS July   Israel Potter *is reviewed & summarized, by Émile Monté-gut, in the first article (51 pages) in* Revue des Deux Mondes, *"Israël Potter, une légende démocratique américaine":*
  Depuis la préface . . . jusqu'aux dernières pages, qui sont réellement touchantes, ce livre semble en effet une tentative pour déployer dans le cadre d'un récit populaire deux qualités essentielles de l'esprit américaine, l'amour-propre démocratique et l'orgeuil national. Pour ne parler que du cadre d'abord, M. Melville a procédé comme tous les légendaires; chez lui comme chez eux, on retrouve l'amour du héros poussé en quelque sorte jusqu'à la susceptibilité, la narration lente et détaillée, la calque fidèle et minutieux de la réalité, l'apothéose et la *sublimisation*, si nous pouvons ainsi parler, des faits les plus humbles . . . il le présente comme le type de ces vertus sur la terre ennemie, comme le symbole de la démocratie dans un pays aristocratique.

PITTSFIELD August 1 [M's 36th birthday]   *The Valuation Book for Pittsfield is completed; in M's estimate:*
                              [Money]   2,500

NEW YORK August [1]   *Publication of* [M's story] *"The Bell-Tower,"* in Putnam's Monthly Magazine:
  So the blind slave obeyed its blinder lord; but, in obedience, slew him. So

the creator was killed by the creature. So the bell was too heavy for the tower. So the bell's main weakness was where man's blood had flawed it. And so pride went before the fall.

PITTSFIELD   Before August 8   *M writes to Dix & Edwards, inquiring about payment [for "The Bell-Tower"?] in* Putnam's Monthly Magazine.

NEW YORK   August 8   *Dix & Edwards writes to M.* (I have just received yours of the 8th. — The explanation explains all . . . I was not aware of your arrangement as to sending your check regularly to contributors on the 1st of the month. — *M to Dix & Edwards, Aug 10*)

PITTSFIELD   August 10   *M writes to Dix & Edwards:*
The [postal?] expences are inconsiderable. I have paid them.

August 21   *M writes to G. P. Putnam & Co.:*
   By reference to our agreement about *Israel Potter,* I see there is to be a payment (by note) during the present month.
   Could you conveniently send me the acct: & note by the beginning of next week . . .

MARQUESAS   August 23   *Journal of Alfred G. Jones:*
About 10 o'clock entered the harbor of Taio-hae or Nuka-hiva . . . Called upon *Te Moena* the King or Chief of this bay his name signifies "The Ocean" He is said to be a well disposed person and when young was exhibited in London — of which occurrence he is now much ashamed — he occasionally gets tight & then loses all control of himself during one of his drunken fits he killed the "Typee" Chief whom Melville in his book speaks of as the Chief of that tribe . . . Te Moena receives an annual stipend of 2000 francs and a ration a day from the French — When he killed the Typee Chief — this pay was discontinued and his flag hauled down — about a year since he was restored to favor after two years of disgrace.

August 24   At 6 o'clock started in the Barge for a visit to the "Typee" valley . . . passing by the Valley of the "Happars" this tribe so much feared by the "Typees" in Melvilles account were by the latter almost exterminated 12 years ago — they killed of one tribe about 700 men women & children leaving only 5 decrepit or deformed "Happars." They roasted and devoured the slain — that they were Cannibals until a very late period and are still upon the other islands of this group there is not a shadow of doubt. We saw the Island upon which the Happars had a grand feast upon the bodies of the Typees killed by Commodore Porter on his expedition against them in 1813 . . . we did not enter the eastern valley which was the one where Melville was confined — our curiosity was the less in this point from the fact — that although we had evidence that such persons as Kory-Kory and Tinor and the one eyed chief had once existed — they were now however dead and their homes abandoned or destroyed. "Moreta" recollected Melville and had seen the personages alluded to in his book — but there was no one of the name of "Fayaway" indeed their language does not admit of such a name . . . I am very well convinced that Melville drew altogether upon his imagination for the Lake he speaks of — for no such lake exists upon the island and no pool large enough for a boat . . .

Our conclusions were that Melville had a truthful basis for his book but that his imagination was very largely drawn upon for the attractive features of the same — his manufacture of cocoa-nut oil into a perfumed cosmetic fit to grace the toilet of a queen is a specimen of the strength of his olfactories as well as of his imagination.

PITTSFIELD August 28 *M orders from Harpers:*
    1 Waikna [by Samuel A. Bard (E. G. Squier)] ⎫
    1 Panama [in 1855, by Robert Tomes] ⎬ 1.30
                                ⎭

Late August?

And this reminds me of a little excursion which Darley, the artist, and myself once made together from Stockbridge. We started in a buggy to call upon Melville, intending to go from there to Dr. Holmes's, then to the hotel at Pittsfield to dine, and thence home. We found Melville, whom I had always known as the most silent man of my acquaintance, sitting on the porch in front of his door. He took us to a particular spot on his place to show us some superb trees. He told me that he spent much time there *patting them upon the back.* When we were about to start for Dr. Holmes's, we invited Melville to accompany us, and he accepted. We found the poet-physician, to whom I was presented for the first time, at home, and he took us into a room at the back of his house, which overlooked the mountains. For some time the talk, in which we all tried to participate, dragged . . . At length, somehow, the conversation drifted to East India religions and mythologies, and soon there arose a discussion between Holmes and Melville, which was conducted with the most amazing skill and brilliancy on both sides. It lasted for hours, and Darley and I had nothing to do but listen. I never chanced to hear better talking in my life. It was so absorbing that we took no note of time, and the Doctor lost his dinner, as we lost ours. (Maunsell B. Field, *Memories of Many Men* [1874])

August 31 *An item in the* Berkshire County Eagle:

Messrs. Bell and Stanly, of the Insane Asylum Commission, arrived in town on Wednesday afternoon, and will remain through today (Thursday). Mr. Stanly is going over the ground a second time, accompanied by Dr. Bell . . . whose great experience in matters pertaining to the insane, renders his opinion too valuable to be lost . . . The Commissioners have examined the farms of Mess. Hermann Melville, E. R. Colt, Justus Merrill, and others, and appear most anxious to do everything in their power to obtain data upon which to decide wisely upon the location of the new Asylum.

NEW YORK August 31 *G. P. Putnam invites M to attend the Compli-*
mentary Fruit & Flower Festival of the New York Book-Publishers As-
sociation, to be given at the Crystal Palace on September 27.

PITTSFIELD September 7
. . . on the morning of last Friday, tables and seats had been erected [beside
Melvill Lake], and a platform for dancing laid. The day had been fixed for a
fancy dress pic nic, a startling novelty in this region, and one which the timid
ones feared would not succeed. But it did.
    [Among the pic-nickers are:] Mrs. J. R. M[orewood] as an old lady . . .
Mrs. E[llen] B[rittain] of Broadhall, and Mrs. J. H. T. as squaws . . .
Mrs. H[erman] M[elville] as Cypherina Donothing, in a costume of cyphers
was no cypher, and although continually adding up cyphers to get at a sum of
cyphers, found naught to amuse her; and was one of the most successful
characters of the day, although she did nothing well.
    Miss A[ugusta] M[elville] as a market woman of the olden times, in a red
cloak and hood.
    . . . T[haddeus] C[lapp] 3d., as Hiram Hunkins, a Yankee . . . J. E. A.
S[mith], a "Friar of Orders Grey," proved his title to monkship by showing
himself a trenchant man at the trencher . . .
    Master M[alcolm] M[elville], about eight years old, as Jack the Giant
Killer, with sword and buckler, marched about bravely, bearing on his belt
the inscription,
>   "I am the gallant Cornishman,
>   Who slew the giant Cormogan." . . .
During the day we were pleased to see on the ground, and apparently
greatly enjoying the scene, the authoress [Catherine Sedgwick] of Hope Leslie
and the author of Typee — the latter just recovering from a severe illness.
([J. E. A. Smith?], *Berkshire County Eagle*, Sept 14)

Life is a pic-nic *en costume;* one must take a part, assume a character, stand
ready in a sensible way to play the fool. To come in plain clothes, with a long
face, as a wiseacre, only makes one a discomfort to himself, and a blot upon
the scene. (*The Confidence-Man*, XXIV)

M responds to G. P. Putnam's invitation:
    If in my power I shall be most happy to be present at so attractive a
festival.

NEWPORT September 7 *G. W. Curtis writes to J. H. Dix:*
    I return all the *Mss.*
1 — "I & my chimney" is a capital, genial, humorous sketch by Melville,
thoroughly magazinish . . .
    If you can squeeze Melville into oct. it would be great . . .
    Sam. Ward, (formerly of Wall St.) dined with Longfellow yesterday,
and said that he dined just before leaving London in company with
Thackeray, & that Thack asserted before the whole table that "Putnams"
was much the best Mag. in the world, — and was better than Blackwood
is or ever was! Hooray for our side.

PITTSFIELD Before September 14   *M & his mother leave Pittsfield, on "a few days jaunt." — M to Peter & Susan Gansevoort, Sept 18*

NEWPORT September 14   *G. W. Curtis writes to J. H. Dix:*
I return the *Mss* . . . The Benito Cereno is ghastly & interesting. How much will it make?

PITTSFIELD September 14   *Lemuel & Hope Shaw arrive at Arrowhead. (her diary)*

September 17   *Hope Shaw writes to her son, Lemuel, from "Herman's Study":*
As expected, Mrs Melville & Herman are away and, when they return its uncertain. Elizabeth & her children are remarkably well, The children are bright & noisy.
Miss Augusta is *all* energy, united with much kindness — anticipates wishes — You know that is my *idol*, to have a thing done — without a hint when my friend knows, exactly what I wish . . .
Your father is making a Kite for Malcolm to day — I cannot imagine, it will be like the one for twenty years to my knowledge he has been wishing to make — as it would be larger than Lizzy & her four children all together.

ALBANY September 18   *M, with his mother, calls upon Peter & Susan Gansevoort (in their absence), & leaves a note for them:*
Mama & I, on our return towards home from a few days jaunt, arrived at the depot here this morning, intending to greet you and dine with you, and then take the afternoon train for Pittsfield. But as it proved very stormy, we thought that, unless it cleared off, we might stay overnight. At any rate, up *here* we came — you were gone — for which, need we say, we felt much regret. However your people have kindly cared for the travelers, so after a pleasant lunch we are off on the afternoon train, spite of the storm.

Before leaving Albany M buys, at Sprague's bookstore, Don Quixote de la Mancha, *translated from the Spanish of Miguel de Cervantes Saavedra by Charles Jarvis (Philadelphia, 1853), in which he subsequently reads (on the cars?) & marks this passage in Vol. II, p 216:*
". . . a knight-errant without a mistress is like a tree without leaves, a building without cement, a shadow without a body that causes it."
M's comment: **X** or as Confucius said 'a dog without a master,' or to drop both Cervantes & Confucius parables — a god-like mind without a God.

BUFFALO September   *The* Western Literary Messenger *prints "Ethan Allen's Captivity" [a condensation of Chapters XXI & XXII of M's* Israel Potter].

NEW YORK October [1]   *Publication of the first installment of [M's story]* "Benito Cereno" *in* Putnam's Monthly Magazine:

The morning was one peculiar to that coast. Everything was mute and calm; everything grey. The sea, though undulated into long roods of swells, seemed fixed, and was sleeked at the surface like waved lead that has cooled and set in the smelter's mold. The sky seemed a grey mantle. Flights of troubled grey fowl, kith and kin with flights of troubled grey vapors among which they were mixed, skimmed low and fitfully over the waters, as swallows over meadows before storms. Shadows present, foreshadowing deeper shadows to come.

October 8   G. P. Putnam & Co. submits a statement to M:
             "Israel Potter" — Printed
                 1st Edition   1400
                 2d   "   800
                 3   "   1500   3700

                 Less Shorts on 3 Editions   25

                         Copies Bound   3675
                 Given to Editors   192
                 1855
                 July 1 On hand   906   1098

                             Sold   2577
           2577 @ ⁶75 = $1932.75 @ 10% =   — $193.27
[Another hand has noted a figure, $241.58, which, when $193.27 is subtracted from it, leaves a total for M of: $48.31.]

PITTSFIELD   October 24   Priscilla Melvill writes to Lemuel Shaw:
    Herman call'd to see me, this afternoon — left all well, at home — Augusta was preparing to attend a grand party, this Eveᵍ — at Mrs Learneds — 100 invitations — & I think they will literally have a great "blow out," as the Sailors say, for the winds are howling fiercely, & the air is full of Snow —

GANSEVOORT   October 27   M arrives to watch by the death-bed of Herman Gansevoort's wife, Catherine.

October 29   Herman Gansevoort's remembrancer:
    The faithful and beloved Catherine S. Gansevoort wife of Herman Gansevoort, departed this life on the 29th day of October 1855 at 7 O.clock and 30 minutes in the evening —

Maria Melville & her daughter Frances Priscilla remain at Gansevoort to keep house for Herman Gansevoort.

NEW YORK   November [1]   Publication of the second installment of "Benito Cereno" in Putnam's Monthly Magazine.

Publication of [M's sketch] "Jimmy Rose" in Harper's New Monthly Magazine:

Though at the first onset of his calamity, when creditors, once fast friends, pursued him as carrion for jails; though then, to avoid their hunt, as well as the human eye, he had gone and denned in the old abandoned house; and there, in his loneliness, had been driven half mad, yet time and tide had soothed him down to sanity. Perhaps at bottom Jimmy was too thoroughly good and kind to be made from any cause a man-hater. And doubtless it at last seemed irreligious to Jimmy even to shun mankind.

December [1]   *Publication of the third & last installment of "Benito Cereno" in* Putnam's Monthly Magazine:
. . . said Don Benito, sadly; "You were with me all day; stood with me, sat with me, talked with me, looked at me, ate with me, drank with me; and yet, your last act was to clutch for a villain, not only an innocent man, but the most pitiable of all men. To such degree may malign machinations and deceptions impose. So far may even the best men err, in judging the conduct of one with the recesses of whose condition he is not acquainted . . ."

Late December   *J. H. Dix writes to G. W. Curtis, asking his advice on the wisdom of publishing a volume of M's stories.*

Publication of Cyclopædia of American Literature, *edited by Evert & George Duyckinck, with a biographical sketch of M, concluding:*
Pierre, or the Ambiguities, was published in 1852. Its conception and execution were both literary mistakes. The author was off the track of his true genius . . .
Since the publication of this volume, Mr. Melville has written chiefly for the magazines of Harper and Putnam. In the former, a sketch, entitled *Cock-a-doodle doo!* is one of the most lively and animated productions of his pen; in the latter, his *Bartleby the Scrivener,* a quaint, fanciful portrait, and his reproduction, with various inventions and additions, of the adventures of *Israel Potter,* an actual character of the Revolution, have not met with deserved success.

*

1 8 5 6

*

STATEN ISLAND January 2   *G. W. Curtis replies to J. H. Dix:*
I don't think Melville's book will sell a great deal, but he is a good name upon your list. He has lost his prestige, — & I don't believe the Putnam stories will bring it up.
But I suppose you can't lose by it.
I like the Encantadas, and Bartleby, very much.

NEW YORK   January 3   *Dix & Edwards notify M of their acceptance of a volume of his stories, thus far published in* Putnam's.

PITTSFIELD   January 7   *M replies to Dix & Edwards:*
Since you are disposed to undertake the book, were it not well to have a written Agreement? Such, if you please, you may prepare & send me for signature. I am ready to sign one of the same sort made concerning "I. Potter" with Mr Putnam.

In your note you state *12 per cent* as the terms I mentioned. But I meant to say *12 &1/2 per cent;* that is, the same terms as I had for "I Potter" . . .

Upon looking over my set of the Magazine, I find two Nos., that I want sent: — Dec. N° 1853, & Ap. N° 1854. Will you be kind enough to send those two nos. to me by mail, so that I can do my share of the work without delay.

January 24   [Thomas Melville's 36th birthday]   *A paragraph in* The Pittsfield Sun:
☛ A new work by Herman Melville, the author of "Typee," "Omoo," &c., is announced as in preparation and soon to be issued from the New-York press.

SEATTLE, TERRITORY OF WASHINGTON   January 26   *The officers & crew of the U. S. Sloop-of-war* Decatur, *Guert Gansevoort Commander, defend the community & port of Seattle from a force of some 2000 Indians.*

DUBLIN   January   The Dublin University Magazine *publishes a critical article, "A Trio of American Sailor-Authors," on Cooper, Dana, & Melville:*
Herman Melville completes our Trio. A friend has informed us that "Herman Melville" is merely a *nom de plume,* and if so, it is only of a piece with the mystification which this remarkable author dearly loves to indulge in from the first page to the last of his works . . .

. . . [In *Mardi*] all the author's unrivalled powers of diction, all his wealth of fancy, all his exuberance of imagination, all his pathos, vigor, and exquisite graces of style, cannot prevent the judicious reader from laying down the book with a weary sigh, and an inward pang of regret that so much rare and lofty talent has been so wilfully wasted on a theme which not anybody can fully understand . . . It is, in our estimation, one of the saddest, most melancholy, most deplorable and humiliating perversions of genius of a high order in the English language . . .

The last work we have to notice is a large one, entitled "The Whale," and it is quite as eccentric and monstrously extravagant in many of its incidents as even "Mardi" . . .

Such is Herman Melville! a man of whom America has reason to be proud, with all his faults; and if he does not eventually rank as one of her greatest giants in literature, it will be owing not to any lack of innate genius, but solely to his own incorrigible perversion of his rare and lofty gifts.

We have Mr. Melville's own authority for saying that he was sensitive to the criticism of foreign reviews, for once when reading one of them [as reprinted in *Littell's Living Age*, Mar 1?], he looked up to say, "Well, it is pleasant to read what those fellows over the water say about us!" And he was greatly amused when he found the critic, thinking that his name was altogether too fine for common use in America, concluded it was a pseudonym. (Smith, *Biographical Sketch*)

NEW YORK   February 9   Life Illustrated *publishes an editorial on "benevolent societies":*
For our own part, we would rather be the means of effectually helping or enlightening *one* of our own countrymen or countrywomen, than of seducing ten thousand darky savages from their natural way of life into the baptized unnaturalness so well described by Herman Mélville in his immortal "Typee."

PITTSFIELD   Before February 16   *M sends his corrected magazine sheets to Dix & Edwards, & writes "The Piazza," an introductory sketch for the volume of stories:*
. . . and, indeed, was become so sensitive through my illness, as that I could not bear to look upon a Chinese creeper of my adoption, and which, to my delight, climbing a post of the piazza, had burst out in starry bloom, but now, if you removed the leaves a little, showed millions of strange, cankerous worms, which, feeding upon those blossoms, so shared their blessed hue, as to make it unblessed evermore — worms, whose germs had doubtless lurked in the very bulb which, so hopefully, I had planted . . .

"But, do you not go walk at times? These woods are wide."
"And lonesome; lonesome, because so wide. Sometimes, 'tis true, of afternoons, I go a little way; but soon come back again. Better feel lone by hearth, than rock. The shadows hereabouts I know — those in the woods are strangers."

February 16 [Malcolm's seventh birthday]   *M notifies Dix & Edwards that the title chosen for the volume of stories is* The Piazza Tales, *& encloses the introductory piece for the volume, "The Piazza":*
I think, with you, that *"Bartleby"* had best come next. So that, as amended, the order will be
> The Piazza
> Bartleby
> Benito Cereno
> Lightning-Rod Man
> Encantadas
> Bell Tower

NEW YORK   February 20   The Piazza Tales *is ready for the printer.*

March [1]   *Publication of [M's sketch] "I and My Chimney," in* Putnam's Monthly Magazine:

But it is within doors that the pre-eminence of my chimney is most mani-fest. When in the rear room, set apart for that object, I stand to receive my guests (who, by the way, call more, I suspect, to see my chimney than me), I then stand, not so much before, as, strictly speaking, behind my chimney, which is, indeed, the true host . . . From this habitual precedence of my chimney over me, some even think that I have got into a sad rearward way altogether; in short, from standing behind my old-fashioned chimney so much, I have got to be quite behind the age, too, as well as running behindhand in everything else. But to tell the truth, I never was a very forward old fellow, nor what my farming neighbors call a forehanded one . . . As for my belong-ing to the rearguard in general, certain it is, I bring up the rear of my chim-ney — which, by the way, is this moment before me — and that, too, both in fancy and fact. In brief, my chimney is my superior . . . yet never does it minister, or incline over to me; but, if anything, in its settlings, rather leans the other way . . .

It is now some seven years since I have stirred from home. My city friends all wonder why I don't come to see them, as in former times. They think I am getting sour and unsocial. Some say that I have become a sort of mossy old misanthrope, while all the time the fact is, I am simply standing guard over my mossy old chimney; for it is resolved between me and my chimney, that I and my chimney will never surrender.

Publication of [M's sketch] "The 'Gees," in Harper's New Monthly Magazine:

In relating to my friends various passages of my sea-goings, I have at times had occasion to allude to that singular people the 'Gees, sometimes as casual acquaintances, sometimes as shipmates . . . My auditors have opened their eyes as much as to say, "What under the sun is a 'Gee?" To enlighten them I have repeatedly had to interrupt myself, and not without detriment to my stories. To remedy which inconvenience, a friend hinted the advisability of writing out some account of the 'Gees, and having it published. Such as they are, the following memoranda spring from that happy suggestion . . .

BOSTON March 1 Littell's Living Age *reprints "A Trio of American Sailor-Authors" from the* Dublin University Magazine.

WASHINGTON March 6 *J. C. Dobbin, Secretary of the Navy, writes to Commander Guert Gansevoort:*

Your communications to the Department dated 10th and 31 of January last, have been received; that of the latter date has been perused by the Secretary of War, who has expressed his appreciation of the judicious measures taken by you under the circumstances in which you were placed, and his thanks for the very efficient aid [to] the Military in their efforts to protect the inhabitants of the Territory of Washington from the incursions of the Indians.

NEW YORK March 6 *Harper's sends M its eleventh account:*
Balance due Harper & Bros. $348.51

March 7   *Dix & Edwards sends M the agreement (to sign) for the pub-*
lication of The Piazza Tales; *M's royalties are to be* "*12 1/2 per cent, per*
copy on each copy sold."

PITTSFIELD March 24   *M returns the signed agreement & corrected*
proofs on The Piazza Tales *to Dix & Edwards, along with a note:*
There seems to be a surprising profusion of commas in these proofs.
I have struck them out pretty much; but hope that some one who understands punctuation better than I do, will give the final hand to it.

GALENA April 1   *Mary A. A. Melvill writes to Lemuel Shaw:*
My son John's wife became deranged after her last confinement, more
than two months ago, and was taken to the asylum I brought the three
children home; last week she was pronounced cured and came to see
her children, with the expectation to remain here some time; but I fear
that she was sent home too soon, perhaps meeting with her husband and
family (for whom, she manifested all the dislike and a suspicion common
I believe to all deranged persons) may have caused a partial relapse, but
I cannot but hope that it may wear off after a time . . .

PITTSFIELD April 5   *M writes a letter introducing Samuel Shaw to*
J. M. Langford in London.

NEW YORK April 5   *Dix & Edwards' advertisement in* The Criterion:
In Press.
Herman Melville. "Piazza Tales,"
A New Book. (Shortly.)

PITTSFIELD April 14   *M inserts a running ad in* The Pittsfield Sun:
FOR-SALE,
PART of the FARM now occupied by the subscriber, being 80 acres, more than
half well wooded, within a mile and a half of Pittsfield village by the County
road.
HERMAN MELVILLE.

[First printed on April 17.]

BOSTON April   *Richard Henry Dana, Jr's journal:*
The truth is, Judge Shaw is a man of intense & doating biasses, in religious, political & social matters. Unitarianism, Harvard College, the
social & political respectabilities of Boston are his idola specus & fori.

NEW YORK May [1]   *Publication of [M's sketch]* "The Apple-Tree
Table, or Original Spiritual Manifestations," *in* Putnam's Monthly Magazine:
Wishing to shed a clearer light through the place, I sought to withdraw
the scuttle-slide. But no sign of latch or hasp was visible. Only after long
peering, did I discover a little padlock, imbedded, like an oyster at the bottom
of the sea, amid matted masses of weedy webs, chrysalides, and insectivorous

eggs . . . As if incensed at this invasion of their retreat, countless bands darted up from below, beating about my head, like hornets. At last, with a sudden jerk, I burst open the scuttle. And ah! what a change. As from the gloom of the grave and the companionship of worms, man shall at last rapturously rise into the living greenness and glory immortal, so, from my cobwebbed old garret, I thrust forth my head into the balmy air, and found myself hailed by the verdant tops of great trees, growing in the little garden below — trees, whose leaves soared high above my topmost slate.

Refreshed by this outlook, I turned inward to behold the garret, now unwontedly lit up. Such humped masses of obsolete furniture . . . broken-down old chairs, with strange carvings, which seemed fit to seat a conclave of conjurors. And a rusty, iron-bound chest, lidless, and packed full of mildewed old documents; one of which, with a faded red ink-blot at the end, looked as if it might have been the original bond that Doctor Faust gave to Mephistopheles. And, finally, in the least lighted corner of all, where was a profuse litter of indescribable old rubbish — among which was a broken telescope, and a celestial globe staved in — stood the little old table, one hoofed foot, like that of the Evil One, dimly revealed through the cobwebs. What a thick dust, half paste, had settled upon the old vials and flasks; how their once liquid contents had caked, and how strangely looked the mouldy old book in the middle — Cotton Mather's *Magnalia*.

PITTSFIELD May 12 *M drives into town to pay his Town, County & State Taxes for 1855: a Total Tax of $38.73.*

NEW YORK May 20 *Registered at the Clerk's Office of the Southern District of New-York:*
THE | PIAZZA TALES. | BY | HERMAN MELVILLE, | AUTHOR OF "TYPEE," "OMOO," ETC., ETC., ETC. | NEW YORK; | DIX & EDWARDS, 321 BROADWAY. | LONDON: SAMPSON LOW, SON & CO. | 1856.

BUFFALO May 30 *Henry Sanford Gansevoort writes to his father:*
Have you read Cousin Hermans new work   There are I perceive one or two capital pieces in it but the rest are a rehash of former dishes —

PITTSFIELD May 30 The Piazza Tales *is reviewed* [*by J. E. A. Smith?*] *in the* Berkshire County Eagle:
This new work of our fellow citizen is decidedly the most readable which he has published since Omoo and Typee. It consists of several graphic tales, some of which have been before admired by us. The title is derived from the piazza on the north of the author's residence and the introduction will be especially interesting to Pittsfield readers for its description of familiar scenery. The first story, "Bartleby the Scrivener," is a portrait from life and is one of the best bits of writing which ever came from the author's pen.

Without so many striking passages as "Moby Dick" and some others, the "*Piazza Tales*" is more uniformly excellent and is more free from blemishes than any of Mr. Melville's later books.

NEW YORK May 31 The Piazza Tales *is reviewed in* The Criterion:

The volume contains *The Piazza*, an introduction; *Bartleby*, a quaint tale, based upon living characters; *Benito Cereno*, a thrilling, weird-like narrative, which, read at midnight, gives an uncomfortable feeling to a powerful imagination; *The Lightning-Rod Man*, that shows that Mr. Melville can, if he so chooses, write a very indifferent paper; *The Encantadas*, a series of charming descriptions; and *The Bell Tower*, which, when we read some time since, rang in our mind for days after.

BOSTON   June 4   The Piazza Tales *is noticed in the* Boston Post.

NEW YORK   June 14   *To Allan & Sophia Melville is born a fifth daughter [Lucy].*

SANDUSKY   June 16   *Richard Tobias Greene writes to M:*
I have just been reading the "Piazza Tales," which my brother-in-law, [C. L.] Derby [of the Cosmopolitan Art Association], presented me. The "Encantadas" called up reminiscences of days gone by – the *Acushnet* – the "turpin" &c . . .
By the way do you remember Haynor, the steward? Well I found him in New Orleans last winter keeping a Hotel! He wished to be remembered to you, should I write you . . .
I am determined to keep you in remembrance, so you would think if you could see my little son, two years old, who glories in the name of "Herman Melville" –

NEW YORK   June 23   The Piazza Tales *is reviewed in the* New-York Daily Tribune:
In these stories . . . we find the peculiar traits of the author's genius, though in a less decided form, than in most of his previous compositions. They show something of the boldness of invention, brilliancy of imagination, and quaintness of expression which usually mark his writings, with not a little of the apparent perversity and self-will, which serve as a foil to their various excellences. "Bartleby," the Scrivener, is the most original story in the volume . . .

SALEM   June 26   The Piazza Tales *is reviewed in the* Salem Register:
The characteristics of Melville's style, and the peculiar turn of his mind are known to a multitude of readers, who will recognize in these tales their true paternity.

PITTSFIELD   June 28   *The Valuation Book for Pittsfield is completed; in M's estimate:*

> [Money]   2,500
> 80 Acres set to Geo S. Willis   1857

RICHMOND   June   The Piazza Tales *is reviewed [by John R. Thompson?] in the* Southern Literary Messenger:
For some time the literary world has lost sight of Herman Melville, whose

last appearance as an author, in "Pierre or the Ambiguities," was rather an unfortunate one, but he "turns up" once more in "The Piazza Tales," with much of his former freshness and vivacity . . . the preference must be given to the "*Encantadas*" . . . "The Lightning Rod Man" is a very flat recital which we should never have suspected Melville of producing . . .

LONDON   June   *The English edition of* The Piazza Tales (*composed of American printed sheets*) *is published by Sampson Low, Son & Co.*

NEW YORK   July [1]   The Piazza Tales *is noticed in* Mrs. Stephens' New Monthly.

LONDON   July 1   The Westminster and Foreign Quarterly Review *publishes an article* [*by John Chapman?*], "*Christian Missions: their Principle and Practice*," *containing liberal citations from* Typee & Omoo.

PITTSFIELD   July 12?   *M writes to the Shaw family.* (Herman writes that he has sold [to George S. Willis] the western half of his farm at Pittsfield — upon pretty good terms . . . — *Lemuel Shaw, Jr to his brother, Samuel, July 15*)

CHARLESTOWN, N. H.   July 12   *Henry G. Webber writes to M:*
I have heard once or twice from Mr Geo P. Putnam of N. York that you wished to possess some illustrations of your tale of the Bell Tower, drawn by me, which were at Mr. Putnam's last fall. But, as I understood, you did not feel like paying such a price as you supposed would be asked. The drawings are in pretty good preservation now, but are of no particular use to me, and I shall be glad to have you take them, if you wish, at any price that you may set . . . I had rather you should have them than any one else.
I authorized Mr Wells (of the firm of G. P. P. & C°) to tell you this when he first spoke to me on the matter, but he told me this spring he had not seen you since.

BOSTON   July 15   *Lemuel Shaw, Jr sends news to his brother, Samuel, of the completion of* The Confidence-Man:
. . . I believe he [M] is now preparing another book for the press — of which Augusta is making a fair copy for the printer & which will be published before long — I know nothing about it; but I have no great confidence in the success of his productions —

. . . his general method of literary work was to shut himself up in his library, having his luncheon, if needed, placed at the door in order to avoid interruption. Often he submitted his manuscript to one of his sisters for revision. Probably it came from her hand somewhat toned down from what he left it in the heat of composition; but not essentially changed. This solitary labor continued until he was wearied, when he would emerge from his "den," join in family or social intercourse, indulge in light reading — which was not so very light; as it included much less of what we commonly call "light literature," than it did of profound reviews, abstruse philosophy in prose or verse, and the like — visit or entertain his friends, or otherwise enjoy himself. But no more formal serious work for him until the next morning, although, consciously or unconsciously, his mind was always gathering material for it. (Smith, *Evening Journal*, Dec 16, 1891)

LONDON July 26   The Piazza Tales *is reviewed in* The Athenæum:

That the Americans excel in short tales, the mention of Irving, Poe, Hawthorne, will remind our readers. That Mr. Melville might deserve to be added to the list is also possible; but in these 'Piazza Tales' he gives us merely indications, not fulfilment. Under the idea of being romantic and pictorial in style, he is sometimes barely intelligible . . . The author who "flames amazement" in the eyes of his readers . . . must content himself with a very young public. Elder folk, however tolerant of imagery, and alive to the seductions of colour, will be contented with a few such pages and phrases, and lay by the rhapsody and the raving in favour of something more temperate. The legends themselves have a certain wild and ghostly power; but the exaggeration of their teller's manner appears to be on the increase.

PITTSFIELD July?   *M discards a chapter of* The Confidence-Man:

As the word Abraham means the father of a great multitude of men so the word Mississippi means the father of a great multitude of waters. His tribes stream in from east & west, exceeding fruitful the lands they enrich. In this granary of a continent this basin of the Mississippi will not the nations be greatly multiplied & blest?

Above the Falls of St: Anthony for the most part he winds evenly in between banks of flags or tracts of pine over marble sands in waters so clear that the deepest fish have the [?] flight of the bird. Undisturbed as the lowly life in its bosom feeds the lowly life on its shores, the coronetted elk & the deer, while in the walrus form of some couched rock in the channel, furred over with moss, the furred bear on the marge seems to eye his amphibious children. Wood & wave wed, man is remote.

GANSEVOORT August 1   [M's thirty-seventh birthday]   *Herman Gansevoort's remembrancer:*
Herman Melville arrived here this evening.

M brings to his uncle a gift, presented by his mother, The Piazza Tales.

NEW YORK August [1]   *An article, "The Islands of the Pacific," in* Putnam's Monthly Magazine, *mentions* The Piazza Tales:

The author of that volume, in his Typee and Omoo, and other books, whose coloring is the blue South Sea and its green islands, has charmed thousands upon thousands of readers, so playing with fact and imagination that a world has admired the cunning of his pen.

COLOGNE August 4 *Samuel Shaw writes to his half-sister, Elizabeth Melville:*
I was just filling up the blank in my pocket diary for the 4th of August with the memorandum "From Dusseldorf to Cologne," when it occurred to me that it must be the ninth anniversary of your wedding day . . . How distinctly I remember the blue jacket I wore on that solemn occasion, and how disgusting wedding cake got to be! Subtract 9 from 22 and you have 13. Can it be possible that I was only 13 then?
. . . Remember me kindly to Herman, and tell him that I am pained to hear that he suffers so much from ill health.

GANSEVOORT August 7 *Herman Gansevoort's remembrancer:*
Herman & Allan [Melville] gone to Lake George, expected to meet D[aniel] Shepherd in the Carrs to join them on an excursion of pleasure.

PITTSFIELD August 8 *The* Berkshire County Eagle *reprints a portion of "A Trio of American Sailor-Authors" from the* Dublin University Magazine, *(via* Littell's Living Age) *to which an editorial post-script [by J. E. A. Smith?] is added:*
P.S. Since the above article appeared in the Dublin *Magazine*, Mr. Melville has published "The Piazza Tales" . . . "The Bell Tower" is a picturesque and arabesque tale well fitted to inspire an artist, as it did one [Webber] in New York who has made four striking sketches from it, which we trust will be engraved.
Mr. Melville is now in the prime of his life and in the freshness of his genius, and it is far from improbable will yet write something much better than any of the works upon which his reputation now rests.

LONDON August 8 *The Rev Arthur Tidman, Foreign Secretary of the London Missionary Society writes to the Rev Rufus Anderson, Secretary of the American Board of Commissioners for Foreign Missions:*
The last number of the Westminster Review, — a publication which is not only hostile to Evangelical religion, but has also a decided leaning to infidelity, — contained an article animadverting in no measured terms upon Christian Missions in general, and more particularly in application to the Islands of the Pacific. The author of the article appears to have derived his information, and to have grounded his strictures, chiefly on two works of an American Writer, Mr Herman Melville . . .
As these works have probably come under your notice, I need scarcely observe that they contain statements in regard to the working and results of Missionary operations in Polynesia, calculated to give pain to the

Christian friends of Missions, and to furnish a pretext for the sneers and insinuations of their opponents, as in the instance of the attack in the Westminster Review. I should therefore feel obliged by your informing me whether, any reply has yet been issued in America in refutation of the injurious representations contained in Mr Melville's books, and if such be the fact, I should be glad, through your friendly medium, to be favoured with a copy of the reply, of course at our expense, or perhaps you can inform me whether the reply is to be met with in this Country.

That Mr Melville's statements respecting the Missions, both at Tahiti and the Sandwich Islands, are for the most part gross misrepresentations, having no more substantial foundation than the idle and malevolent rumours of the worst portion of the foreign settlers in the Islands, we are firmly persuaded, but it may be worth consideration whether, in the event of their remaining unrefuted, it will not be to the prejudice of the good cause both in America and in this Country.

GANSEVOORT August 9 *Herman Gansevoort's remembrancer:*
Herman & Allan returned this morning in first train on R.R.

August 12 Herman Melville went to Sar[atoga] Spgs. by 1st train — to return this evening.

August 13 Herman rec^d letter from Allan, who is expected to leave Lake George the beginning of next week, Aug[ustus] Peebles came here in afternoon train.

August 14 Aug Peebles left here this morning Herman M. left with him to return this evening from Sar Springs —

August 16 Herman Melville left here in first train, for Arrowhead . . .

ALBANY August 16 *Peter Gansevoort's diary:*
Herman Melville called at the office & is to dine with us.

August 20 *Peter Gansevoort reserves his "whole house for [M], Lizzie & the Children," during the Albany meeting of the American Association for the Advancement of Science. [his letter to M, Oct 9]*

PITTSFIELD August 25 *M writes to Dix & Edwards, inquiring about the progress of sales on* The Piazza Tales. (*Dix & Edwards to M, Aug 30*)

August 30 *Dix, Edwards & Co sends M in reply a statement & a letter:*
        Costs $1048.62
        2500 Copies bound
        1047 Copies sold @ 60 ¢ $628.20
. . . we beg to enclose a statement of sales of Piazza Tales to this date, by which you will see that it has not yet paid expenses.

We published late in May, and business has been dull since that time, but is reviving with the opening of fall trade, and we feel the good influence upon sales of all our books.

The statement of Cost does not include any advertising or incidental expenses — We hope our next statement will show a handsome return.

BOSTON   September 1   *Lemuel Shaw writes to his son, Samuel:*

I suppose you have been informed by some of the family, how very ill, Herman has been. It is manifest to me from Elizabeth's letters, that she has felt great anxiety about him. When he is deeply engaged in one of his literary works, he confines him[self] to hard study many hours in the day, with little or no exercise, & this specially in winter for a great many days together. He probably thus overworks himself & brings on severe nervous affections. He has been advised strongly to break off this labor for some time, & take a voyage or a journey, & endeavor to recruit. No definite plan is arranged, but I think it may result, in this that in the autumn he will go away for four or five months, Elizabeth will come here with her younger children, Mrs Griggs & Augusta will each take one of the boys, their house at Pittsfield will be shut up. I think he needs such a change & that it would be highly beneficial to him & probably restore him.

NEW YORK   September [1]   *The Piazza Tales is reviewed in* The United States Magazine and Democratic Review:

The author of "Typee" and "Omoo" requires none of "the tricks of the trade" to secure a favorable audience for a collection of tales upon which he seems to have lavished even more than his usual care . . . All of them exhibit that peculiar richness of language, descriptive vitality, and splendidly sombre imagination which are the author's characteristics. Perhaps the admirers of Edgar Poe will see, or think they see, an imitation of his concentrated gloom in the wild, weird tale, called "Bartleby:" in the "Bell Tower," as well, there is a broad tinge of German mysticism, not free from some resemblance to Poe.

PHILADELPHIA   September 2   *The Rev John W. Dulles writes to the Rev Rufus Anderson:*

May I trespass upon your time so far as to ask for information as to where I can find *facts* in refutation of the South Sea statements of Melville in his Omoo &c — In the last (July) number of the Westminster Review there is an article on For[eign] Missions full of misrepresentation & old accusations — The subject as to the avowed failure of modern missions is up before our Pastoral Association & I am expected to be booked up on the question —

PITTSFIELD   September 3   *Sarah Morewood stages a second fancy dress pic-nic.*

Mrs. H[erman] M[elville], as the Genius of Greylock, was original and unique, her head being shrouded in nests and her dress decorated with leaves, pine cones, and other mountain trophies. Miss A[ugusta] M[elville] originated a new style of Berkshire fashions, the material being the leaves of the grove and the flowers of the field. Miss B[essie] M[elville], a miss of three years, as Little Bo-Peep . . . (*Berkshire County Eagle*, Sept 5)

BOSTON September 5   *The Rev Anderson replies to the Rev Dulles, providing him with a reading list to combat "that mischievous Review in the Westminster."*

HONG KONG September 10   *Thomas Melville writes to his mother.*

GANSEVOORT September 15   [?] *M & his family visit here.*

PANAMA September 18   *Commodore William Mervine writes to the Secretary of the Navy:*
Captain Farragut, Commandant of the Navy Yard, Mare Island Cal: informed me that he suspended Commander Guert Gansevoort on the 18th ultimo, for being intoxicated at 11 o'clock A M. of that day; and that he had appointed Lieut Edw Middleton to succeed him in the command of the Decatur . . .

I was not surprised to hear of the circumstances having long known indirectly that his habits in this respect are bad; but there is such a strong disposition generally prevailing among the younger officers to screen such acts, that it is seldom that any officer so offending can be brought to proper accountability.

PITTSFIELD September 24   *M presents his sister Augusta with a copy of* The Piazza Tales.

Before he left home he was convinced that a residence in the country was not the thing for him, & could he have met with an opportunity of disposing of his place he would have done so. — *Augusta Melville to Peter Gansevoort, Apr 7, 1857*

GANSEVOORT September 27   *Herman Gansevoort's remembrancer:*
Herman Melville brot his little son Stanwix to remain with us to stay untill his father returns from Europe.

September 28   Sister Maria, Fannie, Stanwix and Kate, attended Church — Self and Herman at home —

September 29   Herman Melville left here for New York, to take passage from there to Europe — I accompanied him to Saratoga Spgs —

NEW YORK September   The Piazza Tales *is noticed in* The Knickerbocker:
This series of stories, though partaking of the marvellous, are written with the author's usual felicity of expression, and minuteness of detail. The tale entitled 'Benito Cereno,' is most painfully interesting . . .

PHILADELPHIA September The Piazza Tales *is reviewed in* Godey's Lady's Book:
Herman Melville has numerous admirers, and perhaps his writings render him worthy of them; but — unfortunately, it may be, for ourselves — we cannot read his productions with much satisfaction. His style has an affectation of quaintness, which renders it, to us, very confused and wearisome.

NEW YORK September? *Publication of new edition of S. G. Good-rich's* Personal Recollections . . . :
   Most of the authors which we have named as belonging to the preceding era, shed their luster upon this. Among those who now first entered the lists, we may name . . .
   In Fiction — Melville, Kimball, Mayo, Mrs. Stowe . . .

October 1 *Evert Duyckinck's diary:*
Herman Melville passed the evening with me — fresh from his mountain charged to the muzzle with his sailor metaphysics and jargon of things unknowable. But a good stirring evening — ploughing deep and bringing to the surface some rich fruits of thought and experience — Melville instanced old Burton as atheistical — in the exquisite irony of his passages on some sacred matters; cited a good story from the Decameron the *Enchantment* of the husband in the tree; a story from Judge Edmonds of a prayer meeting of female convicts at Sing Sing which the Judge was invited to witness and agreed to, provided he was introduced where he could not be seen. It was an orgie of indecency and blasphemy. Said of Bayard Taylor that as some augur predicted the misfortunes of Charles I from the infelicity of his countenance so Taylor's prosperity 'borne up by the Gods' was written in his face.

GANSEVOORT October 5? Two days ago I went to Gansevoort to bid Mamma good bye, and in returning from there would have stopped to bid *you* also good bye & Aunt Susan, had not engagements forbid. — *M to Peter Gansevoort, Oct 7*

NEW YORK October 6 *Evert Duyckinck writes to his brother, George:*
   Herman Melville starts on another European pilgrimage in a few days by one of the Glasgow steamers — I think the 'Glasgow' on the 12ᵗʰ. He passed an evening with me last week. He goes to Italy — for a vacation I suppose. I hope you will meet in London. I shall send him to Barings for your address.

October 7 *M writes to Peter Gansevoort:*
   I think of sailing for the other side of the ocean on Saturday next, to be gone an uncertain time . . . Pray make my adieus to Aunt Susan & to Kate & Henry . . .

M picks up his passport & fills in a description of himself:

DESCRIPTION

Age 37 Years
Stature 5 Feet 8¾ Inches Eng^t
Forehead   medium
Eyes   Blue
Nose   Straight
Mouth   medium
Chin   Round
Hair   Dark Brown
Complexion   Fair
Face   oval

———— >•< ————

Signature of the Bearer

Herman Melville

October 8   *Allan Melville writes to Evert Duyckinck:*
Accompanying this I send you a copy of Saratoga written by Mr
Daniel Shepherd my friend and late partner . . .
    Mr. Shepherd is a friend of Hermans and is desirous of your further
acquaintance and [?] I propose to call with him upon you to night
& take the chance of your being at home.

Evert Duyckinck's diary:
In the evening home: Allan Melville brought his friend David Shepherd
whose novel just published 'Saratoga a Tale of 1787' he had sent me in the
afternoon.

October 9   In the evening at Mr Shepherd's, in 14th str with Herman
and Allan Melville and [Robert] Tomes. Good talk — Herman warming
like an old sailor over the supper — He is going to Italy for the winter.

ALBANY   October 9   *Peter Gansevoort replies to M's letter of Oct 7:*
I regret that your engagements prevented your stopping with us on y^r
return from G[ansevoort]. It would have not only gratified us but have
removed the edge of the disappt. during the Scientific Convention when
we reserved the whole house for you, Lizzie & the Children . . .
    Your Mother arrived yesterday we hope for a long visit . . .
    She unites with Susan, Kate & myself in best wishes & sincere prayers

for a pleasant & safe voyage & the restoration of your health & your return to your family & friends —

PITTSFIELD   October 10   *A paragraph in the* Berkshire County Eagle:
   Mr. Melville will sail from New York in the steamer of Saturday with intention of spending some months in Europe. — Mr. Melville much needs this relaxation from his severe literary labors of several years past, and we doubt not that he will return with renovated health and a new store of those observations of travel which he works [writes?] so charmingly. The literati of Europe will also have the opportunity to learn that Herman Melville is the real name of a man, and a real man all over.

BOSTON   Before October 11   When you went to Europe in the fall of 1856 I advanced the money necessary for your outfit and the expenses of your tour. This was done through your brother Allan and amounted to about fourteen or fifteen hundred dollars. In my own mind, though I took no note or obligation for it, I treated it like the other advances, to be regarded as advance by way of loan or a gift according to some future arrangement. — *Lemuel Shaw to M, May 15, 1860*

NEW YORK   October 10   *Dix & Edwards' first draft agreement with M to publish* The Confidence-Man.

October 11   *M's contracted delivery date for the manuscript of* The Confidence-Man *to Dix & Edwards.*

Elizabeth Melville's memoir of M:
   In Oct. 1856 his health being impaired by too close application he again sailed for London — taking manuscript books with him for publication there . . .

Evert Duyckinck's diary:
Another, yet another of the series of extraordinary fine days; sunny, mellow, quiesent. Saw Herman Melville off in the propeller Glasgow for Glasgow . . . Melville right hearty — Pleasant fates to him on his Neapolitan way.

BERLIN   October 19   *Samuel Savage Shaw writes to his mother:*
I was anxious to hear if Herman had sailed on the 4th as Lem intimated he might do. However I suppose that if he comes he will communicate with me through the Barings, if he does not get the letter which I have sent to Havre in time to meet him.

THE ATLANTIC   Before October 25   *M's journal:*
Conversations with the Colonel [George C. Rankin?] on fixed fate &c. during the passage.

The Glasgow had fourteen days passage encountered a gale, which made her lay to for sixteen hours, otherwise the passage was a favorable one. — *Maria Melville to Peter & Susan Gansevoort, Nov 11*

October 25   *M's journal:*
In 15 days made the north of Ireland, — Rathlin isle — passed Arran, Ailsa Crag &c (see map). Ailsa looming up in the mist. Got to Greenoch 10 at night, lay there at anchor . . .

GALENA   October 25   *Mary A. A. Melvill writes to Lemuel Shaw:*
We saw by the papers that Herman had sailed for Europe; I most sincerely hope that his health may be permanently benefited by the journey; doubtless he will while in Scotland visit the places that have long been the homes of his name & family.

GLASGOW   October 26   *M's journal:*
. . . next morning, Sunday, went up the Clyde to Glasgow. Great excitement all along. Banks like tow-paths — narrow channel — immense steamer — green heights — received by acclamation — Lord Blantyre's place — opposite mud cottage — cattle tenders — women — face like cattle — places for building iron steamers.

October 27   Next morning went to old cathedral, — tombs, defaced inscriptions — others worn in flagging — some letters traced in moss — back of cathedral gorge & stream — Acropolis — John Knox in Geneva cap frowning down on the cathedral — dimness of atmosphere in keeping — all looked like picture of one of the old masters smoked by Time — Old buildings about the hill, stone walls & thatch roof — solid & fragile — miserable poverty — look of the middle ages — west end & fine houses — the moderns — contemporary. — The University. The park — the promenade (Seychill street) — at night population in the middle of the street. High Street.

M sends newspapers to his mother, & a letter to his wife. (Elizabeth has received but one letter from her husband, written soon after his arrival at Glasgow. He expected after a few days in Scotland to proceed to Liverpool & thence to London, where he would inquire for you at Baring Bro. & Co. & thus probably be enabled to put himself in communication with you. I hope you will meet him, and so make your arrangements, as to travel together. — *Lemuel Shaw to his son, Samuel, Nov 23*)

LOCH LOMOND   October 28   *M's journal:*
Next morning took steamer down the Clyde to Loch Lomond — R.R. part of the way — thick mist, just saw the outline of Ben Lomond — like Lake George . . . — came back & stopped at Dumbarton Castle — isolated rock, like Ailsa — promontory at the juncture of the Clyde & Levern — covered with sod & moss — a cleft between — stone stairs & terraces — W. Wallace's broadsword — great cleaver — soldiers in red coats about the Rock like flamingoes among the cliffs — some rams with smoky fleeces — grenediers — smoked by the high chimneys of furnaces in Dumbarton village —

NEW YORK   October 28   *The agreement with Dix & Edwards to pub-lish* The Confidence-Man *is signed on M's behalf by Allan Melville:* 12½ *cents a copy to M after expenses are deducted.*

EDINBURGH   After October 28   *M stops here, begins a letter to his mother, & has his washing done:*

        9 Shirts
        1 Night shirt
       7 Handkerchiefs
        2 Pair stockings
        drawers & under shirt

Streets [of Genoa] like those of Edinburgh; only still more steep & crooked. — *M's journal, Apr 11, 1857*

[?] *M visits literary shrines at Abbotsford and/or the Isle of Wight; on the reverse of the business card of Henry Mew, Newport, is an itinerary sketched by M.*

YORK   Before November 8   *M stops here.*

LIVERPOOL   November 8   *M's journal:*
Arrived from York, through Lancaster, at 1.P.M., having passed through an interesting country of manufactures. A rainy day. Put up at "White Bear Hotel" Dale St:. Dined there at ordinary. Before sitting down, asked bar-maid, "How much?" Curious to observe the shrinking expression, as if shocked at the idea of anything mercenary having part in the pure hospitality of an ordinary. Host & hostess at table. Comical affectation of a private dinner party. All thought of the public house banished. Enter-taining his friends. "Will you have some ale?" — But charged in the bill. — Affectation of the unstinted bounty of a Christmas party, but great economy. — Capital bed. — After dinner went to Exchange. Looked at Nelson's statue, with peculiar emotion, mindful of 20 years ago. — Stayed at hotel during the evening. Rain. Made acquaintance with an agreeable young Scotchman going to the East in steamer "Damascus" on Monday. Wanted me to accompany him. Sorry that circumstances prevented me.

November 9   Rain. Stayed home till dinner. After dinner took steam-boat for Rock Ferry to find Mr Hawthorne. On getting to R.F., learned he had removed thence 18 months previous, & was residing out of town. — Spent evening at home.

November 10   Went among docks to see the Mediterranean steamers. Explored the new docks "Huskisson" &c. Saw Mr Hawthorne at the Consulate. Invited me to stay with him during my sojourn at Liverpool. — Dined at "Anderson's" a very nice place, & charges moderate.

Hawthorne's journal:
A week ago last Monday, Herman Melville came to see me at the Con-sulate, looking much as he used to do (a little paler, and perhaps a little

sadder), in a rough outside coat, and with his characteristic gravity and reserve of manner. He had crossed from New York to Glasgow in a screw steamer, about a fortnight before, and had since been seeing Edinburgh and other interesting places. I felt rather awkward at first; because this is the first time I have met him since my ineffectual attempt to get him a consular appointment from General Pierce. However, I failed only from real lack of power to serve him; so there was no reason to be ashamed, and we soon found ourselves on pretty much our former terms of sociability and confidence. Melville has not been well, of late; he has been affected with neuralgic complaints in his head and limbs, and no doubt has suffered from too constant literary occupation, pursued without much success, latterly; and his writings, for a long while past, have indicated a morbid state of mind. So he left his place at Pittsfield, and has established his wife and family, I believe, with his father-in-law in Boston, and is thus far on his way to Constantinople. I do not wonder that he found it necessary to take an airing through the world, after so many years of toilsome pen-labor and domestic life, following upon so wild and adventurous a youth as his was. I invited him to come and stay with us at Southport, as long as he might remain in this vicinity . . . [entry of Nov 20]

He appeared one day in Hawthorne's consulate at Liverpool, when [I] chanced to be present, and sat talking for an hour. But his talk was not in the improvisatorial style of the red-cottage days, it was for the most part unintelligible to me, a boy of eight or nine, and he seemed depressed and aimless. He said goodbye at last, and wandered away . . . (Julian Hawthorne, "Herman Melville," *The Dearborn Independent*, Sept 24, 1922)

SOUTHPORT November 11 *M's journal:*
Went among the steamers in the morning. Took afternoon train with Mr Hawthorne for Southport, 20 miles distant on the seashore, a watering place. Found Mrs. Hawthorne & the rest awaiting tea for us.

Hawthorne's journal:
. . . and, accordingly, he did come, the next day, taking with him, by way of luggage, the least little bit of a bundle, which, he told me, contained a night-shirt and a tooth-brush. He is a person of very gentlemanly instincts in every respect, save that he is a little heterodox in the matter of clean linen.
He stayed with us from Tuesday till Thursday . . .

GANSEVOORT November 11 *Maria Melville writes to Peter & Susan Gansevoort:*
We had two Newspapers from Glasgow this morning, sent by Herman . . .
I suppose Lizzie has received letters, which we shall soon have.

SOUTHPORT November 12 *M's journal:*

An agreeable day. Took a long walk by the sea. Sands & grass. Wild & desolate. A strong wind. Good talk. In the evening Stout & Fox & Geese. — Julian grown into a fine lad, Una taller than her mother. Mrs Hawthorne not in good health. Mʳ H. stayed home for me.

Promenade & beach at Southport, Lancashire

Hawthorne's journal:
. . . on the intervening day, we took a pretty long walk together, and sat down in a hollow among the sand hills (sheltering ourselves from the high, cool wind) and smoked a cigar. Melville, as he always does, began to reason of Providence and futurity, and of everything that lies beyond human ken, and informed me that he had "pretty much made up his mind to be annihilated;" but still he does not seem to rest in that anticipation; and, I think, will never rest until he gets hold of a definite belief. It is strange how he persists — and has persisted ever since I knew him, and probably long before — in wandering to and fro over these deserts, as dismal and monotonous as the sand hills amid which we were sitting. He can neither believe, nor be comfortable in his unbelief; and he is too honest and courageous not to try to do one or the other. If he were a religious man, he would be one of the most truly religious and reverential; he has a very high and noble nature, and better worth immortality than most of us.

LIVERPOOL November 13   *M's journal:*
At Southport till noon. Mʳ H. & I took train then for Liverpool. Spent rest of day pressing inquiries among steamers, & writing letters, & addressing papers &c.

[*529*]

M completes the letter to his mother. (. . . I am happy to learn, his health is improving & that he is aware of the necessity of cessation from writing — & is convinced that by travelling he is renovating his system — *Peter Gansevoort to Maria Melville, Nov 27*)

November 14   *M's journal:*
Took 'buss for London Road, — "Old Swan" Passed grealry [?]. Returning, called at Mr Hawthornes. Met a Mr Bright. Took me to his club & lunched there. Then to view Unitarian church, & Free Library & Cemetery.

M has his passport endorsed:
Exhibited at the Consulate of the United States of America at Liverpool this 14th November 1856
    Good for Constantinople (via Malta & Gibraltar) Egypt & a tour about the Continent   Nathl Hawthorne

M gets his Turkish visa at the Consulat Ottoman.

CHESTER November 15   *M's journal:*
Rode in the omnibus. Went out to Toxteth Park &c — Grand organ at St. George's Hall.

Hawthorne's journal:
On Saturday, Melville and I went to Chester together. I love to take every opportunity of going to Chester; it being the one only place, within easy reach of Liverpool, which possesses any old English interest. It was a fitful and uncertain day; and began to shower just as we left the Landing Stage in crossing the Mersey; but, arriving at Chester, we had glimpses of sunshine, and walked round the wall with hardly a spatter of rain . . .
    It being now one °clock, or thereabouts, we walked through some of the Rows, in quest of a dinner, and found one in a confectioner's shop . . . We were shown upstairs, into an antique room fronting on the street, with cross-beams, panelled walls, a large table and some smaller ones, and a good fire. The waiting maid brought us some little veal-pies on a tray, and some damson tarts on another tray; and we had, besides, some Bass's ale, and made a very comfortable meal at the cost of a shilling and two-pence each. And then we went to the Cathedral . . .
    [In the Refectory] we went through a small room in which Melville opened a cupboard and discovered a dozen or two of wine-bottles; but our guide told us that they were now empty, and never were meant for jollity, having held only sacramental wine. In the Chapter House we saw the library, some of the volumes of which were antique folios . . .
    After leaving the Cathedral, we sought out the Yacht Inn, near the Water Gate. This was, for a long period of time, the principal inn of Chester, and was the house at which Swift once put up, on his way to Holyhead, and where he invited the clergy of the Cathedral to come and sup with him. We sat down in a small snuggery, behind the bar, and

smoked a cigar and drank some stout, conversing the while with the landlord . . .

We left Chester at about four °clock; and I took the rail for Southport at half-past six, parting from Melville at a street-corner in Liverpool, in the rainy evening.

LIVERPOOL November 16   *M's journal:*
In the morning packed trunk. To church in the afternoon, & evening.

November 17   *Hawthorne's journal:*
I saw him again on Monday, however. He said that he already felt much better than in America; but observed that he did not anticipate much pleasure in his rambles, for that the spirit of adventure is gone out of him. He certainly is much overshadowed since I saw him last; but I hope he will brighten as he goes onward.

M's journal:
Was to sail to day in "Egyptian" Captain Tate, but put off till tomorrow. Great disappointment. Tired of Liverpool.

November 18   *Hawthorne's journal:*
He sailed from Liverpool in a steamer on Tuesday, leaving his trunk behind him at my consulate, and taking only a carpet-bag to hold all his travelling-gear. This is the next best thing to going naked; and as he wears his beard and moustache, and so needs no dressing-case — nothing but a tooth-brush — I do not know a more independent personage. He learned his travelling habits by drifting about, all over the South Sea, with no other clothes or equipage than a red flannel shirt and a pair of duck trowsers. Yet we seldom see men of less criticizable manners than he.

M's journal:
Sailed about three o'clock. Fine sight going out of harbor.

NEW YORK November 18   *Evert Duyckinck writes to his brother, George:*
Melville will, probably has been to see you. I have heard of him at Glasgow on his way to London. His publishers here announce 'The Confidence Man' a new volume which he left behind him — a fine playful subject for a humorist philosopher.

IRISH SEA November 19   *M heads his subsequent entries, "Voyage from Liverpool to Constantinople," to be written up later for publication(?):*
Saw Tusca [Tuskar] Rock, on Irish Coast.

November 20-22   Fair wind & fine weather. Passed Cape Finisterre.

November 23   Passed within a third of a mile of Cape St: Vincent. Light house & monastery on bold cliff. Cross. Cave underneath light house. The whole Atlantic breaks here. Lovely afternoon. Great procession of ships bound to Crimea must have been descried from this point.

November 24   Strong wind ahead. Sighted Cape Trafalgar. Entered the Strait of Gibraltar at 4.P.M. . . . Insular Rock. Sunset. Rock strongly lit, all the rest in shade. England throwing the rest of the world in shade. Vast heigth. Red sky . . . Calm within Straits. Long swell took us. The Mediterranean.

November 25   Beautiful morning. Blue sea & sky. Warm as May. Spanish coast in sight. Mountains, snow capped, always so Captain says. Mate came out with straw hat. Shirt sleeves. Threw open my coat. — Such weather as one might have in Paradise. Pacific. November too! Like sailing on a lake.

November 26   At sunrise close to African Coast. Mountains, in parts crested with snow. Peeps of villages. Wild looking. At noon, off Algiers. In the vicinity beautiful residences among the hills. White house among gardens. Reminded one of passages in Don Quixotte, "Story of the Morisco." Saw the mole & light house — the town built up a hill — latteen boats in view. The sun hot. High mountains all around. Fine bay. Piratical corsair look. — Leaving it in the distance the town looked like a sloping rock, covered with bird lime — the houses all white. — In the afternoon passed a detached group of very high mountains covered a long way down with snow — Alpine heights. The most solitary & dreariest imaginable.

GANSEVOORT   November 26   *Maria Melville receives M's letter & forwards it to Peter Gansevoort:*
    I received the enclosed letter from Herman this morning, knowing you feel an interest in all that concerns him, I thought you would like to read this letter the first I have had from him . . .
    I received a pleasant letter from Helen this morning, they are all well, & take their Thanksgiving dinner tomorrow at Judges Shaws — Lizzie & the children are well and most agreeably & comfortably accommodated at her Fathers for the winter or until Hermans return from abroad . . .
    Please do not fail to return this letter by the next days mail.

MEDITERRANEAN   November 27   *M's journal:*
Same glorious weather. In the evening passed Isle Galeta — uninhabited. Clear nights, stars shining with brilliancy.

ALBANY   November 27   *Peter Gansevoort writes to Maria Melville (returning M's letter):*
    I thank you my dear Sister for yr favor enclosing a letter from Herman at Edinburgh & Liverpool, which I have read with very great pleasure . . .
    I am glad that he has gone to the Mediterranean, & I hope he will remain absent until his health is re-established.

MEDITERRANEAN November 28   *M's journal:*
Bright & blue as usual. At noon passed close to Pantalaria . . . Cultivated slopes & plains all round a mass of lofty rock. Beautiful landscapes inland. A town & scattered houses. A large castle. Belongs to Naples. Convicts here. — Went to bed at 8.P.M. and at 1.A.M. dressed & went on deck, the ship about entering Malta harbor. To bed again when anchor was down.

GANSEVOORT November 28   *Maria Melville writes to Peter Gansevoort:*
I received your letter this morning enclosing Hermans from abroad & the circular —
I hope Herman will feel content to remain away for six months at least for he has sadly overworked his strength — & requires recreation, freedom from care, from writing, & the little petty cares, & annoyances, of the farm which are ever recurring & are so distasteful to him.

MALTA November 29   *M's journal:*
Lying in the harbor of Malta. Ashore all day. At 6.P.M. got under weigh, with two passengers in cabin, a Greek & Austrian, very gentlemanly men.

November 30   Cross sea, ship rolling very bad. G[reek] & A[ustrian] quite sick. Rather dismal day. At night had to secure myself in berth against being rolled out.

SOUTHPORT November 30   *Una Hawthorne writes to her aunt, Elizabeth Peabody:*
Mr. Melville was here a day or two, and Mamma overtired herself during his visit, and was quite unwell for a day or two afterwards.

MEDITERRANEAN December 1   *M's journal:*
Sea less cross. At 12.M. pleasant, & made the coast of Greece, the Morea. Passed through the straits, & Cape Matapan.

SYRA December 2   At daylight in the midst of Archipelago; 12 or 15 islands about. Came to anchor at Syra about 8 A.M. Port of the Archipelago. Much alarmed lest we should have a quarantine of eleven days. Saw the quarantine house — lonely place among bare hills; opposite the shipping. At the Custom house with the Captain & his papers; at a grating, took the ship's papers with pair of wooden tongs. Meantime an officer off to the ship to muster the crew; if one was dead, or missing, — quarantine! All right, though. — Went ashore. New & Old Town. Animated appearance of the quay. Take all the actors of opera in a night from the theatres of London, & set them to work in their fancy dresses, weighing bales, counting codfish, sitting at tables on the dock, smoking, talking, sauntering, — sitting in boats &c — picking up rags, carrying water casks, lemonade &c — will give some notion of Greek port . . . Went to Old Town

. . . Climbed up. Complete warren of stone houses or rather huts, built without the least plan, zig-zag, little corrals in front of each, sometimes overhead, crossing the track. Paved with stone, roofs flat & m'cadamed. Up & up, only guide was *to mount.* At last got to the top, a church, from court of which, fine view of archipelago & islands (name them) — Looks very old; — probably place of defence. Poor people live here. Picturesque. Some old men looked like Pericles reduced to a chiffonier — such a union of picturesque & poverty stricken. — Streets of stairs up the Old Town. As if made for goats. The donkeys climb them. All round barren tawny hills, here & there terraced with stone. Saw a man ploughing with a peice of old root . . .

December 3   *M again goes ashore at Syra.*

December 4   *M's journal:*
On the last day I did not go ashore. Several steamers arrived. Got my sovereigns back from Loyd's. Our two passengers sailed for Athens.

December 5   At 2 A.M. got under weigh for Salonica. Passed various islands. First bad weather encountered since leaving England. Rain & wind. About sunset passed through very narrow passage into the Gulf of Salonica. In the cabin had a Greek gentleman & wife for passengers . . .

SALONICA December 6   At day break roused by the Captain to come on deck. Did so. Saw Mount Olympus, covered with snow at the summit, & looking most majestic in the dawn. Ossa & Pelion to the South . . . Mount Athos (rather conical) on the opposite shore. About nine o'clock came to anchor before Salonica. A walled town on a hill side. Wall built by Genoese. Minarets & cypress trees the most conspicuous objects. Two Turkish men of war in harbor. Olympus over against the town far across the water, in plain sight. Went with Captain with papers to the quarantine. All right & shook hands. (Usual ceremony of welcome). Went to the Abbots, ship's agents. Politely received. One of their employees took me a stroll through the town. Went into the mosques . . . Went into the Bazaar. Quite large, but filthy. Streets all narrow, like cow lanes, & smelling like barn-yards. Very silent. Women muffled about the face. All old. No young. Great numbers of Jews walking in long robes & pelisses. Also Greeks mixed with the Turks. Aspect of streets like those of Five Points [in New York City]. Rotten houses. Smell of rotten wood . . .

December 7   Purposed going with Captain Tate to the Protestant missionaries, but learned they were absent at Cassandra. Duckworth, the English resident, came off early. Talked with him. Said he had been *a day's shooting in the Vale of Tempe* — Ye Gods! whortleberrying on Olympus, &c. — Went ashore with Captain. Started from Abbots' on horseback with a guide & guard to the Abbots place three miles inland. On emerging from gate met the first troop of camels. Passed an immense cemetery. Turbanded tombstones. Rode over bleak hills — no verdure — here & there an old sycamore . . . Abbots place enclosed by high thick stone wall. On knocking, after a good time, gate was opened, & we were repulsed. But presented letter. Guards came running with muskets. Letter read at last by a handsome, polite Greek, who then led us through the grounds . . . Served with sweetmeats & liquers & coffee. Bath rooms. Thick dome perforated — light but no heat. — Returned at 3 P.M. & dined aboard . . . In the evening Captain told a story about the heat of arms affecting the compass.

BERLIN December 7 *Samuel S. Shaw writes to his mother:*
I received your letter week before last, and one from Elizabeth this last week, in which she gives me Herman's direction — I have a letter ready for him & hope to get some news from him . . .

SALONICA December 8 *M's journal:*
Lovely day. Ashore & visited the walls. Was repulsed from a tower by a soldier who refused money. Went through the bazars. At the landing watched for an hour or two a vast crowd & tourist [?]. An Austrian steamer from Constantinople just in, with a great host of poor deck passengers, Turks, Greeks, Jews &c . . . After dinner on board, several deck passengers came off to us to go to Constantinople. Turkish women among others. Went right aft on deck & spread their carpets . . . Heard a rumor by way of Trieste that Louis Napoleon had been assassinated . . .

December 9 Remained on board, observing the arrival of deck passengers for Constantinople. A large number in all costumes. Among others two "beys effendi" in long furred robes of yellow, looking like Tom cats. They had their harems with them. All on deck. At 1½ P.M. got under weigh. Lovely day. A calm. Ship steady as a house. Like a day in May. A moonlight night followed . . . Got up tents for the two harems. Guard set up over them. Fine old effendi wounded at Sinope. Some very pretty women of the harem . . .

December 10 [John C. Hoadley's 38th birthday] Up early, fine morning, off "Lemnos, the AEgean isle". Passed to the north of it, between it & Imbros. About 11 A.M. entered the Helespont . . . 8½ P.M. Tomorrow morning I must rise betimes to behold Constantinople, where it remains to be seen how long I shall sojourn.

December 11 Thick fog during the night. Steamed very slowly, ringing the bell. Ere daylight came to anchor in the Sea of Marmora, as near as the Captain could determine, within but three miles or less of Constantinople. All day the fog held on. Very thick, & damp & raw. Very miserable for the Turks & their harems . . . Old Turk ("Old Sinope") I said to him "This is very bad" he answered "God's will is good, & smoked his pipe in cheerful resignation.

CONSTANTINOPLE December 12 About noon fog slowly cleared away before a gentle breeze. At last, as it opened around us, we found ourselves lying, as in enchantment, among the Prince Islands, scores of vessels in our own predicament around us . . . The fog only lifted from about the skirts of the city, which being built upon a promontory, left the crown of it hidden wrapped in vapor. Could see the base & wall of St. Sophia, but not the dome. It was a coy disclosure, a kind of coquetting, leaving room for imagination & heightening the scene. Constantinople, like her Sultanas, was thus seen veiled in her "ashmack." Magic effect of the lifting up of the fog disclosing such a city as Constantinople. — At last rounded Seraglio Point & came to anchor at 2 P M in the Golden Horn. Crossed over to Tophanna in a caique . . . No demand made for passport nor any examination of luggage. Got a guide to Hotel du Globe in Pera. Wandered about a little before dinner. Dined at 6 P.M. 10 F per day for 5th story room without a carpet &c. Staid in all night. Dangerous going out, owing to footpads & assassins . . .

December 13 Up early; went out; saw cemeteries, where they dumped garbage. Sawing wood over a tomb. Forrests of cemeteries. Intricacy of the streets. Started alone for Constantinople and after a terrible long walk, found myself back where I started . . . Just like getting lost in a wood. No plan to streets. Pocket-compass. Perfect labyrinth. Narrow. Close, shut in. If one could but get *up* aloft, it would be easy to see one's way out. If you could but get up into tree. Soar out of the maze. But no. No names to the streets no more than to natural allies among the groves. No numbers. No anything. — Breakfast at 10 A.M. Took guide ($1.25 per day) and started for a tour. Took caique for Seraglio. Holy ground . . . Saw the mosque of St Sophia. Went in. Rascally priests demanding "baksheesh". Fleeced me out of ½ dollar; following me round, selling the fallen mosaics. Ascended a kind of horse way leading up, round & round. Came out into a gallery fifty feet above the floor. Superb interior . . .

— To the Hippodrome, near which stands the six towered mosque of Sultan Achmet; soaring up with its snowy spires into the pure blue sky (like lighthouses) . . . Then to the Cistern of 1001 columns. You see a rounded knoll covered with close herbage. Then a kind of broken cellar way, you go down, & find yourself on a wooden, rickety platform, looking down into a grove of marble pillars, fading away into utter darkness. A palatial sort of Tartarus . . . Used to be a reservoir. Now full of boys twisting silk. Great hubbub. Flit about like imps. Whir of the spinning jennies. In going down, (as into a ship's hold) and wandering about, have to beware the innumerable skeins of silk. Terrible place to be robbed or murdered in . . . To the Bazarr. A wilderness of traffic. Furniture, arms, silks, confectionery, shoes, saddles — everything . . . You loose yourself & are bewildered & confounded with the labyrinth, the din, the barbaric confusion of the whole. — Went to the Watch Tower within a kind of arsenal . . . From the top, My God, what a view! Surpasses everything

. . . Went down to Golden Horn. Crossed bridge of pontoons. Stood in the middle & not a cloud in the sky. Deep blue & clear. (Sultan's sloop in colors — no atmosphere like this for flags.) Delightful elastic atmosphere, altho December. A kind of English June, cooled & tempered sherbet-like with an American October . . . Came home through the vast suburbs of Galata &c . . . You feel you are among the nations. Great curse that of Babel; not being able to talk to a fellow being, &c. — Have to beware of your pockets. My guide went with his hands to his. — The horrible grimy tragic air of these streets. The rotten & wicked looking houses. So gloomy & grimy seems as if a suicide hung from every rafter within.

December 14   Three Sabbaths a week in Constantinople. Friday, Turks; Sat, Jews; Sunday, Romanists, Greeks, & Armenians. — At 8. A M crossed over the 2^d bridge to Stamboul to ride round the Walls. Passed between wall & Golden Horn through Greek & Jew quarters, and came outside the land wall in view of Sweet Waters, which run inland & end in beautiful glades. Rode along the land wall . . . A beautiful cave chapel — a fountain of holy water — Greeks come here & wash & burn a candle. All round under the trees people smoking nargiles, drinking & eating, & riding. Gay crowds. Greek Sunday. Rode to the wall-end at Sea of Marmora . . . Immensely long ride back within the walls. Lonely streets . . . Recrossed the 2d bridge to Pera. Too late for the Dancing Dervishes. Saw their convent. Reminded me of the Shakers. — Went towards the cemeteries of Pera . . . saw a woman over a new grave — no grass on it yet. Such abandonment of misery! Called to the dead, put her head down as close to it as possible; as if calling down a hatchway or cellar; besought — "Why dont you speak to me? My God! — It is I! Ah, — speak — but one word! — All deaf. — So much for consolation. — This woman & her cries haunt me horribly. ——
Street sights. — The beauty of the human countenance. Among the women ugly faces are rare. — Singular these races so exceed ours in this respect . . .

December 15   Utterly used up last night. This morning felt as if broken on the wheel. — At eleven oclock went out without guide. Mounted the Genoese Tower . . . After much study succeeded in understanding the way to the two great bridges. Came down, & crossed the first bridge. There took a boy-guide to the bazar. (All the way from the G. Tower down steep hill to bridge, a steady stream of people) . . . After dismissing my boy, was followed for two or three hours by an infernal Greek, & confederates. Dogged me; in & out & through the Bazaar. I could neither intimidate or elude them. Began to feel nervous; remembered that much of the fearful interest of Schiller's Ghost-Seer hangs upon being followed in Venice by an Armenian. The mere mysterious, persistent, silent following. At last escaped them. Went to the Aga Janissary's . . . Strange books in the Mosque bazaar. — Englishman at dinner. Invited me to Buyukderre — give me a shake down &c. Said nothing would tempt him to go by night through Galata.

NEW YORK December 15   *Contracted publication date for* The Confidence-Man.

CONSTANTINOPLE December 16   *M's journal:*
At 8½ A.M. took steamer up the Bosphorus to Buyukdereh. — Magnificent! The whole scene one pomp of Art & Nature. Europe & Asia here show their best . . . Myrtle, Cyprus, Cedar — evergreens. — Catch glimpse of Euxine from Buyukdereh. The water clear as Ontario . . . One peculiarity is the introduction of ocean into inland recesses. Ships anchor at the foot of ravines, deep among green basins, where the only canvas you would look for would be tents. — A gallery of ports & harbors, formed by the interchange of promontory & bay. Many parts like the Highlands of the Hudson, magnified . . . "Royal Albert" Euxine in sight from Buyukdereh. A chain of Lake Georges. No wonder the Czars have always coveted the capital of the Sultans . . . Wandered about in vicinity of Hippodrome till nearly dusk; lost myself, & finally came out at a gate on the Sea of Marmora. Returned to Tophanna by kayeck . . . At dinner to day the French attache estimated the population of Constantinople, suburbs, & banks of Bosphorus at 1,500,000.

December 17   Spent the day revisiting the Seraglio &c . . . The courts & grounds of Seraglio have a strange, enchanted sort of look. — *The dogs*, roam about in bands like prairie wolves . . . Wandering about came across Black Hole in the street. Did not enter far. — Harem (sacred) on board steam boats. Lattic division. Ladies pale, slight noses, regular features, fine busts. Look like nuns in their plain dress, but with a roundness of bust not belonging to that character. Perfect decorum between sexes. No ogling. No pertness. No looking for admiration. No Cyprians. No drunkards. Saw not a single one, though liquor is sold.

SCUTARI December 18   In morning took caique, & crossed the Bosphorus to Scutari. Luxurious sailing. Cushioned like ottoman. You lie in the boat's bottom. Body beneath the surface. A boat bed . . . Great barracks at Scutari; Noble view of Constantinople & up Bosphorus.

CONSTANTINOPLE December 18   At 4 P.M. sailed in steamer Acadia for Alexandria, via Smyrna. It was sunset ere we rounded Seraglio Point. Glorious night. Scutari & its heights, glowed like sapphire . . . Out into Sea of Marmora.

MYTELENE December 19   Passed through Dardenelles at daybreak. Showers of rain. Cleared off. Passed Plain of Troy, Mount Ida beyond. Passed the tumulus of Achilles &c. Steered in between Tenedos & the main. Passed a town & harbor of Tenedos . . . The Asiatic coast all along lofty with ranges of mountains in the background — a yellow look.

Steered in between Mytelene & the main. A large & lovely island, covered with olive trees. They make much wine. The whole island green from beach to hill-top. — a dark rich bronzy green, in marked contrast with the yellow & parched aspect of most other isles of the Archipelago — Asia looks in color like those Asiatic lions one sees in menageries . . . Near sunset came to anchor for the night in a little bay of Mytelene, so as to have the benefit of daylight for getting into Smyrna, a ticklish harbor. Sent a boat off to get soundings. A boat came from shore; brought olives & figs.

SMYRNA   December 20   At two in the morning up anchor at Mytelene, and by daylight were entering the bay of Smyrna . . . Met the steamer Egyptian in port; saw Cap. Tate . . . Went ashore & called up[on] American Consul [E. S. Offley], a Greek. Spent an hour conversing with him & his brother, Got a guide . . . and went to Bazarr, to see the slaves. Failed. Went up Mt Pagus. A large circuit . . . An old ruinous mosque within. A Boston name written there. Descended, & went to the Caravan Bridge . . .

December 21   Called with Captain Tate upon his agent [Eustace?] living in a handsome house upon the Marinar. Married to a Greek lady, with a child that speaks as yet only Greek, her father a Scotchman. With reference to the American Mission here the agent said it was about discontinued; a hopeless affair; all the converts male, mercenary ones. Attended chapel at the English Consulate. Very flat affair; the chaplain, however, a curiosity. — There dined today on board "Arcadia" C. Orpheus, C Tate, C. Eustace & self. Much talk of India voyages.

December 22   Went ashore in the morning, interested in the curious appearance of strings of loaded camels passing through the narrow & crowded covered ways of the Bazaar. Heard a good deal about the commerce of England with Turkey . . . Altho' it was a little rainy the morning of our arrival here, yet ever since, the weather has been very beautiful, like fine Spring days at home. This evening an odd affair between C Orpheus & his first officer, to which I was an unavoidable listener.

December 23   Expect to sail to day for Syra, so did not go ashore. Two passengers came off to day, one a Greek officer, a comical looking fellow. — Got under weigh for Syra about 3. P. M. Fine sail down the bay.

SYRA   December 24   Came on blowing a gale outside, but by morning pleasant weather. Strong winds of short continuance here. Approached Syra by Myconi Passage between the islands of Myconi & Tinos. Many other isles scattered about. Among others, Delos, of a most barren aspect, however flowery in fable. I heard it was peculiarly sterile. Patmos, too, not remote; another disenchanting isle . . . Came to anchor at 12. M. Put us in quarantine for 24 hours (to begin from time of leaving Smyrna) tho' no case of illness on board. C. storms at the nuisance.

December 25   *Christmas* . . . Went ashore to renew my impressions of the previous visit . . . They have quite a ship-yard here. Two Greek men-of-war lie here; little fellows, yawls-of-war one might call them . . . In the afternoon some Greek ladies came off, passengers for Alexandria. At five P.M. got under weigh — Farewell to Syra and the Greeks & away for Egypt & the Arabs.

Last night the Captain mildly celebrated the day with a glass of Champagne . . . [entry of Dec 26]

BOSTON   December 25-27   *Hope Shaw writes to her son, Samuel, in Berlin:*
Elizabeth's children so far has been much blessed with health — may this scourge [of scarlet fever] not enter this house . . .
   Elizabeth has not heard one word from Herman since her husband left Liverpool, for Constantinople.

AEGEAN SEA   December 26   *M's journal:*
This morning was invited by Chief Engineer to inspect his department. The furnaces were a fearful scene. A hell in the hull. All day a head wind & bad sea. Passengers mostly laid up. The Greeks invisible. Passed pretty close to Scarpanti, — rugged & barren — Rhodes in sight.

December 27   Sea gone down with the wind. Towards noon fine weather, transparent air & a Syrian sun, rather scortching to the cheek. Expect to reach Alexandria tomorrow early.

ALEXANDRIA   December 28   At early morning came in sight of Alexandria Light-house, and shortly after, saw Pompey's Pillar. Landed at 10.A.M. Donkey to hotel, near which garden of the date palm . . . Rode along banks of Canal of Mohammed, and to Garden of the Pasha.

December 29   Called at Consul's for my passport. M^r [Edwin] De Leon formerly political literary man at Washington. Met officers of the U.S.F. Constellation. Went to the Catacombs on the sea.

Wonderful appearance of the sea at noon. Sea & sky melted into each other. Pompey's Pillar like long stick of candy, well sucked. Cleopatra's needles close by hovels. One down & covered. Sighing of the waves. Cries of watchmen at night. Lanterns. Assassins. Sun strokes. [entry of Jan 3]

BOSTON   December 29   *Lemuel Shaw, Jr writes to his brother, Samuel:*
   We have heard nothing from Herman since I last wrote you, when he was on the point of leaving Liverpool for Constantinople — we do not know whether he will go from there to Trieste & Venice or Naples or Ancona & cannot put you in the way of meeting him, when we do hear from him we will let you know — Lizzie & her two youngest children are still with us . . .

THE DELTA December 30   *M's journal:*
Ride to Cairo from Alexandria. The Delta. Like Mohawk Flats in Spring.
Soil like moist pulverized manure. Seems spaded over. Barn-yard. 4 crops
a year. Sugar, wheat, cotton. — Villages of unbaked brick. Wasps nests
& mud pies . . . Buffalo, camel, donkey. Palms. Villages like sand banks
at distance. Approaching Cairo long avenues (raised above level) pro-
cessions of people, crossing & recrossing at long distances . . . From the
car (1st class) you seem in England. All else Egypt. Seems unreal & a
panorama, beginning with Pompey's Pillar & ending with Cheops. [entry
of Jan 3]

To Cairo, arrived there at 4 P.M. put up at Shepherd's. Walked about
the square with Dr [John A.] Lockwood [of the *Constellation*].

. . . [Cairo] seems one booth and Bartholemew Fair — a grand masquerade of mortality . . . The houses seem a collection of old orchestras, or-
gans, proscenium boxes, — or like masses of old furniture (grotesque)
lumbering a garret & covered with dust . . . Great numbers of uninhabited houses in the lonelier parts of the city. Their dusty, cadaverous
ogerish look. Ghostly, & suggestive of all that is weird. Haunted houses
& Cock Lanes. Ruined mosques, domes knocked in like stoven boats.
Others, upper part empty & desolate with broken rafters & dismantled
windows; (rubbish); below, the dirty rites of religion. Aspect of the
thoroughfares like London streets on Saturday night. All the world gos-
sipping & marketing, — but in picturesque costumes. Crookedness of the
streets — multitudes of blind men — worst city in the world for them.
Flies on the eyes at noon. Nature feeding on man. Contiguity of desert &
verdure, splendor & squalor, gloom & gayety; numerous blind men going
about led. Children opthalmic. Too much light & no defence against it. —
The antiquity of Egypt stamped upon individuals. — Appearance of the
women. Thing for the face. Black crape hanging like trunk of elephant.
Profusion of jewelry. Brass on face . . .

Life at hotel. Magnitude of Shepherds, lofty ceilings, stone floors, iron
beds, no carpets, thin mattresses, no feathers, blinds, moscho curtains. —
All showing the tropics. And that you are in the East is shown by fresh
dates on table for desert, water in stone jars — (cool) waited on by
Arabs — dragomen — clap your hands for servants. — Brilliant scene at late
dinner — hard to believe you are near the pyramids. Yet some repose in
fastidiousness. [entries of Jan 3]

December 31   To the Pyramids; through the town to the Citadel & back
to Shepherd's at night fall. — Never shall forget this day. It racks me that
I can only spend one day in Cairo, owing to steamer.

The Sphynx. back to desert & face to verdure. Solid rock. — You ride
through palms to the pyramids. You are carried across the mire &c by
Arabs. The two black Sheiks in black robes. ——

The Pyramids . . . As with the ocean, you learn as much of its vastness by the first five minutes glance as you would in a month, so with the pyramid. Its simplicity confounds you . . . The tearing away of the casing, though it removed enough stone to build a walled-town, has not one whit subtracted from the apparent magnitude of the pyramid. It has had just the contrary effect. When the pyramid presented a smooth plane, it must have lost as much in impressiveness as the ocean does when unfurrowed. A dead calm of masonry. But now the ridges majestically diversify it.

Pyramids from distance purple like mountains. Seem high & pointed, but flatten & depress as you approach. Vapors below summits. Kites sweeping & soaring around, hovering right over apex. All angles, like broken cliffs . . . Pyramids on a great ridge of sand. You leave the angle, and ascend hillock of sand & ashes & broken mortar & pottery to a point, & then go along a ledge to a path &c. Zig-zag routes, As many routes as to cross the Alps — The Simplon, Great St: Bernard &c. Mules on Andes. Caves — platforms. Looks larger midway than from top or bottom. Precipice on precipice, cliff on cliff. Nothing in Nature gives such an idea of vastness. A ballon to ascend them. View of persons ascending, Arab guides in flowing white mantles. Conducted as by angels up to heaven. Guides so tender. Resting. Pain in the chest. Exhaustion. Must hurry. None but the phlegmatic go deliberately. Old man with the spirits of youth — long looked for this chance — tried the ascent, half way — failed — brought down. Tried to go into the interior — fainted — brought out — leaned against the pyramid by the entrance — pale as death. Nothing so pathetic. Too much for him; oppressed by the massiveness & mystery of the pyramids. I myself too. A feeling of awe & terror came over me. Dread of the Arabs. Offering to lead me into a side-hole. The Dust. Long arched way, — then down as in a coal shaft. Then as in mines, under the sea. (At one moment seeming in the Mammoth Cave. Subterranean gorges, &c.) The stooping & doubling. I shudder at idea of ancient Egyptians. It was in these pyramids that was conceived the idea of Jehovah. Terrible mixture of the cunning and awful. [entries of Jan 3]

> [Slant from your inmost lead the caves
> And labyrinths rumored. These who braves
> And penetrates (old palmers said)
> Comes out afar on deserts dead
>   And, dying, raves.
>
> Craftsmen, in dateless quarries dim,
> Stones formless into form did trim,
> Usurped on Nature's self with Art,
> And bade this dumb I AM to start,
>   Imposing him.
>   ("The Great Pyramid")]

*

1 8 5 7

*

ALEXANDRIA January 1 *M's journal:*
From Cairo to Alexandria. Put up at Victoria Hotel.

January 2 Expected to have sailed to day for Jaffa. But steamer not arrived. Spent day reading a book on Palestine.

M gets his passport visaed at the American Consulate, "buono per Jaffa e Smirna."

January 3 *M's journal:*
Steamer for Jaffa will not sail till tomorrow, so that I am wearied to death with two days in Alexandria which might have been delightfully spent in Cairo. But travellers must expect these things. — I will now without any order jot down my impressions of Cairo, ere they grow dim . . . Pyramids still loom before me — something vast, indefinite, incomprehensible, and awful. Line of desert & verdure, plain as line between good & evil. An instant collision of the two elements. A long billow of desert forever hovers as in act of breaking, upon the verdure of Egypt. Grass near the pyramids, but will not touch them — as if in fear or awe of them. Desert more fearful to look at than ocean.

[?] M writes to his mother.
(The friends of Herman Melville, who sailed for Europe in October to recruit his health, will be glad to learn that by letters from Egypt, received by the last steamer, he speaks of being so much restored in health and strength that he "climbed Cheops the other day, an enterprise of prodigious exertion." He was to go to Jerusalem, and expected to be in Rome in the course of a few weeks. (The Albany *Atlas*, Feb[?])

January 4 *M's journal:*
Sailed from Alexandria for Jaffa. 2ᵈ class passage. Many deck passengers Turks &c.

January 5 Fine day & warm. On deck all the time.

JAFFA January 6 Early in the morning came in sight of Jaffa. A swell rolling, and saw the breakers before the town. Landed, not without some danger, — boatmen (Arabs) trying to play upon my supposed fears. Cunning dogs! — Employed a Jew dragoman to take me to Jerusalem. — Crossed the plain of Sharon in sight of mountains of Ephraim. Arrived at Ramla & put up at alleged (hotel). At supper over broken crockery & cold meat, pestered by moschitos & fleas, dragoman said, "Dese Arab no know how to keep hotel" I fully assented.

JERUSALEM   January 7   After horrible night, at 2 in the morning in saddle for Jerusalem. The three shadows stalking over the plain by moonlight. Moon set, all dark. At day break found ourselves just entering the mountains. Pale olive of morning. Withered & desert country. Breakfast by ruined mosque — cave. Hot & wearisome ride over the arid hills. — Got to Jerusalem about 2 P.M. Put up at Meditterranean hotel, kept by a German converted Jew, by name, *Hauser*. Hotel overlooks on one side Pool of Hezekiah (balconies) is near the Coptic Convent, is on the Street called Street of the Patriarchs leading out of Street of David. From platform in front of my chamber, command view of battered dome of Church of Sepulchre & Mount Olivet . . . Walked out to the North [?] of the city, but my eyes so affected by the long days ride in the glare of the light of arid hills, had to come back to hotel.

> [With infirm intent
> He sought the house-top. Set of sun:
> His feet upon the yet warm stone,
> He, Clarel, by the coping leant,
> In silent gaze . . .
>   . . . There where he stood,
> Was Acra's upper neighborhood.
> The circling hills he saw, with one
> Excelling, ample in its crown,
> Making the uplifted city low
> By contrast — Olivet . . .
> The inn abutted on the pool
> Named Hezekiah's, a sunken court
> Where silence and seclusion rule . . .
> As a three-decker's stern-lights peer
> Down on the oily wake below,
> Upon the sleek dark waters here
> The inn's small lattices bestow
> A rearward glance. And here and there
> In flows the languid evening air
> Stirs the dull weeds adust, which trail
> In festoons from the crag, and veil
> The ancient fissures, overtopped
> By the tall convent of the Copt,
> Built like a light-house o'er the main.
>   (*Clarel*, 1:1)]

January 8   All day with dragoman roaming over the hills.

January 9   [Lemuel Shaw's 76th birthday]   The same.

January 10   Thought I should have been the only stranger in Jerusalem, but this afternoon came on from Jaffa, a M[r] Frederick Cunningham of Boston, a very prepossessing young man who seemed rejoiced to meet a companion & countryman.

January 11-17   Spent the remaining days till Jan. 18th in roaming about city & visiting Jordan & Dead Sea.

Jerusalem

Village of Lepers — houses facing the wall — Zion, their park, a dung-heap. — They sit by the gates asking alms, — then whine — avoidance of them & horror . . .
Wandering among the tombs — till I began to think myself one of the possessed with devils . . . [entries of Jan 21]

I often passed the Protestant School &c on Mt Zion, but nothing seemed going on. The only place of interest there was the Grave Yard. I attended a Missionary meeting in Jerusalem (to raise money for some other far-away place) but was not specially edified. [entry after Jan 21]

The old Connecticut man [Roberts] wandering about with tracts &c — knew not the language — hopelessness of it — his lonely batchelor rooms . . .
Warder Crisson of Philadelphia — An American turned Jew — divorced from former wife — married a Jewess &c — Sad . . . And in the afternoon, I would stand out by St Stephen's Gate, Nigh the pool likewise named after him, occupying the spot where he was stoned, and watch the shadows slowly sliding (sled-like) down the hills of Berotha & Zion into the valley of Jehosophat, then after resting a while in the bottom of the ravine, slowly begin creeeping up the opposite side of Olivet, entering tomb after tomb & cave after cave . . . The Holy Sepulchre . . . Near by is a blind stair of worn marble, ascending to the reputed Calvary where among other things they show you by the smoky light of old pawnbrokers lamps of dirty gold, the hole in which the cross was fixed and through a narrow grating as over a coal cellar, point out the rent in the rock! On the same level, nearby is a kind of gallery, railed with marble, overlooking the interior entrance of the church; and here almost every day I would hang, looking down upon the spectacle of the scornful Turks on the divan, & the scorned pilgrims kissing the stone of the anointing. — The door of the church is like that of a jail — a grated window in it . . . A sort of plague-stricken splendor reigns in the painted mildewed walls around. In the midst of all, stands the Sepulchre; a church in a church . . . It is like entering a lighted lanthorn. Wedged & half-dazzled, you stare for a moment on the ineloquence of the bedizened slab, and glad to come out, wipe your brow glad to escape as from the heat & jam of a show-box. All is glitter & nothing is gold. A sickening cheat. The countenance of the poorest & most ignorant pilgrims would seem tacitly to confess it as well as your own . . .
Talk of the guides. "There is the stone Christ leaned against, & here is the English Hotel." Yonder is the arch where Christ was shown to the people, & just by that open window is sold the best coffee in Jerusalem. &c &c &c . . .

[545]

The color of the whole city is grey & looks at you like a cold grey eye in a cold old man. — its strange aspect in the pale olive light of the morning . . .

In the emptiness of the lifeless antiquity of Jerusalem the emigrant Jews are like flies that have taken up their abode in a skull.

From Jerusalem to Dead Sea &c . . . Mount of Temptation — a black, arid mount — nought to be seen but Dead Sea, mouth of Kedron — very tempting — foolish feind — but it was a display in vision — then why take him up to Mount? — the *thing itself* was in vision . . . Ride over mouldy plain to Dead Sea — Mountains on their side — Lake George — all but verdure. — foam on beach & pebbles like slaver of mad dog — smarting bitter of the water, — carried the bitter in my mouth all day — bitterness of life — thought of all bitter things — Bitter is it to be poor & bitter, to be reviled, & Oh bitter are these waters of Death, thought I. — Old boughs tossed up by water — relics of pick-nick — nought to eat but bitumen & ashes with desert of Sodom apples washed down with water of Dead Sea. — Must bring your own provisions, as well, too, for mind as body — for all is barren.

Shore of the Dead Sea

Barrenness of Judea . . . Crossed elevated plains, with snails, flat tracks of slime, all over . . . wall of stone on ravine edge — Monastery (Greek) rode on with letter — hauled up in basket into hole — small door of massive iron in high wall — knocking — opened — salaam of monks — Place for pilgrims — divans — St Saba wine — "racka" — comfortable. — At dusk went down by many stone steps & through mysterious passages to cave & trap doors & hole in wall — ladder — ledge after ledge — winding — to bottom of Brook Kedron — sides of ravine all caves of recluses — Monastery a congregation of stone eyries, enclosed with wall — Good bed & night's rest . . . numerous terraces, balconies — solitary Date Palm midway in precipice — Good bye — over lofty hills to Bethlehem . . . In chapel, monk (Latin) took us down into cave after cave, — tomb of saints — lights burning (with olive oil) till came to place of Nativity (many lamps) & manger with lights . . . On way to Bethlehem saw Jerusalem from distance — unless knew it, could not have recognized it — looked exactly like arid rocks.

Stones of Judea . . . no wonder that stones should so largely figure in the Bible. Judea is one accumulation of stones — Stony mountains & stony plains; stony torrents & stony roads; stony vales & stony fields, stony homes & stony tombs; [effaced: stony eyes & stony hearts.] Before you & behind you are stones. Stones to right & stones to left . . . stone walls of immense thickness are thrown together, less for boundaries than to get them out of the way. But in vain; The removal of one stone only serves to reveal those stones still lying, below it. It is like mending the old barn; the more you uncover, the more it grows . . . To account for the abundance of stones, many theories have been started; *My* theory is that long ago, some whimsical King of the country took it into his head to pave all Judea, and entered into contracts to that effect; but the contractor becoming bankrupt mid-way in his business, the stones were only dumped on the ground, & there they lie to this day. [entries of Jan 24]

RAMLAH   January 18   Quitted Jerusalem with Mʳ Cunningham & his dragoman — The Druze, Abdallah — Stayed at Greek convent at Ramlah. No sleep. Old monk like rat. Scurvy treatment.

LYDDA-JAFFA   January 19   Rode from Ramlah to Lydda . . . We rode to Lydda in train of the Governor's son. A mounted escort of some 30 men, all armed. Fine riding . . . Entering Lydda, Governor's son discharged all his barrels (Revolver) into a puddle — & we went to see the ruined church of Lydda. Evidently of the time of the Crusaders. A delightful ride across Plain of Sharon to Jaffa . . . Found the *Petra Party* at Jaffa. In the afternoon had a bath in the Meditteranean. Inspected some old ruins of walls by & in, the sea.

January 20   Mʳ Cunningham & the Petra party left this afternoon in the French steamer for Alexandria. Very rough getting off. After their departure, returned to the place called "the hotel," and ascended to the top of the house — the only promenade in the town . . . I am the only traveller sojourning in Joppa. I am emphatically alone, & begin to feel like Jonah. The wind is rising, the swell of the sea increasing . . .

M gets his passport visaed at the American Vice-Consulate, "buono per Alexandria," which M corrects to read "Smyrna and Athens."

January 21   *M's journal:*
Could not sleep last night for the fleas. Rose early & to top of the house. The wind & sea still high . . . Wrote in this diary (Jerusalem) to day. In the afternoon called upon Mr & Mrs Saunders, outside the wall, the American Missionary. — Dismal story of their experiments. Might as well attempt to convert bricks into bride-cake as the Orientals into Christians . . . Mrs S, an interesting woman, not without beauty, and of the heroine stamp, or desires to be. A book lying on her table, entitled "Book of Female Heroines," I took to be the exponent of her aspirations. She talked to me, alone, for two hours; I doing nothing but listen. Mʳ S.

came in. A man feeble by Nature & feebler by sickness; but worthy. A Seventh Day Baptist — God help him! A Miss Williams, an elderly English woman, a kind of religious teacher, joined us in a walk through the orange groves.

At Joppa, M^r & Mrs Saunders from Rhode-Island. Mr Saunders a broken-down machinist & returned Californian out at elbows . . . Mr S. now does nothing — health gone by climate. Mrs S. learning Arabic from a Sheik, & turned doctress to the poor. She is waiting the Lord's time, she says. For this she is well qualified, being of great patience. Their little girl looks sickly & pines for home — but the Lord's work must be done. [entry of Jan 25?]

January 22   No sleep last night — only resource to cut tobacco, and watch the six windows of my room, which is like a light-house — & hear the surf & wind. The genuine Jonah feeling, in Joppa too, is worth experiencing in the same sense that, according to Byron, the murderer sensations were worth a trial . . . I have been to the alleged home of Simon the Tanner — "by the sea" & with a wall . . . I have such a feeling in this lonely old Joppa, with the prospect of a prolonged detention here, owing to the surf — that it is only by stern self-control & grim defiance that I contrive to keep cool & patient. — The main beam crossing my chamber overhead, is evidently taken from a wreck — the trenail holes proving it.

January 23   Thank God got some sleep last night. Wind & sea subsided. Lovely day, but wet underfoot . . . Walked on top of the house. Read Dumas's "Diamond Necklace" — Excellent, Cagliostro's talk in opening chapter. — Walked out & looked at rocks before town. After dinner went with Mr Saunders to Mr Dickson's.

Deacon Dickson of Groton, Mass . . . Mr Dickson a thorough Yankee, about 60, with long oriental beard, blue Yankee coat, & Shaker waistcoat. — At the house we were ushered into a comfortless — barn-yard sort of apartment & introduced to Mrs D. a respectable looking elderly woman. We took chairs. After some introductory remarks the following talk ensued —

H.M. "Have you settled here permanently, Mr Dickson?"

Mr D. "Permanently settled on the soil of Zion, Sir."
        with a kind of dogged emphasis.

Mrs. D (as if she dreaded her husband's getting on his hobby, & was pained by it) — "The walking is a little muddy, aint it?" — (This to M^r S[aunders].)

H.M. to Mr D. "Have you any Jews working with you?"

Mr D. No. Can't afford to hire them. Do my own work, with my son. Besides, the Jews are lazy & dont like work.

H.M. "And do you not think that a hindrance to making farmers of them?"

Mr D. "That's it. The Gentile Christians must teach them better. The fact is the fullness of Time has come. The Gentile Christians must prepare the way.

Mrs D. (to me) "Sir, is there in America a good deal of talk about Mr D's efforts here?

Mr D. Yes, do they believe basically [?] in the restoration of the Jews?

H.M. I can't really answer that.

Mrs D. I suppose most people believe the propheseys to that effect in a figurative sense — dont they?

HM. Not unlikely. &c &c &c . . .

Old Dickson seems a man of Puritanic energy, and being inoculated with this preposterous Jew Mania, is resolved to carry his Quixotism through to the end. Mrs D. dont seem to like it, but submits, — The whole thing is half melancholy, half farcical — like all the rest of the world. [entry of Jan 25?]

January 24 [Thomas Melville's 27th birthday] Bravo! — This moment, sitting down to jot awhile, hear that the Austrian steamer is in sight, & going to the window, beheld her. — Thus there will end nearly six days in Joppa . . . 11.A.M. Just returned from stroll. Steamer drawing nigh. Was again pleased with the queer school kept in chicken-coop under dim arcade nigh Gate . . . Took boat & rowed off to rocks (Jonah's pier) off harbor . . . While by the water saw men emptying sacks of rubbish into the harbor, such as it is. Vastly improving, this. — Amused with the autographs & confessions of people who have stayed at this hotel. "I have *existed* at this hotel &c &c." Something comical could be made out of all this. Let the confessions being of a religious, penitential resigned & ambiguous turn, apparently flattering to the host, but really derogatory to the place. — Bright sun & sea. You seem to look through a vaccum at every thing. The sea is like a great daub of Prussian Blue.

Got on board the Austrian steamer "Acquile Imperiale" at 1.P.M. yesterday, but did not sail till late in the evening. Much wind & sea all night. [entry of Jan 25]

BEIRUT January 25 In morning coast in view . . . At 2.P.M. came to anchor at Beyrout. — Hotel Bel View — dragoman to Warburton — Sirocco blowing . . . Town between desert & sea — both eating at it . . .

January 26 Fine day — warm. Strolled about. Lazy heave of sea on rocks. Beautiful walk to town. Consuls books. Interesting man. Luckless discussion at dinner. Young Prussian.

January 27-31 At the hotel. Mt Leabonon — snow — sun — tropic & Pole brought into one horizon. *The gate.* Tartar couriers rushing in with tidings of war. — Quiet days — stroll out on sea shore — dash of billows — what is all this fuss about? . . .

January 28 *M gets his passport visaed (gratis) by Henry Wood, Consul at Beirut, for Smyrna & Athens.*

GENOA January 29 *Samuel L. Breese, Commander of the Mediterranean Squadron, writes to J. C. Dobbin, Secretary of the Navy:*
The Constellation arrived at Messina, Sicily, on the 24th inst. from Alexandria, and will remain there until 1st March . . .

HONG KONG January 30 *Thomas Melville writes to his family.* (We have just received letters from Tom, dated Hong Kong January 30th There was some probability of his being placed in command of the vessel, as Captain Pike thought of returning home from that port in case the Meteor was to prolong her voyage. — *Augusta Melville to Peter Gansevoort, Apr 7*)

BEIRUT February 1 *M's journal:*
Fine day — sea & wind abated. Paid passage (cheated) in Austrian Loyds steamer "Smirne" to Smyrna. Went on board at 3.P.M. Did not have chance to bid Mr Wood good bye. Sailed at sunset. One week at Beyrout. — Very slow boat — foul bottom: poor accomodations. — Unmannerly captain — scene at dinner table.

February 2 At 10.A.M. sighted Cyprus. on starboard bow. Coming near long reach of whitish & yellowish coast with lofty mountains inland. From these waters rose Venus from the foam. Found it as hard to realize such a thing as to realize on Mt Olivet that from there Christ rose. — About 5.P.M. came to anchor off Larnaca the port of Cyprus. Could not well go ashore. But saw pretty much all worth seeing from deck.

February 3 At 11.A.M. came wind ahead with a very violent squall. Continued blowing for rest of day, ship horribly pitching & rolling. Seas coming from all directions. Poor devils of pilgrims seasick.

Yesterday, during squall, amusing conduct of *Panurge* a Greek — thought his hour was come. Also, amusing scene in cabin at dinner. Democracy of Captain & officers. Engineer came in — sat down — drank to "The Queen!" — All Lloyds & M.J. [?] built in England. [entry of Feb 4]

February 4 Sudden change to very fine weather. The coast of Caramania in sight all day . . . Beautiful evening — moonlight. Came up with Rhodes, but did not touch (though we had some Turk passengers for it) owing to the Captain's wanting to use the moonlight for getting through intricate part of the Sporades. Rhodes looked a large & high island with some few lofty mountains inland . . . One finds that, after all, the most noted localities are made up of common elements of earth, air, & water. — English (Cornish) engineer invited me down to his department, and afterwards to supper in his mess. He was somewhat under stimulants. Said (pointing to his engines) "A fine pair of tools, Sir." Quite in love with his engine. — Beautiful moonlight detained me on deck late, as well as dread of my birth. Retired about 11. but at 2 A.M. was fairly goaded on deck by intolerable persecutions of bugs. Have suffered beyond telling from this cause. Not a wink of sleep now for four nights, & expect none till I get to Smyrna. This affliction of bugs & fleas & moschitos fully counterbalance to me all the satisfactions of Eastern travel. —

February 5   In among the Sporades all night. Standing on t'gallant fore-castle by the bright moon, Captain & officers steered us through the en-tanglements of channels. At dawn were completely landlocked by islands & islets . . . Would think this were navigation for a skiff . . . A fine sail upon the whole. But the scenery is all outline. No filling up. Seem to be sailing upon gigantic outline engravings . . . Serene morning. Pale blue sky. — Steered out from intricasies & saw Samos ahead, and Patmos — quite lonely looking . . . Patmos is pretty high, & peculiarly barren look-ing. No inhabitants. — Was here again afflicted with the great curse of modern travel — skepticism. Could no more realize that St: John had ever had revelations here, than when off Juan Fernandez, could believe in Robinson Crusoe according to De Foe. When my eye rested on arid heigth, spirit partook of the barrenness. — Heartily wish Niebuhr & Strauss to the dogs. — The deuce take their penetration & acumen.

> [Sail before the morning breeze
> The Sporads through and Cyclades
> They look like isles of absentees —
>   Gone whither? . . .
>
> 'Tis Polynesia reft of palms,
> Seaward no valley breathes her balms —
> Not such as musk thy rings of calms,
>   Marquesas!
>   ("The Archipelago")]

A cold rainy night, last night. Choice between shivering & scratching. Took both. Horrible night. — Slept awhile on settee, awoke chilled through. — Another time was all but frantic with the fleas. — The Scratch-ing ship. Captain with back-scratcher — two men leaning up & rubbing against each other &c. Main diversion. [entry of Feb 6]

SMYRNA   February 6   In the rain entered Smyrna bay at day break. Nearly two months since here before . . . Ashore to hotel & break-fast . . . While at breakfast felt very bad neuralgic pain top of head — owing to utter sleeplessness of last five nights. — At 5.P.M. sailed in Paddle steamer "Italia" of Lloyd's Austria Co for Pireus.

SYRA   February 7   Came to anchor at Syra — after stopping at Scio — this afternoon. Blowing hard & remained through the night.

GREEK COAST   February 8   At dawn got under weigh. Head wind, head sea — cold, comfortless. Turned in to berth till four o'clock. Could not view the islands, though passing many. — Towards sunset approached Pireus . . . Came to anchor at 7.PM . . . Got into boat & ashore, & into

old hack, and through a settlement like one on tow path of canal, to a
McAdamed road, straight as die, — & into Athens . . . Tomorrow prepare
for the Acropolis. — I saw it by moonlight from road. Trying to be
serious about St. John when from where I stood figure of Santon a Arab
holy man came between me & island — almost naked — ludicrous chased
away gravity — solemn idiocy — lunatic — opium-eater — dreamer — yet
treated with profoundest respect & reverence — allowed to enter any-
where. — Wretched imbecile! base & beggarly Santon, miserable stum-
bling-block in way of the prophecies . . . Hotel d Angleterre. Alexander,
guide — with Boyd who wrote Murray's G[uide] B[ook]. —

ATHENS   February 9   Viewed the ruins with Alexander . . . Mr Mar-
shall of Boston or N.Y. at hotel. Been all over Meditteranean on ice business. Cut ice at Black Sea. — I imagined his story of life. Called on Dr
King Consul. Greek wife. Invited to tea. His daughter been in America.
Pleasant evening.

February 10   Among the ruins — revisited them all. *Temple of Theseus*
well preserved. Yellowish look — saffron — burnt in slow fire of Time . . .
Spent evening conversing with young English officer from Zephalonia —
Told story of Lindy Foote's son, &c. — Saw the sunset from *Lyccabacus*.
Lovely climb.

*M gets his passport visaed at the American Consulate by Jonas King
"Good for Messina and Naples," & takes it to the Sicilian Consulate for
a visa "Buono per Herman Melville americano che si reca a Napoli via di
Messina."*

February 11   *M's journal:*
Clear & beautiful day. Fine ride on box to Piraeus. Acropolis in sight
nearly whole way. Straight road. Fully relieved against the sky . . .
Ruins of Parthenon like North River breaking up, &c — At 2 P.M. embarked in French steamer "Cydnus" for Messina. Noble vessel & French-
built. Two or three Englishmen on board — young men. Talk with them.
Misseri (Eothen's) on board, going to England. Talk with him. — Sailed
along coast of Morea — mountains. Good bed & slept well.

MESSINA   February 13   Coasts of Calabria & Sicily ahead at day break.
Neared them at 10 o'clock . . . At 1 P.M. anchored in harbor of Messina . . . Rainy day. Landed at Police. Searched for papers &c. [*A stamp
on M's passport: Messina Polizia Marittima 13 Febb. 1857.*]

Last night went to Cafe near opera-house to meet, if I might, Dr [John
A.] Lockwood of the frigate [*Constellation*]. But did not. [entry of
Feb 14]

February 14   This morning pleasant weather. Many American vessels in
port for fruit. This the season. Went on board one. Went off to friggate.
Called on Cap. Bell. Saw Dr Lockwood. Went with him on donkeys to a

high hill four miles distant. The telegraph. Dined with him & officers in ward-room of friggate. Passed off pleasantly. Then walked through the town with the Dr, and in evening went to the opera of Macbeth [conducted by its composer, Verdi] with him.

M has his passport visaed at the American Consulate "Buono per Napoli."

February 15 *M's journal:*
Dr Lockwood called at hotel, sat, and then proposed long walk. Walked out in lovely suburbs skirting the sea. Calabria's mountains in sight. Salvator Rosa look of them. Met masques on the road. Carnival. Walked 7 or 8 miles. Sat on stones, much talk. Fine day. Enjoyed it considerably. Back to dinner at hotel by 6 P.M. Street very lively in evening. Walked about with/Dr. till 10 o'clock.

February 16 [Malcolm's 8th birthday] Neapolitan steamer for Naples started at 1 P.M. to day. Took 2d cabin passage. Repented it sorely in the end. Crossed the Straits to Reggio (St. Paul) lay there till midnight.

February 17 By day break stopped at another place [Pizzo], high on hill, (Murat shot) and at noon at a third place on coast . . . Scenery very fine. Sailed close in shore. Suffered again horribly from sleeplessness. (Saw Etna from Reggio)

NAPLES February 18 Ere day break we passed between Capri & main & entered bay of Naples. I was on deck. Dim mass of Vesuvius soon in sight. Recognized it from picture of mother's. Soon, *smelt* the city. Brilliant lights. — Detained on board till 9 A.M. by Police being dilatory. Went to *Hotel de Geneve* with some others . . . At breakfast Rhinelander & Friedman said they were going to Pompeii. Joined them . . . Pompeii like any other town. Same old humanity. All the same whether one be dead or alive. Pompeii comfortable sermon. Like Pompeii better than Paris. Guards there. Silent as Dead Sea. — To Vesuvius on horseback . . . Modern crater like old abandoned quarry — burning [?] — Red & yellow. Bellowing. Bellows. flare of flame. Went into crater. Frozen liquorice. — Came down with a rush . . . Cold ride, no coat, — back to hotel by midnight.

February 19 Sallied out for walk by myself . . . To Capo di Monte in cab . . . Catacombs — old man with lanthorn. Great extent. Old times. Grimy. Could'nt get away. Thought crazy. — Walked about again. Bought good coat for $9 . . . Walked to Villa Real — hotels — at Brittanique happened to see Townsend's name. — Dined there. Releived by hearing (tho' but indirectly) from home. To San Carlo at 10 o'clock. Fine house. Met English banker. [*M writes letters.*]

February 20 Walked to Post Office with letters. Then took voiture for eastern part of bay. Posilipo — beautiful promontory of villas — along the sea — new road — till came in sight of bay of Pozzuoli. Went through

Grotto of Sejanus to remains of School of Virgil & other ruins of villas
. . . Sulphur & aridity, the end of the walk. (At Posilipo found not
the cessation [of pain] which the name expresses.) . . . Drove to Cafe
de la Europe for cheap dinner. Row with cabman. Dined & walked for
a hour in Strada de Toledo. Great crowds. Could hardly tell it from
Broadway. Thought I was there. — Cafes well filled. — Many lottery shops,
all with little shrine of Virgin & child, lit — cheap decoration. Curious
reflections. Religious inducement to wickedness. — Home by 9 & to bed.

February 21   Went to Rothschild's for £20. No scrutiny as at other
places. Went to Museums. A collection of them . . .
Hall of bronze statuary. Plato (hair & beard & imperial) Nero (villainous)
Seneca (caricature.) . . .

To look at the statue of Nero one might fancy him to be a genteelly dissipated
youth — a fast young man; and Plato, with his long locks parted like those of
a lady, supposed meditating on the destinies of the world while under the
hands of his hair dresser. (M's lecture, "Statuary in Rome," reported in the
Boston Post, Dec 3)

Paintings Madonna [del divino Amore] by Raffael — a Domenichino.
Two small Correggios — (could not see anything so wonderful in these
last) but face of Raffael's Madonna touchingly maternal.
. . . a promiscuous drive through the older & less elegant part of town.
Long narrow lanes. Arches, crowds. —
Tumblers in narrow street. Blocked way. Balconies with women. Cloth
on ground. They gave way, after natural reluctance. Merriment. Turned
round & gave the most grateful & graceful bow I could. Handkerchiefs
waved from balconies, goodhumored cries &c — Felt prouder than an
Emperor. Shabby old hack, but good fellow, driver.

> [. . . His rug or bed
> In midmost way a tumbler spread,
> A posturing mountebank withal . . .
> Reversed in stature, legs aloft,
> And hobbling jigs on hands for heels —
> Gazed up with bloodshot brow that told
> The tension of that nimble play —
> Gazed up as martyred Peter might;
> . . . tickled at my puzzled plight,
> Yet mindful that a move was due,
> And knowing me a stranger there,
> With one consent the people part
> Yielding a passage, and with eyes
> Of friendly fun — how courteous, too!
> Catching an impulse from their air,
> To feet I spring, my beaver doff
> And broadcast wave a blithe salute.
> ("Naples in the Time of Bomba")]

M has his passport visaed for Rome at the American Consulate (paying $1 or L1.25) & at the Papal Nunzio.

February 22   *M's journal:*
Breakfasted early and at 9 o'clock took train for Castleamare (In the corner) with Mr Rows of Brunswick (N.J.) and young Englishman . . . Three hours, with coach berths, at least. To Sorrento for about a dollar. — Grand drive . . . Got man to speak English & engaged 1st seat in coupe [to Rome] for 24th Feb. — Mr R. a little queer at dinner. His sister affable.

February 23   Went to Museum after breakfast. Shut. Took hack and went on Pausilipo road . . . to Lake Avernus . . . Curious they should have fabled hell here. Cave of Sybil. Gate. (Narrow one to hell, here) Torches. Long grotto, many hundred feet, fast walk. Came to sudden dive down — very narrow — Descent to Infernal regions, guide said — Came to pool — took me on his shoulder across — bath & bed of Sybil — oracle-place — landed me on ledge of rock. — Many other caves to right & left. Infernal enough. — What in God's name were such places made for, & why? Surely man is a strange animal. Diving into the bowels of the earth rather than building up towards the sky. How clear an indication that he sought darkness rather than light . . . Scene at dinner table tonight. Comments &c. The young Parisian, the fair young lady, the French judge with black cap on. (Sentencing cap)

February 24   [*M's passport is stamped: "Visto a partira."*]
At 8 A.M. started in diligence from P.O. in Naples for Rome. Only Frenchman & self in coupe . . . Smart postillion — one continual gallop & crack of the whip from post to post. Change horses 8 miles. At least 100 horses at this diligence . . . At night fall entered among mountains. The tower & sea at Terracina. Night. [*Twice on the road M's passport is stamped: "Buono per Roma."*]

ROME   February 25   At daybreak were on the Alban mount. At 10 A.M. were in Rome . . . Stopped at hotel de Minerva . . . Walked to Capitol. Took view from tower. Whether it is having coming from the East, or chafed mood, or what, but Rome fell flat on me. Oppressively flat. — Did'nt sleep any last night, though. — Tiber a ditch, yellow as saffron. The whole landscape nothing independent of associations . . . Exhausted at 3.P.M. Dined at 6 & to bed.

February 26   To Tortoni's, banker, to find out about S. Shaw or letters. Learnt nothing. To Capitol & Coliseum. — Coliseum like great hollow among hills. Hopper of Greylock. Slope of concentric ruins overgrown. Mountainous. Museum of Capitol. Hall of Emperors. "That Tiberius? he dont look so bad at all" — It was he. A look of sickly evil, — intellect without [effaced: manhood] manliness & sadness without goodness. Great brain overrefinements. Solitude. — Dying Gladiator. Shows that humanity existed amid the barberousness of the Roman time, as it now among Christian barberousness. Antinous, beautiful . . . In the evening walked to Cafe Greco, in Via Condotti. "English sculptor" with dirty hands &c. Dense smoke. Rowdy looking chaps, &c — Home & to bed. (Stopped at evening in picture dealers; offered a Cenci for $4. Surprisingly cheap). *[M purchases engraving of Beatrice Cenci:]*

February 27   Tried to find A[merican] Consul, [William] Page, & Jarves. Failed in all. — Went to Baths of Caracalla. — Wonderful. Massive. Ruins form, as it were, natural bridges of thousands of arches. There are glades, & thickets among the ruins — high up. — Thought of Shelley. Truly, he got his inspiration here. Corresponds with his drama & mind. Still majesty, & desolate grandeur. — After much trouble & sore travel without a guide managed to get to Protestant Burial Ground & pyramid of Cestius under walls. Read Keats' epitaph . . . Thence to Cenci Palace . . . Orsini Palace & Ghetto. Tragic looking place enough . . . Thence to Farnese Palace . . . St. Angelo Bridge & St. Peters . . . Remarked the banks of Tiber near St: Angelo — fresh, alluvial look near masonry — primeval as Ohio in the midst of all these monuments of the centuries.

M writes to his family at Gansevoort. (Another letter received from Herman dated Rome Feby 27th, announcing his return home next month . . . — *Augusta Melville to Peter Gansevoort, Apr 7*)

February 28   *M's journal:*
Lost time going after Consul &c. At 12 M. was at Borghese villa. Extent of grounds — peculiar odor of Italian gardens — Deep groves — cold splen-

dor of villa — Venus & Cupid — mischievous look of C. — Thence to Villa Albani — along the walls — Antinous — head like moss-rose with curls & buds — rest all simplicity — end of fillet on shoulder — drapery, shoulder in the marble — hand full of flowers & eyeing them — the profile &c . . . Silence & loneliness of long streets of blank garden walls.

March 1   To Monte Cavallo — colossal equestrian group, found in Baths, basin also, obelisk — most imposing group of antiques in Rome. — People these Caracalla baths anew with these colossal figures — Gigantic Rome. — St. Peters in its magnitude & colossal statuary seems an imitation of these fragments . . . The mossy pillars & green ooze of loneliness. — The poor old statues in their niches — the gardens. — San[ta] Maria Maggiore. — (The picture at home) Gold from Peru . . . Cloaca Maxima — gloomy hole — trailing ruins into the sewer. — Lost my way getting back. Stopped in at church. Animated preacher. Home by 5 P.M. Dinner & to bed.

March 2   [Frances's second birthday]   Vatican Day (Monday)   From 12 to 3 in Museum; previously visiting the Loggie of Raphael & Sistine Chapel . . . Adam & Eve — The Eve — Faded bloom of the paintings. — Staid in Vatican till closed. Fagged out completely, & sat long time by the obelisk, recovering from the stunning effect of a first visit to the Vatican. — Went to Piazza de Espagna, & home. — Sat awhile in the Rouses' room ere retiring.

March 3   Started with Mr & Miss R. to ascend St. Peters. Too late for time . . . Rode to Palazza Barberini to see Cenci [by Guido Reni?] — Expression of suffering about the mouth — (appealing look of innocence) not caught in any copy or engraving. — Lovely little painting of Galatea in car — Two swimmers in dark blue shadowed water — gleam of limbs . . . A cold rain, windy, dirty & horribly disagreeable day.

GALENA   March 3   *Mary A. A. Melvill writes to Lemuel Shaw:*
I suppose that Herman finds travelling a more pleasant medecine than any that the Dr can prescribe, hope that it may prove beneficial and that he may return home in safety with his health restored.

ROME   March 4   *M's journal:*
Ascended St. Peters. feilds & paddocks on top — figures of saints. — Met Mr & Mrs C. & brother on the church. — To Corsini Palace . . . church of St. Pietro in Montorio . . . Early to bed.

March 5   To Coliseum . . . To Capitol. Through gallery a second time. Bronze wolf. To Borghese Gallery . . . Cold grey windy day. Eye so bad had to go to room & to bed at 5 P.M. minus dinner.

March 6   Eye prevented me from doing or seeing much to day. To St. Peters — Borghese Gallery — Pincian — Saw the Pope in carriage . . . Talk with Mr R. in his room.

March 7   To Sciarra Gallery. Faded splendor — balcony over Corso — closeness of a closet — The Cheating Gamblers (Honesty & Knavery — the self-possession & confidence of knavery — the irresolution & perplexity of honesty) — The Gloaming (to apply a Scotch word) of a scene between dusk & dark of Claude. Other Claudes (his finest manner) All their effect is of atmosphere. He paints the air. Curious Holy Family of Albert Durer (The old nurse) A Lady by Titian — The crimson & white sleeves — The golden haze of his pictures (Danae) The Sciarra have been in Chancery. — *To the Rospigliosi Gallery . . . To the Quirinale Palace of Pope . . . The Gardens* — A Paridise without the joy — freaks & caprices of endless wealth — rheumatics in gardener — As stone is sculptured into forms of foliage, so here foliage trained into forms of sculpture — walls, niches, arches, casements, columns, bases, chambers (quarried out of foliage) . . . *To Church out of Bath* . . . Dined on 19 cents at Lepri's in Via Condotti & home & to bed. Eye very troublesome. Hope it wont stay so.

March 8   To Jesuits Church — To Gibbon's Church nigh Capitol — various columns rifled from ancient edifices — Gibbon's meditations — Christianity. — To Baths of Titus — overgrown — dark & intricate — resort of banditti once . . . Dined on 17 cents & to bed at 11 P M after a talk with Mͬ R. in his room.

March 9   Vatican day. — Deliberate walk through the galleries. — Hall of Animals — Wolf & lamb, paw uplifted, tongue — fleece. Dog on stag, eying him. Lion on horse. — But Playing Goats — the goat & kid — show a Wordsworthian appreciation of the gentle in Nature. — Frescoed ceilings, which, like starry skies, no man regards — so plentiful are the splendors. — Coronation of the Virgin — Raphael — The faces so like his masters Perugino's in the next room. — Review of troops in St Peters piazza. — With Mr & Miss Rouse to St. Onofrio, church & monastery, where Tasso expired. On the Janiculum, fine view of Rome. Sad corridors, cloisters . . . Doleful old chamber — wax casts. — Little sad garden, moulding gateways. — Quaint church — damp & doleful. — New monument in wretched taste. — Stopped in at some churches & to Lepri, to soup & meat.

March 10   I begin writing here after more than one week's abstinence, owing to state of my eyes and general incapacity. On the day of this date I went to the Doria Pamfili palace in the morning . . . Breughel's pictures much pleased me. The Elements & animals. — Lucretia Borgia — no wicked look about her. Good looking dame — rather fleshy . . . To the studios. The English sculptor, Gibson. His colored Venus. Talk with him. The 7 branched candlestick &c. Art perfect among Greeks. Limit to human power, — perfection. — To Bartholomew's. His Eve . . .

March 11   Started for Appian Way. Narrow, — not like Milton's Way

— not suitable to dignity &c. Old pavement. Tomb with olive trees on it. Sown in corruption, raised in olives . . . To St. Pauls, outside walls. Magnificent. Malaria among the gilding. Building against Nature. Pet of Pio's. The Catacombs — labyrinth of them. — Home at 3, changed room, had fire, and prepared for being laid up. No dinner.

M has his passport visaed by the American Consul, A. Ardisson: "Buono per Firenze e Venezia" (paid $1).

March 12   *M's journal:*
Crept out at 12 M. to Coliseum. Repeopling it, &c. The arch. Dined on fig & bread.

[When I stood in the Colosseum, its mountain-chains of ruins waving with foliage girdling me round, as in some great green hollow in the Appenine range, the solitude was like that of savage nature; but restoring the shattered arches and terraces, I re-peopled them with all the statues from the Vatican, and in the turfy glen of the arena below, I placed the Fighting Gladiator from the Louvre, confronting him with the dying one from the Capitol. And as in fancy I heard the ruffian huzzas for the first, rebounded from the pitiless hiss for the last, I felt that more than one in that host I had evoked, shared not in its passions; that some hearts were there that felt the horror keenly as any of us would have felt it. (M's lecture, "Statuary in Rome," reported in the Boston *Daily Courier*, Dec 3[?], 1857)]

March 13   Fine day. To grounds of Villa Borghese. Great beauty of them. Fine rich odours of bushes & trees. The laurel &c. The closed villa, statues seen thro' railing. Silence & enchantment. "Glitter wide the halls, high the laurel groves &c — Taken from scenery of Italian Villa. — Called on Page. Long lecture. Swedenburgh. Spiritualist. Thin socks. Dined on a plate at Lepri's.

March 14   Walked about [?] to Trinita di Monte. Second [?] went [?] to Albani Villa. Father Murphy [in Tahiti?]. Mrs. S.   Caryatide.

March 15   Attacked by singular pain across chest & in back. In my room till 5½ P.M. Dined at table d'hote. This day saw nothing, learned nothing, enjoyed nothing, but suffered something.

March 16   Vatican day. — Afterwards to Pincian. Could not engage seat in coupe of diligence. Have to go to Florence by Civita Vechia.

March 17   To Frascati by R.R. Crossing Campagna by R.R. — Villa Aldobrandini. Charming day & grounds . . . Mellow aspect of all. Willows advanced as far as middle of May with us. Felt the bracing, reviving air of these hills very sensibly. Air of Rome hypochondriac. — Fine neglect of ground of villa. Omnibus ride, through Rome to & from R.R.

March 18   Breakfasted on 16 pennies at Caffe Nuovo. To Torlonia Villa . . . Crawfords studio — Colossal America & various statues . . . Indian, Backwoodsman &c &c

March 19   Engaging vetturino for C[ivita] Vechia. Old stables &c. —
To Villa Doria Pamfili . . . The Ghetto. The market (butcher) in old
temple . . . In the evening at Caffe Nuovo — old palace. Deep recesses
of windows. Crowd of orderly well-dressed people. Magical guitar man.
Hush & applause.

March 20   At 6.A.M. started for Tivoli. Chill, grey ride across Campagna. Lake Tartarus. Travertine. — Villa of Hadrian — solemn scene &
solemn guide . . . Guide philosophizing . . . Chill ride home in the
evening. —

LONDON March 20   *The agreement with Messrs Longman, Brown,
Green, Longmans, & Roberts to publish* The Confidence-Man *is signed
by "Nath¹ Hawthorne, U.S. Consul, on behalf of Herman Melville." The
publishers agree to publish at their own risk and divide profits equally
with the author.*

ROME   March 21   . . . I have seen Herman. When I arrived I learned
that he was at the Hotel de Minerve, and the first thing I did was to call
there, but he was out. Returning to my own hotel in the course of the
forenoon I found that he had been there and left a note for me stating
that all his arrangements were made to leave for Florence in the afternoon
and that I must see him between 3 and 4 or not at all. Accordingly I went
and saw him off. He has been almost entirely alone but has found travelling companions, who are of service to him — Although his general health
is much improved, yet at Rome, the climate and the dampness have affected him somewhat. He is considerably sunburnt and is stout as usual.
It was a very great disappointment that things should have happened as
they have both for him and me. He expects to sail for America by the
1st of May, and doubtless you have heard his plans from himself before
this. — *Samuel Shaw to his father, Mar 24*

*M has his passport visaed for Florence at the Police & at the Legazione
Toscana, & gets a visa for Venice at the Austrian Embassy.*

M's journal:
Rainy. Run about getting my *vises.* Sam left his card. Saw him. Had letter
from home to 20ᵗʰ Feb. All well. Met to part. — At 4 P.M. started in
veturino for Civitta Vecchia in company with Mʳ & Miss R. of New
Jersey and an Italian lady. Desolate ride across desolate country . . . At
midnight stopped for three hours at lonely inn. Heard Mediteranean
near. Rode on.

CIVITA VECCHIA March 22   Arrived at C. Vecchia at 6 A.M. Crowd
in streets. Sheepskin leggins &c. At 3 P.M. went aboard French steamer
"Aventime," small craft. Great crowd. Turkish flag hoisted in honor of
Turk envoy to Sardinia. Talked with him. His views of Mohammedanism
&c. Upper classes of Turkey indulge philosophical opinions upon re-

ligion &c. Repeated story of Abbots fire at Salonica. Same as I heard from Abbot himself. — Slept on settee (no berth).

LEGHORN-PISA March 23 At Leghorn by daylight. Pleasant morning, though damp. Passports. [*Vista buono per Firenze*]. Nothing special about Leghorn. At 10½ took 2ᵈ class cars for Pisa. Walked at once to the Duomo &c — One end of it looks like coral grottos in sea, — pearl diver, pillars in tiers . . . Campanile like pine poised just ere snapping. You wait to hear crash. Like Wadsworth's moon cloud, it will move all together if it move at all, for Pillars all lean with it. About 150 of 'em. There are houses in wake of fall. —

[THE LEANING TOWER AT PISA

The Tower in tiers of architraves,
Fair circle over cirque,
A trunk of rounded colonades,
The maker's marvellous work,
Imperils with all its pillared tribes
And poising them, debates:
It thinks to plunge, but hesitates;
Shrinks back — yet fain would slide!
Witholds itself — itself would urge;
Hovering, shivering on the verge —
A would-be suicide!]

Campo Santa . . . Frescoes. Wags who painted them. Tartarus — toothpulling — serpent looking in eye. Impudent — mouth. Esop might have designed it. The three kings. — The four monuments stand in commons — grass. grown out of ground. Came upon them as upon bouquet of architecture . . . At 5½ P.M. took cars for Florence . . . At 8 P.M. arrived at Florence. Hote du Nord. Caffe Doney near it. To bed early, no sleep for 2 nights past.

FLORENCE March 24 Cold & raining all day. To Pitti Palace — "It's as bad as too much pain: it gets to be pain at last" Heard this broken latter part of sentence from wearied lady coming from Uffizi Palace. — She was talking no doubt about excess of pleasure in these galleries. — Florence is a lovely city even on a cold rainy day . . . Wandered about after leaving gallery Pitti. To the Duomo & Campanile. Came upon them unexpectedly. Amazed at their magnificence.

M purchases a hand-book, Historical Literary and Artistical Travels in Italy . . . *by M. Valery (Paris, 1852).*

March 25 *M's journal:*
Festa, galleries closed . . . Strolled about generally to churches, piazzas, &c. At Santa Croce saw tombs of Dante, M. Angelo, Alfieri, and Machiavelli. Preacher near M.'s tomb. M. said naught. Crucifix held out towards him.

March 26   Sunned myself after breakfast in Grand Ducal square. To the Uffizi Gallery. Idle to enumerate . . . Not pleased with the Venus de Medici, but very much astonished at the Wrestlers [Diomedes & Ajax] & charmed with Titian's Venus [of Urbino] . . . Raining pretty much all day, at times violently. — At dinner table accosted by singular young man who speaks 6 or 8 languages. He presented me with a flower, and talked like one to whom the world was delightful. May it prove so.

M gets his passport visaed at the Papal Nunzio ("Buono per Bologna") & at the Austrian Legation ("Buono per Venezia").

March 27   *M's journal:*
At Caffe after breakfast sat musing upon caffes in general, & the young men frequenting them. Something good might be written on the "Caffe Doney," including that "Henry" & the flower-girls. — To the Museum of Natural History . . . The Sicilian's work. N° 1 . . . crown & sceptre among bones — medallions — Death & scythe — pointing — tossed skeletons & tools. horrible humiliation . . .
N° 2. Vault — heaps — all colors from deep green to buff — all ruins — detached bones — mothers children old men, intricacy of heaps. Man with cloth over face bringing down another body whose buff contrasts with the putrid green.
N° 3. In a cavernous ruin. Superb mausoleum like Pope's, lid removed shows skeleton & putridity. Roman sarcophagus — joyous triumphal procession — putrid corpse thrown over it. — grating — rats, vampires — insects, slime & ooze of corruption. — Moralist, this Sicilian. (H. [?]) . . . Revisited Pitti Gallery. The 3 Fates of M. Angelo. Admirable expression. The way the one Fate looks at other — Shall I? — The expectancy of the 3ᵈ. (Transition of splendid humanity of gallery to the Sicilian) . . . S[alvator] Rosa's portraits (one autograph) Battle Peice. — To [Hiram] Powers' studio. His America. Il Penseroso, Fisher Boy. — Saw him. Open, plain man. Fine speciman of an American. — To the Cascine. — Dined at the Luna with the young Polyglot. Walk along river & home.

March 28   Before breakfast ascended Duomo. Entered Ball. Fine morning & noble view . . . After breakfast at Caffe Doney, did some business & then to Ufizzi gallery for last look . . . After dinner packed carpet bag & wrote this.

NEW YORK   March 28   The American Publishers' Circular and Literary Gazette *prints an advertisement of Dix & Edwards, announcing that* The Confidence-Man *is in press.*

FLORENCE   March 29   *M's journal:*
Porter forgot to wake us at 3.A.M. Diligence started without us. Ran round the Duomo to the Gate. All day among hills. Crossed the Appenines. Grand scenery . . . No woods. No heartiness of scenery as in

New England. Drawn by oxen part of the way . . . Lonely houses. Villages. Grave & decorous people: breakfast in the huts. Nothing of talk in the coupe: But much smoking.

BOLOGNA March 30   Stopping at the "Three Moons." Fine day. Saw the leaning tower — black & grimy — brick . . . First thing at Bologna, tried Bologna sausage, on the principle that at Rome you first go to St. Peters.

In the Valery hand-book M scores various details on paintings in Bologna, as well as an inscription of Michael Apostolius:
     The king of the poor of this world wrote this book for his bread.

The Bolognese police stamp M's passport: "Buono pro siguire il viaggio a Venezia."

March 31   *M's journal:*
After breakfasting with the young C. Traveller at caffe, started alone in diligence for Padua. — Polite elderly gentleman in diligence . . . At one P.M. came to Ferrara, where diligence stopped till 3. Went to see cathedral. Interesting old pile. Portico sustained by pillars resting on old hunchbacks. — The Last Judgement sculptured overhead. The Father in the angle of pediment. Below to right & left the elect & reputable. The four figures stepping out of their stone graves, as out of bed. The legs thrown out in various attitudes. Capital. Grotesque figures. — Fine bell-tower, but incomplete . . . Tasso's prison. Mere cider-cellar. Grated window, but not strong.

In the Valery hand-book M checks:
   On the walls of Tasso's prison are the names of Lord Byron, Casimir Delavigne, and Lamartine's verses on Tasso . . . The perusal of the different lives of Tasso and his correspondence, (the best of them all) has convinced me that his confinement at the hospital of Saint Anne bears much greater resemblance to what is now called detention in a *maison de santé* . . .

M's journal:
From Ferrara to Padua went by smaller post. Austrian. Old fashioned vehicle. Mysterious window & face. Secret recesses. Hide. Old fashioned feelings. Crossed the Po, quite a broad stream & very turbid & rapid. Yellow as Mississippi. Alluvial look. Old ferry boat. Austrian frontier. At dusk came to Rovigo, a considerable town . . . At midnight came to Padua, & to the hotel "Star of the East."

NEW YORK March 31   *Evert Duyckinck writes to his brother, George:*
   Allan Melville has just this moment sent me Herman's 'Confidence Man.' It is a grand subject for a satirist like Voltaire or Swift — and being a kind of original American idea might be made to evolve a picture of our life and manners. We shall see what the sea dog philosophy of Typee makes of it.

In his copy of The Confidence-Man *Evert Duyckinck marks, in Chapter*
XXXIII:
. . . so precious to man is the approbation of his kind, that to rest, though
but under an imaginary censure applied to but a work of imagination, is no
easy thing.

PADUA   April 1   *In the Valery hand-book M scores:*
In the saloon is now kept the stone (*lapis vituperii*) seen by Addison at the
town hall, by which any debtor was delivered from the pursuits of his creditors, on swearing, after having been seated on it bare-breeched three times
by the officers, before the assembled crowd, that he had not the value of five
francs. It is a kind of stool of black granite, not in the least worn . . .

M's journal:
Rainy day. To the famous caffe of Pedrocci . . . Got a grave dark guide
& started with great-coat & umbrella to see the sights — To the town hall.
Wonderful roof (India) . . . Pleasant aspect of Brenta winding through
town. To Giotto's chapel. — The Virtues & Vices. Capital . . . Old palaces & old arcades & old streets.

> [IN A CHURCH OF PADUA
> In vaulted place where shadows flit,
> An upright sombre box you see . . .
>
> Who bendeth here the tremulous knee
> No glimpse may get of him within,
> And he immured may hardly see
> The soul confessing there the sin;
> Nor yields the low-sieved voice a tone
> Whereby the murmurer may be known.
>
> Dread diving-bell! In thee inurned
> What hollows the priest must sound,
> Descending into consciences
> Where more is hid than found.]

At 2.P.M. took cars for Venice. Raining hard . . . Approaching Venice
like approaching Boston from the West. — Into gondola to Hotel Luna.
Dined . . . & sallied out to piazza of St. Marco, & about there till 8 P.M.

NEW YORK   April [1]   Putnam's Monthly *publishes a critical essay [by
Fitz-James O'Brien], "Our Authors and Authorship. Melville and Curtis":*
Mr. Melville was not only a young man, but a young American, and a young
American educated according to the standard of our day and country. He
had all the metaphysical tendencies which belong so eminently to the American's mind — the love of antic and extravagant speculation, the fearlessness of
intellectual consequences, and the passion for intellectual legislation, which
distinguish the cleverest of our people. It was inevitable that he should have
stamped himself pretty clearly on his book [*Typee*], and his book was all the
more interesting that he had so stamped himself upon it. Still we waited anxiously for number two . . . Had not Mr. Melville been impelled to a good

deal of sharp, sensible writing in "Omoo," by his wrath against the missionaries, it is clear, we think, that he would have plunged headlong into the vasty void of the obscure, the oracular, and the incomprehensible . . .

We frankly own here, and now, and once for all, that we have not, and never expect to have, the faintest notion of why we took a voyage to "Mardi" . . . Do we believe, then, that Mr. Melville meant nothing by taking us to "Mardi" . . . ? Not a bit of it; for, dull of perception, and still more dull of instinct must the critic be who does not recognize in every page of Mr. Melville's writings, however vague and obscure, and fantastic, the breathing spirit of a man of genius, and of a passionate and earnest man of genius. It is precisely because we are always sure that Mr. Melville *does* mean something, and something intrinsically manly and noble, too, that we quarrel with him for hiding his light under such an impervious bushel . . .

The sum and substance of our fault-finding with Herman Melville is this. He has indulged himself in a trick of metaphysical and morbid meditations until he has perverted his fine mind from its healthy productive tendencies. A singularly truthful person — as all his sympathies show him to be — he has succeeded in vitiating both his thought and his style into an appearance of the wildest affectation and untruth. His life, we should judge, has been excessively introverted . . .

As with the larger so it is with the smaller works of Mr. Melville. He balances the charm, and truth, and hazy golden atmosphere of "Las Encantadas" against the grotesque absurdity and incomprehensible verbiage of the "Lightning-Rod Man."

The two latest published books of our author differ considerably from their predecessors, in the degree in which they exhibit the characteristics of the classes of writing to which they respectively belong. "Israel Potter" is a comparatively reasonable narrative . . .

The "Confidence Man," on the contrary, belongs to the metaphysical and Rabelaistical class of Mr. Melville's works, and yet Mr. Melville, in this book, is more reasonable, and more respectful of probabilities . . . than he usually is when he wraps his prophetic mantle about him . . .

. . . We desire him to give up metaphysics and take to nature and the study of mankind. We rejoice, therefore, to know that he is, at this moment, traveling in the Old World, where, we hope, he will enjoy himself heartily, look about him wisely, and come home ready to give us pictures of life and reality.

VENICE April 2 *M's journal:*
Breakfasted at Florian's, on roll. Went into St. Mark's. Ducal Palace. Oily looking interior, reeking look, disappointed. Repairing dome — scaffold. To Rialto. Up Bell Tower. In gondola to Grand Canal & round by Guidecca . . . In the evening met in Ducal Palace (the court) affable young man (Antonio) engaged him to meet me for guide tomorrow.

My Guide. How I met him, & where. Lost his money in 1848 Revolution & by travelling. — To day in one city, tomorrow in next. Fine thing to travel. When rich, plenty compliment How you do, Antonio — hope you very well, Antonio — Now Antonio no money, Antonio no compliment. Get out of de way Antonio. Go to the devil, Antonio. Antonio you go shake yourself. You know dat Sir, dat to de rich man, de poor man hab always de bad smell? You know dat Sir?

Yes, Antonio, I am not unaware of that. Charitably disposed. Old blind man, give something & God will bless you Will give, but doubt the blessing. Antonio good character for Con[fidence] Man. Did not want to die. Heaven. You believe dat? I go dere, see how I like it first. — His rich anecdote. Byron swimming over by nunnery to watch a lady in palace opposite. The Prussian countess, candle sends. Very wicked lady but very happy. — Floating about philosophizing with Antonio the Merry. [entry of Apr 5]

April 3   To Glass bead manufactury . . . To Gold chain manufactury . . . To Church St. Giovanni Paoli . . . To the Arsenal . . . On the canals . . . After dinner in Piazza.

April 4   Breakfast at Mindel's. Took gondola at Piazzetta for Murano . . . Back & to Jesuit Church. Marble drapery of pulpit. Astonishing what can be done with marble. Into Grand Canal . . . To Gallery, Titian's Assumption. The great black heads & brown arms. St. Mark coming to rescue . . . After dinner, took gondola till dark on Canals. Old Palace with grinning monsters &c. Bought coat. To bed at 9½.

April 5   Breakfast on St. Marks . . . The charm of the square: The snug little breakfast there . . . Took gondola . . . To the Lido . . . Through the grassy lagoon to Armenian Convent. Admirable retirement from the world, asleep in the calm Lagoon, the Lido a breakwater against the tumultuous ocean of life . . . Chapel. 8 worshippers. & 8 priests. Superb vestments, blended with superb light streaming in from shining lagoon through windows draped with rosy silks. Chaunting, swinging silver censers — puff of incense at each worshipper. Great gorgeousness of effect . . . Back to the city . . . Walked to Rialto. Looked up & down G. Canal. Wandered further on. Numbers of beautiful women. The rich brown complexions of Titian's women drawn from Nature, after all. (Titian was a Venetian.) The clear, rich, golden brown. The clear cut features, like a cameo. — The vision from the window at end of long, narrow passage . . . On these still summer days the fair Venetians float about like in full bloom like pond lillies.

April 6   [Maria Melville's 66th birthday]   Left Venice at 5½ A M for Milan. Through Padua & Vicenza to Verona, where bride & groom entered the cars . . . Farm houses so unlike ours. No signs of hard work as with us. This region the scene of Napoleon's campaigns. At Coccaglio took diligence for Treviglio (18 m. from Milan). Rode from 1 P M till 6. In coupe. Arrived at Milan at 7½ P.M. Omnibus to Hotel de le Ville . . . Walked out to see the cathedral by night.

SALEM April 6   *The* Salem Register *quotes the* Albany Evening Journal's *review of* The Confidence-Man.

MILAN   April 7   [Allan Melville's 34ᵗʰ birthday]   *M's journal:*
To the Gallery . . . To the Camp d'Armo. Arch. To the picture of
Leonardo da Vinci . . . Some trouble finding the refectory. At last directed to an archway where stood trumpeters. *Not* for Leonardo, though.
Led through passages . . . Catching last hues of sunset. Whole picture
faded & half gone . . . Significance of the Last Supper. The joys of the
banquet soon depart. One shall betray me, one of you — men so false —
the glow of sociability is so evanescent, selfishness so lasting. — Leonardo
& his oil, case of a great man (Wordsworth) & his theory. To the cathedral. Glorious. More satisfactory to me than St. Peters. A wonderful
grandeur. Effect of burning window at end of aisle. Ascended, — Far below people in the turrets of open tracery look like flies caught in cobweb.
— The groups of angels on points of pinnacles, & everywhere. Not the
conception but execution. View from summit. Might well [stand?] host
of heaven upon top of Milan Cathedral. Dined at 5 P.M. at table d hote of
the Hotel de la Ville. Curious old gentleman there. Prided himself upon
filling his glass. Young man. Talk. About cathedral.

> [Of Art the miracles
>   Its tribes of pinnacles
> Gleam like to ice-peaks snowed; and higher,
> Erect upon each airy spire
>   In concourse without end,
> Statues of saints over saints ascend
> Like multitudinous forks of fire.
>   ("Milan Cathedral")]

GANSEVOORT   April 7   *Augusta Melville writes to Peter Gansevoort:*
   Another letter received from Herman dated Rome Febʸ 27ᵗʰ, announcing his return home next month, leads me to write you upon the subject
of which we were speaking the day before I left Albany. We all feel that
it is of the utmost importance that something should be done to prevent
the necessity of Herman's writing as he has been obliged to for several
years past. Were he to return to the sedentary life which that of an author
writing for his support necessitates, he would risk the loss of all the
benefit to his health which he has gained by his tour, & possibly become
a confirmed invalid. Of this his physicians have warned him . . . Now in
order to induce him to lay aside his pen it would be necessary to secure
to him some position which would give him occupation, & to some extent, means of support. The Custom House seems the only quarter for
us to look to. And it is believed that if a strong effort were made by his
influential friends in Albany Mr Corning & others an office there could be
secured to him. Indeed it has been suggested to us that your intimacy
with Judge Parker might be the means of affecting it, since from his
position as Candidate for Governor, he commands influence with the Collector in New York in securing some appointments. To be sure Herman

has never been a politician, but he belongs to a Democratic family, &
one which has done much for its party, & receive little from it. Then
aside from these facts, Herman is just one of those persons who should be
considered in filling these places, for he has done honor to, & reflected
credit upon his country.

I did not, my dear Uncle, intend to occupy so much of your time as
I have done, but in my deep anxiety for the future well-being of a beloved
brother I could not be more brief . . .

Mamma desires me to say, dear Uncle, that her heart echoes all I have
said about Herman, & that for any effort you may make in his behalf you
have a sister's gratitude.

We have just received letters from Tom, dated Hong Kong January
30th There was some probability of his being placed in command of the
vessel . . . So there is a possibility that *Captain* Melville is now on the
broad seas bound to San Francisco.

LAKE COMO April 8 *M's journal:*
Up at 5.A.M. At 6½ started for Lake Como. Ride of hour & half in cars
over dead rich plain. Took steamer at Como. Like going to Lake George.
— Wonderful populousness of shores of Lake . . . Villages upon all kinds
of sites. Some midway upon steep slopes as if they had slipped there in a
land-slide. Churches on isolated peaks. Group of hamlets — pinfolds. Villages by scores, or hundreds. Terraced vegetation. Lone houses way up,
here & there. Cascades, (under house) No trees. Back to Milan at 7 P.M.

BOSTON April 8 The Confidence-Man *is noticed in the* Boston Daily
Advertiser:
The grand *morale* of the book appears to be that the world is full of knaves
and fools, and that a man who ventures to believe what is told him, neces-
sarily belongs to the latter class.

MILAN April 9 *M's journal:*
Up at 5. Scribbled here, and down to breakfast at 6½. at hotel. Young
Parisian and lady there. At 9. o'clock started in diligence for Novara.
Smart postilions, bugles under arm, glazed hat, metal band, jack boots.
Over dead flat Lombardy plain, Alps in sight to the North. Passed many
populous villages & towns. High cultivation of a most fertile soil. Crossed
noble granite bridge of the Ticino. Came to Novara at 1½. Lunched
there. Remained, waiting for train, 4 hours. Walked in boulevard on old
walls — ancient brick fortress with deep, broad moat — Old duomo.
Thorvaldsen's angels. Old court. Baptistry. Wax work. Nails & hammer,
hair &c. At 5½ took train for Turin. Fell in with Greek from Zephalonia
("English subject") . . . saw church with wooden architecture before
it. Within, altar made into stage, where were pasteboard figures of scriptural characters. Exactly as in theatre. And lighted. Arrived at Turin
9.P.M. Adventure with omnibus, porter, and Hotel d la Europe.

PITTSFIELD April 9 *An item in* The Pittsfield Sun:
☞ HERMAN MELVILL, *Esq.*, the author, is expected soon to return from his European tour to his residence in Pittsfield, in greatly improved health.

ALBANY April 9 *Peter Gansevoort writes to Augusta Melville:*
Your suggestion of a place in the Custom House New York I readily adopted; & prepared to enlist the influence of my friends in the matter; but this morning was met by an objection considered a serious obstacle viz, that he is not a Citizen of this State, but resides in the State of Mass^ts . . .

TURIN April 10 *M's journal:*
Very rainy. Breakfasted at caffe (gilded octagonal saloon) in Via di Po. Walked under the great arcades. Took view across to Colina. Visited Gallery. Admirable painting of "A Confessional". Some heads of Titian. 4 fine allegorical paintings [by Francisco Albani] — Earth, Air, Fire, Water. Rubens' Magdalen — excellently true to nature, but very ugly. Groups of children by Van Dyke — six in a row, heads — charming. Teniers tavern scenes. The remarkable Teniers effect is produced by first dwarfing, then deforming humanity. Breughel — always pleasing. — Piazza Castello, where hotel is, is the centre of Turin. Interesting old pile, with various fronts, and grotesque assemblage of various architectures. Turin is more regular than Philadelphia. Houses all one cut, one color, one heigth. City seems all built by one contractor & paid for by one capitalist . . . Boulevards around the town. Many caffes & fine ones — Laboring people & poor women taking their frugal breakfast in fine caffes. Their decorum, so different from corresponding class at home. — In the evening it cleared off. Went down to the Po again. Stood on steps of church there. To bed early.

April 11 Bright weather. Up early to see Mont Rosa from the street. Saw it. Breakfasted on chocolate (Turin famous for it) on bank of Po. At 10/A.M. took cars for Genoa, over 100 miles. Pleasant for some time & passed through pleasant country. Very populous & highly cultivated. Approaching Appennines, noble scenery. Road built with great skill & cost. Numerous tunnels through hills at base of Appennines, till at last comes the Grand Tunnel — 2 miles long. Arrived at Genoa in rain at 3 P.M. Carpet bag fell from shoulder of clumsy porter. Afraid to look at Kate's affairs. — Stopped at hotel Feder on water side. Walked through Strada Nuova &c. Palaces inferior to those of Rome, Florence, & Venice. One peculiarity is the *paintings of architecture* instead of the reality. All kinds of elaborate architecture represented in fresco. — Machiavelli's saying that the appearance of a virtue may be advantageous, when the reality would be otherwise. — Streets like those of Edinburgh; only still more steep & crooked. Ascended one for view. — Dined at table 'dhote. Fine room. The hotel occupies old palace.

[*569*]

NEW YORK April 11 *In the* New-York Evening Times, *the "Books of the Week" column* [*by Fitz-James O'Brien?*] *replies to an article in the November issue of* North British Review, *on "Modern Style":*

The next show we made in style, after Hawthorne, was in *Typee,* and, after that delightful vision came the *Nile Notes* [by G. W. Curtis] . . . They were alike only in their sensuous originality, their freedom of feeling, their purity of form, and independence of all the conventionalities of style before known and recognized in the old world of literature . . . They were new writers in a new country; neither English, French, nor classical, but American. *Typee* and the *Nile Notes* are not noticed by the *North British* reviewer, but they will exact attention by and by.

The author of *Typee* has again come upon us in one of his strange vagaries, and calls himself *The Confidence Man* . . . Mr. Melville's *Confidence Man* is almost as ambiguous an apparition as his *Pierre,* who was altogether an impossible and ununderstandable creature. But, in the Confidence Man, there is no attempt at a novel, or a romance, for Melville has not the slightest qualifications for a novelist, and therefore he appears to much better advantage here than in his attempts at story books . . . It is, in short, a Rabelaisian piece of patchwork without any of the Rabelaisian indecency . . . the oddities of thought, felicities of expression, the wit, humor, and rollicking inspirations are as abundant and original as in any of the productions of this most remarkable writer. The volume has an end, but there is no conclusion to the book; the last chapter might have been the first, and the author intimates that there is more of the same sort to come.

LONDON April 11 The Confidence-Man *is reviewed in* The Athenæum:

The Confidence Man' is a morality enacted by masqued players. The credulous and the sceptical appear upon the stage in various quaint costumes, and discourse sententiously on the art of human life, as developed by those who believe and those who suspect . . . Mr. Melville is lavish in aphorism, epigram, and metaphor. When he is not didactic, he is luxuriously picturesque; and, although his style is one, from its peculiarities, difficult to manage, he has now obtained a mastery over it, and pours his colours over the narration with discretion as well as prodigality . . .

Full of thought, conceit, and fancy, of affectation and originality, this book is not unexceptionally meritorious, but it is invariably graphic, fresh, and entertaining.

The Confidence-Man *is reviewed in* The Leader:

. . . festoons of exuberant fancy decorate the discussion of abstract problems; the controversalists pause ever and anon while a vivid, natural Mississippi landscape is rapidly painted before the mind; the narrative is almost rhythmic, the talk is cordial, bright American touches are scattered over the perspective . . . In his Pacific stories Mr. Melville wrote as with an Indian pencil, steeping the entire relation in colours almost too brilliant for reality; his books were all stars, twinkles, flashes, vistas of green and crimson, diamond and crystal; he has now tempered himself, and studied the effect of neutral tints. He has also added satire to his repertory, and, as he uses it scrupulously, he uses it well . . . the charm of the book is owing to its originality and to its constant flow of descriptions, character-stretching, and dialogue, deeply toned and skilfully contrasted.

The Confidence-Man *is reviewed in* The Literary Gazette:
Those who, remembering the nature of the author's former performances, take it up in the expectation of encountering a wild and stirring fiction, will be tolerably sure to lay it down ere long with an uncomfortable sensation of dizziness in the head . . . A novel it is not, unless a novel means forty-five conversations held on board a steamer, conducted by personages who might pass for the errata of creation . . .
. . . We should be sorry, in saying this, to be confounded with the cold unimaginative critics, who see nothing but extravagance in some of our author's earlier fictions — in the first volume of 'Mardi,' that archipelago of lovely descriptions is led in glittering reaches of vivid nautical narrative — the conception of 'The Whale,' ghostly and grand as the great grey sweep of the ridged and rolling sea. But these wild beauties were introduced to us with a congruity of outward accompaniment lacking here . . .
. . . It is, of course, very possible that there may be method in all this madness, and that the author may have a plan, which must needs be a very deep one indeed . . . It may be that he has chosen to act the part of a mediaeval jester, conveying weighty truths under a semblance antic and ludicrous; if so, we can only recommend him for the future not to jingle his bells so loud.

The Confidence-Man *is reviewed in* The Spectator.

GENOA April 12 *M's journal:*
Breakfasted at Caffe. Chocolate. To the Public promenade on ramparts. Look off. Troops. Unhandsome set of men. To the Cathedral. White & black marble in alternate courses. The steps . . . All the world out. Numbers of women. The Genoese head dress. Undines and Maids of the Mist. Simple & graceful. Receipt for making a plain woman look lovely. Took omnibus (2 sous) to end of harbor. Light house (300 feet high) Ascended. Superb view. Sea coast to south. Promontory. All Genoa & her forts before you. The heigth & distances of these forts, their outlying lonelinesses. The bleakness, the savageness of glens between, seem to make Genoa rather the capital and fortified camp of Satan fortified against the Archangels. Clouds rolling round ramparts aerial, &c. Took the East side of harbor, and began circuit of the 3ᵈ line of defences . . . Up & up. Finer & finer, till I got to the apex fort . . . With great fatigue descended irregular path, coming out by Doria palace. Dined at table d hote. Greek next me. Gigglers opposite. — Walked over the port. Stopped in with Greek at garden-caffe.

April 13 Chocolate at Caffe. Old Wall of the Custom House. Visited the palaces . . . Was shown thro' some palaces in great haste. Rosso palace in particular. Very windy. To hotel early, effects of yesterday's walk. Met Purser of Constitution at dinner. In bed by eight.

THE ALPS April 14 Took cars at six A.M. for Arona on Lake Maggiore.

Met Lieutenant Fauntleroy at station. Pleasant ride across new country. At 2 P.M. sailed from Arona in (Passed thro' Allessandria & Novara) small steamer. Cold passage. Scenery fine. White-wash brush. Confusion of seasons. Pourings of cascades. Numbers of hamlets. The terraced isle. Came to Magadino at 7 P.M. Diligence to Bellizzona. Entered defile at dusk, and kept in it. Shadowy & vague approach among the roots of Alps. At Bellizona out jumped Dr Lockwood just from Simplon.

April 15   At 2.A M started in diligence for crossing the San Gothard. Bow window. Silence, mystery. Steady roll of wheel. Dawn, zig-zags, Gorge, precipice, snow. At Airolo breakfasted. Mr Abbot accosted me. Storming violently. Hand sleds. Parties waiting at Airolo for three days. Started. Long train. Zig-zag. Houses of refuge. Discussion of the gods &c . . . Descent. Like coming from the clouds. Noses of crags thrusting out — 10000 feet. Down at Andermatt. Wet through. Diligence. Devil's Bridge. Scenery through Gorge. Green & white of grass & snow. Lima torrent. Alt[d]orf. Fluellen at 7 P.M. —

GANSEVOORT   April 15   *Augusta Melville writes to Peter Gansevoort:*
I have waited before writing you again until I should be able to ascertain whether in New York his being a non-resident of the state would be considered an obstacle to his obtaining an appointment there. And I have been informed that custom has settled this question in the negative, & that there exists no necessity that the person applying for office should be a citizen of the state where the post is located . . .

And then too we have in Herman's favor the recent decision in this state which holds that a person doing business in New York who only sleeps out of the state is not a non-resident within the attachment laws. Now Herman by birth & from his residence in the city of New York is known as a New Yorker; all his books are published in that city; all his interests are there except the land in Massachusetts. Then it is well known that he has never voted in Mass., or taken any part in state matters. With some of these facts Mr Schell, the Collector is acquainted for he is personally known to him . . .

Mother received the morning Times [of April 8] containing an allusion to Herman's improved health & desires her acknowledgements. To-day's mail brought us several highly complimentary notices of Herman's new book "The Confidence Man."

LONDON   April 15   The Confidence-Man *is reviewed in* The Critic:
That prosiness is the last crime of which Herman Melville can be accused, will be admitted by all who are familiar with "Omoo," "Typee," "Mardi," "White Jacket," and "Moby Dick." On the contrary, there is a vividness and an intensity about his style which is almost painful for the constant strain upon the attention; and *The Confidence Man* is that of all his works which readers will find the hardest nut to crack.

We are not quite sure whether we have cracked it ourselves — whether there is not another meaning hidden in the depths of the subject other than that which lies near the surface. There is a dry vein of sarcastic humour running throughout which makes us half suspect this.

LAKE LUCERNE   April 16   *M's journal:*
Before breakfast next morning went out for view of Lake Lucerne — Bay of Uri. Chapel. (seats Methodists) At 9.A.M. started for Lucerne in steamer. Entrance of Bay of Uri. Tell's Chapel. At 11 came to Lucerne. — Thorwaldsen's lion — living rock. Ramble with Abbot & fine views. Old Bridges.

April 17   At 8 A M started in diligence for Berne. Coupe, only Abbot & me. Charming day & charming country . . . At 7 arrived at Berne, putting up at "The Crown". Went to terrace of cathedral for view of Bernese Alps. There they were — seen over the green.

ALBANY   April 17   *Peter Gansevoort writes to Augustus Schell & to Augusta Melville:*
. . . I called on Judge Parker who has this morning, written to Augustus Shell the new collector N.Y. strongly recommending the appointment of Herman to some appropriate place in the Custom House —
   I have also seen Mr Corning on the subject, who is friendly . . .
   Hermans numerous friends in N.Y. ought without delay to write in a recommendation

BOSTON   April 17   *Lemuel Shaw writes to his son, Samuel:*
   We are strongly in hope that you will meet Herman in Rome. It appears by letters received from him, that he was in Rome, about the same time you were at Geneva. A new work of Herman's has just been published at N. York entitled the "Confidence Man." He left the M.S. ready for publication, when he went out, last autumn, but it was not issued untill within a week or two. I have it but have not yet read it.

BERNE   April 18   *M's journal:*
Walk on terrace. Cathedral. Spent whole day about with Mr [Theodore] Fay & Abbot & daughter. Ride. Noble view of Alps. Rail Road building.
Fay gives M's passport a visa "pour la France et l'Angleterre" & the French Legation gives him a French visa.

LONDON   April 18   The Confidence-Man *is noticed in* The Examiner:
   Mr. Herman Melville, a clever American author, whose Marquesas Island story no reader can have forgotten, has published a fanciful work which he calls a "Masquerade" . . .

BERNE-BASLE   April 19   *M's journal:*
At 10.A.M. started in diligence (interior) for Basle. Fine day. At Soleure dined. Encountered a Mr Smyth[e] merchant of N.Y. . . . Beyond

Soleure drew near Jura, — palisades — About high as Saddle Back . . .
Took R.R at L[augenbruch] and at 8 P.M. put up at "The Wild Man" in
Basle. Walked out, crossed the Rhine by bridge of boats. Deep, broad,
rapid.

STRASBURG April 20 At 5 A.M. off by R. R. for Strasbourgh — 90
miles. To the Cathedral. Pointed — pinnacles — All sprouting together
like bed of asparagus . . . Ascent. Not fine as Milan. Platform on top.
The Spire. inscriptions (1500) At 2 P.M. crossed with Mr Smyth[e] to
Kiel. Passports. French & German. Baden. Took cars for Heidelburgh.
Californians. Lovely afternoon . . . At 8 P M arrived at Heidelburgh.
Hotel Adler.

HEIDELBERG April 21 Up at 5 and mounted to Castle. Blossoms, grass,
all things fresh round the charming old ruin . . . The university. — The
cloven ruin. trees sprouting. defile in ruins. — Flower bed in banquet hall.
Knights in green niches. — Students. Daguerreotypes. At 2 P.M. took cars
for Frankfort on Maine. At station encountered Dr Abbot again — bound
to Frankfort . . . At 4 P M came to Frankfort, stopping at Hotel
[?]. After dinner Smythe invited us to ride about town. — Goethe's
statue. Faust's.

BOSTON April 21 *Lemuel Shaw, Jr writes to his brother, Samuel:*
  Elizabeth has gone to Pittsfield to set her house in readiness to receive
her husband whom she expects sometime in May. A new book by Herman called "The Confidence Man" has recently been published. I have not
yet read it; but have looked at it & dipped into it, & fear it belongs [to]
that horribly uninteresting class of nonsensical books he is given to
writing — where there are pages of crude theory & speculation to every
line of narritive — & interspersed with strained & ineffectual attempts to
be humorous. I wish he could or would do better, when he went away
he was dispirited & ill — & this book was left completed in the publisher's
hands.

FRANKFORT April 22 *M's journal:*
After breakfast went in to see Abbot — found him smoking in bed &
better. Went to Rothschilds. — Eminent hard-ware merchant . . . Drove
about the town. Faust's statue. The "Ariadne" of H [Dannecker?]. Rose
light. Beauty and Deformity contrasted. At half past eleven A.M. started
in cars for Weisbaden, but by mistake arrived at Mayence — at 2 P.M.
Took boat for Cologne . . . Got to Cologne at 10 P.M. Rainy & cold all
day. My practical companion. (from Boston?) Stopped at Hotel de
Cologne.

COLOGNE April 23 At 5 o'clock got up, breakfasted & went to R.R.
station, across river for Amsterdam. Through Dusseldorf & Utrecht.
Rainy, cold, hail at times & sleet . . . Adventure after hotel in Amster-

dam, where we arrived at 3½ P.M. Put up at last at the "Old Bible," upon which something good might be written in the ironical way.

M's passport is stamped: RIJKSPOLITIE ZEVENAAR.

A great grievance from first to last is the passport. You soon learn by official demands what becomes to you an adage, — open passport, open purse. Its endless crosses at the close of your travels remind you of the crosses it has cost you all the way through. (*M's lecture, "Travel," reported in the* Cambridge Chronicle, *Feb 25, 1860*)

AMSTERDAM   April 24   *M's journal:*
At ordinary a number of sea captains. This morning got a queer little old Dutchman for guide & went to Picture Gallery. Wonderful picture of Paul Potter — The Bear[-hunt] . . . The Syndics of Rembrandt & The Night Watch (shadows) — Portrait [by Hals] of a painter & his wife — admirable (Old Peddlers) The abandonment of good humored content. Dutch convivial scenes. Teniers & Breughel. — Streets of Amsterdam like long lines of old fashioned frontispieces in old folios & old quartoes . . . To the "Garden" & "Plantation." The pink-mouthed dog. The "Sloth". — View of city from cupola of palace. Red tiles of houses. The Port. The drop of gin . . . At 4½ took train for Rotterdam. Smoking cars. One all to myself . . . Arrived at Rotterdam at 7½. Got guide & went to Dance Houses. Into three of them. Striking & pathetic sight. The promenading girls — music — their expressions & decorum. — Villiany of the guide. To bed by 9½.

ROTTERDAM   April 25   With guide went to cathedral of St. Lawrence . . . Fine view of Rotterdam & environs. House of Erasmus. At 11 oclock went on board steamer [*Fyenoord?*] for London. Fair wind, but chilly.

NEW YORK   April 25   The Confidence-Man *is noticed in* Porter's Spirit of the Times.

LONDON   April 26   *M's journal:*
Made the mouth of Thames early, & steamed up, passed many objects of interest. The mammoth ship "Great Eastern." At 7 A M were at St. Catherine Wharf. Cab, & to Tavistock Hotel. Dreary Sunday in London. Walked to Hyde Park & in Kensington Gardens. Got an idea of them.

April 27   To the Longman's [publishers of *The Confidence-Man*] &c

NEW YORK   April 27   *The firm of Dix, Edwards & Co. is dissolved, by the retirement of Messrs Dix & Edwards; a new firm is formed, allying the senior partner of a printing firm & a portion of the old house: Miller & Company.* (American Publishers' Circular)

LONDON   April 28   *M's journal:*
To Madame Tussaud's. No where else in particular.

April 29-May 1   Lay a sort of waterlogged in London. — Reverie at the "Cock." Chrystal Palace — digest of universe. Alhambra — House of Pansi — Temple of [?]. &c &c &c. — Comparison with the pyramid. — Overdone. If smaller would look larger. The Great Eastern. Pyramid. — Vast toy. No substance. Such an appropriation of space as is made by a rail fence. Durable materials, but perishable structure. Cant exist 100 years hence . . . Rode out in omnibus to Richmond. Several evenings at Hyde Park to see the equestrians. Free & bold riding of the ladies. Poor devil looking over the rail. — Visited the Vernon & Turner galleries. Sunset scenes of Turner. "Burial of Wilkie." The Shipwreck. "The Fighting [Temeraire] taken to her last berth."

BATH   May 1   *Amos Nourse writes to Lemuel Shaw:*
I was glad to hear so good accounts of Herman & Elizabeth. The latter seems to have become quite a business character — She always proves just equal to the emergency whatever it may be.

OXFORD   May 2   *M's journal:*
At 11½ arrived at Oxford. — Most interesting spot I have seen in England. Made tour of all colleges. It was here I first confessed with gratitude my mother land, & hailed her with pride . . . Pulpit in corner of quadrangle. Deer. Garden girdled by river. — Meadows beyond. Oxen & sheep. Pastoral & collegiate life blended. — Christ Church Meadow. Avenue of trees. — Old reef washed by waves & showing detached parts — so Oxford. Ivy branch over portal of St. John intertwining with sculpture. Amity of art & nature. Accord. Grotesque figures. Catching rheumatism in Oxford cloisters different from catching it in Rome. Contagion in Pamfili Doria but wholesome beauty in Oxford. Learning lodged like a faun. Garden to every college . . . Each college has dining room & chapel — on a par — large windows. Soul & body equally cared for . . . I know nothing more fitted by mild & beautiful rebuke to chastise the presumptuous ranting of Yankees. — In such a retreat old Burton sedately smiled at men.

NEW YORK   May 2   *Deposited for copyright:*
THE | CONFIDENCE-MAN: | HIS MASQUERADE. | BY | HERMAN MELVILLE . . .

STRATFORD-BIRMINGHAM   May 3   *M's journal:*
Left Oxford at 9 A. M for Stratford on Avon. Changed for horse rail road. Stopped at the "Red Horse." — Shakspeare's house — little old groggery abandoned. — cheerless, melancholy Scrawl of names. — The church. Tomb stones before altar, wife, daughter son-in-law. — New Place. — Walk to Hathaway cottage at Shottery. Level country. —
    At 3½ went on stage to Warwick. Cold & windy. Wonderfully beautiful country. — (Edge Hill). — Aspect of Castle nigh Avon. Walked about Warwick. Entrance very fine. Old gate &c. At 6½ took R.R.

for Birmingham. Arrived before dark. Mob of chimneys. Like Newcastle-upon-Tyne. Stopped at Queen's, by R.R. Drove around town.

LIVERPOOL May 4 At 6 A.M. took R R for Liverpool. Like riding through burnt district — standing columns of pines, smoking or with stars of flame from top. — The Chimneys. Arrived at Liverpool at 12.M. — Secured my berth on "City of Manchester" by paying balance. Got letters from Brown, Shipley & Co. Saw Hawthorne. Called on Mr Bright. Got presents. Trunk. Packed.

May 5 Fine day. At 10 A.M. got on board tender for steamer. — At 11½ — off for home.

ATLANTIC After May 5? *M reads in the Valery hand-book, & scores:*
On the front of the Lanfreducci palace [in Pisa] are the words *Alla giornata* (day by day), under which hangs a captive's chain, no less difficult to understand than the inscription. These words and this chain on the front of a fine marble palace have always inspired me with a singular melancholy. One feels that such a combination has something of romance and poesy, and may perhaps hide the secret of some touching tale.

In the back pages of his journal, M notes some projects:

Frescoes of Land
&
Three Brothers
Poet, Painter, and Scholar Adler.

Ronsan ⎫ Venice
Cicero ⎬ Olympus
Byron ⎨ Parthenon
Haydon ⎭ Seamen

Subjects for Roman Frescoes.
⎰A group of cypresses in Villa D'Este.
⎱Whispering apart like Angelo's "Fates"
⎰From *Tartarus to Tivoli*
⎱is but a step or two.
⎰The Cenci portrait.
⎰Sixtus V^{th} — His obelisks &c
Sprung from the people — What it was to be
Pope in those days. No democracies —
Only way of rising to preeminence — & rich
preeminence. — What he did in order
to be this.

LONDON May 9   The Confidence-Man *is noticed in* John Bull:
. . . The conflict between the feeling of trust, enjoined by every nobler sentiment and higher principle, and the feeling of distrust engendered by the experience of life, of which every human breast is, however unconsciously, the perpetual battle-field, has not often been so forcibly as well as amusingly illustrated as it is in the incoherent ramblings of "the confidence-man."

ALBANY May 11   *Amasa J. Parker replies to Lemuel Shaw's request:*
. . . I am happy to assure you, it will give me pleasure to do all in my power to secure a place in the New York Custom house for Mr Melville.
Before your letter was rec^d, I had, already, on the suggestion of some of his friends here, written to Mr Schell our newly appointed collector, urging his appointment, & I will do any thing further in my power.

46.58 42   May 13
. . . signalized Norw[egian] brig Allecto, and bark Daedalus, of Falmouth, for Quebec . . . (*City of Manchester* report, May 21)

PORT ARBROATH, SCOTLAND May 13   *Eliza Gordon writes to M, praising* White-Jacket, *& promising a visit to the United States:*
I have for this many a day been wishing to see you "to hear you speak to breathe the same air in which you dwell" Are you the picture of him you so powerfully represent as the Master peice of all Gods works Jack Chase? —

CHICAGO May 15   *The* Chicago Magazine *prints "The Sandwich Islands," By an American Resident:*
It will give some idea of the immense gulf between chiefs and common people to review some of their "tabus," or prohibitions . . . For these statements, incredible as they seem, there is abundance of the best authority, viz: the unanimous testimony of intelligent natives. They describe a state of things very different from the Paradisiacal innocence and happiness ascribed to the aborigines by Hermann Melville & Co.

43.12 56.17   May 16
. . . spoke Brem[en] bark Copernicus, for New-York; 18th, in lat. 41 17, lon. 65 47, passed a steamer, supposed the Hermann. (*City of Manchester* report, May 21)

NEW YORK May 20
ARRIVED.
Steamship City of Manchester (Br. screw), Petrie, Liverpool May 6, mdse. and pass. to J. G. Dale. (*New-York Daily Tribune*, May 21)

Elizabeth Melville's memoir of M:
. . . came home about the time The Confidence Man was published in 1857 — and with much improved health. In 13 years he had written 10 books, besides much miscellaneous writing.

LONDON May 23 The Confidence-Man *is reviewed in* The Saturday Review:

There is one point on which we must speak a serious word to Mr. Melville before parting with him. He is too clever a man to be a profane one; and yet his occasionally irreverent use of Scriptural phrases in such a book as the one before us, gives a disagreeable impression. We hope he will not in future mar his wit and blunt the edge of his satire by such instances of bad taste. He has, doubtless, in the present case fallen into them inadvertently, for they are blemishes belonging to a far lower order of mind than his . . .

. . . The money-getting spirit which appears to pervade every class of men in the States, almost like a monomania, is vividly portrayed in this satire . . . we gladly hail the assistance of so powerful a satirist as Mr. Melville in attacking the most dangerous and the most debasing tendency of the age.

CAMBRIDGE May 25 *Henry Gansevoort's diary:*
Yesterday Cousin Herman & Lem Shaw [Jr] visited me [at Harvard]. Walked with them to Fresh Pond etc. [entry of May 26]

BOSTON May 27 [Herman] says he is better than at any time while absent, but still he is not perfectly well; he staid with us about a week & I gave a dinner-party for him & had a very pleasant one, Dr Holmes & the two Danas &c . . . —*Lemuel Shaw, Jr to his brother, Samuel, June 2*

Henry Gansevoort's diary:
Dined at 6 P.M. with Chief Justice Shaw and his son. There were present Dr Holmes, the poet, Herman Melville the author, R H Dana the jurist, and several others, including Dr Inches of Boston — After a short conversation in the parlour we were seated at a sumptous repast, presided over by the Chief Justice. First Course Salmon in French style Mock Turtle soup, Spring chicken, squabs, broiled turkey, mutton chop sweetbread, Canvass back duck and too many other things to enumerate. Every kind of dessert, useless to name and Bergundy Hock Claret, Madara Heidsick Sherry Ancette and other wines cordials, etc Seltzer water etc. Wit circled the board, repartee flashed and humor, thundered until 11 P.M. when the joyous company seperated. This is a memorable day for me — Holmes remarked in the course of the conversation that a lecturer was a literary strumpet subject for a greater than whore's fee to prostitute himself. Many good things were said which I shall ever treasure in my memory and therefore need not transcribe to paper.

PITTSFIELD May 28 *A paragraph in* The Pittsfield Sun:
HERMAN MELVILL, *Esq.*, of this town, returned on the 20th inst . . . after a seven months' absence abroad. His last book, the "Confidence Man," was brought out in London in April, by the Longmans, and is critically noticed at large in most of the London literary papers.

LIVERPOOL May? *Hawthorne writes to M about* The Confidence-Man.

NEW YORK June [1]   The Confidence-Man *is reviewed [by Ann S. Stephens] in* Mrs. Stephens' New Monthly:
    It is the most singular of the many singular books of this author. Mr. Melville seems to be bent upon obliterating his early successes . . . This is the more to be condemned, because in many important points he has sensibly advanced. His style has become more individualized — more striking, original, sinewy, compact; more reflective and philosophical . . .

BOSTON   Before June 2   Herman says he is not going to write any more at present & wishes to get a place in the N.Y. Custom House — Lizzie & her children returned to Pittsfield with Herman . . . — *Lemuel Shaw, Jr to his brother, Samuel, June 2*

PITTSFIELD   June 19   *The* Berkshire County Eagle *quotes* The Saturday Review *on* The Confidence-Man, *adding:*
We need not say to those who have read the book that as a picture of American society, it is *slightly* distorted.

BROOKLINE?   June 21   I spent a pleasant Sunday at Mr Griggs' with Aunt [Maria] Melville I never have seen her look better. She seems to have renewed her youth and to have quaffed the elixier of life. She informed me that Cousin Herman and herself intended visiting you at Albany sometime this week. — *Henry Gansevoort to his sister, Catherine, June 22*

ALBANY   After June 21   *M & his mother call at Peter Gansevoort's.* (I understood that you had gone west from Mr Griggs, who learned the fact from Aunt Melville. It seems that she found you absent when arrived with Cousin Herman to pay you a visit. — *Henry Gansevoort to his father, July 9*)

PITTSFIELD   June 23   *The Valuation Book for Pittsfield is completed; in M's estimate:*

[Money] $5000

June 24   *M places a running advertisement in the* Berkshire County Eagle:

FOR SALE.

THE PLACE now occupied by the sub-scriber (two miles and a half from Pittsfield village by the east road to Lenox,) being about seventy acres, embracing meadow, pasture, wood, and orchard, with a roomy and comfortable house. For situation and prospect, this place is among the pleasantest in Berkshire, and has other natural advantages desirable in a country residence.   H. MELVILLE.
June 24, 1857.   tf48

[*First printed in issue of June 26*]

NEW YORK   June 30   *Harper & Bros. sends M their 12th account:*
Balance due Harper & Bros. $352.11

LONDON   June   *Longman, Brown & Co. send M a statement:*
1000 copies [of *The Confidence-Man*] printed
343   "   sold
[amount short of expenses, £29.2.3]

NEW YORK   July [1]   Putnam's Monthly *prints a communication from Richard Tobias Greene:*
To the Editor:
  In the April number of *Putnam*, I saw an article on our authors — among others Herman Melville is spoken of. As I am the veritable "Toby" of· which he wrote in "Typee," I would like to correct an error which many have fallen into respecting myself. I am often spoken of as Melville's valet, his "man Friday," etc., and by some as a myth. Now that I exist is true, and the book "Typee" is true, but I was not Herman Melville's valet, man Friday, or anything of the sort. I stood on the same footing with Melville. We both shipped as foremast hands on board a whale ship, in one of the whaling ports in Massachusetts, and from there made the romantic trip from which he wrote his "Typee." I was his companion from the time of our entering on board the whaler, until our separation on the Marquise islands, as related by himself in "Typee." A friendly communication exists between us, and I presume it is amusing to him to see "Toby" spoken of as his valet.

LONDON   July 1   The Confidence-Man *is reviewed in* The Westminster and Foreign Quarterly Review:
  We are not among those who have had faith in Herman Melville's South Pacific travels so much as in his strength of imagination. The "Confidence-Man" shows him in a new character — that of a satirist, and a very keen, somewhat bitter observer . . . It required close knowledge of the world, and of the Yankee world, to write such a book and make the satire acute and telling . . . we are conscious of a certain hardness in the book, from the absence of humor, where so much humanity is shuffled into close neighborhood. And with the absence of humor, too, there is an absence of kindliness. The view of human nature is severe and sombre . . . It wants relief, and is written too much in the spirit of Timon . . . Few Americans write so powerfully as Mr. Melville, or in better English, and we shall look forward with pleasure to his promised continuation of the masquerade. The first part is a remarkable work, and will add to his reputation.

PITTSFIELD   July 13   *M inserts his running advertisement also in* The Pittsfield Sun, *first printed in the issue of July 16.*

BOSTON   August 17?   *Francis H. Underwood writes to M, inviting him to contribute an article to the projected* Atlantic Monthly.

PITTSFIELD   August 19   *M replies to Francis Underwood's invitation:*

[581]

I shall be very happy to contribute, though I cannot now name the day when I shall have any article ready.

August 31   *M drives into town to pay his Town, County & State Tax: a Total Tax of $42 (less $1.11 for prompt payment).*

NEW YORK   September 4   *G. W. Curtis writes to Allan Melville:*
Mr. [Francis G.] Shaw desires me to say that if you think fit to petition the Court to allow him to arrange the settlement of "The Confidence Man" upon the terms of the contract, he will not oppose the petition.

Mr. Dix informs me that you were right in your interpretation of the "Piazza Tales" contract.

PITTSFIELD   September 8?   *M writes to G. W. Curtis.* (I had also a note from him yesterday. He thinks well of lecturing, and wants to be hung for the whole sheep, and go the entire swine. His animal tastes can easily be gratified, I presume. — *G. W. Curtis to Allan Melville, Sept 10*)

ALBANY   September 9   *Peter Gansevoort writes to his son, Henry:*
Herman Melville was at my office when I opened yr letter of the 6th . . .
Herman is to dine with us, & I am to see him on Business at the house before Dinner —

NEW YORK   September 10   *G. W. Curtis writes to Allan Melville:*
I enclose your note from your brother, and await further events.

PITTSFIELD   September 12   *Hope Shaw's diary:*
Left Boston Saturday 12 of Sept went to Pittsfield — staid there until the next Monday [14]

September 15   *M writes to G. W. Curtis:*
I said the other day in my note that I would soon tell you about the plates [of *The Confidence-Man?*]. Well, I have now to say that I can not at present currently make arrangements with regard to them.

It strikes me though, that under the circumstances (copyright &c) they can bring but little at the Trade Sale, or any other sale. Whereas, if held on to for a while, they might be transferred to me to the common advantage of all concerned. But I do not wish to suggest anything in the way of a prompt settling up of the affairs of the late firm. Do with the plates whatever is thought best.

— I have been trying to scratch my brains for a Lecture. What is a good, earnest subject? *"Daily progress of man towards a state of intellectual & moral perfection, as evidenced in history of 5th Avenue & 5 Points"*

NEW YORK September 19 *At 11 A.M. the stereotype plates of Miller & Curtis are sold at the sales-rooms of George A. Leavitt & Co.:*
The competition was solely between Derby & Jackson, Rudd & Carleton, Leavitt & Allen, Dick & Fitzgerald, and the authors, two or three of whom were represented. The first lot offered was the plates of Geo. W. Curtis's Works . . . Two volumes by Herman Melville were withdrawn . . . (*New-York Daily Tribune*, Sept 21)

PITTSFIELD September 29 *M pays his Town, County & State Tax for 1856: a Total of $38.88.*

NEW YORK Late September? *The stereotype plates of* Israel Potter *are sold by Putnam to Peterson, Philadelphia, for $218.66.*

BOSTON? September? Kiana, *by James Jackson Jarves, is reviewed:*
Where is Melville? Will he not leave the mazes of Pierre or the Ambiguities, and the eccentricities of the Confidence Man, and with some such charming tradition as this bring back the days and the delights of beautiful Fayaway, or take us voyaging to another Mardi.

NEW YORK October *The* New-York Daily Tribune *announces the names of lecturers available for this winter season, including M.*

It is said that several of the American writers who were at that time popular in the lecture field, Mr. [George William] Curtis among them, helped to start him [M] in his first course by referring to him in their own lectures before country audiences. (Stedman, New York *World*, Oct 11, 1891)

CLARKSVILLE, TENN. October 12 *The corresponding committee of the Clarksville Literary Association writes to M:*
We . . . are instructed to tender you the earnest invitation of our Society to address them at whatever time during the coming Fall or Winter as may best suit your convenience. We are anxious that it is the impression with our Northern Brethren that Literary men meet with poor appreciation in the South, but we can assure you, there are many amongst us who have delightedly perused your productions, and who are eager to render personal, that charming acquaintance they have formed with you through the medium of your genial pen. Presuming that your Steps have never wandered this far West, we indulge the hope that this opportunity of seeing our portion of the Union and our forms of society will induce you to accept the invitation. The facilities for reaching our city are both pleasant and expeditious . . .

PITTSFIELD October 20 *On their letter M drafts his reply to the Clarksville Literary Association:*
Accepted — cannot name precise day but it will probably be some time in the latter part of January — $50 is considered average sum — will write again — as soon as arrangements are completed

GALENA October 31   *Mary A. A. Melvill writes to Lemuel Shaw:*
I hope with you that Herman may succeed in lecturing his arrangements are probably fixed for the season, so that we can not expect to see him so far west, which we should rejoice to do.

BOSTON November [1]   *The first issue of* The Atlantic Monthly *appears, on the back cover of which is printed a "list of literary persons interested in [this] enterprise," including M.*

PITTSFIELD November 6   *An item in the* Berkshire County Eagle:
JOHN C. HOADLEY, formerly of the firm of McKay & Hoadley in this town, is chosen a representative from the city of Lawrence on the Republican ticket.

BOSTON November 19   *Lemuel Shaw writes to Peter Gansevoort:*
We expect Herman & his wife on Saturday evening. He is to make his first essay at lecturing at Lawrence on Wednesday next.

November 21   *Hope Shaw's diary:*
Mr & Mrs Melville arrived from Pittsfield.

LAWRENCE November 23   *For the first time M reads his lecture on "Statuary in Rome," a benefit at City Hall for the Lawrence Provident Association:*
. . . most admirable studies were presented of a great number of characters; studies marked throughout by keen insight, honest independence, bold originality, and great justness of vision.
Of the style, nervous and vigorous, yet easy and flowing, and falling constantly into the most melodious cadences; it can only be said in dispraise that it was perhaps too highly wrought, and too uniformly excellent . . .
The Lecturer, like many others unacquainted, with our City Hall, was baffled by its echoes. Though endowed with a voice which could shake the roof, he feared to speak too loud, lest he should be out-shouted by the mocking wall, and the consequence was that he spoke so low, in general, as to be heard with difficulty except by those on the front seats.
The rain, which fell in torrents, accompanied by thunder and lightning, detained many from attending, and many who came got thoroughly wet.
The poor, in whose behalf Mr. Melville lectured gratuitously, therefore received less. — The net proceeds, however, were over thirty dollars.
All success attend the warm hearted and gifted Lecturer. (*Lawrence Courier*, Nov 25)

MALDEN? November 23   *A. D. Lamson [?] invites M to lecture in December at Malden.*

CAMBRIDGE November 23   *Henry Gansevoort writes to his father:*
[M] has numerous engagements to lecture in Boston and its vicinity. I understand his subject to be "Roman Statuary." He is able to treat this finely if he will follow "crassa Minerva," but if he aims at metaphysical

disquisitions he will surely fail. His forte is narration or description in other words a wild, bold word painting — When he essays philosophy he seeks to ascend by waxen wings from his proper sphere only to find his mind dazzled his wings melted and his fall mortifying —

CONCORD, N. H.   November 24   *M reads his lecture on "Statuary in Rome" in the Phenix Hall for the Pennacook Lyceum (fee, $30).*

BOSTON   November 26   *The Melvilles spend Thanksgiving at the Shaws.*

November 27   *M answers the enquiry [of A. D. Lamson?] of Nov 23:* I am very sorry that it will be quite impossible for me to be with you in Dec. and must therefore regret that our negotiation must, for this season at least, fall through.

Mr Mackay's lectures have, I hear, given very great pleasure.

BROOKLYN   November   *Commander Guert Gansevoort writes to the Secretary of the Navy:* Being very desirous of obtaining sea service, I respectfully request, that I may be ordered to the Command of any sea going ship, that the Hon. Secretary of the Navy may think proper.

If I should fail in obtaining orders to sea, I would beg leave to ask, that I may be detailed for the U.S. Naval Rendezvous at this place, when made vacant by its present Commander.

BOSTON   December 2   *M reads his lecture on "Statuary in Rome" at Tremont Temple for the Mercantile Library Association (fee, $40):* A large audience assembled last evening to listen to the author of "Omoo" and "Typee." He began by asserting that in the realm of art there was no exclusiveness. Dilletanti might accumulate their technical terms, but that did not interfere with the substantial enjoyment of those who did not understand them. As the beauties of nature could be appreciated without knowledge of botany, so art could be enjoyed without the artist's skill. With this principle in view, he, claiming to be neither critic nor artist, would make some plain remarks on the statuary of Rome. (*Boston Daily Journal*, Dec 3)

Passing through the gate of St. John, on the approach to Rome by Naples, the first object of attraction is the group of colossal figures in stone, surmounting, like storks, the lofty pediment of St. John Lateran. Standing in every grand or animated attitude, they seem not only to attest that this [is] the Eternal City, but likewise, at its portal, to offer greeting in the name of that great company of statues, which, amid the fluctuations of the human census, abides the true and undying population of Rome. (*Daily Courier,* Dec 3[?])

The speaker then vividly described the statues of Demosthenes, Titus Vespasian, Socrates, looking like an Irish comedian, Julius Caesar, so sensible and business-like of aspect that it might be taken for the bust of a railroad president, Seneca, with the visage of a pawnbroker . . . (*Boston Daily Journal,* Dec 3)

Yet in all these we saw but the men of to-day, so that we might believe that if a hundred men of that age should be transplanted to this, we would perceive that humanity was the same to-day as ever, — in what went to make up the basis of human character. We might learn that then, as now, appearances were deceptive. "That Tiberias," said a lady, "it does not look bad." If he did, he would not be Tiberias. That arch dissembler wore a sad, intellectual look, in which only deep attention perceived the sinister lines . . . (*Daily Evening Traveller*, Dec 3)

Thus these statues confessed, and, as it were, prattled to us of much that does not appear in history and the written works of those they represent. They seem familiar and natural to us — and yet there is about them all a heroic tone peculiar to the ancient life. It is to be hoped that this is not wholly lost from the world, although the sense of earthly vanity inculcated by Christianity may have swallowed it up in humility. (*Boston Daily Journal*, Dec 3)

In the Vatican Museum one meets old acquaintences which the historian has introduced to him in times past. The Apollo, the masterpiece of the place seems to respond to those aspirations of beauty and perfection that we only can hope to fully enjoy in another world. It seems to breathe divinity. It awes to silence. The Venus de Medeci is lovely but the Apollo is divine. The Venus seemed to blend the actual & ideal. He had authority for the assertion, as one day from his mat in the Typee valley he saw a maiden surprised in the bath retreating with the grace of nature to a friendly covert. These beautiful figures he contended showed that the violence of the Romans as a conquering race did not engross them wholly. — *Henry Gansevoort to his father, Dec 9*

. . . the lecturer said that as instinct is below reason, so is science below art — a proposition which caused some little discussion in several groups of homeward-bound listeners, after the lecture was closed. (*Daily Evening Traveller*, Dec 3)

The pleasant book-maker proved himself as much at home in the lecture-room as in prosecuting his peculiar vocation . . . The lecture contained many trenchant passages, similar to those which have made Mr. Melville's works so highly prized by the large class whose literary appetite relishes only richly-flavored dishes. (*Boston Evening Transcript*, Dec 3)

The lecture was quite interesting to those of artistic tastes, but we fancy the larger part of the audience would have preferred something more modern and personal. (*Boston Daily Journal*, Dec 3)

BROOKLINE December 6 *M visits his sister, Helen Maria & her husband, George Griggs.* (Herman Melville seems considerably improved in health and spirits by his interspersing the spice of variety with the reality of life I met him at Mr Griggs last Sunday evening. He was in a fine flow of humor which I enjoyed exceedingly. There is doubtless positive originality in him. Brilliancy but misanthropy. Genius but less judgement. He evidently mistakes his sphere. He has dropped the pen of candid narration for that of captious criticism. He does the latter well but he can do the former much better. —*Henry Gansevoort to his father, Dec 9*)

BOSTON December 8   *M dines at the Shaws.* (Yesterday I visited Judge Shaw. I there saw Herman Melville. Both desired me to remember them particularly to you. The Judge is the same droll but earnest man as ever. He is indefatigable in business and at the age of eighty [seventy-seven] still presides on the bench and at his table with the same lynx eye and compressed lip as characterised him of yore . . . —*Henry Gansevoort to his father, Dec 9*)

December 9   *M leaves to fill a lecture engagement in Montreal, & begins an itemized account of his expenses:*

Fare from Boston to Montreal	$9.
Apples	3
Dinner	42
R. R. Guide	15
Lodging & Breakfast at Rut[land]	1.

Henry Gansevoort sends his father a report on M's lecture, a paraphrase of the account in the Daily Courier.

MONTREAL December 10   [John C. Hoadley's 39th birthday]   *M reads his lecture on "Statuary in Rome" (fee, $50).*

RUTLAND December 11   *M stops here, on his way to his mother's at Gansevoort, & purchases some gifts:*

2 lodges & 3 meal at R[utland?]	2.50
Post[age] Stamp (Mama)	1.
Presents for Uncle, (Tobacco & pipe 12.)	3.25

ALBANY December 17   *Peter Gansevoort replies to his son Henry's letter of Dec 9:*
Altho° persuaded he will be an interesting & successful lecturer, I entirely accord with your opinion, that he would be more "at home" in Narrative than in criticism.
It would be a luxury to hear from him a Narrative of his recent tour on the borders of the Mediterranean & Constantinople &c
I am surprised that he has not made his travels the subject of a Lecture, to be hereafter woven into a Book; which would be not only instructive to others, but very profitable to him. [draft of this letter continued: Such work would not make a requisition on his imagination]
Make the suggestion to him when you see him.

SARATOGA SPRINGS Before December 28 (Christmas?)   [?] *M takes his mother & sister, Augusta, to the Springs:*
Fare from Saratoga, & Augusta's   1.20

6 Fares to & from Saratoga Spgs	2.40
Coffee & Blacking	64
Candy	10

M composes a new lecture, "The South Seas."

ALBANY December 28 *Peter Gansevoort's diary:*
Met my Nephew Herman Melville on my way to the office — He had just returned from "Gansevoort" & is on his way to Springfield —
  Went with him to the Studio of [Erastus Dow] Palmer, the Sculptor — He afterwards called at my office & left at 2³⁰ PM

NEW HAVEN December 30 *M arrives, via Springfield, to read a lecture at The College Street Church, for the Young Men's Institute (fee, $50). An editorial in the* Journal and Courier *of this date announces the engagement:*
His subject, "Roman Statuary," is purely artistic, and of course can arouse no jealous solicitude in regard to any possible connection between it and questions of current politics, or the vexed questions of theological dispute.
  We know little of Mr. M. personally — farther than that he is a native of Pittsfield, Mass., where he now resides — a farmer of staid and sober demeanor, and a gentleman of scholarly tastes, and connected by birth and marriage with some of the first families of the country. Without the best advantages of culture in his early youth, he has advanced over difficulties of considerable magnitude, to a position of peculiar elevation as an American literary man.

*

1 8 5 8

*

EN ROUTE Early January *M lists some miscellaneous expenses:*

Tea on R.R.	18
Books	6.62
Rubbers	.80

AUBURN January 5 *M reads his new lecture, on "The South Seas" (fee, $40).*

ITHACA January 7 *M reads his lecture, on "Statuary in Rome," at the Town Hall (fee, $50):*
His subject, "Ancient Sanctuary," must, from the necessity of the case, be an unattractive one to the masses . . . (*Journal and Advertiser*, Jan 13)

SANDUSKY January 9 *Richard Tobias Greene writes to M:*
Dear Old Shipmate:
  Hearing that you were to be in Cleveland and wife being there on a

visit, I wished her to see you. Were it at all possible I would go down myself for I would like much to see you. Cant you take this place in your route?

CLEVELAND January 11 *M reads his lecture, on "Statuary in Rome"* (*fee, $50*):
  The fact that we Western people, have not got sufficiently beyond the influence of the prevailing *practicality* of pioneer society, and are therefore, to a great extent destitute of that cultivation of nature and taste necessary to a fine and general appreciation of Art will undoubtedly account for the fact that the hall was not crowded to its utmost capacity, as it should have been by the announcement of the subject "Roman Statuary" in connection with the name of Melville. (Cleveland *Morning Leader*, Jan 12)

  Mr. Melville has a musical voice, and a very correct delivery, but a subdued tone and general want of animation prevents his being a popular lecturer. The same essay, read by him in a parlour as from the pages of a book, would give far greater satisfaction than it conveyed last evening when delivered under the guise of a popular lecture. We repeat our axiom — good writers do not make good lecturers. (Cleveland *Daily Herald*, Jan 12)

I once had the pleasure of listening to Mr. Melville lecture on his travels in Cleveland while I was living in Sandusky and Mr Greene himself delivered some lectures on travel, in parts of Ohio and Westfield N.Y. my old home. — *Mary J. Greene to Elizabeth Melville, Nov 14, 1892*

DETROIT January 12 *M reads his lecture, on "Statuary in Rome," for the Detroit Young Men's Society (admission twenty-five cents); M is paid fifty dollars for his lecture.*

PITTSFIELD January 21 *M's subscription to* Harper's Magazine *is renewed for one year.*

EN ROUTE Before January 22 *Items (& comments) extracted from M's expense account:*

Tobacco [at Lafayette]	· 5
[Buss at] Greencastle (Mud to the hub)	.25
Supper [at Vincennes] (ale)	· 5
Evansville to Southland [?] (River)	3.
Bill at " (damned rascal)	1.50
Hat [at Nashville]	5.
More cut [tobacco]	.25
Bill at [Clarksville] (landlord fat & honest)	2.50
Washing Do (40 cts overcharge)	1.
Porter (Not Brown Stout, but stout black)	25
[Total expenses paid through Clarksville]	$89.19

In one of the books bought in January M writes a poem about the passing landscape of the Mississippi[?] shores.

CLARKSVILLE January 22   *M reads his lecture, on "Statuary in Rome,"
for the Clarksville Literary Association (fee, $75):*
The expression of doubt, and dark groping of human speculation, in the ideal
statuary of that age, when the old mythology was passing away, and men's
minds had not yet reposed in the new faith, was finely portrayed. A most
striking and beautiful thought was introduced, when speaking of the equestrian
statues of Rome, and the expression of untamed docility, rather than con-
quered obedience which their artists have given to the horse, the lecturer de-
duced the enlarged humanity of that elder day, when man gave himself none
of those upstart airs of superiority over the brute creation which he now as-
sumes. (*Clarksville Daily Enquirer*, Feb 3)

EN ROUTE TO CINCINNATI Before February 2   *Items extracted from
M's expense account:*

Clarksville to Paducah	$5.
Cigar (Dinner Sunday night)	5
Bath (Buffalo)	.37
From Paducah to Louisville (U[nited] S[tates])	8.
Boot black (boat)	10
Car from Portland to Louisville	10
Solace — (Anderson's) [for his cold?]	10
From Louisville to Cincinnati	2.50
Cigar & candy	.20
Theatre at Cincinnati	.50

M attends the National Theatre to see Mazeppa; or, The Wild Horses of
Tartary *and* Karmel, the scout; or, The Rebel of the Jerseys.

CINCINNATI February 2   *M's lecture is announced in the Cincinnati
Daily Commercial:*
Herman Melville, "who," said an enthusiastic Athenian admirer of his beautiful writings — "entranced the American public by freshness and mellow style
of his South Sea adventures . . . who *dazed* us still more with the white gleam
of *Moby Dick*, through whose five hundred weird pages 'all thoughts, all
passions, feelings and delights,' chase each other 'like shadows o'er the plain' —
and in whom we have the wildest and strangest mysticisms, mingled with the
frankest and freest common sense and practical knowledge of the world and
its ways, and the truest, most genuine American Democratic feeling" — will
appear to-night before a Cincinnati audience to discourse in the lectorium
(Smith & Nixon's Hall,) of the Young Men's Mercantile Library Association
upon the Statuary of Rome.

M reads his lecture, on "Statuary in Rome" (fee, $50):
Smith & Nixon's Hall was about two-thirds filled with a highly intelligent and
cultivated auditory, when the lecturer, an unremarkable, quiet, self-possessed-
looking man, seemingly about thirty-five or six years of age, with brown hair,
whiskers and mustache, bronze complexion, about the medium stature, appear-
ing not unlike the captain of an American merchantman, presented himself
before them . . .

His delivery was, in some respects, agreeable, but not in others — it was monotonous and often indistinct, but not devoid of impressiveness, which sometimes approached the ministerially solemn. (*Cincinnati Enquirer*, Feb 3)

Mr. Melville is rather an attractive person, though not what anybody would describe good looking. He is a well built, muscular gentleman, with a frame capable of great physical exertion and endurance. His manner is gentle and persuasive, while a certain indefinable sharpness of features, with small twinkling blue eyes under arched brows, and a rather contracted and rugged forehead, indicates the spirit of adventure which sent him roving a sailor's sturdy life. His face, three parts obscured by a heavy brown beard and moustache, still glistens duskily with the Polynesian polish it received under the tawny influences of a Southern sun, and his voice is as soft and almost as sweet, barring a slight huskiness proceeding from a cold, as the warbling of the winds in cocoa groves. His style of delivery is earnest, though not sufficiently animated for a Western audience, and he enunciates with only tolerable distinctness. (Cincinnati *Daily Commercial*, Feb 3)

Mr. Melville, in appearance, is about such a man as one might see from reading his works . . . He makes no attempts at eloquence, but appears upon the rostrum as though reading from one of his descriptive works of what he saw . . .
The lecturer closed by a very beautiful description of the villas and private gardens of Rome, in which every breath of air that stirs is perfumed, and which reminded us that in a garden originated the dread sentence, DEATH — that it was amid such perfumed grottoes, bowers and walks, the guests of a Lucretia Borgia were welcomed to a feast, but received with a pall.
The lecture throughout was rather interesting than otherwise, although the interest excited in the opening passages was not maintained to the close. The manner of Mr. Melville is too quiet, common-place and unobtrusive for a popular audience, but he talks as he writes — without the pretension of those who make lecturing a business. (*Cincinnati Daily Gazette*, Feb 3)

CHILLICOTHE February 3 *M gives the fourth lecture of the first annual course under the auspices of the Gymnasium & Library Association, at the Second Presbyterian Church, "Statuary in Rome" (fee, $40):* Altogether, to those familiar through writers of the day with Rome and its attractions, the lecture was a string of indifferent Pearls, genuine indeed, but sadly wanting in that polish which gives even to trite common places a passing interest . . . If the lecture was faulty, the delivery can hardly be said to have been less so. Perhaps we do injustice to Mr. M by expressing any opinion in regard to his delivery, since any one who has tried to speak in public, must know how a slight cold will entirely untune the voice, and so diminish his control over it as to render the speaker timid and reserved in his utterance, and it was quite apparent that Mr. M was afflicted with quite a severe cold, was aware that he could not command his voice and therefore afraid to trust it. (Chillicothe *Advertiser*, Feb 5)

Although laboring under a severe cold, his voice was still rich and mellow, and he had the most complete control of it. He speaks with earnestness and ennunciates distinctly; even when he descended, as he sometimes did, almost to a whisper, his words were audible in the remotest parts of the room. (*The Scioto Gazette,* Feb 5)

EN ROUTE TO CHARLESTOWN, MASS. Before February 7 *Items extracted from M's expense account:*

Breakfast (R.R.)		2
Police Gazette		5
Dinner — Pittsburgh		75
Cigar —	do	5
Ale	do	10
Supper	do	35
Breakfast — (Washington)		10
Dinner	Philad.	18
Supper	(boat)	50
omnibus	N.Y.	6
Cars	3ᵈ Av. Sunday	10

NEW YORK February 7? *M draws up his account thus far:*

Recᵈ from Lectures	— $355
Travelling Expen &c	155.85 [later revised]
On hand — New York	214.50
	$ 370.35

CHARLESTOWN February 10 *M reads his lecture, "Statuary in Rome," in the course of Mishawum Lectures, at the City Hall (fee, $20):*
. . . a well written but particularly dull lecture by Herman Melville, Esq. If it had been announced before hand that some distinguished 'Professor' of phrenology would lecture on his favorite science in the City Hall, we may safely say hardly a baker's dozen would have ventured out to hear him on such an evening as last Tuesday. What then must have been the 'sell' inflicted upon the holders of tickets to these lectures to be compelled to listen to a monotonous description of such 'dead heads' as Demosthenes, Julius Caesar, Seneca, Plato, Tiberius and Apollo, and that too by one neither a 'Professor' nor 'Artiste' by his own confession? Still Mr. Melville's fault was rather in the selection of his subject than in his treatment of it. No man could reasonably hope to interest a common audience upon such a subject . . . They have, moreover as we have some reason to believe an instinctive dread to hear a man either lecture or talk, who would begin by telling them that "when he was in Italy he saw" &c. Such an opening is always the precussor of a painful *bore* . . . His draughts upon the classical Dictionary were frequent and heavy, too heavy for the comfort and edification of his auditors. Some nervous people, therefore, left the hall; some read books and newspapers; some sought refuge in sleep, and some, to their praise be it spoken, seemed determined to use it as an appropriate occasion for self-discipline in the blessed virtue of patience. ("Reporter," *Bunker Hill Aurora,* Feb 13)

ROCHESTER February 18

The Athenaeum Course of lectures is drawing to a close. Herman Melville gives the one to-night . . . [fee, $50.] (*Union and Advertiser*)

The author of those very entertaining narratives of adventures in some of the far-off islands of the sea, and various fictions smacking of salt-water and mystic philosophy, was very well received by the lecture-goers of this city . . . To a miscellaneous audience like that assembled to hear it, however, the lecture was not particularly in[t]eresting . . . The audience generally, were disappointed; and we think that the lecturer erred in his choice of a theme in this instance. MR. MELVILLE is capable of doing better . . . (*Democrat and American*, Feb 20)

ALBANY February 19 *M visits Peter Gansevoort.* (Herman passed last evening with me, on his return from Rochester & intended to take the Cars for Boston early this morning — His next engagement is at New Bedford — He is stalworth, in excellent health & very fine spirits — *Peter Gansevoort to Maria Melville, Feb 20*)

BOSTON February 20 *Charged to Shaw's membership, at the Boston Athenaeum:* The Life of Beethoven . . . *by Anton Felix Schindler (London, 1841)*

NEW BEDFORD February 23 *M reads his lecture, on "Statuary in Rome," for the course of Lyceum Lectures (fee, $50):*
Here [at the Villa Albani], were the remains of antiquity from Pompeii, and we might bring back the guests to the rooms where they sat at the feast on the eve of the fatal eruption of Vesuvius. They spoke of topics which were forbidden to modern ears at such scenes, and dared to allude to their mortality, even while at the banquet. Yet the gardens around the villas were the abodes of malaria, and the laurel and the myrtle in their beauty concealed the seeds of death. (*New Bedford Morning Mercury*, Feb 24)

GANSEVOORT March *Elizabeth Melville's memoir of M:*
A severe attack of what he called crick in the back laid him up at his Mothers in Gansevoort in March 1858 — and he never regained his former vigor & strength.

BROOKLYN April 9 *Commander Guert Gansevoort writes to his uncle, Peter, asking for his help in making the transfer to the Naval Rendezvous.*

LONDON June *Longman, Brown & Co. sends M a statement informing him that 34 more copies of their edition of* The Confidence-Man *have been sold, reducing the amount short of expenses to £24.8.0.*

PITTSFIELD July 4 The afternoon Geo & I passed with Herman Melville 'bathing' as he called it in these divine breezes. The Morewoods

drove over to his house, remained to tea and walked home at dusk . . .
— *Evert Duyckinck to his wife, Margaret, July 5*

July 7   *George Duyckinck writes to Mrs Rosalie Baker:*
We have some good friends resident here. One, Herman Melville you
know well by his books. I wish you knew, perhaps you do, the man,
with his offhand hearty sailor grace. He has a pleasant farm house looking
directly at the "Monarch of Mountains" — of Berkshire — Saddleback or
Greylock.

July 14   After an early tea Mrs Morewood took us all in her wagon
across the fields to Arrowhead. Herman & wife were out but we met them
on our way home, and interchanged a few words. — *George Duyckinck
to his brother, Evert, July 15*

July 21   *The Valuation Book for Pittsfield's taxpayers is completed; in
M's estimate:*
                    [Money] $1,000

Before July 26   I passed a very pleasant afternoon recently with your
friend Typee Melville. He is busy on a new book. — *George Duyckinck
to Mrs Baker, July 26*

August 14   *Samuel Shaw arrives from Boston. (his diary)*

August 24   *George Duyckinck writes to his brother, Evert:*
. . . This morning the thermometer stood at 50° I warmed myself by a
walk to Herman Melville's over the railroad and enjoyed it greatly, but
missed my chief object as both Melville and [Samuel] Shaw were off on
a tramp in the woods.

August 25   *Samuel Shaw returns to Boston. (his diary)*

September 12   I was about answering your invitation to join you on the
Greenport expedition when Herman Melville came along with a pro-
posal for a two days trip in the mountains. It was too tempting an offer
to be declined and I was a few minutes after seated along side of him in
a buggy and "off" — . . .
Melville was very genial during our ride and we both enjoyed it
greatly. The chief features of the trip were the Greenfield river valley,
in the adjoining county of Franklin (almost a rival to Berkshire in verdure and picturesqueness) and the Hoosic tunnel. We walked through
the mud to the end of the excavation, a little over a thousand feet. It
was like a scene in the Mammoth Cave, with German [?] for actors.
The tallow dips stuck beside the workmen gave a dull yellow light and
the ring of the heavy sledge hammers on the drills was nerve-jarring and
unearth[l]y. As we stood at the entrance we heard the blasts within,
like the distant report of cannon.

We crossed the mountain passing the night at a little inn near the summit, for the sake of the picturesque and to avoid those knaves, the North Adams publicans. The views on either side were magnificent.

We got within Mr Aspinwall's iron gates yesterday morning [September 13] and enjoyed an exquisite drive of miles in his grounds. We ascended his tower and paced his piazza. It was almost like an extra dividend of Pacific Mail. A capital idea would it not be, for him to throw open his doors and entertain the stockholders. — *George Duyckinck to his brother, Evert, Sept 14*

September 12-14   I had a delightful three days ride last week with your sailor friend Herman Melville. He was in good spirits; we passed through delightful scenery with constantly beautiful skies; and, as you may imagine, with good talk. He is as robust and fine looking as Evert, but somewhat impaired in health by an affection of the spine brought on by too many hours of brain work day after day, following a life of great bodily activity. — *George Duyckinck to Mrs Baker, Sept 17*

September 19   *Lemuel Shaw writes to his son, Lemuel:*
The family here are on the whole very well. Herman is as well as I have seen him for years, & Elizabeth was quite well, & [?] all her household cares with great care and satisfaction. The four children are, or it appears to me, greatly improved, in appearance and conduct.

NEW YORK   October 3   *Sophia Melville dies, aged 30 years.*

October 4   *George Duyckinck writes to Mrs Baker:*
I am sorry to see in today's paper the death of Mrs Allan Melville. She was a very gentle, sweet woman. He is as fine, though not as talented a man, as his brother Herman. Her disease . . . was consumptive. She was kept alive for months by an egg and a small glass of whiskey, her only nourishment, a day. — speaking but a few words and those in a whisper.

PITTSFIELD   October 20   *Priscilla Melvill dies.* .

NEW YORK   November [1]   *In the serial account of her trip to Niagara,* "The Seven Travelers," *published in* Emerson's Magazine and Putnam's Monthly, *Elizabeth Oakes Smith quotes Mrs Sarah Helen Whitman:*
"I am inclined to think that where the conditions for spiritual intercourse are favorable, as at present they seldom are, the character of the communications is proportionate to the character of the recipients. 'From without,' says Herman Melville [in *Pierre*] 'no wonderful effect is wrought within ourselves, unless some interior, corresponding [responding] wonder welcome [meets] it.'"

Early November?   *George Duyckinck sends M a five-volume set of George Chapman's translations of Homer (London, 1857).*

PITTSFIELD November 6 *M thanks George Duyckinck for his gift:*
Indisposition has prevented me from writing you ere now. Your gift is very acceptable — could not have been more so. I am glad to have a copy of Chapman's Homer. As for Pope's version (of which I have a copy) I expect it, — when I shall put Chapman beside it — to go off shrieking, like the bankrupt deities in Milton's hymn. —— Thus far I have been mostly engaged in cutting the leaves by way of pastime — as I must do to read at present.

BOSTON November 8 *Lemuel Shaw writes to M:*
Believing that in providing your family supplies for the approaching winter, some pecuniary assistance may be wanted by you. I enclose you above my check, on the New England Bank above for $100 . . .

We shall really miss your visit with that of Elizabeth & your children as Thanksgiving approaches. Our family circle will show a large vacancy. We expect a visit from you however, whether Elizabeth will accompany you or not, as I presume you have an engagement to deliver a lecture here . . .

PITTSFIELD November 11 *A paragraph in* The Pittsfield Sun:
"THE LECTURE SEASON." — Under this caption, our exchanges in various parts of the country are mentioning the names of gentlemen who are ready to lecture upon interesting subjects when applied to, and we presume upon reasonable terms. The Rev. Dr. TODD of this town . . . is one of the best and most attractive of the lecturers. HERMAN MELVILL, Esq., of this town, the author, is also ready, as is reported, to receive applications to lecture.

November 19 *A paragraph in the* Berkshire County Eagle:
LECTURES. — By invitation of a large number of his fellow citizens of Pittsfield, Herman Melville will give his new lecture upon the South Seas, in this town, December 14th . . . an effort is making, under the charge of the originator of the movement, Mr. Edwin F. Sandys, to sell a sufficient number of tickets to secure [several of the best lecturers in the country] . . . otherwise, other arrangements will be made by the gentlemen who invited him.

CHICAGO December 1 *James G. Wilson invites M to lecture in Chicago for the Young Men's Association.*

YONKERS December 6 *M begins his second lecture season, reading his "South Seas" lecture before the Yonkers Library Association, at the Getty House (fee, $30):*
Before last Monday evening . . . we doubt whether [M] was recognized as a humorist. His success in this field, if it be newly tried, is such as should encourage him, for his audience was not only large, but very sympathetic . . . The facetious tone of Mr. Melville is beyond description . . .

Mr. Melville's delivery is any thing but pleasant. To use a common simile, the close of his sentences have a descending and rising cadence, which can be likened to nothing on earth but the graceful twist in a porcine after part

. . . his voice is susceptible of a modulation, which cannot be acquired without much care. (*Yonkers Examiner*, Dec 9)

NEW YORK   After December 6   I called to see Mr Davidson the day I saw you in Clinton Place, but he was out. After waiting for him awhile, I went away. If by chance you should meet him, wont' you mention that I called?

I should like to procure an engagement through Mr Davidson, especially if it could be moved to fall about the time of my lecture before the Historical Society. — *M to George Duyckinck, Dec 13*

December 8   *M replies to James Wilson's inquiry of December 1:*
I am willing to come for the amount which the other lecturers you name receive — $50; hoping that, as you suggest, you will be able to make additional appointments for me in your quarter; for which I shall be much obliged to you.

PITTSFIELD   December 10   [John C. Hoadley's 40th birthday]   *An item in the* Berkshire County Eagle:
The opening lecture in Mr. Sandys' course was delivered on Monday evening last, by Rev. T. Starr King, of Boston . . .
Next *Tuesday* Herman Melville will give his lecture upon "the South Seas" and we need say nothing to induce Pittsfield people to hear such a man upon such a subject. Mr. Melville is a familiar speaker, abounding in quaint and original thoughts, which adorn and enliven a story told with extraordinary powers of narrative and description.

NEW YORK   Before December 13   *George Duyckinck writes to M.* (Upon getting home, I was greeted by your note. — *M to George Duyckinck, Dec 13*)

PITTSFIELD   December 13   *M writes to George Duyckinck:*
Would it make too much trouble if for the two days in February I named to you (to choose from) for my lecture before your Society, I should substitute the 10th & 17th of January?, either of which, would, as I now see, be more convenient to me. —

December 14   *M reads his lecture on "The South Seas"* (fee, $50):
Burbank's hall was filled on Tuesday evening to listen to the lecture of Herman Melville . . . although the night was the most stormy and uncomfortable of the winter. The lecture was a pleasant and instructive outline of the geography, natural history, "civilization," and other general characteristics of the "South Seas," enlivened with incidents of personal adventure. It is written in the style of Mr. Melville's best books, quaint, simple and polished; redolent of the spicy odors of the South Seas, and sparkling with original thoughts. (*Berkshire County Eagle*, Dec 17)

LAWRENCE   December 17   *To John & Catherine Hoadley is born a daughter [Charlotte].*

BOSTON Before December 25   *John Oakes Shaw sends his two Melville nephews, for Christmas, the Aimwell Stories. (Malcolm Melville to his cousin Maria, Feb 13, 1859)*

NEW YORK December 29   *George Duyckinck writes to Mrs Rosalie Baker:*
How do you like the article on 'Sailors' in the January *Atlantic*. I took it to be Melville's; but is by a Mr Mitchell an Episcopal Clergyman of Connecticut *raised* in Nantucket, but who has never been at sea.

.   .   .   .   .

PHILADELPHIA   *Publication of Samuel A. Allibone's Critical Dictionary with a biographical sketch of M.*

*

1 8 5 9
*

BOSTON January   *Thomas Melville arrives as master of the clipper ship Meteor.*

NEW YORK January 28?   *George Duyckinck writes to M, asking for the title of his lecture.*

PITTSFIELD January 30   *Elizabeth Melville writes to George Duyckinck:*
Mr Melville is absent in Boston, and in reply to your letter (which I open in accordance with his instructions) I am happy to give you the desired information. The title of his lecture is "The South Seas," and may be so advertised.
It was Herman's intention to pass a few days in New York before the lecture appointment, but the arrival of his brother, Capt. Melville, in Boston, from a long voyage has decided him to pass the intervening time in his company at their mother's in Gansevoort, where they will probably go immediately after the Boston lecture of tomorrow evening . . .

BOSTON January 31   *A notice in* The Boston Herald:
Mechanic Apprentices' Lectures
The Ninth Lecture of this Course will be delivered in Tremont Temple on Monday Evening, Jan. 31st by Herman Melville, Esq. [fee, $50] Subject — "South Sea Adventures." Single tickets, 25 cents each . . .

It is only since 1848 — since the discovery of gold in California — that the civilized world has been brought to a sensible knowledge of this vast expanse of waters. Even now its geography is but illy known. The ships which plough it for the most part go in established routes, and those vessels who leave these old roads continually run upon some island or cluster of islands unknown to the charts or geographers. (*Boston Daily Courier*, Feb 1)

In conclusion, the lecturer spoke of the projects recently set on foot for annexing the Sandwich Islands to the United States. As a philanthropist in general, and a friend to the Polynesians in particular, he hoped, that these Edens of the South Seas, blessed with fertile soils and peopled with happy natives, would long be preserved from the contaminating influence of foreign powers. (*Boston Daily Advertiser*, Feb 1)

The hall was not more than half full. (*Boston Daily Traveller*, Feb 1)

NEW YORK January 31 *George Duyckinck writes to Mrs Rosalie Baker:*
You should be here next Monday evening to hear Herman Melville. Cannot you get him an invitation to lecture at Sag Harbor? He would come for fifty dollars and his travelling expenses.

GANSEVOORT February 1? *M & his brother, Thomas, arrive at their mother's home.*

BOSTON February 1 *Norman W. Stearns writes to M:*
Last evening I was present at your lecture . . . and as I have recently returned from Polynesia where I lived in various localities for nearly six years, I feel assured I am in possession of valuable information . . .
. . . I am satisfied if you intend to enlarge on your favorite theme I can furnish you with abundant material for an interesting yarn.

LYNN February 2 *W. H. Barry writes to M.* (Absence from home has prevented an earlier reply to your notes of the 2nd and 8th inst. I should be very happy to lecture at Lynn, if we can agree upon the time, &c. — *M to W. H. Barry, Feb 12*)

CORFU, N. Y. February 4 *Oliver Russ writes to M:*
. . . first of all I will let you know who I am you probably have not forgotten all of the crew of the Old Frigate United States and more especialy our visit to the city of Lima. my name is Oliver Russ, although I went by another name when at sea to conceal from my friends the unwise step I had taken and that name was Edward Norton I assumed my right name on coming home. Now what I wish to say is that I in the course of the next year after our return from sea I took to wife one of the fair daughters of the state of Maine and in two years from that day a son was born to us a substancial token of our mutual love and to manifest the high regard in which I have ever held yourself I named him Herman Melville Russ at that time I did not expect ever to hear of you again or that you would be numbered among the literary writers of the day. I say this to let you know that it was not

the almost universal desire to name after great men that led me to do it, but a regard for those qualities which an acquaintance of eighteen month with you led me so much to admire.

NEW YORK February 7 *Henry Gansevoort writes to his father:*
Cousin Herman Melville is in town. He lectures before the Historical Society tonight. I understand that Thomas Melville will visit New York in his clipper ship "The Meteor" during the present week.

An announcement in the New-York Daily Tribune:
New-York Historical Society Lecture. — HERMAN MELVILLE, Esq., author of "Typee," "Omoo," &c., will deliver the Fourth Lecture of the series in the Hall of the Library, 2d-av., corner of 11th-st., on MONDAY EVENING, Feb. 7, at 7½ o'clock. Subject: South Sea Islands [fee, $55]. Tickets, 50 cents . . . The number of tickets to be sold is limited to 500.

. . . I assure you it was a treat long to be remembered. The rooms were about half filled owing to the want of proper advertising but those who were present evinced their gratification by applause and attention. He treated the subject in so unpretentious a manner, so originally and so carelessly if I may say so that I assure you it was really refreshing. Its very semplicity was its success. He spoke ably for one hour of the phenomena of those unfrequented regions . . . He presented the habits of the islanders, their religion their tatto-ing — their dispositions and their institutions in such glowing and gentle colors that every mind seemed to quit its local habitation the while for a short journey through the countries he described. — *Henry Gansevoort to his sister Catherine, Jan [Feb] 8*

He adopts "The South Seas" as a title for his lecture in preference to "The Pacific;" he finds it more relishing of the old, antique exploring and buccaneering adventures of the fresh, imaginative days of voyaging in those waters; and he, probably from old experience, has a lurking distrust of the pacific qualities of the great ocean. It got its name up at a favorable moment, and in spite of pouting, storms, tempests and hurricanes, has lain abed upon it ever since.

A map gave no idea of the extent of the islands. Polynesia, hinted in its very name, at the immensity of their number. After a brief description of the appearance of these islands, of their excellent natural facilities, the lecturer glanced at the character and habits of the inhabitants, their progress in civilization, &c. In 1824 several buccaneers first cherished the idea of creating a home in the South Sea Islands and emigration thither had since rapidly increased. Parties of Fourierites had looked to Typee as their future paradise, but the natives would never tolerate any new fangled notions of the social state; they would reject all "fillibusters," and resist their encroachments as did the Staten Islanders that of Quarantine.

There were two places in the world, said Mr. Melville, where a man might lie concealed — in London and the South Seas. Various and extraordinary were the waifs and strays of humanity which turned up in traversing these waters. He remembered once, after five months weary navigation out of sight of land, turning to a secluded island in search of fruit. The pensive natives lay upon the bank, gazing listlessly, hardly turning on their mats at their landing, for they had seen white men before. There, in that remote island, among its sixty or seventy lazy inhabitants, he found an American, not imposing in his breech cloth and the scanty shreds of tappa which hung from his shoulders as signals of distress, which, it appeared to the traveller, the assiduous diligence of three wives — for the ill-clothed gentleman was blessed with that number — might have remedied. On conversation it came to light that this virtuous exile from civilization had been Professor of Moral Philosophy in a college in his own land; though, for the credit of the country, he did not mention the name of the institution.

The results of civilization, at the Sandwich Islands and elsewhere, Mr. Melville found productive to the civilizers, destructive to the civilizees. It was said to be compensation — a very philosophical word; but to the lecturer it appeared very much on the principle of the old game, "You lose, I win;" good philosophy for the winner. With a humorous and well wrought out exhibition of the various fashions and stripes of tattooing in the different islands, Mr. Melville concluded a very interesting lecture, none the less so for its modest and unpretending composition and delivery.

The Hall [at the Library in Second Avenue] was nearly filled by an audience highly respectable, and comprising some of our most eminent *literati* . . . The lecture was . . . delivered with ease and grace. (unidentified New York newspaper, Feb 8)

BALTIMORE February 8 *M delivers his "South Seas" lecture in the Universalist Church, for the Mercantile Library series (fee, $100):*
Mr. M. began by saying:
The subject of our lecture this evening, "The South Seas," may be thought perhaps a theme if not ambitious at least somewhat expansive, covering according to the authorities, I am afraid to say how much of the earth's surface — in short, more than one-half. We have, therefore, a rather spacious field before us, and I hardly think we shall be able, in a thorough way, to go over the whole of it to-night.

And here (to do away with any erroneous anticipations as to our topic) I hope you do not expect me to repeat what has long been in print touching my own casual adventures in Polynesia. I propose to treat of matters of more general interest, and, in a random way, discuss the South Seas at large and under various aspects, introducing, as occasion may serve, any little incident, personal or other, fitted to illustrate the point in hand. (*Baltimore American*, Feb 9)

NEW YORK February 8 *Henry Gansevoort reports last night's lecture to his sister, Catherine:*
It was in Cousin Hermans true vein. He was emphatically himself, and the lecture was to me like a quantity tied together — of his vivid and colloquial sketches (always too short) told under the inspiration of Madeira after dinner or drawn forth by some proper association elsewhere. He should be invited to deliver it at Albany.

PITTSFIELD February 12   *M drives into town to pay his Town, County & State Tax: a Total of $20.57 (with 21 cents discount).*

M replies to W. H. Barry's inquiries:
I have two lectures: "The South Seas"
"Statues in Rome"
If, as you intimate, you should like me to deliver both, well and good.
My terms, of course, I find it necessary to adapt to the means of various Societies. I should think that, in the present case, thirty dollars for each lecture would not be too much.

February 13   *Malcolm Melville writes to his cousin, Maria Melville:*
I got your letter a good while ago, and I thought I would write to you. I go to school and I study arithmetic, with cyphering, geography, spelling and reading, and every Friday we have to speak a piece.
We have a firstrate coasting place, and my clipper sled beats all the other boys.
We made a snowhouse at noon big enough for 15 boys to go into. Bessie and Fanny go out every day to play with their sleds, and Saturday we all have a nice time together. I wish you and the little girls were here too.
I have been reading the Rollo Books all through, and Stanny has read some of them, and we liked them very much, and now I am reading the Aimwell Stories, they are firstrate, have you read them? Uncle Oakes sent them to us Christmas. I have the Childs Paper every month, aunt Augusta sends it to me.
We have a Skating place at school, and another one at home, and I can skate pretty well.
Can you skate yet?

ALBANY February 18   *Peter Gansevoort's diary:*
Damp & unpleasant
My nephew Herman Melville passed the evening with us, being on lecturing Tour West as far as Chicago.

CHICAGO February 24   *M delivers his "South Seas" lecture in Metropolitan Hall, for the Young Men's Association (fee, $50):*
He said he would direct the gas to be turned down, and repeat to his audience in a whisper the mysterious rites of the "Taboo," but the relation would so far transcend any of Mrs. Ratcliffe's stories in the element of the horrible, that he would not willingly afflict any one with its needless recital. (*Daily Press and Tribune*, Feb 25)

MILWAUKEE February 25   *M delivers his "South Seas" lecture at Albany Hall.*
Albany Hall was filled at an early hour with an unusually large audience.

Precisely at half past seven, the President of the Young Men's Association introduced the Lecturer, Herman Melville . . .

As a lecturer, Mr. Melville sustains the idea we have formed of him in "Typee" a soft, voluptuous ease is the predominant characteristic. Romance is breathed into the sterile topography of his subject, and the same drowsy enchantment that makes his writings so fascinating radiates from the speaker . . . (*The Daily Sentinel* [?], Feb 26)

The modes in which seamen disappear in the Pacific are various.

Some fall overboard, some are left by unprincipled captains, some are killed in brawls, &c. He alluded to the class known as Beech-combers, who infest the shores of the Pacific, who are ready for anything, for a war in Peru, a whaling voyage, or to marry a Polynesian princess. They were among the first in California in the gold times, and afforded subjects for strange newspaper stories. They were also the occasion, as much as anything, of the Vigilance Committee in California. Spoke of many strange characters he had met, whose experiences if written out, would form volumes of weird, wild and fanciful interest. Spoke of a manuscript tradition he had seen that was told by a King of one of those Islands. It had much of the grace, strangeness and audacity of the Grecian Fables. (report by Mr & Mrs William Cramer [possibly assisted by M's manuscript lecture], *The Daily Wisconsin*, Feb 26)

Minutes of the Young Men's Association of the City of Milwaukee:
[Feb] 25 Rec^d at door — H.Mellville — "South Seas" 50.45
        [in addition to subscribers]
[Paid] Herman Melville 50
      expenses   29.50   79.50

ALBANY February 26 *Peter Gansevoort's diary:*
My sister Mrs Melville & her son Thomas, Captain of the Ship Meteor in the East Indias Trade & recently from Manilla after 5 years absence, arrived at my House at 2 P.M. on a visit to us —

ROCKFORD February 28 *M delivers his "South Seas" lecture in Warner's Hall, for the Young Men's Association (fee, $50):*
It has rarely been our lot to witness a more painful infliction upon an audience . . . We had expected to hear a personal narrative of sight scenes . . . the relation of real personal adventures — always pleasing — which so emphatically marks the fact of the narrator's having actually been in the places described, and seen and known for himself. Instead of these there was a simple presentation of historical facts, few in number, very common placed, and to be found in books on the shelves of almost any library; the facts slightly exaggerated . . .

Mr. Melville is a youngish man, of good physique, apparently enduring constitution, slightly billious temperament, and a very good external make up in general. He lacks depth, earnestness, consecutiveness, and finish, without which qualities no man need hope of being a permanently successful lecturer. Lecturing is evidently not his forte, his style as well as the subject matter being intensely "Polynesian" and calculated to "Taboo" him from the lecture field in the future. (*Republican*, Mar 3)

. . . we expected to hear an interesting personal experience of one who had travelled in one of the most delightful portions of the world . . . But we were disappointed in this, and instead we received a record in *manuscript* of a few general historical facts . . . And no man has a right to set himself up as a lecturer at $50 per night, who cannot for one minute take his eyes from his manuscript. (*Register,* Mar 5)

LONDON February? *Publication of* Two Journeys to Japan, 1856-7, *by Kinahan Cornwallis; pp 209-300 (Vol. II) entitled "The After Journey, A Single Glimpse," is a bald & unacknowledged condensation of* Typee.
Herman Melville, the American author, has been robbed of his literary property by the author of a book lately published in London, entitled "Two Journeys to Japan, &c." (unidentified clipping)

QUINCY March 2 [Frances's fourth birthday] *M delivers his "South Seas" lecture in the City Hall, for the Lyceum series; he is paid $23.50.*

Diary of Orville H. Browning:
. . . Mrs. Cox came in to tea, and she and I went to City Hall, and heard Herman Melville Esqr lecture on the South Sea Islands — Erratic but interesting

LYNN March 16
The first lecture by the celebrated adventurer, Herman Melville, Esq., will be delivered in Sagamore Hall . . . Subject — The South Seas and the Cannibal Islands. (*Lynn Weekly Reporter,* Mar 12)

Herman Melville's first lecture was tolerably well attended, but didn't touch the innermost, as did those of Emerson [who "gave us a most felicitous discourse on 'Success' . . ."] and Lowell. It was more "of the earth, earthy," or rather of the water, aqueous. It was good, though, of its kind, and went off very well. ("Noggs," *Lynn Weekly Reporter,* Mar 19)

[?] M gives a second lecture, "Statues in Rome."

NEW YORK March 26 *The* Meteor *sails on her fourth voyage, Thomas Melville, Commander, for San Francisco, taking along:*
      1 set Works, 8 vols.   5.85
      (From *me* to Tom) (*Harpers statement, annotated by M*)

PITTSFIELD April 15 *John Brewster & George Willis grant M deeds of discharge on the Arrowhead property.*

April 20 *Journal of John Thomas Gulick:*
Our vacation commenced last week, the 19th of April. Coan and myself departed from Williamstown by the afternoon stage reaching Pittsfield about 6 o'clock.
Wednesday morning we called on Herman Melville, author of Typee, etc. We found him on a comfortable farm occupying a fine site about

two miles south of Pittsfield. From his north piazza he has a fine view of Greylock, while to the south lie the Berkshire hills with Washington peak in the centre. He has a form of good proportions, is about 5ft. 9″ in height, stands erect and moves with firm and manly grace. His conversation and manner, as well as the engravings on his walls, betray little of the sailor. His head is of moderate size with black hair, dark eyes, a smooth pleasant forehead and rough heavy beard and mustache. His countenance is slightly flushed with whiskey drinking, but not without expression. When in conversation his keen eyes glance from over his aquiline nose. Though it was apparent that he possessed a mind of an aspiring, ambitious order, full of elastic energy and illumined with the rich colors of a poetic fancy, he was evidently a disappointed man, soured by criticism and disgusted with the civilized world and with our Christendom in general and in particular. The ancient dignity of Homeric times afforded the only state of humanity, individual or social, to which he could turn with any complacency. What little there was of meaning in the religions of the present day had come down from Plato. All our philosophy and all our art and poetry was either derived or imitated from the ancient Greeks. Three of his children (the eldest about 10 or 12) were at home with him but his wife was absent with the youngest on a visit to Boston. After a noon lunch he took us in his wagon to the village where he was expecting to meet his lady on the arrival of the next train.

Titus Munson Coan tells his mother of the visit:

I have made my first literary pilgrimage — a call upon Herman Melville, the renowned author of "Typee," &c. He lives in a spacious farm-house about two miles from Pittsfield, a weary walk through the dust. But it was well repaid. I introduced myself as a Hawaiian-American and soon found myself in full tide of talk — or rather of monologue. But he would not repeat the experiences of which I had been reading with rapture in his books. In vain I sought to hear of Typee and those Paradise islands, but he preferred to pour forth his philosophy and his theories of life. The shade of Aristotle arose like a cold mist between myself and Fayaway. We have quite enough of Greek philosophy at Williams College, and I confess I was disappointed in this trend of the talk. But what a talk it was! Melville is transformed from a Marquesan to a gypsy student, the gypsy element still remaining strong in him. And this contradiction gives him the air of one who has suffered from opposition, both literary and social. With his liberal views he is apparently considered by the good people of Pittsfield as little better than a cannibal or a "beach-comber." His attitude seemed to me something like that of an Ishmael; but perhaps I judged hastily. I managed to draw him out very freely on everything but the Marquesan Islands, and when I left him he was in full tide of discourse on all things sacred and profane.

But he seems to put away the objective side of life and to shut himself up in this cold North as a cloistered thinker.

April 23 *M grants George Willis a deed of discharge on the Arrowhead property.*

LONDON April *Publication of Charles Reade's* Love Me Little Love Me Long, *including a whaling narrative (related by Frank Dodd to Mr Fountain & to his lovely niece) influenced by* Moby Dick.

PITTSFIELD May 18 *M submits "two Pieces" (poems?) to a magazine:*
  Here are two Pieces, which, if you find them suited to your Magazine I should be happy to see them appear there. — In case of publication, you may, if you please, send me what you think they are worth.

NEW YORK May 23 *Henry Gansevoort writes to his father:*
  P.S. Cousin Herman is in town looking well and hearty.

June 18 *M orders, through Harpers:*
  1 Poets [of the Nineteenth Century], full mor to A Melville 3.85

June 20 *M subscribes, on his Harpers account, for two years of* Harpers Weekly, *to be sent to Mrs Maria G. Melville. ($3.34)*

NEW ROCHELLE June 23 *Evert Duyckinck visits "Winyah," the country estate of Richard Lathers:*
  I noticed in his Library a copy of Hazlitt's Abridgement of Tucker's Light of Nature with a presentation inscription from Herman Melville [dated August 1853]. Mr. Lathers married Miss Thurston sister of Allan Melville's wife — through whom my acquaintance with Mr L comes.

PITTSFIELD July 6 *M addresses a poem "To Daniel Shepherd":*
  Come, Shepherd, come and visit me:
  Come, we'll make it Acady:
  Come, if but for charity.
  Sure, with such a pastoral name,
  Thee the city should not claim.
  Come, then, Shepherd, come away,
  Thy sheep in bordering pastures stray.

  Come, Daniel, come and visit me:
  I'm lost in many a quandary . . .
  But other visions stir my head;
  No poet-problems, fancy-fed —
  Domestic prose of board and bed.
  I marvel oft how guest *unwined*
  Will to this farm-house be resigned.
  Not a pint of ruby claret
    Cooleth in our cellar-bin;

And ripening in our sultry garret,
    Otard glows no flask within . . .
— Of bourbon that is rather new
I brag a fat black bottle or two. —
Shepherd, is this such Mountain-Dew
As one might fitly offer you?

NEW YORK July 30 *Evert Duyckinck writes to his brother, George:*
Allen Melville has been here with an entertaining account of his Virginia travels . . . Herman is doing nothing in particular.

PITTSFIELD Summer *Samuel Shaw presents to M a copy of Emerson's*
Poems (*seventh edition, Boston, 1858*), *in which M reads; on "The Humble-Bee" M notes, without further comment:*
    "Happy thing! thou seem'st to me
        Almost a little god to be!"
                    Anacreon — 'The Grasshopper.'

In "Merlin" M scores two passages:
            He shall not seek to weave,
            In weak, unhappy times,
            Efficacious rhymes;
            Wait his returning strength . . .

            Nor profane affect to hit
            Or compass that, by meddling wit,
            Which only the propitious mind
            Published when 'tis inclined.

August 16 *M subscribes, on his Harpers account, for two more years of* Harpers Magazine (*$4*), *& orders two books to be sent to his brother, Allan:*
    1 Land & Book [by William McClure Thomson], full mor. to A. Melville   4.50
    1 Clouded Happiness [by the Countess d'Orsay] to A. Melville   .30

THE ATLANTIC August
From first to last "Mocha Dick" had nineteen harpoons put into him. He stove fourteen boats and caused the death of over thirty men. He stove three whaling vessels so badly that they were nearly lost, and he attacked and sunk a French merchantman and an Australian trader. He was encountered in every ocean and on every known feeding ground. He was killed off the Brazilian banks in August, 1859, by a Swedish whaler, which gathered him in with scarcely any trouble, but it was always believed that poor old "Mocha Dick" was dying of old age. He measured 110 feet long; his girth was 57 feet; his jaw was 25 feet 6 inches long. Eight of his teeth were broken off and all others badly worn down. His big head was a mass of scars, and he had apparently lost the sight of his right eye. ("The Career of Mocha Dick")

[607]

PITTSFIELD Early fall *Lemuel Shaw visits Arrowhead, on which occasion M hands him the deeds to the estate, with a view to settling his financial obligations to his father-in-law. (Lemuel Shaw to M, May 15, 1860)*

NEW YORK September 6 *Evert Duyckinck writes to his brother, George, vacationing in Pittsfield:*
You will of course see Melville and as certainly give him my regards.

September 8 *Harper & Bros. sends its thirteenth account to M:*
      Balance due Harper & Brothers $287.53

PITTSFIELD September *M writes to G. W. Curtis.*

M acquires Hesperides: or the Works Both Humane and Divine of Robert Herrick, Esq. (*Boston, 1854-1856*); *among other poems checked in Vol I:*
      TWO THINGS ODIOUS.
      Two of a thousand things are disallow'd:
      A lying rich man, and a poore man proud.
M's comment: X Pride is in none becoming. But it is less unbecoming in the poor than in the rich. Good Herrick, however, was an Englishman.

In Vol II, M checks "His Letanie to the Holy Spirit":
      In the houre of my distresse,
      When temptations me oppresse,
      And when I my sins confesse,
            Sweet Spirit, comfort me!
      When I lie within my bed,
      Sick in heart, and sick in head,
      And with doubts discomforted,
            Sweet Spirit, comfort me!

M acquires English and Scottish Ballads, *selected & edited by Francis James Child (Boston, 1854-1858); among the ballads scored in Vol VI is this stanza in "The Raid of the Reidswire":*
      To deal with proud men is but pain;
            For either must ye fight or flee,
      Or else no answer make again,
            But play the beast, and let them be.

In Vol VIII, M double-scores this stanza in "The Gentleman in Thracia":
      Away he goes with heavy heart;
            His griefs he did conceale,
      And like a wise and prudent man,
            To none did it reveale.
& scores this stanza in "George Barnwell":
      "For without money, George,
            A man is but a beast:
      But bringing money, thou shalt be
            Always my welcome guest . . ."

October 7   *M orders [duplicate?] numbers 105-122 of* Harpers Weekly
sent to his mother (54¢) &
            1 Christmas Books to Allan Melville   .50

October 13   *M orders from* Harpers *[for his brother, Allan?]:*
            1 Adam Bede *[by George Eliot]*   .75

Before November?   *M writes a third lecture, "Travel."* (I had not an
opportunity of hearing it [at Flushing], but I read it in M S. & thought
it highly interesting . . . — *Augusta Melville to Catherine Gansevoort,
Jan 4, 1860*)

FLUSHING November 7   *At the Young Men's Association M opens his
third & last lecture season with a new lecture (fee, $30):* "Travelling:
Its Pleasures, Pains, and Profits."

November 8?   He stayed over night and part of a day at Mr [William
R.] Prince's where he was most hospitably entertained, & presented with
a bouquet of lovely flowers. — *Augusta Melville to Catherine Gansevoort,
Jan 4, 1860*

NEW YORK Mid-November?   *M borrows from Evert Duyckinck's
library, seven volumes: Giorgio Vasari's* Lives of the Most Eminent
Painters, Sculptors, and Architects *(London, 1850-52); Luigi Lanzi's*
History of Painting in Italy *(London, 1847)*

Herman & Bessie passed a week in New York while I was there. He was
feeling much stronger then. — *Augusta Melville to Catherine Gansevoort,
Jan 4, 1860*

PITTSFIELD November 21   *Mrs Sarah Morewood writes to George
Duyckinck:*
Herman Melville is not well — do not call him moody, he is ill.

LAWRENCE November 30   *John C. Hoadley writes to a business associate, George A. Gordon, in Charleston, South Carolina:*
   My Brother-in-law, Herman Melville, has prepared a lecture, entitled:
"Travel, its pains, pleasures and profits," which he is now engaged in
delivering. —
   Can't you manage him an invitation? — an engagement? — You can't
do a better action, for a better fellow; nor oblige me more deeply. —

NEW YORK Before December 14   *George Duyckinck writes to M,
asking for information about a book belonging to M,* The Temple, *by
George Herbert.*

PITTSFIELD December 14   *M replies to George Duyckinck:*
   Certainly: — Pages, 384; Price, 25 cts (at least that's all I gave for
it) . . .

As to the size — there you have me. But by *rule*, it is 5½ In. by 4¼, and 1 In. thick. I am a sorry arithmetician; but, seems to me, if you figure this up by cord-measure and compound reduction, the result will be the size of the book, technically expressed.

BOSTON Before December 29 *Lemuel Shaw asks A. M. Livingston to have M lecture in Salem.*

SALEM December 29 *A. M. Livingston replies to Lemuel Shaw:*
I put myself in communication with the managers of our Lyceum at once . . . and find the list of lecturers for the "Young Mens Union", so called, is already filled . . . The old Salem Lyceum . . . has one or two vacancies, and I have reason to believe that Mr. Melville will be invited to fill one of them — I think also he will be invited to lecture before the Peabody Institute, in So Danvers . . . If Mr. M. shall come here, or to the Peabody Institute, I shall be very happy to have him stop at my house.

1860 **VII** 1869

1860: *Feb 21, Melville delivers his last lecture; May, he prepares a volume of poems to be offered to publishers, & sails on a long voyage on the* Meteor, *captained by his brother Thomas; Oct 12, the* Meteor *arrives at San Francisco & Melville leaves her, to return, via the Isthmus, to New York, where he arrives on the* North Star *on Nov 12*

1861: *Feb, Allan Melville, his two brothers-in-law, & Lemuel Shaw make a second effort to obtain a consular post for Melville; Mar, with this aim Melville visits Washington & leaves, without success, on hearing of the last illness of his father-in-law; Apr, on outbreak of Civil War Melville seeks a naval appointment, without success; Dec, he leaves Pittsfield to spend the Winter in New York*

1862: *Mar 12, Herman Gansevoort dies but Melville is too ill with rheumatism in New York to attend the funeral; Apr, returns to Pittsfield to move the family out of Arrowhead to the village, in preparation for a later move to New York; Nov 7, Melville is seriously injured in a road accident*

1863: *June, Melville participates in the semi-centennial anniversary of the Albany Academy; Oct, the family moves from Pittsfield to 104 East 26 Street, New York*

1864: *Apr, via Washington, Melville visits his cousin, Col. Henry Gansevoort, in his camp on the Virginia front, resulting in a severe attack of neuralgia; Nov, Capt. Thomas Melville retires from the sea*

1865: *Mar, Melville protests, in vain, against the re-issue of the* Israel Potter *plates under a new title, "The Refugee"; Apr, after the fall of Richmond, Melville plans a volume of war verse*

1866: Harper's Monthly *publishes four of Melville's war poems in advance of the volume,* Battle-Pieces, *in Aug; Dec 5, Melville takes the oath of office as Inspector of Customs at the Port of New York*

1867: *Sept 11, Melville finds his son Malcolm dead of a self-inflicted pistol-shot; Nov 19, Thomas Melville is elected Governor of Sailors' Snug Harbor on Staten Island*

1869: *Apr 4, Melville's surviving son, Stanwix, goes to sea on the* Yokohama, *sailing for China*

NEW YORK January 26 & 31 *Evert Duyckinck's diary:*
Herman Melville called for some volumes of the Essayists to take with him to his winter reading at Pittsfield. Says that the mealy mouthed habit of writing of human nature of the present day would not tolerate the plain speaking of Johnson, for instance, in the Rambler — who does not hesitate to use the word *malignity!*

M borrows:
The Tatler; a Daily Journal of Literature and the Stage (*4 vols, 1830-32*)
The British Essayists, *edited by Alexander Chalmers (3 vols of* The
 Observer, *& 3 vols of* The Looker-On)

DANVERS February 14 *M delivers one of his lectures (fee, $25).*

CAMBRIDGEPORT February 21 *M delivers his new lecture, "Travel," at the Dowse Institute (fee, $55):*
 Every man's home is in a certain sense a "Hopper," which however fair and sheltered, shuts him in from the outer world. Books of travel do not satisfy; they only stimulate the desire to see. To be a good traveller, and derive from travel real enjoyment, there are several requisites. One must be young, care-free, and gifted with geniality and imagination. Without these last he may as well stay at home. (*Cambridge Chronicle,* Feb 25)

BOSTON February *M acquires* The Poetical Works of Andrew Marvell . . . (*Boston, 1857), in which he scores this passage in "Upon the Hill and Grove at Billborow":*
>Learn here those humble steps to tread,
>Which to securer glory lead.

& this passage is underscored throughout:
>Nor he the hills, without the groves,
>Nor height, but with retirement, loves.

PITTSFIELD Before March 1 *M lends $600, to the town of Pittsfield*
[*Extracts from* The Annual Report of the Selectmen . . .]:
>Settlement with the Treasurer.
>Borrowed of H. Melville $600.00
>Liabilities to March 1, 1860.
>Note to Lemuel Shaw $1144.00
>Note to H. Melville   .   600.00

NEW YORK   April 9   *Giovanni Spaggiari writes to M:*
I take the liberty of addressing this letter to you, desirous as I am
of knowing whether the enclosed apostrophe to America, which I found
a few years ago in the "Mondo Illustrato," a magazine of Turin, as a
translation from the English of "Ermanno Meiville" is really yours; and
. . . where I can find the English original? . . . and then I could avail
myself of it for the Latin-English-Italian translated Anthology which
I am preparing: a specimen of which I had the honor to show to your
brother, Allan Melville, Esq.

PITTSFIELD   April 9   *Mrs Sarah Morewood writes to George Duyckinck:*
I am so sad to hear of Allan Melville's engagement to be married so
soon — God help his dear little family. I am disappointed in Allan Melville — he is now only an acquaintance of the past.

PHILADELPHIA   April 18   *Allan Melville is married to his second wife,
Jane Louisa Dempsey, by the Rev H. A. Boardman; now or later the
bride acquires a copy of the Rev Boardman's* The Bible in the Family: or,
Hints on Domestic Happiness (*Philadelphia, 1859*).

BOSTON   April 28   *Thomas Melville returns on the* Meteor.

PITTSFIELD   April 30   *M drives into town to pay his Town, County &
State Tax for 1859: a Total of $20.25 (less 70 cents discount).*

Early May   *M decides to accompany his brother, Captain Thomas
Melville, on the next voyage out of the clipper ship* Meteor. (If you
have met Allan lately he has perhaps informed you that in a few days
I go with my brother Tom a voyage round Cape Horn. It was only
determined upon a short time since; and I am at present busy, as you may
imagine in getting ready for a somewhat long absence, and likewise in
preparing for type certain M.S.S. — *M to Evert Duyckinck, May 21*)

Before May 15   *M writes to Lemuel Shaw.* (I am very glad to learn
from your letter that you intend to accept Thomas' invitation to go on
his next voyage. — *Lemuel Shaw to M, May 15*)

BOSTON   May 15   *Lemuel Shaw writes to M:*
I think [the voyage] affords a fair prospect of being of permanent
benefit to your health, and it will afford me the greatest pleasure to do
any thing in my power to aid your preparation, and make the voyage
most agreeable and beneficial to you.
The prospect of your early departure renders it proper and necessary
to bring to a definite conclusion the subject we have had a considerable
time under consideration, a settlement of the matter of the Pittsfield

estate, with a view to which you handed me your deeds, when I was in Pittsfield last autumn.

You will recollect that when you proposed to purchase a house in N. York I advanced to you $2000. and afterwards, when you purchased the Brewster place, I again advanced you $3000. For these sums, as well as for another loan of $500. afterwards, I took your notes . . . and I put these advances upon the footing of loans until some future adjustment . . .

What I now propose is to give up to you the above mentioned notes in full consideration of your conveyance to me of your present homestead, being all the Brewster purchase except what you sold to Mr. Willis. This being done and the estate vested in me, I propose to execute a deed conveying the same in fee to Elizabeth. This will vest the fee as an estate of inheritance in her, subject of course to your rights as her husband during your life . . . I do not see any advantage in giving the business any more notoriety than will arise from putting the deeds on record . . .

. . . The effect of the arrangement [turning M's notes over to Elizabeth's share of the Shaw estate] will be to cancel and discharge all debt and pecuniary obligation of every description from you to myself. You will then leave home with the conscious satisfaction of knowing that you are free from debt: that if by a Providential dispensation you should be prevented from ever returning to your beloved family some provision will have been made at least for a home, for your wife and children.

Two conveyances are written:
Know all Men by These Presents,
That I Herman Melville of Pittsfield, in the county of Berkshire, Gentleman in consideration of five thousand and five hundred dollars, paid by Lemuel Shaw of Boston in the county of Suffolk Esquire . . . do hereby give, grant, bargain, sell and convey unto the said Lemuel Shaw . . . a certain tract of land, situated in said Pittsfield . . .

. . . I Lemuel Shaw of Boston . . . in consideration of affection and goodwill, and also of one dollar paid by my daughter Elizabeth S. Melville, wife of Herman Melville of Pittsfield in the county of Berkshire Gentleman . . . do hereby give, grant, bargain, sell and convey unto the said Elizabeth S. Melville . . . all that tract and parcel of land, with the dwelling house and buildings standing thereon, being the homestead on which the said Herman and Elizabeth, now reside . . .

PITTSFIELD May 21 *M writes to Evert Duyckinck:*
Now may I with propriety ask of you, conditionally, a favor? Will you, upon the arrival of the M.S.S. in New York — that is, in the course of two weeks, or less — look over them and if they seem of a sort

that you care to be any way concerned with, advice with Allan as to a publisher, and form of volume, &c . . . In short, may I, seeming too confident, ask you, as a veteran & expert in these matters, and as an old acquaintance, to lend something of an overseeing eye to the launching of this craft — the committing of it to the elements?

May 22 [Bessie's seventh birthday] *M jots down:*

Memoranda for Allan

concerning the publication of my verses.

1 — Don't stand on terms much with the publisher — half profits after expenses are paid will content me — not that I expect much "profits" — but that will be a fair nomical arrangement . . .

2 — Don't have the Harpers. — I should like Appletons or Scribner — But Duyckinck's advice will be good here.

3 — The sooner the thing is printed and published, the better. The "season" will make little or no difference, I fancy, in this case.

4 — After printing, dont let the book hang back — but publish & have done.

5 — For God's sake don't have *By the author of* "*Typee*" "*Piddledee*" *&c* on the title-page.

6 — Let the title-page be simply,

Poems

by

Herman Melville.

7 — Dont have any clap-trap announcements and "sensation" puffs — nor any extracts published previous to publication of book — Have a decent publisher, in short.

8 — Don't take any measures, or make inquiries as to expediency of an English edition simultaneous with the American — as in case of "Confidence-Man."

9 — In the M.S.S. each piece is on a page by itself, however small the piece . . . Of course in printing two or more pieces will sometimes appear on the same page — according to length of pieces &c . . .

10 — The poems are divided into books as you will see; but the divisions are not *called* books — they are only numbered . . .

11 — Anything not perfectly plain in the M.S.S. can be referred to Lizzie . . .

12 — Lizzie should by all means see the printed sheets *before* being bound, in order to detect any gross errors consequent upon misconstruing the M.S.S.

These are the thoughts which hurriedly occur to me at this moment. Pardon the abruptness of their expression, but time is precious. — Of all human events, perhaps, the publication of a first volume of verses is the most insignificant; but though a matter of no moment to the world, it is still of some concern to the author, — as these *Mem.* show . . .

[?] *From the poems copied by Elizabeth, M discards one before his departure:*

* A Reasonable Constitution

What though Reason forged your scheme?
'Twas Reason dreamed the Utopia's dream:
'Tis dream to think that Reason can
Govern the reasoning creature, man.

* Observable in Sir Thomas More's "Utopia" are First its almost entire reasonableness. Second its almost entire impracticability The remark applies more or less to the Utopia's prototype "Plato's Republic"

Before May 26   *M leaves for Boston, taking several books with him, including a gift from Mrs Morewood:* The Marble Faun: or The Romance of Monte Beni, *by Nathaniel Hawthorne*

NEW YORK   Before May 26   *Evert Duyckinck replies to M's letter of May 21.* (I am glad that the postponement of the ship's day of sailing gives me a chance to answer your letter, received, in reply to mine, on the eve of my leaving Pittsfield. It was a very welcome one — quite a wind from the fields of old times. — *M to Evert Duyckinck, May 28*)

PITTSFIELD   May 27   *Sarah Morewood writes to George Duyckinck:* Our neighbour Herman Melville sailed yesterday with his brother Capt. Tom — on a year's voyage.

BOSTON   Before May 28   *Before boarding the* Meteor, *the two brothers have an ambrotype taken at Davis & Co.* [See Pl. XI]

BOSTON HARBOR   May 28   *M writes Evert Duyckinck, from on board the clipper ship* Meteor:
My wife will send you the parcel in the course of a week or so — there remaining something to be finished in copying the M.S.S.

As my wife has interested herself a good deal in this matter, and in fact seems to know more about it than I do — at least about the *merits* of the performance — I must therefore refer you to her in case of any exigency requiring information further than you are in possession of.

If your brother George is not better employed, I hope he will associate himself with you in looking over my scribblings.

That is enough in the egotistic way. Now for something else.

I anticipate as much pleasure as at, at the age of forty, one temperately can, in the voyage I am going. I go under very happy auspices so far as ship & Captain is concerned. A noble ship and a nobler captain — & he my brother. We have the breadth of tropics before us, to sail over twice; & shall round the world. Our first port is San Francisco, which we shall probably make in 110 days from Boston. Thence we go to Manilla — & thence, I hardly know where. — I wish devoutly you were going along. I think it would agree with you. The prime requisite for enjoyment in sea voyages, for passengers, is 1ˢᵗ health — 2ᵈ good-nature. Both first-rate things, but not universally to be found. — At sea a fellow comes out. Salt water is like wine, in that respect.

I have a good lot of books with me — such as they are; — plenty of old periodicals — lazy reading for lazy latitudes. —

May 30 *The* Meteor *weighs anchor:*
At 10½ A.M. Tom, Fanny, George Griggs, and I went off to ship in the stream. Beautiful day, and pleasant sail down the harbor. Mʳ Peabody was on board, and lunched in the cabin. We bade Fanny good bye, and I assisted her into the tug-boat, preparatory to its going ahead to tow. At ¼ past one P.M. pilot and tug-boat left us. Waved our handkerchiefs to Fanny, and the voyage began. — Quite sea-sick at night. — *M's* Meteor *journal*

PITTSFIELD May 31 *A paragraph in the* Berkshire County Eagle:
HERMAN MELVILLE. — This gentleman left home last week for a voyage round the world, in pursuit of relaxation, renewed vigor, and, we hope, material for another charming volume on sea-life, which he will now see in a new phase. He was to have sailed yesterday, from Boston, in the fine clipper ship *Meteor,* which is commanded by his brother, Capt. Thomas Melville. She sails direct for San Francisco, and thence across the Pacific. The voyage will occupy about a year, and can hardly fail to be a pleasant one.

June 1 *Elizabeth Melville writes to Evert Duyckinck:*
On Monday or Tuesday of next week I shall forward to you by Express, the manuscript of which Herman wrote you — and with this I enclose a copy of the memoranda which he jotted down for Allan, — according to his request —
To this also should have been added an item which Herman omitted in his haste — and that is, that the book should be plainly bound, that is, not over-gilt — and to "blue and gold" I know he has a decided aversion —

June 4 *Elizabeth Melville sends Evert Duyckinck the manuscript & a letter:*
. . . Herman was obliged to leave much in an unfinished state, and I should feel much easier, as I know he would, if you would overlook the sheets for these little inaccuracies —
When you have read the manuscript, I should be very glad to have your opinion of it, as a whole, and you need not be afraid to say *exactly* what you think, — I am the more desirous of this, because as yet, no one has seen the sheets, excepting two of Herman's sisters, who are now with me — and I want to know how they would strike an unprejudiced person — If your brother also would add his impressions, so much the better —

THE ATLANTIC June 8 *M's* Meteor *journal:*

During the past days, cloudy, foggy rainy weather, with good breeze generally, and sailing Eastward, or little south of East. — Gulf Stream disagreeable. But this [day] there is a change. Clear & bright — light breeze. Wind still from the South. Sent up skysail yard. Crew busy in rigging &c.

33.21N 41.37W June 9   The same bright, clear weather, growing warmer each day. Feel very sensibly improving in appetite &c, after seasick qualmishness. Have seen flying-fish, weed, Portuguese men-of-war, and several sail lately. This afternoon had a collision with an English brig [*Elizabeth Baxter*] from Pernambuco bound for Liverpool. She blundered down across our bow, & was locked with us for a time; ripping & tearing her sails. We also were damaged in fore-yard & main. At the moment of collision the Steward of the brig being in jeopardy, leaped aboard of us, and the vessels separating, remained aboard, till taken off by boat sent from the brig. He told me that the Captain was asleep in his berth when we came together, and added the Mate was half-blind &c. It was altogether an instance of the grossest heedlessness possible on the part of the brig — quite unaccountable. — When it was plain that she purposed crossing our bow, and that it was out of the question for her to do so, Tom at once put his helm up, and by so doing, we came off with less damage than could have been anticipated.

June 10   Came out to day in light clothes.

PITTSFIELD June 11   *The Valuation Book for Pittsfield's Taxpayers is completed; in M's estimate:*
[Money] $1,000

THE ATLANTIC Before June 17   *M's* Meteor *journal:*
During the past week took the Trades — crossed the Northern Tropic . . . [entry of June 18]

June 17   . . . Last night saw the Southern Cross — the North Star sensibly sinking. Unvarying fine weather. [entry of June 18]

LAT. 18.30N June 18   *M's* Meteor *journal:*
  Went out to flying-jib-boom end this morning. Glorious view of the ship. Spent the day dipping into the "Quarterlies," — Find methodical reading out of the question. Not yet completely settled in my stomach. Head all right, tho'.

NEW YORK June 19   *Charles Scribner returns M's manuscript to Evert Duyckinck with a letter:*
  I have looked over Melville's Poems. I have no doubt they are excellent, they seem so to me, and I have confidence in your judgment — But I have not got the heart to publish them — I doubt whether they would more than pay expenses, and as I have issued two vols of Poems [by

E. C. Stedman & G. P. Morris] this season and the prospect is that neither of them will pay I don't feel like making another venture in that line

Evert Duyckinck sends the manuscript to Rudd & Carleton, & writes to Elizabeth Melville. (Elizabeth Melville to Evert Duyckinck, June 23)

PITTSFIELD   June 23   *Elizabeth Melville writes to Evert Duyckinck:*
I . . . hasten to thank you for your kind endeavors about the manuscript, regretting that its course does not run smoothly, thus far — For myself, I am willing to wait patiently for the result, so that the publication is eventually accomplished — and do not consider its rejection by the publishers as any test of its mint in a literary point of view — well-knowing, as Herman does also, that *poetry* is a comparatively uncalled-for article in the publishing market — I suppose that if John Milton were to offer "Paradise Lost" to the Harpers tomorrow, it would be promptly rejected as "unsuitable" not to say, denounced as dull —
I think infinitely more of yours and your brother's opinion of it, and feel more confidence in its worth, since it has been looked at by persons of judgment and taste, than ever before — it has been such a profound secret between Herman and myself for so long, that I rejoice to have my own prejudice in its favor confirmed by some one in whose appreciation we can feel confidence — for I do not believe you would speak favorably of it, unless you could do so sincerely . . .
I feel that you and Allan will do everything that is suitable and proper about it and am deeply sensible of your kindly efforts to further its success — indeed I feel that it is in better hands than even with Herman's own management for he might be disheartened at the outset, by its rejection, and perhaps withhold it altogether, which would be a great disappointment to me —

00.15N   June 25   *M's Meteor journal:*
For four days past have been in the Doleful Doldrums. — The whole ship's crew given up to melancholy, and meditating darkly on the mysteries of Providence. But this morning we have a wind, and feel better.

29.00W   June 29   *Crossed the Line* last evening. Saw bonetoes under the bow.

M gives a book to his brother, Thomas: Sketches of Life and Character, by Alexander Campbell (Edinburgh, 1842).

Beginning of July   *M's Meteor journal:*
For the last five or six days — Calm — profound at times. Few or no fish seen. A comet made its appearance to the N.W. the other night, and was still visible last night . . . Some ten days since the Carpenter

made a set of chessmen; and Tom and I have played a game or two every evening. [entry of July 8]

July 7   At 4½ P.M. yesterday the Calcutta sow commenced delivering her pigs, and about 6½ P.M. concluded. Eleven were born, but two were dead; thus, nine "souls" have been added to our company. [entry of July 8]

18.30s 33.30w   July 8   This morning sprang up a breeze — I hope it will continue.

41.00s   July   *M reads in* The Marble Faun: *Chapter XII. "The Emptiness of Picture-Galleries"*
& comments: Most original & admirable, and, doubtless, too true.
Continuing in the chapter, he reads: "Perugino was evidently a devout man . . ."
& comments: On the contrary, if I remember right, he is said, in [Vasari's] "Lives of the Painters," to have been a jeerer at all religion, — a . . . (Lat. 41° South Atlantic)

July 21   *M's Meteor journal:*
Put up cabin-stove yesterday . . . [entry of July 22]

43.30s 49.00w   July 22   Clear fine mild day. Speckled haglets & other birds about. Since writing last, have had two hard blows. Have a stove up in the cabin. Play chess every evening . . . Quite comfortable & domestic in the cabin now.

50.00s   August 1   [M's 41st birthday]
. . . crossed 50 S in the Atlantic Aug 1st; Aug 2d, while running with wind NE, a gale sprung up suddenly from ESE, with snow and hail; continuing three days . . . ("Meteor" report, San Francisco *Daily Evening Bulletin*, Oct 13)

August 6   *M's Meteor journal:*
Since last date have had several gales, with snow, rain, hail, sleet, mist, fog, squalls, head-winds, refractory stove, smoky cabin, drunken ship &c &c. — In one gale, several men washed off the t'gallant forecastle, and the boy Charlie was sent flying into the pig-pen which was stove, & the sow & little pigs came, with the deluge, aft. One (pigling) drowned, poor fellow. — A man hurt by a sea; assisted his chum in getting him into his berth, the crew being engaged taking in sail. — One of the gales lasted three days. In one we split the mainsail all to pieces, & the mizzen topsail, and a staysail — Days short — but not sweet. Winter.

CAPE HORN   August 7   At daylight made the land — Fair wind & pleasant. — Made Staten Land & N.W. Coast of Terra del Fuego. Two sail in sight. Entered the Strait of Le Maire, & through the short day had a fine view of the land on both sides — Horrible snowy mountains — black, thunder-cloud woods — gorges — hell-landscape. Signalled ship "Black Prince" from New York. — There are three on the Sick List. The man hurt by the sea — one with a fever — the third, a boy with general debility. —

At last we came in sight of land all covered with snow — uninhabited land, where no one ever lived, and no one ever will live — it is so barren, cold and desolate. This was Staten Land — an island. Near it, is the big island of Terra del Fuego. We passed through between these islands, and had a good view of both. There are some "wild people" living on Terra del Fuego; but it being the depth of winter there, I suppose they kept in their caves. At any rate we saw none of them. — *M to his son Malcolm, Sept 1*

August 8   *M's* Meteor *journal:*
Moderate breeze & fair, but thick. Could not see the land, tho' to be wished. Just before sunset, in a squall, the mist lifted & showed, within 12 or fifteen miles the horrid sight of Cape Horn — (the Cape proper) — a black, bare steep cliff, the face of it facing the South Pole; — with[in] some miles were other awful islands and rocks — an infernal group. Tried to weather Cape Horn, as sloops weather Castle Garden Point N.Y. — but were headed off. Tacked ship to the southward.

The next day we were off Cape Horn, the Southernmost point of all America. Now it was very bad weather, and was dark at about three o'clock in the afternoon. The wind blew terribly. We had hail-storms, and snow and sleet, and often the spray froze as it touched the deck. The ship rolled, and sometimes took in so much water on the deck as to wash people off their legs. Several sailors were washed along the deck this way, and came near getting washed overboard. — *M to his son Malcolm, Sept 1*

August 9   *M's* Meteor *journal:*
A gale of wind, with snow & hail & sleet. —
[Benjamin] Ray, a Nantucketer, about 25 years old, a good honest fellow (to judge from his face and demeanor during the passage) fell this morning about day-break from the Main topsail yard to the deck, & striking his head foremost upon one of the spars was instantly killed. His chum, Macey (Fisher) of Nantucket, I found alone in the upper cabin sitting over the body — a harrowing spectacle. "I have lost my best friend," said he; and then "His mother will go crazy — she did not want to let him go, she feared something might happen." — It was in vain to wash the blood from the head — the body bled incessantly & up to the moment of burying; which was about one o'clock, and from the poop, in the interval between blinding squalls of sharp sleet. Tom read some lines

from the prayer-book — the plank was sloped, and — God help his mother. — During the brief ceremony, made still the more trying from being under the lee of the reefed spanker where the wind eddies so — all stood covered with Sou-Westers or Russia caps & comforters, except Macy — who stood bareheaded.

It was just about day-light; it was blowing a gale of wind; and Uncle Tom ordered the topsails (big sails) to be furled. Whilst the sailors were aloft on one of the yards, the ship rolled and plunged terribly; and it blew with sleet and hail, and was very cold & biting. Well, all at once, Uncle Tom saw something falling through the air, and then heard a thump, and then, — looking before him, saw a poor sailor lying dead on the deck. He had fallen from the yard, and was killed instantly. — His shipmates picked him up, and carried him under cover. By and by, when time could be spared, the sailmaker sewed up the body in a piece of sailcloth, putting some iron balls — cannon balls — at the foot of it. And, when all was ready, the body was put on a plank, and carried to the ship's side in the presence of all hands. Then Uncle Tom, as Captain, read a prayer out of the prayer-book, and at a given word, the sailors who held the plank tipped it up, and immediately the body slipped into the stormy ocean, and we saw it no more. — Such is the way a poor sailor is buried at sea. This sailor's name was Ray. He had a friend among the crew; and they were both going to California, and thought of living there; but you see what happened. — *M to his son Malcolm, Sept 1*

August 10   *M's* Meteor *journal:*
— Calm: blue sky, sun out, dry deck. Calm lasting all day — almost pleasant enough to atone for the gales, but not for Ray's fate, which belongs to that order of human events, which staggers those whom the Primal Philosophy hath not confirmed. — But little sorrow to the crew — all goes on as usual — I, too, read & think, & walk & eat & talk, as if nothing had happened — as if I did not know that death is indeed the King of Terrors — when thus happening; when thus heart-breaking to a fond mother — The King of Terrors, not to the dying or the dead, but to the mourner — the mother. — Not so easily will his fate be washed out of her heart, as his blood from the deck.

50.00S 88.00W   August 16
. . . crossed 50 S in the Pacific in lon 88 W . . . ("Meteor" report, *Daily Evening Bulletin*, Oct 13)

PITTSFIELD   August 16   *An item in the* Berkshire County Eagle:
    Chief Justice Shaw is on a visit to his daughter, Mrs. Herman Melvill of this town.

THE PACIFIC Summer?   [*?*] *M composes "The Admiral of the White," a first version of "The Haglets":*
> Proud, O proud in his oaken hall
> The Admiral walks to-day,
> From the top of his turreted citadel
> French colors 'neath English play . . .

I cant help thinking what a luckless chap you were that voyage you had a poetaster with you. You remember the romantic moonlight night, when the conceited donkey repeated to you about three cables' length of his verses. But you bore it like a hero. I cant in fact recall so much as a single *wince*. To be sure, you went to bed immediately upon the conclusion of the entertainment; but this much I am sure of, whatever were your sufferings, you never gave them utterance. Tom, my boy, I admire you. I say again, you are a hero. — *M to his brother, Thomas, May 25, 1862*

Many [sea-birds] have followed the ship day after day. I used to feed them with crumbs. But now it has got to be warm weather, the birds have left us. They we[re] about as big as chickens — they were all over speckled — and they would sometimes, during a calm, keep behind the ship, fluttering about in the water, with a mighty cackling, and wherever anything was thrown overboard they would hurry to get it. But they never would light on the ship — they kept all the time flying or else resting themselves by floating on the water like ducks in a pond. These birds have no home, unless it is some wild rocks in the middle of the ocean. — *M to his daughter, Bessie, Sept 2*

CAPRICORN September 1   *M writes the first installment of a letter to his son, Malcolm:*
I suppose you have followed out on the map (or my *globe* were better — so you get Mama to clean it off for you) the route from Boston to San Francisco. The distance, by the straight track, is about 16000 miles; but the ship will have sailed before she gets there nearer 18 or 20000 miles. So you see it is further than from the apple-tree to the big rock.

September 2   *M writes to his daughter:*
My Dear Bessie: I thought I would send you a letter, that you could read yourself — at least a part of it. But here and there I propose to write in the usual manner, as I find the printing style comes rather awkwardly in a rolling ship. Mamma will read these parts to you. We have seen a good many sea-birds. Many have followed the ship day after day . . . They never see any orchards, and have a taste of the apples &, cherries like your gay little friend in Pittsfield Robin Red Breast Esq. — I could tell you a good many more things about the sea, but I must defer the rest till I get home . . .

I suppose you have had a good many walks on the hill, and picked the strawberries.

I hope you take good care of little

FANNY

and that when you go on the hill, you go this way:

That is to say, hand in hand.

By-by

Papa.

[*?*] *M composes the first version of*

WILD-STRAWBERRY HUNTERS.
Through the orchard I follow
Two children in glee:
In the apple tree hollow
They startle the bee.
The white clover throws
Perfume in their way
To the hedge of red rose:
Tween roses and clover
The strawberry grows.
'Tis Lilly and Cherry
Hunt the red and white berry
Companioned by butterflies,
Madcaps as merry.

19.00S   September 4   *M reads in* The Songs of Béranger (*Philadelphia, 1844*).

117.30W   September 13
. . . crossed the Equator Sept 13th, lon 117 30 W; have had light airs all the way up . . . ("Meteor" report, *Daily Evening Bulletin,* Oct 13)

Before September 16   The other day we saw a whale-ship; and I got into a boat and sailed over the ocean in it to the whale-ship, and stayed there about an hour. They had eight or ten of the "wild people" aboard. The Captain of the whale-ship had hired them at one of the islands called Roratonga. He wanted them to help pull in the whale-boat when they hunt the whale. — *M to his son, Malcolm, Sept 16*

ON THE LINE   September 16   *M continues his letter to his son, Malcolm:*
. . . I hope that you have called to mind what I said to you about your behaviour previous to my going away. I hope that you have been obedient to your mother, and helped her all you could, & saved her trouble. Now is the time to show what you are — whether you are a good, honorable boy, or a good-for-nothing one. Any boy, of your age, who disobeys his mother, or worries her, or is disrespectful to her — such a boy is a poor shabby fellow; and if you know any such boys, you ought to cut their acquaintance.

Now, my Dear Malcolm, I must finish my letter to you. I think of you, and Stanwix & Bessie and Fanny very often; and often long to be with you. But it can not be, at present. The picture which I have of you & the rest, I look at sometimes, till the faces almost seem real. [*See Pl. XI*]

13.00N   September 19   *M reads in his volume of Schiller's* Poems and Ballads *as far as "To Emma":*
> Can those sweet longing hopes, which make
>   Love's essence, thus decay?
> Can that be love which doth forsake? —
>   *That* love — which fades away?
> That earthly gifts are brief, I knew —
> Is that all heaven-born mortal too?

September 22   [*?*] *M writes to his wife, Elizabeth, to be mailed Oct 19.*

September 25   *M reads in his volume of Schiller, "The Diver, A Ballad,"* *scoring this stanza:*
> Dark-crawl'd — glided dark the unspeakable swarms,
>   Clump'd together in masses, misshapen and vast —
> Here clung and here bristled the fashionless forms —
>   Here the dark-moving bulk of the Hammer-fish pass'd —
> And with teeth grinning white, and a menacing motion,
> Went the terrible Shark — the Hyæna of Ocean.

700 MILES FROM SAN FRANCISCO   October 3   *M reads in the set of Chapman's translation of Homer:*
In The Odysseys, *Fifth Book, p 129, M underscores & checks*
> ⤹ The sea had soak'd his heart through . . .

In The Odysseys, *Sixth Book, p 143, M underscores & checks*
> In soul more rich the more to sense decay'd . . . ✔

In The Iliads, *Fourth Book, p 94, M underscores*
> But Gods at all times give not all their gifts to mortal men.
> If then I had the strength of youth, I miss'd the counsels then
> That years now give me; and now years want that main strength
> > of youth . . .

In Batrachomyomachia *[&c]* . . . , *M underscores & checks the opening line of Chapman's concluding verses:*
> The work that I was born to do is done! ✔

October ?   *M reads in his* New Testament *& underscores this passage in* Romans XIV:
> 22 Hast thou faith? have it to thyself before God. ✔

M's comment: ✔ The only kind of Faith — one's own.

OFF CALIFORNIA Early October   *M continues to read in the second volume of* The Iliads *in view of the clipper* Derby, *Captain Hutchinson.*

. . . was becalmed four days 160 miles W S W of Point Reyes . . . ("Meteor" report, *Daily Evening Bulletin*, Oct 13)

M makes a drawing of Arrowhead [see Pl. IX] & writes a note:
> Drew this at sea one afternoon on deck — & when in the calm. — Made me feel as if I was there, almost — Such is the magic power of a fine artist. — Be it known I pride myself particularly upon "Charlie" & the driver. — It is to be supposed that *I* am in the carriage; & the figures are welcoming me.

OFF SAN FRANCISCO October 11
. . . anchored on the bar at 8:30 P M, 11th inst . . . ("Meteor" report, *Daily Evening Bulletin*, Oct 13)

October 12
> By Telegraph — Point Lobos — 1:30 P.M.
Weather hazy — wind light from West, Ship Meteor, Melville, 134 days from Boston, mdse, to C. T. Meader & Co, off the heads . . . (*Daily Evening Bulletin*, this date)

A paragraph in the Daily Evening Bulletin:
A Noted Author Coming to San Francisco. — Private letters from Boston advise us that Herman Melville . . . is coming to San Francisco — indeed that he may now be daily expected to arrive here, having sailed on the *Meteor*, which ship has been out 130 days. Mr. Melville is traveling in pursuit of health, and new experiences to turn to account in a literary way. He will remain in San Francisco some time; and our Mercantile Library Association, or some other society, might possibly secure his services for a series of lectures. We like to taste the quality of all the celebrities who fall upon our shores . . .

The Meteor *comes to anchor at the Vallejo street wharf.*

After October 12? *M writes to his mother & sisters in Gansevoort, & to his wife, Elizabeth.* (By Pony Express, Lizzie had a letter saying he was not at all benefitted by the Voyage . . . He had written us to come by Steamer — Lizzie writes — *Maria Melville to Peter Gansevoort, Nov 5*) [Mr. Melville's health is better in some particulars than when he left home, but we regret to learn that he has not experienced the full benefit hoped from the trip, and as the voyage will be prolonged beyond what was first anticipated, Mr. Melville will return via the Isthmus, and reach home early in the winter. (The *Berkshire County Eagle*, Nov 8)]

October 15 [?] *M acquires* The Book of English Songs, *edited by Charles Mackay (London, 1857), which he subsequently reads & marks; on "This Bottle's the Sun of Our Table," by Richard Brinsley Sheridan, M comments:* **X** Good for "Old Sherry."

October 16 *M writes to Lemuel Shaw, enclosing this note to Samuel Shaw:*
My Dear Sam: In a few days I shall be at sea again, and as I want to see what I can while here, you may imagine I have not much idle time. I have just written to your father, and slip this little note in, just to say that your letter received here was really interesting to me, and merits a longer & more communicative reply than I shall be able to make. Indeed, as I write by night (rather unusual for me) and my eyes feel tired, all I can add here is, that I hope you are a good enough Christian in this matter of correspondence to be willing cheerfully to give much and receive little.

October 18 *A paragraph in the* Daily Alta:
HERMANN MELVILLE — This well known author arrived here on board the ship *Meteor,* a few days since, from New York, and, as we learn, intends to return by the next steamer to New York . . . Like Dana, he is on a tour of observation, and has made the trip around Cape Horn to benefit his health. Perhaps some of the literary Institutions might prevail on him to favor us with a lecture or two before his departure.

October 19 *M writes to Elizabeth by overland mail.*

October 20 *M leaves San Francisco.*
The *Cortes* [Richard H. Pearson, master] left for Panama between 9 and 10 o'clock this morning, with the mails, 250 passengers, and $1,022,566 in specie . . . The reader will note among [the cabin passengers], Herman Melville, the author of "Omoo" and "Typee," who arrived here but a few days since from around Cape Horn . . .
An unusual number of stowaways were sent ashore after the steamer got into the stream. (*Daily Evening Bulletin,* this date)

MANZANILLO October 27
. . . 6½ A.M., arrived at Manzanillo, took on board $315,000 in silver and

left at 10 o'clock the same morning; October 28th, 5 P.M., arrived at Acapulco, took in coal, water and provision, and sailed same evening at 9 o'clock, arriving at Panama, November 4th, at 2.15 P.M. ("Cortes" report, *Daily Evening Bulletin*, Nov 26)

M, with the other passengers, crosses the Isthmus to Aspinwall, New Granada, where their connection waits.

ASPINWALL November 5 *Departure of the Vanderbilt Steamship* North Star, *A. G. Jones, master, for New York; among the passengers in the First Cabin is:*

Herman Melville [age] 40 [profession] Author

Steamship North Star

GANSEVOORT November 5 *Maria Melville writes to Peter Gansevoort:* [Herman] was not at all benefitted by the Voyage —

I feel so much disappointed, I had fondly hoped that a Voyage to India under kind Tom's care would have quite brought Herman back to health —

CARIBBEAN SEA November 8 *On the* North Star *M reads in his volume of Schiller:*

THE POET TO HIS FRIENDS
Friends, fairer times have been
(Who can deny?) than we ourselves have seen;
And an old race of more majestic worth.

PITTSFIELD November 8   *A paragraph in the* Berkshire County Eagle:
  HERMAN MELVILLE . . . We trust and think that the trip home will be
of more benefit than out, and that Mr. M. will reach us in the full vigor of
health that used to distinguish him.

NEW YORK November 12   *M arrives in the Port of New York on the*
S. S. North Star.

After November 12   [?] *M calls on Henry T. Tuckerman.* (*Tucker-*
man to Evert Duyckinck, Jan 17)

[?] *M & Catherine Gansevoort attend services at Grace Church.*

SAN FRANCISCO November 16   *The* Meteor, *Melville, master, sails for*
Falmouth, England.

PITTSFIELD November 23   *Mrs Sarah Morewood writes to George*
Duyckinck:
Were you not surprised at Mr Herman's return. I am glad that we
shall have them for Neighbors again this winter.

December 12   *M drives into town to insert a running advertisement in*
the Berkshire County Eagle:
                              WANTED.
A WOMAN to do cooking and general Housework in a small family three miles
  from Pittsfield Village.

                                        HERMAN MELVILLE.
                                     [*first printed*, Dec 13]

December 18   *M writes to Oliver Russ.* (I recd your kind favour of the
18 inst in due time and its perusal gave me the greatest pleasure posable
its reception was altogether unexpected but not unwelcomed . . . If I
understand your letter aright you have been enjoying another trip
around Cape Horn to the ever delightful Pacific did its scenes appear
to you as they did when we were there then has sixteen years wrought
no change there, if not I fear it has with you and me . . . You ask me
to write what I am doing out here . . . — *Oliver Russ to M, Dec 24*)

RICHVILLE December 24   *Oliver Russ replies to M's inquiries:*
. . . I will tell you with the greatest pleasure I have been farming on a
small scale for a few years . . . I keep a boot & shoe store and shop for
making and repairing . . . by this you may infer that I live like yourself in rather primitive stile only a little more so.
  . . . I live but a short distance from Mr Green the father of Toby
I often see the old gentleman but have never seen Richard (Toby) but
learn that he is now in Mishagan, and that he is not a very desirable patern
for a husband and father but perfection is not to be found in man

PITTSFIELD December 25?   *M composes:*

TO TOM.

Thou that dost thy Christmas keep
Lonesome on the torrid deep,
But in thy "Meteor" proudly sweep
O'er the waves that vainly comb —
  Of thee we think,
  To thee we drink,
And drain the glass, my gallant Tom!

Thou that, duty-led, dost roam
Far from thy shepherd-brother's home—
Shearer of the ocean-foam!
To whom one Christmas may not come, —
  Of thee I think
  Till on its brink
The glass shows tears, beloved Tom!

PITTSFIELD End of December? *M writes to Richard Tobias Greene, announcing that he has properly engraved spoons to send to Greene's son (Herman Melville Greene) & Greene's nephew (Richard Melville Hair), & inviting Greene to visit him at Arrowhead. (Richard T. Greene to M, Jan 4, 1861)*

·   ·   ·   ·   ·

NEW YORK *Publication, by Polhemus & De Vries, of* Life in the South Seas; History of the Whale Fisheries; Habits of the Whale; Perils of the Chase . . . , *by Captain E. C. Williams, containing the following portions of* Moby Dick: *"Extracts" [no credit], "The Line" [credited to Herman Melville], "Forty Years" [credited to Moby Dick. Herman Melville].*

[?] *M composes:*

MISGIVINGS.

When ocean-clouds over inland hills
  Sweep storming in late autumn brown,
And horror the sodden valley fills,
  And the spire falls crashing in the town,
I muse upon my country's ills —
The tempest bursting from the waste of Time
On the world's fairest hope linked with man's foulest crime.

Nature's dark side is heeded now —
  (Ah! optimist-cheer disheartened flown) —
A child may read the moody brow
  Of yon black mountain lone.
With shouts the torrents down the gorges go
And storms are formed behind the storm we feel:
The hemlock shakes in the rafter, the oak in the driving keel.

*

1 8 6 1

*

PITTSFIELD   January 1   *M gives Lizzie his copy of* The Works of the Late Edgar Allan Poe (*New York, 1859*).

CHICAGO   January 4   *Richard Tobias Greene replies to M's letter:*
Hope you enjoy good health, and can yet stow away your "five shares of duff"! I would be delighted to see you and "freshen the nip" while you would be spinning a yarn as long as the Maintop bowline. I shall most certainly avail myself of your kind invitation if ever I travel that way . . .
. . . I often have the pleasure of seeing our future President. "Old Abe" looks all right, and its my opinion, he will take the oath of office on the Capitol Steps in spite of all fire eating bragadocios.

PITTSFIELD   Early January   *M sends a letter & a gift to Oliver Russ.*

January 10   M writes to Richard Tobias Greene.

PEMBROKE, N. Y.   January 14   *Oliver Russ acknowledges M's remembrances:*
. . . your letter and present arrived in due time all safe and were received with the greatest satisfaction and delight by us all, and after a thourough inspection by all the house hold were consigned to a secluded corner of a drawer there to be kept for years to come, but its occasional appearance will ever revive those kindly feelings which we have ever cherished for the giver, it brings to mind anew all those circumstances which made us acquainted and all the incidents which hapened while we were togather.

CHICAGO   January 16   *Richard Tobias Greene replies to M's note of the 10th:*
The name of my Nephew is "*Richard Melville Hair*" . . .
My son's name is Herman Melville Greene . . .

NEW YORK   January 17   *Henry T. Tuckerman writes to Evert Duyckinck:*
Do you ever see Herman Melville? If so, will you be so kind as to explain to him that the reason I have not returned his call, is that I have been laid up for several weeks with a severe neuralgic attack. Had I known his address I should have sent him a line.

16° s. 23° w   January 24   [Thomas Melville's 31st birthday]   *Captain Thomas Melville writes to his niece, Florence Melville:*
I left San Francisco on the 19th of November and reached Cape Horn after a very pleasant passage of fourty five days. We saw the land on the morning of the 3th of January, & in a few hours had passed Cape Horn and where in the South Atlantic.

ALBANY   February 2   *Peter Gansevoort's diary:*
My Nephew Herman Melville came from Pittsfield to day to make us a visit —

February 3   Sue Mrs [Maria] Melville, Herman Melville & Kate at church AM

Catherine Gansevoort's diary:
Cold day — All went to the N.D. church in the morning after service walked over to the New Cathedral St Josephs . . .

February 5   Aunt Melville & Cousin Herman left for Gansevoort in the 4:30 Train.

February 11   *Peter Gansevoort's diary:*
Herman Melville returned from Gansevoort — Dined with the family, & at 4³⁰ left for Pittsfield

BUFFALO   February 13   *Richard Melville Hair, Toby's nephew, thanks M for the "really nice and appropriate present" which had been forwarded to his present residence.*

PITTSFIELD   February 16   [Malcolm's twelfth birthday]   *Elizabeth Melville receives $90, "semi-annual interest on trust fund accruing to Feby 4th 1860 [?] —"*

NEW YORK   February 18   *Allan Melville writes to Lemuel Shaw & to George Griggs, respecting a consulship at Florence for M.*

BOSTON   February 20   *George Griggs replies to Allan Melville's inquiry:*
. . . I have made some inquiries about the consulship at Florence and I learn it is worth only about $500 per year.

Perhaps if that is the fact it will not be desirous to make any great effort to secure it for Herman. What think you.

I have not yet seen Judge Shaw. He is now unwell and I feel disinclined to call on him to make exertions for what may not be worth the trouble it would occasion him

Would not a knowledge of the French and Italian languages be essential to our consul?

Lemuel Shaw replies to Allan Melville:

I am as deeply impressed as you possibly can be of the necessity of Herman's getting away from Pitts. He is there solitary, without society, without exercise or occupation except that which is very likely to be injurious to him in over-straining his mind. I therefore have hoped that some situation may be found for him, where he has easy employment and moderate exercise of mind & body, and give him an opportunity to associate habitually with others.

But even with all this earnest desire for his removal, I could not have consented to co-operate in procuring his appointment to an office at the Sandwich Islands, especially without his own consent and desire . . .

But if Herman can get the appointment of Consul at Florence, I think it would be extremely beneficial to him. I suppose he does not understand the language of Italy; but as the business is small there, I should think he might engage a clerk . . . I think he would be able to perform the duties of the office satisfactorily.

. . . I will do anything in my power to promote this appointment . . .

I have been very ill, and quite confined to my room, all winter, though my physicians inform me that I am convalescent . . .

. . . I hope you will not fail to take some measures, if the consulship cant be obtained, to get an office in the N.Y. Custom House. I should hope that he could do the moderate daily labor required there, & thus be enabled to live in N.Y. & remove him from Pittsfield.

WASHINGTON February 28 *Alexander Rice, Representative from Boston, writes a recommendation of M for the Consulship at Florence.*

PITTSFIELD Early March *M writes to his mother. (her letter to Catherine Gansevoort, Mar 12)*

NEW YORK March 11 *John C. Hoadley writes to Charles Sumner, requesting his influence in support of M's appointment:*
His appointment, as a literary man, would be thought a graceful act by men of all classes and parties, and would add to the popularity and support of the Administration.

GANSEVOORT March 12 *Maria Melville writes to Catherine Gansevoort:*
The enclosed part of a letter from Herman & the printed paper you will please give to your Father for his amusement & when you write please send it back to me.

PITTSFIELD March 14 *A group of Pittsfield citizens (Julius Rockwell, James D. Colt, P. L. Page, E. H. Kellogg, Robert Campbell, William Pollock, J. D. Adamson, & Thomas Pomeroy) sign a recommendation to President Lincoln for M's appointment.*

March 15 *M writes to his uncle, Peter Gansevoort:*
It has been suggested to me that I might procure some foreign ap-

pointment under the new Administration — the consulship at Florence, for example. In many respects such an appointment would be desirable for me, altho' the emoluments are not very considerable. At all events, it is my purpose to apply . . . early next week (perhaps on Monday) I shall leave here for New York, and have thought it advisable to take Albany on my way, for the purpose of seeing & consulting with you, touching my design.

ALBANY   March 18   *Peter Gansevoort's diary:*
We had a pleasant Dinner, returned at 6 P.M. & found Herman Melville at the House —

March 19   Herman staid with us last night & left at 10.³⁰ A.M. for New York by Hudson R. Road —

LAWRENCE   March 19   *Organized by John C. Hoadley, a group of prominent Lawrence citizens write to President Lincoln, recommending M for the Florence appointment.*

NEW YORK   Before March 20?   *Alexander W. Bradford writes to the President, recommending M:*
I have known him from his youth, and believe him competent to oc-cupy any post . . . He is a gentleman of accomplished mind, excellent character and pure purpose.
& joins other signers (E. P. Hurlburt, Samuel Blatchford, R. M. Blatch-ford, John A. Dix ["in case a new appointment is to be made"], George F. M. Davis & David Dudley Field) in a letter to President Lincoln:
We believe that Mr. Melville is not only highly competent to fill the Station referred to, but that he is a patriot, & a gentleman of fine attain-ments, & would do honor to his country abroad.

March 20   *M writes to Richard Henry Dana, Jr:*
I am persuaded, from all I hear, that if Senator Sumner could be earnestly enlisted in the cause, I should, in all likelihood, succeed. May I therefore ask your good services in that quarter? I should be greatly obliged to you for a strong letter from yourself, and for procuring for me other strong letters from suitable persons in Boston.

M writes to Thurlow Weed:
I have thought that you might remember me sufficiently to justify my asking your friendly aid. — I desire to obtain the appointment of Consul at Florence.
I have taken steps to secure strong letters to Senator Sumner of Massachusetts — the state of my present residence. But, above all, an earnest letter from yourself to Gov. Seward would further my design.
I am aware, of course, that in your position you must be harassed by similar applications, but yet I am not without hope of your assistance.

& encloses this in a letter to Peter Gansevoort:

Upon inquiring for Mr Weed at the Astor this morning, I find the bird flown back to its perch — Albany.

. . . may I ask you to write him a note, enclosing mine? I think you can thus greatly aid me. *But it ought to be done immediately.*

Richard Henry Dana, Jr writes to Charles Sumner:

In my tour around the world, I made some observations on our foreign posts, — which, in a patriotic spirit, I offer to the Chairman, with reference to appointments.

Aspinwall. If you have a friend you wish to kill, send him to A. as Consul.

Sandwich Islands, Commissioner to. A post with handsome salary, no duties, few expenses, delightful climate & good society. Good post for a man of letters, who does not need a library for consultation; or any man who wishes repose, with some profit.

PITTSFIELD March 20   *Sarah Morewood writes to George Duyckinck:* You ask me what is said about Dr. Holme's story [*The Professor's Story (Elsie Venner)*]. *Much,* and that not of the best natured say either — You knew of course many of the localities he meant and Characters too — did you not? It is certain that he has not cared about a strife of winds — for he has created a Storm in many quarters.

BOSTON March 20?   *Lemuel Shaw writes to Stanwix Melville.* (Not more than ten days before his death he wrote Stanwix Melville a beautiful letter full of affection & good advice. Stanwix said he would "always keep Grandpa's Shaws letter, was it not good Grandma to write such a little boy as I am." — *Maria Melville to Catherine Gansevoort, Apr 18*)

NEW YORK March 21   I leave here for Washington tomorrow, and letters will reach me there any time for the next eight or ten days. — *M to R. H. Dana, Jr, Mar 20*

BOSTON March 21   *George Griggs sends a letter introducing M to Charles Sumner:*

I am not quite certain whether you are acquainted with my brother-in-law Herman Melville Esq who will hand this note to you . . .

He is desirous of serving the country, whose literature he has helped to make, in the capacity of consul at Florence, and to diversify the labors of authorship, with those of the consulate.

I know you will be happy to recognize in him, the claims of "the men [of] thought" though I fear you are almost oppressed by the claims of "Men of Action."

Lemuel Shaw writes two letters to Charles Sumner — an official one:

He has suffered somewhat in his health, as his friends believe, by devotion to study, and a life of extreme solitude, and they fully believe, that with the improvement to be derived from a mild climate, a more free social intercourse with artists and men of letters and refinement, he would be able to perform the duties of American Consul at Florence, with great credit to his country.

& a personal one:

I had expected a letter from Rich. H. Dana Jun. Esq. knowing that he & Mr. Melville had been authors of kindred subjects, and believing that they were in fact much acquainted with each other.

But I now learn that Mr. Dana [refuses] under existing circumstances, to volunteer a recommendation to office in favor of any body; but if inquired of will give you all the information in his power. If Sir, you would take the trouble to drop him a line of inquiry, I have no doubt, that you would obtain intelligence favorable to the object Mr. Melville has in view.

Dana writes to M, & to Charles Sumner:

I have told Melville that my rule prevents my giving him a letter or paper; but does not prevent my naming him favorably in my regular correspondence, & that I should do in my letters to you.

I like the notion of such consulships going to men of letters, — of note in the Republic of letters; & Melville is a capital good fellow, good manners & feelings. Duty requires me to suggest a doubt whether his health is sufficient. Of that I know nothing, & you can judge, on seeing him.

WASHINGTON March 22   *M writes to Elizabeth* (I wrote you the other day from here . . . — *M to Elizabeth, Mar 24*), *visits the Senate* (I have attended the Senate twice . . . — *same letter*), *& attends the second levee held by Lincoln at the White House:*

There was a great crowd, & a brilliant scene. Ladies in full dress by the hundred. A steady stream of two-&-twos wound thro' the apartments shaking hands with "Old Abe" and immediately passing on. This continued without cessation for an hour & a half. Of course I was one of the shakers. Old Abe is much better looking [than] I expected & younger looking. He shook hands like a good fellow — working hard at it like a man sawing wood at so much per cord. Mrs Lincoln is rather good-looking I thought. The scene was very fine altogether. Superb furniture — flood of light — magnificent flowers — full band of music &c.

ALBANY March 23   *Peter Gansevoort writes to M, telling him that Weed has returned to Washington:*

He will no doubt, advise you friendly as to your prospects & if the Post at Florence is engaged, suggest some other position —

WASHINGTON March 23   I called last night at Senator's Sumner's, but he was at a dinner somewhere. I shall call again tomorrow After leaving

Sumner's I went with Dr. Nourse to a little sort of party given by the wife of a man connected with one of the Departments. Had quite a pleasant evening. Several Senators were there with wives, daughters &c. The Vice President also & wife. Mrs. Hamlin is in appearance something like you — so she struck me at least. I need not add that she was very pleasing in her manner. — *M to Elizabeth, Mar 24*

March 24   *M writes to Elizabeth:*
    In the first place I must say that as yet I have been able to accomplish nothing in the matter of the counsulship — have not in fact been able as yet so much as even to *see* any one on the subject . . .
    This morning I spent in the park opposite the White House, sunning myself on a seat. The grass is bright & beautiful, & the shrubbery beginning to bud. It is just cool enough to make an overcoat comfortable sitting out of doors. The wind is high however, & except in the parks, all is dust. I am boarding in a plain home — plain fare plain people — in fact all plain but the road to Florence. But if nothing else comes of it, I will at least derive good from the trip at this season. Though, to tell the truth, I feel home-sick at times, strange as it may seem. How long I shall remain is uncertain. I am expecting letters every day, & can do little or nothing till they arrive.
    This afternoon I visited the Washington Monument. Huge tower some 160 feet high of white marble. Could not get inside. Nothing been done to it for long time.

March 25   *M writes a post-script before mailing his letter to Elizabeth:*
Dearest Lizzie: Feel rather overdone this morning — overwalked yesterday. But the trip will do me good. Kisses to the children. Hope to get a letter from you today.

Thine, My Dearest Lizzie,

Herman

PITTSFIELD   March 25   *Julius Rockwell writes to Charles Sumner:*
    Give me credit to say I have not troubled you before for your love & patronage. But my neighbor & friend *Herman* Melvill, author of Omoo — Typee — and many, many, other things which are "joys forever," does want an office. I trust he may have a Consulship. I hope you will aid him in it. Let his genius — his imperfect health — his "res augusti domi" — his noble wife, and his four children — plead, with trumpet tongues for him: and add to them my poor, but earnest, persistent will & wishes. I cannot say more — I will not say less; and if it can be of any use, please say to the President as much as you can in my name, which I trust he may remember with some kindness.

March 27   [?] *Elizabeth writes to M, informing him of her father's illness.*

WASHINGTON   March 28   *M sees Charles Sumner, & writes to him:*

A letter received since my seeing you this morning necessitates my leaving town early tomorrow; and I fear I shall not be able to return verry soon.

I have tried to find you this afternoon and evening without success, and learn that you will not be at your rooms again untill it is too late for me to renew my call.

Permit me to thank you very much for your friendliness, and to hope that you may yet efficaciously exert it in my behalf.

I desire to be considered as an applicant for the consulship at Glasgow.

My affair has thus far been pretty much entirely in your hands, and with you I must now leave it.

PITTSFIELD   March 29   *M returns home.* (Herman returned from Washington, & found Lizzie ready to leave home, she had an hour before got a telegram desiring her to come on — that her father was very ill. She found him dead. — *Maria Melville to Catherine Gansevoort, Apr 18*)

WASHINGTON   After March 29   *Charles Sumner submits M's papers to the State Department, with a memorandum:*

Consul Geneva Glasgow, etc; Papers of Herman Melville; for a Consulship — Geneva — Manchester — I recommend him most cordially.

BOSTON   March 30   *Hope Shaw's journal:*

Mr. Shaw had a bad night. About 12 he rode through the city, came home and took some refreshments such as wine and water. He laid down and appeared very restless. His mind was continually talking about bondages, corporations, and business of all kinds . . . He did not suffer in appearance but his voice I hardly could understand. When I returned from calling Lemuel I found him just rising to sit in his chair. I led him to his chair. He appeared to breathe better, — not one word did he say, but expired Saturday morning about thirty minutes before eight o'clock.

April 3   [?]   *With Elizabeth, M attends Lemuel Shaw's funeral at the New South meeting-house.*

His funeral, notwithstanding a violent snow-storm that obstructed many of the railroads, was largely attended . . . The preacher took for his funeral sermon this text, "A just man and one that feared God." (Chase, *Lemuel Shaw*)

April 8   *Lemuel Shaw's will is probated.*

CHICAGO   April 8   *Richard Tobias Greene acknowledges M's gift to his son:*

In the name of your namesake I thank you sincerely for this pledge of kind remembrance, and hope that the kind feelings which exist between us may never be darkened by a shadow. My mind often reverts to the many pleasant moonlight watches we passed together on the deck of the "Acushnet" as we whiled away the hours with yarn and song till "eight bells"

PITTSFIELD   April 9   *M acquires* The Poetical Works of Shelley (*2 vols, Boston, 1857*) *in which he scores in the Preface to* The Revolt of Islam (*1817*):
Our works of fiction and poetry have been overshadowed by the same infectious gloom. But mankind appear to me to be emerging from their trance. I am aware, methinks, of a slow, gradual, silent change.
M's comment (with irony?): How Prophetic
& on p 389 of Vol II (in Julian and Maddalo), *M double-scores:*
> Me, who am as a nerve o'er which do creep
> The else-unfelt oppressions of this earth . . .

M acquires The Poetical Works of Edmund Spenser (*5 vols, Boston, 1855*), *& checks & underscores this passage in* The Faerie Queene, *Book I, Canto VI:*
> Most senceless man he, that himselfe doth hate
> To love another . . .

CHARLESTON   April 12   *At 4.30 A.M. fire is opened upon Fort Sumter from Fort Moultrie.*

WASHINGTON   April 15
The President of the United States called by proclamation for 75,000 volunteers to suppress insurrectionary combinations; and commanded "the persons composing the combinations aforesaid to disperse and retire peaceably to their respective abodes within twenty days." (*The Rebellion Record,* Vol. I.)

NORFOLK   April 20   *At Gosport Navy Yard, the frigate* United States *is destroyed with other Federal ships, to prevent them from falling into Confederate hands.*

PITTSFIELD   May 22   [Bessie's eighth birthday]   I will now tell you about Aunt Fanny's Lucy's and my visit to Pittsfield. I saw papa on the platform when I was in the cars, he had the great waggon to carry us to the house. I was very glad to see Bessie, and Fannie, but very sorry not to see Mamma, and Mackey. — *Stanwix Melville to Hope Shaw, July 11*

May 23   The next day papa went to Boston. — *Stanwix Melville to Hope Shaw, July 11*

BOSTON   June 3   . . . said Benjamin R. Curtis prays that he may be permitted to resign said trust, and . . . the said Herman and Elizabeth S. Melville have requested the subscribers Lemuel Shaw and Samuel S. Shaw, to act as trustees under said indenture . . . (*request to the Probate Court*)

PITTSFIELD June 10 Papa took me to the cattle show grounds to see the soldiers drill, but we did not see them, because one of the factories [the Pittsfield Woolen Company] was on fire, it was too bad.

But papa took me a ride all through the Cemetery. — *Stanwix Melville to Hope Shaw, July 11*

June   *M presents to his sister, Augusta:* The Bijou; or Annual of Literature and the Arts (*London, 1828*) [*noted in it: Originally Priscilla's*]

M's name reappears on the Militia Roll.

NEW YORK June 28 *Allan Melville invites Evert Duyckinck to spend the day with him at the estate of Richard Lathers:*

July 1 *Evert Duyckinck's diary:*
To the Navy Yard with Hermann Melville. Visited the Savannah, the Iroquois, fresh from the Mediterranean and Garibaldi. Lt Buckner of the former delivered a brief lecture on his Dahlgren gun. On the quarter deck of the [receiving?] ship the North Carolina, the body of Capt [James H.] Ward was lying, with lighted candles at the feet and head, brought from his vessel the Freeborn in the Potomac where he was slain at his gun by a *secessionist's* shot from Matthias Point. Who shall fathom the iniquity of this rebellion?

July 3 *M acquires* The Poetical Works of James Thomson (*Boston, 1854*), *in which he scores, on p lxv of Vol I:*
Blessed is he who expecteth nothing, for he shall never be disappointed.

NEW ROCHELLE July 3 *Evert Duyckinck's diary:*
With Herman & Allan Melville and George [Duyckinck] to Mr Lathers at New Rochelle. Siddons in the cars — joined us for the day at Mr L's. A hospitable open handed entertainment — the beauty of nature, the tranquillity of the landscape stretching to the blue waters of the sound reflecting the azure of the skies a happy relief to the war agitations of the times.

The comet in the evening — a brilliant apparition in the north near the head of the Great Bear which first made its appearance in the heavens a few nights since.

I passed Wednesday very pleasantly with my brother and Herman and Allan Melville. We went out by invitation to pass the day with Mr Lathers at his place at New Rochelle . . .

We had a stroll through the woods . . . a rest on the rocks, a glass of blackberry wine . . . a long talk on the piazza looking out on the Sound — a fine dinner. It was an effort to resist the hospitable invitation to stay all night and tear ourselves away a little after six . . . for the last train to the city. — *George Duyckinck to Mrs Edward Baker, July 5*

July 6   *M subscribes for a year to* Harpers Weekly.

PITTSFIELD Before July 11   *M writes to his sister, Augusta.* (Aunt Augusta had a letter from papa, and he sent me a stamp with Benjamin Franklin head on it . . . I was very glad to hear the Papa, and Mama are coming in the buggy to Gansevoort, I hope they will find some way to bring Mackey along. — *Stanwix Melville to Hope Shaw, July 11;* We are expecting a visit from Herman & Lizzie very soon. Helen has promised to stay with the children. — *Augusta Melville's postscript to same letter*)

ALBANY July 12?   *M stops in Albany on the way to Gansevoort [or writes to Catherine Gansevoort].* (Last eve. I took tea at Uncle G[errit] Y[ates] L[ansing]. Bessie Roger's & I had a very pleasant time . . . Herman M. wishes to be most kindly remembered & hopes you are *sound* on Affairs of the country. — *Catherine Gansevoort to her brother, Henry, July 13*)

PITTSFIELD July ?   *The Valuation Book for Pittsfield's taxpayers is completed:*
>   Melville Herman & wife
>   [Value of cash assets] 600 doubtfull

GANSEVOORT Early August   Lizzie and I have been making a visit here for a few days . . .
   I am glad to say, that Uncle Herman [Gansevoort], although feeble, and almost entirely confined to his sofa during the day, is yet, for the most part, free from pain, has a pretty good appetite, and sleeps well. — *M to Peter Gansevoort, Aug 10*

August 10   *M writes to Peter Gansevoort, asking to see the Gansevoorts between trains on August 14.*

ALBANY August 12   *Peter Gansevoort replies to M's letter, inviting him & Elizabeth to stay for a while at Albany.*

August 14   *M & Elizabeth pass through Albany, but miss seeing Peter Gansevoort.* (*M to Peter Gansevoort, Aug 15*)

While waiting in Albany, M buys, at the shop of B. E. Gray, The Poetical Works of Alfred Tennyson (Boston, 1861) two volumes, in which he subsequently pastes a newspaper clipping about "The Charge of the Light Brigade"; M's comment:
>   Stuff by a swell man ☞

PITTSFIELD August 15   *M writes to Peter Gansevoort:*
I hope, My Dear Uncle, that you will find good weather, good company, and good wine, where you are. Tell Aunt Susan & Kitty that I wish them a continuation of clear cheeks and sparkling eyes, & that the best way to

insure it, is to roll night and morning in the surf at Rockaway. Owing to this sort of exercise, the porpoises, they say, have very fine skin, & enjoy admirable health.

August 19   *M drives into town to pay his Town, County & State Tax for 1861: a total of $20.89 (less $1.04 discount).*

GANSEVOORT   September 5   *Stanwix Melville writes to Peter Gansevoort:*
I think the reason that Aunt Susan did not answere my letter was that I wrote it so badly. I could have written a better letter, and now I write this one to you to show you that I can . . .

ALBANY   September 17   *Catherine Gansevoort writes to her brother, Henry, that Augusta Melville is "fixing a collection of [family] Photographs to send to Tom Melville."*

PITTSFIELD   September 26   *M drives into town to pay his Town, County & State Tax for 1860: a total of $19.80.*

September ?   *For his brother Tom's collection of family photographs M has a new portrait made at Rodney Dewey's studio on North Street. [See Pl. XIII]*

NEW BEDFORD   November 15   *Fifteen old whalers, loaded with stones, sail from New Bedford, to be sunk in the channels of the harbors of Charleston & Savannah, to prevent blockade running:*
The terrible stone fleet, on a mission as pitiless as the granite that freights it, sailed this morning from the harbor of Port Royal, and before two days are past will have made Charleston an inland city . . .
Sixteen vessels will be sunk on the bar at the river entrance . . . all old whalers . . . and cost the Government from two thousand five hundred dollars to five thousand dollars each. (Correspondence, *New-York Tribune*, reprinted in *The Rebellion Record*, Vol. III)

PITTSFIELD   December 12   *Mrs Sarah Morewood writes to George Duyckinck:*
I had hoped to visit New York before this — but I have had so many things to do for the Children to make them comfortable for the winter — and I wanted to stay at home till after the Melvilles left us — but now that all that is over — I am ill in bed . . .

An item in the Berkshire County Eagle:
Hermann Melville, Esq., has left town for the winter, which he is to spend in New York and Boston.

GANSEVOORT   Before December 23   *M & his daughter Bessie are at Gansevoort. (Peter Gansevoort's diary)*

ALBANY   December 23   *Peter Gansevoort's diary:*

Herman Melville, with his daughter Bessie (8 yrs of age) & Fanny Melville came this morning from Gansevoort — dined & remained until 8 P.M. when they went to Stanwix Hall, to lodge & proceed to Boston at an early hour tomorrow morning.

GANSEVOORT December 26 *Augusta Melville writes to Peter Gansevoort:*

Through Herman & Fanny you have the latest news of the farm's members of our family, & sympathize with us, I know, in the prospect of Tom's return home.

. . . . .

M receives, from his uncle, John D'Wolf, a narrative: A Voyage to the North Pacific and a Journey through Siberia more than half a century ago, *by Captain John D'Wolf (Cambridge, 1861).*

*

1 8 6 2

*

PITTSFIELD Early January *Capt Thomas Melville returns by the overland route after selling the* Meteor *at Calcutta.*

LAWRENCE Early January? *M visits his sister & brother-in-law, the Hoadleys.* (Tom & Herman & Helen have been to see them & they have passed a day [in Boston] with Mrs Shaw & Lizzie. — *Maria Melville to Catherine Gansevoort, Jan 6*)

GANSEVOORT January 6 *Maria Melville writes to Catherine Gansevoort:*

I looked at the Diagrams for army socks & army mittens, & if you do not want me to return them, shall like to keep them.

Fannie being away this winter Augusta & myself have much to attend to. However much disposed to knit for our good Soldiers, I cannot promise to do so this winter.

BOSTON January 18 *Samuel Shaw's diary:*
My sister [Elizabeth Melville] left for N.York

NEW YORK Late January *M is ill at their temporary New York residence at 150 East 18 Street.* (For the past week I have been lying here rheumatism-bound, or I should have been to see you to tell you where we are to be found. — *M to Evert Duyckinck, Feb 1*)

February 1 *M asks a favor of Evert Duyckinck:*

[*644*]

I want you to loan me some of those volumes of the Elizabethan drama-tists. Is Deckar among the set? And Webster? If so, please wrap them up and let the bearer have them. — Send me any except Marlowe, whom I have read.

Mrs. Melville and I will be glad to see you & your brother any evening.

February 2 [?] *Evert Duyckinck visits the Melvilles.* (If you have nothing better to do, come round tomorrow (Sunday) evening, and we will brew some whiskey punch and settle the affairs of the universe over it — which affairs sadly need it, some say. — *M to Evert Duyckinck, Feb 1*)

February 14 *M acquires* The Poetical Works of Thomas Hood (*2 vols, Boston, 1860*), *in which he subsequently scores & underscores this passage in R. M. Milnes' "Memoir of the Author":*
. . . the full extent of that poetical vigour which seemed to advance just in proportion as his physical health declined.

In Volume II, M scores "The Poet's Fate":
What is a modern poet's fate?
To write his thoughts upon a slate; —
The Critic spits on what is done, —
Gives it a wipe, — and all is gone.

February 15 *M acquires* The Poetical Works of Thomas Moore (*6 vols, Boston, 1856*), *in which he scores, in the Preface to "Lalla Rookh":*
. . . I have been, at all times, a far more slow and pains-taking workman than would ever be guessed, I fear, from the result, I felt that, in this instance, I had taken upon myself a more than ordinary responsibility, from the immense stake risked by others on my chance of success.

M acquires Poems of James Clarence Mangan (*New York, 1859*), *in which he scores & checks many of Mangan's translations of German poems, & this passage in the introduction (p 8):*
He was a rebel politically, and a rebel intellectually and spiritually, — a rebel with his whole heart and soul against the whole British spirit of the age. The consequence was sure, and not unexpected. Hardly anybody in England knew the name of such a person . . .

February 17 *M acquires* The Works of Robert Fergusson, *edited . . . by A. B. G[rosart] (London, 1857), in which he scores, in Grosart's "Memoir":*
Go, — moralist, light of heart and jovial in intercourse, living at ease, quiet and happy, writing as a recreation in thy study, surrounded with all the deli-cacies, and comforts, and securities of life, on thy gilt-edged, prim-folded sheet, — shut up the kingly eagle in the stancheoned cage of thy court-yard, and bid him 'fly,' *because* his native hills are before him.

February 26 *M pays $5 for* The Works of Isaac Disraeli (*7 vols, Lon-*

don, *1860*), *in which he subsequently reads & marks; in* Curiosities of Literature, *Volume I, M scores & underscores in the chapter on "In-equalities of Genius":*
Faultless mediocrity industry can preserve in one continued degree; but excellence, the daring and the happy, can only be attained, by human faculties, by starts.

& in "Poets" M scores:
[Baron Haller's] house was on fire, and to rescue his poems he rushed through the flames. He was so fortunate as to escape with his beloved manuscripts in his hand. Ten years afterwards he condemned to the flames those very poems he had ventured his life to preserve.

In Vol II, M scores:

VERSES,

Made by Chediock Ticheborne of himselfe in the Tower, the night before he suffered death, who was executed in Lincoln's Inn Fields for treason. 1586.

My prime of youth is but a frost of cares,
My feast of joy is but a dish of pain,
My crop of corn is but a field of tares,
And all my goodes is but vain hope of gain.
The day is fled, and yet I saw no sun,
And now I live, and now my life is done!

My spring is past, and yet it hath not sprung,
The fruit is dead, and yet the leaves are green,
My youth is past, and yet I am but young,
I saw the world, and yet I was not seen;
My thread is cut, and yet it is not spun,
And now I live, and now my life is done!

& M scores a passage removed from Milton's history:
"If there be found in an author's book one sentence of a venturous edge, uttered in the height of zeal, and who knows whether it might not be the dictate of a divine spirit, yet not suiting every low decrepit humour of their own, they will not pardon him the dash."

In The Literary Character; or the History of Men of Genius, *M scores in Chapter X:*
. . . time alone opens discoveries and kindles meditation. This desert of solitude, so vast and so dreary to the man of the world, to the man of genius is the magical garden of Armida, whose enchantments arose amidst solitude, while solitude was everywhere among those enchantments.

& a footnote in Chapter XVI, quoting a letter from Hume to Adam Smith, July 28, 1759:
"This is the first previous agreement ever I made with a bookseller. I shall execute the work at leisure, without fatiguing myself by such ardent application as I have hitherto employed. It is chiefly as a resource against idleness that I shall undertake the work, for as to money I have enough; and as to reputation what I have wrote already will be sufficient, if it be good; if not, it is not likely I shall now write better."

& in Chapter XVII, M scores:
This abandonment of their life to their genius has, indeed, often cost them too dear, from the days of Sophocles, who, ardent in his old age, neglected his family affairs, and was brought before his judges by his relations, as one fallen into a second childhood.

NEW BEDFORD February *John Hoadley moves his family here, in order that he may assume charge of the Copper Rolling Mill.*

NEW YORK March 4 *M buys two volumes (50 cts per vol) of* Germany, *by Madame the Baroness de Staël-Holstein (New York, 1859), & reads in Volume I; in its front cover he comments:*
"It is not French" said Napoleon's Minister of Police, and suppressed this book. — There it is. The Minister said but the truth, &, from his point of view, the suppression was just. —
"You are modernising the laws and are dangerous to the young" said the judges to Socrates. They said the truth, & from their point of view, were just in condemning him. —
What then?
Why, as a self-constituted agent for the conservation of useful persuasions, — I suppress the inference.

On p 190 M triple-scores, checks & underscores:
. . . the effects of poetry depend still more on the melody of words than on the ideas which they serve to express.
M's comment: ✔ This is measurably true of all but dramatic poetry, and, perhaps, narrative verse.
On p 238 M scores:
The ancients, and the poets of the middle ages, were well acquainted with the kind of terror caused in certain circumstances by the repetition of the same words; it seems to awaken the sentiment of inflexible necessity.
On p 355 M scores & checks:
The morbid sensibility of Tasso is well known, as well as the polished rudeness of his protector Alphonso, who, professing the highest admiration for his writings, shut him up in a mad-house, as if that genius which springs from the soul were to be treated like the production of a mechanical talent, by valuing the work while we despise the workman.

March 17 *M acquires* The Poems of Heine, *in a translation by Edgar Alfred Bowring (London, 1861), & scores Heine's prefatory stanzas for* "Histories":

> When vex'd by slander's treacherous breath,
>   Let thy faith soar the higher;
> And when thy soul is sad unto death,
>   Then strike thou the lyre.
>
> A flaming and glowing heroical song
>   The chords breathe discreetly!

[647]

> All anger flies, and thy spirit ere long
> Will bleed to death sweetly.

GANSEVOORT March 18 *Maria Melville telegraphs to Peter Gansevoort:*
Brother Herman died this morning funeral tomorrow . . .
& follows the telegram with a letter:
I have telegraphed to New York, & expect Herman & Allan to night.

March 19 *Herman Gansevoort is buried; M is not present.* (Cousin
Herman is sick in New York & was unable to come up [for the fu-
neral] . . . — *Catherine Gansevoort to her brother, Henry, Mar 20)*

NEW YORK March 22 *M acquires two volumes by Ralph Waldo Emerson:* Essays: First Series (*Boston, 1847*), *&* Essays: Second Series (*Boston, 1844*). *In the* First Series *M marks in Essay IV, "Spiritual Laws,"
p 126:*
[Each man] inclines to do something which is easy to him, and good when it
is done, but which no other man can do. He has no rival. For the more truly
he consults his own powers, the more difference will his work exhibit from
the work of any other.
M's comment: True
His ambition is exactly proportioned to his powers.
M's comment: False
& on p 133:
The good, compared to the evil which he sees, is as his own good to his own
evil. **X**
M's comment: **X** A Perfectly good being, therefore, would see no evil. —
But what did Christ see? — He saw what made him weep. — However,
too, the "Philanthropist" must have been a very bad man — he saw, in
jails, so much evil.
M appends additional comment: * To annihilate all this nonsense read the
Sermon on the Mount, and consider what it implies.
In Essay VII, "Prudence," M marks on p 215:
Trust men, and they will be true to you; treat them greatly, and they will
show themselves great, though they make an exception in your favor to all
their rules of trade. **X**
M's comment: **X** God help the poor fellow who squares his life according to this.
& on p 216:
The drover, the sailor, buffets it [the storm] all day, and his health renews
itself as vigorous a pulse under the sleet, as under the sun of June. **X**
M's comment: **X** To one who has weathered Cape Horn as a common
sailor what stuff all this is.

In the Second Series (*mistakenly inscribed "March 22, 1861"*) *M marks
in Essay I, "The Poet," p 20:*
Also, we use defects and deformities to a sacred purpose, so expressing our
sense that the evils of the world are such only to the evil eye. **X**

M's comment: **X** What does the man mean? If Mr Emerson travelling in Egypt should find the plague-spot come out on him — would he consider that an evil sight or not? And if evil, would his eye be evil because it seemed evil to his eye, or rather to his sense using the eye for instrument?

& on p 24:
As the limestone of the continent consists of infinite masses of the shells of animalcules, so language is made up of images, or tropes, which now, in their secondary use, have long ceased to remind us of their poetic origin. But the poet names the thing because he sees it, or comes one step nearer to it than any other. **X**

M's comment: **X** This is admirable, as many other thoughts of Mr Emerson's are. His gross and astonishing errors & illusions spring from a self-conceit so intensely intellectual and calm that at first one hesitates to call it by its right name. Another species of Mr Emerson's errors, or rather, blindness, proceeds from a defect in the region of the heart.

& on p 30-31:
Hence a great number of such as were professionally expressors of Beauty, as painters, poets, musicians, and actors, have been more than others wont to lead a life of pleasure and indulgence; all but the few who received the true nectar; and, as it was an emancipation not into the heavens, but into the freedom of baser places, they were punished for that advantage they won, by a dissipation and deterioration.

M's comment: No, no, no. — Titian — did he deteriorate? — Byron? — Did he. — Mr E. is horribly narrow here. He has his Dardenelles for his every Marmora. — But he keeps nobly on, for all that!

March 31   *Harper & Bros. sends its 14th account to M:*
            Balance due Harper & Bros. $239.60

April 3   *M acquires* The Poetical Works and Remains of Henry Kirke White (*New York, 1857*) *in which he checks & underscores on p 387:*
Harmonious modulations, and <u>unvarying exactness of measure</u>, totally precluding sublimity and fire, have reduced our fashionable poetry to mere sing-song.

LAWRENCE   April 5   *Frances Priscilla Melville sends Catherine Gansevoort 10 photographs for her collection of American writers:*
   Holme's & Hawthorne's are fine likenesses. I have meet them both several times at Pittsfield when they have been at our house to see Herman. Mr Hawthorne once passed several days with us. (he was then living at Lenox)

NEW YORK   April 6   *M acquires* Poems, *by Matthew Arnold* (*Boston, 1856*); *in the Preface, he underscores a quotation from Hesiod:*
   ". . . <u>a forgetfulness of evils, and a truce from cares</u> . . ."
& disputes a quotation from Schiller on the Laocoon;

M's comment: The "Laocoön" is not dedicated to Joy, neither is "Hamlet." Yet there is a degree of truth in this, only it dont imply that the subjects of true art must be joyful subjects. — Schiller was at once helped & hurt by Goethe. This saying is a Schillerized Goethecism.

In "The Scholar-Gipsy," M scores:
> 'Tis that repeated shocks, again, again,
> Exhaust the energy of strongest souls
> And numb the elastic powers.

In "Morality," M scores:
> But tasks in hours of insight will'd
> Can be through hours of gloom fulfill'd.

M's comment: **X** not always

Before April 15   *M acquires* The Poetical Works of William Collins (*Boston, 1854*).

M acquires The Poetical Works of Charles Churchill (*Boston, 1854*); *in Volume II M scores this passage from "Gotham":*
> Little do such men know the toil, the pains,
> The daily, nightly, racking of the brains,
> To range the thoughts, the matter to digest,
> To cull fit phrases, and reject the rest . . .

In "The Author" M scores:
> When with much pains this boasted learning's got,
> 'Tis an affront to those who have it not:
> In some it causes hate, in others fear,
> Instructs our foes to rail, our friends to sneer.

April 15[?]   *M & Elizabeth leave for Gansevoort.* (You ask for Herman's address — Lizzie wrote a few days ago that they would leave New York for Gansevoort on the 15ᵗʰ (to-day) make a little visit there & early in May return to Pittsfield. — *Frances Priscilla Melville to Catherine Gansevoort, this date*)

LAWRENCE April 15   *Frances Priscilla Melville writes to Catherine Gansevoort:*
I wish you would write & ask him [M] for his photograph — he promises us that he would have it taken while in the city & I have reminded him of this promise very often this winter, but no card have I received as yet — I hope you will be more successful.

PITTSFIELD April 27   *M inserts an advertisement in the* Berkshire County Eagle:

WANTED.

A WOMAN to do the cooking and house-work in a small family, two miles and and a half from Pittsfield village. No dairy-work required. To a competent person the HIGHEST wages will be given.   H. MELVILLE.
[Appears in issues of May 1 & May 8.]

April *M reads the second volume of Madame de Staël's* Germany; *on pp 59-60 he underscores:*
It cannot be denied that there is in Goethe's book [*Elective Affinities*] a pro<u>found knowledge</u> of the human heart, but it is a <u>discouraging knowledge</u> . . .
M's comment: What inadvertence! And what an admission! — "Profound Knowledge" and "discouraging knowledge"
On p 60 he scores & underscores:
. . . the opinions of Goethe are much more profound, but they <u>do not present any greater consolation to the soul</u> . . . it must be agreed that, to think a great deal sometimes leads to the total unsettling of our fundamental ideas . . .
M's comment: **X** It is delightful as well as wonderful to see — passim — such penetration of understanding in a woman, who at the same time possesses so femininely emotional a nature. — Who would one compare Madame De Stael too? — Mrs. Browning? — Mrs B. was a great woman, but Madame De S. was a greater.
On p 71 he scores:
Bayle has somewhere said, that *atheism does not shelter us from the fear of eternal suffering; it is a grand thought, and it offers to us a wide field for reflection.*
M's comment: **X** If we assume that the existence of God makes eternal suffering possible, *then* it may justly be said that Atheism furnishes no defences against the fear of it.
On p 348 his comment for an underscored sentence has been erased:
A man, regarded in a religious light, is as much as the entire human race . . . **X**
M's erased comment: **X** This was an early and innate conviction of mine, suggested by my revulsion from the counting-room philosophy of Paley.

May 1 *Malcolm Melville returns to Pittsfield from Boston. (Samuel Shaw's diary)*

May 15 *M presents to his sister, Helen M. Griggs, his set of Spenser.*

May 19 *M presents to his sister, Frances Priscilla, his set of Cooke editions:* The Poetical Works of Shakspeare (*bound with* The Poetical Works of William Collins), The Poetical Works of Will. Shenstone, The Poetical Works of James Thomson.

May 21 *M drives into town to insert an advertisement in the* Berkshire County Eagle:
FARM FOR SALE.
THE FARM (With large dwelling-house) now occupied by subscriber, two and a half miles from Pittsfield village, on East road to Lenox, embracing about eighty acres, wood, pasture and meadow. H. MELVILLE.
[*Beginning in the issue of May 22, this runs through August 14.*]

May 25 *M writes to his brother Thomas (to the Ship "Bengal," Care, Augustine Heard & Co, Hong-Kong, China):*

My Dear Boy: (or, if that appears disrespectful)

My Dear Captain: Yesterday I received from Gansevoort your long and very entertaining letter to Mamma from Pernambuco. Yes, it was very entertaining. Particularly the account of that interesting young gentleman whom you so uncivilly stigmatise for a jackass, simply because he improves his opportunities in the way of sleeping, eating and other commendable customs. That's the sort of fellow, seems to me, to get along with. For my part I love sleepy fellows, and the more ignorant the better. Damn your wide-awake and knowing chaps. As for sleepiness, it is one of the noblest qualities of humanity. There is something sociable about it, too. Think of those sensible & sociable millions of good fellows all taking a good long friendly snoose together, under the sod — no quarrels, no imaginary troubles, no envies, heart-burnings, & thinking how much better that other chap is off — none of this: but all equally free-&-easy, they sleep away & reel off their nine knots an hour, in perfect amity. If you see your sleepy ignorant jackass-friend again give him my compliments, and say that however others may think of him, I honor and esteem him. — As for your treatment of those young ones, there I entirely commend you. Strap them, I beseech you. You remember what the Bible [Byron's *Don Juan*, Canto the Second] says: —

> "Oh ye who teach the children of the nations,
>   Holland, France, England, Germany or Spain,
> I pray ye *strap* them upon all occasions,
>   It mends their morals — never mind the pain"

In another place the Bible says, you know, something about spareing the strap & spoiling the child. — Since I have quoted poetry above, it puts me in mind of my own doggerel. You will be pleased to learn that I have disposed of a lot of it at a great bargain. In fact, a trunk-maker took the whole stock off my hands at ten cents the pound. So, when you buy a new trunk again, just peep at the lining & perhaps you may be rewarded by some glorious stanza staring you in the face & claiming admiration. If you were not such a devil of a ways off, I would send you a trunk, by way of presentation-copy . . . Do you want to hear about the war? — The war goes bravely on. McClellan is now within fifteen miles of the rebel capital, Richmond. New Orleans is taken &c &c &c . . . But when the *end* — the wind-up — the grand pacification is coming, who knows. We beat the rascals in almost every field, & take all their ports &c, but they dont cry "Enough!" — It looks like a long lane, with the turning quite out of sight. — Guert [Gansevoort] has recently been appointed to the command of a fine new sloop of war [the *Roanoke*]. I am rejoiced to hear it. It will do him good in more ways than one. He is brave as a lion, a good seaman, a natural-born officer, & I hope he will yet turn out the hero of a brilliant victory . . . of late Lizzie has not been very well, tho' she is now getting better. The children are all well. Macky is studying Latin — "Hic — haec — hoc" — "horum, horum, horum," he goes it every night.

June   *M's name is included on the Militia Roll.*

Summer?   [?] *In his house-cleaning of Arrowhead's manuscripts, M copies out the poems he wants to keep & has a prose & poetry bonfire.*

[IMMOLATED.

Children of my Tempe prime,
When One yet lived with me, and threw
Her rainbow over life and time,
Even Hope, my bride, and dame to you;
O, nurtured in sweet pastoral air,
And fed on flowers and light, and dew
Of meads Auroral — spare, Ah, spare
Reproach; spare, and upbraid me not
That, yielding scarce to reckless mood
But jealous of your future lot,
I sealed you in a fate subdued.
Have I not saved you from the drear
Theft and ignoring which need be
The triumph of the insincere
Elect of Mediocrity?
Rest therefore, free from all despite,
Snugged in the arms of comfortable night.]

August 6   *The Valuation Book for Pittsfield is completed:*
Melville Herman & Wife

Money			1500
10 Sh[are]s Boston Fire & Mar[ine] Ins Co		@180.	1,800
10 " Eastern R[ail]Road		@ 40.85	408
5 " New England B[an]k		@ 92.60	463
5 " Washington B[an]k		@100	500
21 " Am[erican] Ins Company		@160.83	3,377
1 Horse			50
3 Carriages			150
[Aggregate of each Person's Ratable Personal Estate]			8,248

[Tax] 44.87

1 Dwelling	600	
1 Barn	200	
House lot 80 acres	3,200	
[Aggregate Value of Real Estate]	4,000	

[Tax on Real Estate]   21.76

[Total]   68.63

ALBANY August 8   *Peter Gansevoort writes to M, notifying him of the death of M's uncle, Wessel Gansevoort, in Danbury, Vermont, on Aug 7.*

PITTSFIELD August 20   *M drives into town to pay his Town, County & State Tax for 1862: $68.63 (less $3.43 discount).*

August 23   *Samuel Shaw arrives from Boston.* (*his diary*)

CARIBBEAN   August 23
. . . on or about the twenty-third day of August . . . the said Captain Guert
Gansevoort, being then in command of the United States steamer, Adirondack,
did, through negligence, suffer the said vessel to be run upon a rock and
wrecked near Man of War Key, Little Bahamas . . . — *specification in the
court martial of Guert Gansevoort, Oct 15*

PITTSFIELD   August 25   *Samuel Shaw's diary:*
Set out with Herman on an Excursion to the mountains. Passed the night
in an old house near Saddle Ball in Cheshire.

August 26   [Frances Priscilla Melville's 35th birthday]   Descended to
Cheshire where we left the horse, lame, and came by rail to Pittsfield —
Hot Day.

September 1   Returned to Boston by the evening train.

ALBANY   September 4   *Peter Gansevoort's diary:*
Herman Melville arrived in the Evg, 5 & after tea took the Boat for New
York.

BOSTON   September 22   *A first & final accounting of Lemuel Shaw's
estate is submitted, these amounts having been paid:*
        [in Item 3] Trustees to Mrs. E. S. Melville   3000.00
        ["   "   6] Mrs. E. S. Melville [approx. ¼]   789.75
        ["   "   8] Mrs. E. S. Melville [approx. ¼]   49.53

NEW YORK   September   *M acquires* The Works of M. de la Bruyère,
in two volumes (London, 1776), *in which he begins his comments on the
fly-leaf of Volume I:*
La Bruyere has never been reprinted in America, and not for many
years, in England. — Why?
On p 58, he scores:
   There are few men so accomplished, or so necessary, but have some failings
or other which will make their friends bear the loss of them with the greater
patience.
M's comment: **X** True, Shakespeare goes further: None die but somebody spurns them into the grave. [*Timon of Athens*, I:2]
On p 182, he scores:
There is nothing at Court so contemptible as a man who can contribute noth-
ing to our fortunes; I wonder such a person dares appear there.
M's comment: **X** What can be finer than the way of saying this.
On p 206, he scores:
He, who in good time, firmly renounces a great name, a great authority, or a
great fortune, delivers himself at once from a host of troubles, from many
restless nights, and, what is still better, from many crimes.
On p 270, he scores & underscores:

Nothing helps a Man more to bear quietly the injuries he receives from parents and friends than a reflection of the vices of humanity.

October 15   *A court martial convenes to try the case of Capt. Guert Gansevoort.*

October 25   *M acquires Volume II of* The Poetical Works of Thomas Moore (*Boston, 1854*).

BOSTON November 1   *M's aunt, Priscilla Melvill, dies at the age of 78 [80?]; her will leaves $900 to M.*

PITTSFIELD Early November?   *The Melvilles move from Arrowhead into the town of Pittsfield.*
(Melville, however, did not leave the place until November, and then not for New York but for the square old-fashioned house on South street in the rear of Backus block. [Smith, *Biographical Sketch*])

November 7
   On Friday forenoon last, as Mr. Herman Melvill, accompanied by Mr. J. E. A. Smith, was riding, in his box wagon, from his house in the village to his farm house, from which he had recently removed, a portion of the iron work of the wagon gave way, letting down the thills about the heels of the horse. The animal, which is a young one, naturally took fright and ran, throwing Mr. Melvill violently to the ground, where he fell into the angle made by the rise of the bank from the road. Mr. M., we regret to say, was very seriously injured, having his shoulder blade broken and several ribs injured, and his whole system badly jarred.
   Mr. Smith was also thrown to the ground and, falling on his head, was stunned and considerably bruised, but not seriously injured.
   Fortunately Col. Geo. S. Willis, near whose farm [on Williams street] the accident occurred, happened to be at hand, and procuring assistance lifted Mr. M., who was in great pain, into his own carriage and conveyed him with the utmost kindness and care to his home, where he was attended by Drs. [O. S.] Root and [Frank A.] Cady. (*Berkshire County Eagle*, Nov 13)

   We cannot but think that an accident which befell him at this time had something to do with his removal [from Pittsfield]; and also with other changes in his life, which accompanied it. A few days after he removed from Arrowhead, he had occasion for some household articles he left behind, and, with a friend, started in a rude wagon to procure them. He was driving at a moderate pace over a perfectly smooth and level road, when a sudden start of the horse threw both occupants from the wagon; probably on account of an imperfectly secured seat. Mr. Melville fell with his back in a hollow of the frozen road, and was very seriously injured. (Smith, *Biographical Sketch*)

Before November 11   *Elizabeth Melville reports the accident in a letter to Catherine Gansevoort.* (I had a letter from Lizzie Melville stating that Herman had been thrown out of his wagon — and his shoulder dislocated besides being dreadfully bruised this occurred last Friday. — *Catherine Gansevoort to her brother, Henry, Nov 11*)

WASHINGTON November 12 *Secretary of Navy Gideon Welles issues a general order relative to the court's findings in the case of Capt. Guert Gansevoort; the specification is not proved & Capt. Gansevoort is not guilty of the charge.*

PITTSFIELD November 13 *M's accident is reported in the* Berkshire County Eagle:
Mr. Melvill, — his friends throughout the country will be pained to learn — still lies very ill, and, although his injuries are not dangerous, we fear they will lead to a somewhat prolonged confinement.

Mid-November I remember that some days after my mishap, when I was able to give the necessary attention, Lizzie read to me the letter you wrote her on that occasion. — *M to Samuel Shaw, Dec 10*

November-December
[M] suffered painfully for many weeks. This prolonged agony and the confinement and interruption of work which it entailed, affected him strangely. He had before been on mountain excursions a driver daring to the point of recklessness; but he always brought his ride to a safe conclusion, and his sometimes terrorized, passengers to a safe landing place. After this accident he not only abandoned the rides of which he had been so fond, but for a time shrank from entering a carriage. It was long before the shock which his system had received was overcome; and it is doubtful whether it ever was completely. (Smith, *Biographical Sketch*)

December 10 *M writes to Samuel Shaw:*
I can not help telling you how sensible I am of the kindness you showed, and write you this that you may have the ocular evidence of my recovery. To be sure, I still carry my arm (the left one, happily) in a sling, and the neuralgia gives me a love-pinch in the cheek now and then. But upon the whole I am now in a fair way of being completely restored to what I was before the accident. — This recovery is flattering to my vanity. I begin to indulge in the pleasing idea that my life must needs be of some value. Probably I consume a certain amount of oxygen, which unconsumed might create some subtle disturbance in Nature. Be that as it may, I am going to try to stick to the conviction named above. For I have observed that such an idea, once well bedded in a man, is a wonderful conservator of health and almost a prophecy of long life. I once, like other spoonies, cherished a loose sort of notion that I did not care to live very long. But I will frankly own that I have now no serious, no insuperable objections to a respectable longevity. I dont like the idea of being left out night after night in a cold church-yard. — In warm and genial countries, death is much less of a bugbear than in our frozen

latitudes. A native of Hindostan takes easily and kindly to his latter end. It is but a stepping round the corner to him. He knows he will sleep warm. ——

Pretty topics there (☠) for a friendly note, you say. (By the way, Death, in my skull, seems to tip a knowing sort of wink out of his left eye. What does that mean, I wonder?)

Lizzie is quite well, though a little jaded by her manifold cares, we not yet being quite in order yet. The children are flourishing as usual.

December 11? *Maria Melville arrives at the new South Street residence for a visit.* (Tomorrow we expect the gratification of a visit from my mother, whom we hope to be able to keep some time with us. — M to Samuel Shaw, Dec 10)

December 25 *M gives a Christmas present to his daughter, Bessie: The Poetical Works of Mrs. Felicia Hemans (Boston, 1859)*

*

1 8 6 3

*

DORCHESTER January 21 *John D'Wolf writes to Mrs Catherine G. Hoadley:*
. . . You are now desirous of having my cart-de visit for your Album and your kind Husband wishes to have one for a frontispiece to his Book, which I now have the pleasure to enclose to you . . . after all they found it difficult to make a Picture of me which entirely satisfies notwithstanding I tryed to look as spruce as I could for I must say I felt some little pride in this matter particularly as I am to become the frontispiece of that *Sublime Narrative,* but it was no go, they could not make the young man of me that performed that Voyage half a Century ago I was young then, full of Blood & blue veins, every trace of which you see time has obliterated . . .

NEW YORK Early February   Cousin Herman has been spending a few days in New York City. — *Col. Henry Gansevoort to his sister, Catherine, Feb 8.*

February 7   *Col. Gansevoort & M meet.* (I saw him yesterday. He seemed to be quite well. — *Col. Henry Gansevoort to his sister, Catherine, Feb 8*)

February 8?   *Sunday dinner at the Allan Melvilles' is attended by M & by Col. Gansevoort.* (. . . I . . . dined with him [Henry Gansevoort] at Allan's one Sunday. — *M to Catherine Gansevoort, Feb 17;* Herman made us a very pleasant visit. — *Jane Melville to Catherine Gansevoort, Feb 13[?]*)

GLENS FALLS February 13   *Katherine Curtis writes to her cousin, Catherine Gansevoort:*
We are enjoying at present, a visit from our dear Aunt Melville — What a wonderful woman she is — I think she is one of the most remarkable persons I ever knew — I look at her with wonder, and astonishment and can not realise, she is over *seventy* — How active she is; and youthful in her feelings — I must say; she is a splendid old lady —

FORT HAMILTON Before February 16   The other day, be it known unto you, Incomparable Kate, I went with Allan and his wife to Fort Hamilton, where we saw Lieutenant Henry Gansevoort of the U.S. Artillery. He politely led us to the ramparts, pointing out all objects of interest. He looked well and war-like, cheerfully embarked in the career of immortality. I saw him upon two other occasions . . . — *M to Catherine Gansevoort, Feb 17*

PITTSFIELD February 17   *M writes to Catherine Gansevoort:*
Upon returning from New York I was made happy by finding your note enclosing the pictures [of General Peter & Catherine Gansevoort]. The one of our grandmother is clear and admirable. But alas for the Hero of Fort Stanwix!
Photographically rendered, he seems under a sort of eclipse, emblematic perhaps of the gloom which his spirit may feel in looking down upon this dishonorable epoch. — But dont let us become too earnest. A very bad habit.

February 25-27   *Samuel Shaw visits the Melvilles.* (*his diary*)

CONCORD March 6   *Sophia Hawthorne writes to Annie Adams Fields:*
P.S. There is a book which was sent to 135 Washington St several weeks ago, directed to Mr Hawthorne. Does Mr Fields know any thing about it. Will the angel Michel look for it? It is "Moby Dick."

PITTSFIELD March 16 *M orders from Harper's two sets of his works for his brother Allan. ($13)*

WASHINGTON March 16 *Secretary of War Stanton allows Lt. Henry Gansevoort to accept the commission of Lieutenant-Colonel.*

NEW YORK March 30 *George Long Duyckinck dies at the age of forty years.*

ALBANY April 4 *M is sent a form letter, signed by Peter Gansevoort, as President of the Board of Trustees of the Albany Academy:*
The Albany Academy during the present year completes half a century of its history. The board of trustees have thought that perhaps this event might not be without interest to the thousands who during that time have been educated within its walls. They have therefore resolved that the semi-centennial anniversary of this institution shall in some suitable way be celebrated, and for this purpose they ask that you, as one of its Alumni, should serve as a member of a committee to make arrangements for the occasion. (*Celebration of the Semi-Centennial Anniversary of the Albany Academy*)

PITTSFIELD May 21 *An item in the* Berkshire County Eagle:
ALLEN MELVILLE, Esq., of New York, has purchased of his brother, Herman Melville, for a summer residence, the fine place, in this town, recently occupied by him, and known as "Arrow-head."

ALBANY June 12 *Along with a circular of the celebration schedule, completed by the committee of arrangements, Peter Gansevoort writes M a personal letter:*
I have much pleasure in sending to you the Circular of the Com. app[ointe]d for the celebration of the semi centennial of the Albany Academy —
You are a member of the Committee; Permit me to indulge the hope, that you will shew your gratitude to the Academy & your appreciation of the services it has rendered the cause of Science by participating in the celebration & favoring us with an expression of your feeling, during the Evening Meeting in the Chapel of the Academy . . .
However I shall be in Albany on 26ᵗʰ inᵗ & if you come you will find my house open to you

June 26 *The semi-centennial anniversary of the Albany Academy:*
Gathering in the Hall of the Academy, the Alumni seemed to revive as to the face of an old friend, their associations with lecture and study rooms, and to recall the memories of the long past hour, when the preparation for the realities of life's work was imparted.
At 10 o'clock the Reunion was duly formed in appropriate order under the direction of Col. FREDERIC TOWNSEND of the United States Army . . . Precedent moved the Trustees, the Faculty, and the Guests, while the Alumni and Students with them, formed an imposing army, which led by the music

of Screiber's band, retraced the streets so familiar in all the incidents of Academical days. It was a procession which commanded the attention and the respect of the citizens . . .

[At 3 P.M. a public meeting was held in Tweddle Hall.]

The meeting was presided over by the Honorable PETER GANSEVOORT, the President of the Board of Trustees, and by his side were his associates and the guests of the festival, among whom was warmly welcomed HERMAN MELVILLE, whose reputation as an author has honored the Academy, worldwide.

Wetron's Grand March was then performed by the band.

The Reverend Doctor FERRIS, now the Chancellor of the New York University . . . made prayer to Heaven, the source of that knowledge which shall not vanish away . . .

At successive periods the exercises were diversified by the music of *Home, Sweet Home,* of *Rest, Spirit, Rest,* and of other appropriate harmonies.

The following Commemorative Oration was then pronounced by the Honorable ALEXANDER W. BRADFORD, LL.D., of New York, a former student of the Academy:

"You have called me to my birth-place, the home of my childhood and my education, the land where my ancestors lived and died, through many generations — and I appear at your summons . . .

"In 1813, Albany was still 'a jewel óf antiquity;' 'all was antique, clean and quiet.' Below the Watering place, and above the Patroon's creek, and on the island where we used to bathe, willows and elms skirted the margin of the river. A short walk, barely a few steps, and you were at Tivoli, or Buttermilk falls. On the opposite side, the Giant's grave towered to the skies covered with ancient trees.

"The twilight stroll was to the Willow walk, to the Hay scales, or to the North gate — the Fishing ground, at the dam, or the creek now spanned by the rail road bridges — the literary culture, at the Apprentices' library, the Albany library, or John Cook's reading room, a man noted for keeping Congress water, and for loud sneezing . .·. The streets were quiet, grave and still — carriages or wagons, by an old ordinance, were forbidden to be driven faster than a walk or a step, for fear of accidents, I suppose, to stray children, pigs and cows. I thought to-day as I was standing in Market street (Broadway), near Maiden lane, I saw a great long red box, which seemed to be gliding through the air. I rubbed my eyes to look again — it was gone. I turned to inquire as to the vision and was told it was a car on a horse rail road.

Steterunt que comæ
Vox hæsit faucibus."

In the evening at 8 o'clock the Alumni gathered in force at the great hall of the Academy [to hear remarks by William H. Bogart & the Reverend Chancellor Ferris] . . .

As there was present some of the very best vocalists, who were also of the Alumni, it was with the highest satisfaction that the songs which are here given, were heard, as while there was a hearty and joyous union in the chorus . . .

> We have come again together
> Here to have a jolly row,
> And to make these old walls echo
> With our merry row-de-dow.
> *Chorus* — Cocachelunk, chelunk, chelaly, etc.
> Loudly, then, upraise the chorus,
> While to-night with memory toys,
> Calling up the hours of pleasure
> When we all were happy boys.
> *Chorus* — Cocachelunk, &c.

And now . . . a recess was taken, to give opportunity for the enjoyment of the collation which the thoughtful liberality of the Committee of Arrangements had provided. (*Celebration*)

June 27   *Peter Gansevoort's diary:*
At 5 P.M. Left Alby for Saratoga Springs, Herman Melville accompanies me on his way to Gansevoort —

PITTSFIELD   July 22   *M is listed on the Militia Roll for the last time.*

BOSTON   July 27   *Samuel Shaw's diary:*
Left for Pittsfield with mother in the afternoon train.

PITTSFIELD   July 28   *Hope Shaw's diary:*
Mr Melville took a carriage and carried us to the top of Mount Washington the road was bad but the scenery was magnificent.

August 1   [M's 44th birthday]   *Samuel Shaw's diary:*
From Pittsfield to Red Hook via Hudson.

August 5   *The Valuation Book for Pittsfield is completed; the last estimate is made for:*
Melville Herman & Wife
  1 [Poll]   2 [tax on Poll]
  [Description Taxable Cash Assets:]

21	[Shares] Am[erican] Ins[urance] Co	1729
8	Shares Conn[ecticut] R.R.R.	528
1	" Boote Cotton Mills	113
10	" Boston F[ire] & M[arine] Ins Co.	2250
1	Carriage	60
	[Aggregate of each Person's Ratable Personal Estate]	4,680

August 11   *M orders Harper's to send three copies of* Typee *to R. T. Greene.*

August 17   *M pays his Town, County & State Tax for 1863: $32.89 (less $1.64 discount); & his Fire District Tax of $3.90 (less 19 cents discount): a last Total of $34.96.*

August 22

Last Saturday saw the return of the long looked for 49th [Regiment] to Pittsfield . . .

The interval before the arrival of the 49th was occupied in inspecting the street decorations . . .

South Street . . .

Herman Melvill. — Flags and festoons.

(*Berkshire County Eagle*, Aug 27)

He rides at their head;
  A crutch by his saddle just slants in view,
One slung arm is in splints, you see,
  Yet he guides his strong steed — how coldly too . . .

There are welcoming shouts, and flags;
  Old men off hat to the Boy,
Wreaths from gay balconies fall at his feet,
  But to *him* — there comes alloy . . .

. . . all through the Seven Days' Fight,
  And deep in the Wilderness grim,
And in the field-hospital tent,
  And Petersburg crater, and dim
Lean brooding in Libby, there came —
  Ah heaven! — what *truth* to him.

("The College Colonel")

The residence of J. R. Morewood, Esq., was handsomely illuminated, and there was a fine display of fireworks on his grounds, on Saturday evening, in honor of the return of the 49th, and of the Colonel of the Regiment, his worthy guest.

The Pittsfield Liederkranz serenaded Col. Bartlett at the residence of J. R. Morewood, Esq., on the evening of his arrival, and were very handsomely entertained by Mrs. Morewood. (*The Pittsfield Sun*, Aug 27)

FIRE ISLAND September 13 *Evert Duyckinck writes to his wife:*

The company is very good — chiefly men of business with fortunes who take the world easily . . . At the end of the table is a fine figure-head of a gentleman at ease in bushy white head and beard with a ruddy glow of good cheer in his portly presence — a Mr. Willoughby who married a Brooklyn fortune and has his home in Saratoga. When he is not telling stories or chuckling or talking with his boy Hugh who has a French governess &c he is reading Moby Dick and is just such a reader as Melville would be delighted with and make a chapter of.

PITTSFIELD September *M writes an entry in his Bible's "Family Record":*

Stanwix, Elizabeth, and Frances Melville were baptized by Rev. Orville Dewey in Pittsfield Village, Mass. Sept. 1863

October 1   *Two items in the* Berkshire County Eagle:

J. C. HOADLEY, formerly of Pittsfield and Lawrence, and now agent of the New Bedford copper company, has gone to England for two months to inspect the cannon and other munitions of war, manufacturing there for the state of Massachusetts.

MRS. HERMAN MELVILLE has presented to the Berkshire Bar a fine bust of her father, the late Chief Justice Shaw . . . It was executed about twenty years ago [1839] by Clevinger, a young Vermont artist, then very popular in Boston . . .

NEW YORK   October 6   *Harper & Bros sends its 15th account to M:* Balance due Harper & Bros. $262.06

PITTSFIELD   Mid-October?

. . . the Pittsfield school system consisted simply of the High and the common district schools and there was no grading beyond this; no Grammar schools such as we now have having then been instituted. The public schools of the town were clearly not such as to invite to it new residents or retain old ones who had children to educate. If Mr. Melville left Pittsfield on that account, his is not the only instance in which it lost or missed getting valuable citizens by its delay in providing the best possible schools and libraries . . . Two other circumstances favored his removal to New York. Chief Justice Shaw died in 1861 . . . leaving his daughter, Mrs. Melville, a moderate fortune, which enabled the purchase of the very pleasant and convenient house, 104 East 26th Street. (Smith, *Evening Journal*, Dec 24, 1891)

Elizabeth Melville's memoir of M:

Lived there [in Pittsfield] till Oct. 1863 when he moved into a house in New York 104 East 26th st bought from his brother Allan giving 7,750 and the Arrowhead estate valued at 3000 and assuming a mortgage of 2000 to Mrs. Thurston which was afterwards paid off by Dr Hayward's legacy to me of $3000 in May 1864 — about $1000 Aunt Priscilla's legacy was spent in repairs. [*In earlier numbering address was 60 East 26.*]

After leaving Pittsfield . . . M[alcolm] went to boarding school in Newton Centre — Stan[wix] went to school in Gansevoort, B[essie] & F[rances] went to Quaker School, Stuyvesant Sq. [New York]

PITTSFIELD   October 16   *Mrs Sarah Morewood dies of consumption at the age of 39.*

MEMPHIS   October 20   *Richard Tobias Greene writes to M:*

I was home on leave of absence when your letter reached Vicksburg . . .

. . . Herman has grown a fine tall boy, and Richard Melville Hair is a Lieutenant in Gen Banks Army, at New Orleans.

. . . We have done a clean job on the Mississippi, and I think we are going to help Rosecrans in this State.

PHILADELPHIA   November 16   *Publication, in the* American Literary

Gazette and Publisher's Circular, *of "Authors in Berkshire," [by Henry T. Tuckerman]*:

Not far from his [Holmes's] old residence lives Herman Melville, author of "Typee," "Omoo," "Moby Dick," and other adventurous narratives, which have more of the genuine Robinson Crusoe spell about them than any American writings. The first and second were entirely new subjects, treated with a mingled simplicity and spirit that at once made the author's name a household and a shipboard word; the last, for curious and eloquent descriptions and details about the whale and whale fishing, rivals Michelet's brilliant and copious brochures on the sea, woman, and other generic themes; but Melville is more scientific as to his facts, and more inventive as to his fiction. "Moby Dick," indeed, has the rare fault of redundant power; the story is wild and wonderful enough, without being interwoven with such a thorough, scientific, and economical treatise on the whale; it is a fine contribution to natural history and to political economy, united to an original and powerful romance of the sea. Melville has written other and more casual things, indicative of great versatility; witness his "Life of Israel Potter," and his remarkable sketch of a Wall street scrivener ["Bartleby"] in "Putnam's Monthly." Impaired health induced him to retire to this beautiful region, and in the care of his fruits and flowers, and the repose of a domestic life, he seems to have forsworn the ambition of authorship, but we trust only for a time.

NEW YORK December 10   *M writes to Miss Sophie Van Matre, Cincinnati:*

Owing to my recent return to this, my native town, after a twelve years' visit in Berkshire, your note was delayed in reaching me.

Though involved in a thousand and one botherations incident to a removal of one's household a hundred and sixty miles, the fitting up & furnishing of a house &c &c, I yet hasten to respond.

I shld be very happy indeed to comply with your request to furnish you with autographs from old letters, were it not that it is a vile habit of mine to destroy nearly all my letters. Such as I have by me would hardly be to your purpose.

With lively remembrances of our pick-nicks, & the warmest wishes for the success of your Fair . . .

PITTSFIELD December 10   The Berkshire County Eagle *reprints Tuckerman's article, with an editorial note of correction:*
Mr. Melville did not come to Berkshire to secure health but to enjoy it. He has now removed to New York to secure its restoration.

NEW YORK December 15 [Henry Gansevoort's 29th birthday]   *M writes to George McLaughlin, Cincinnati:*

The Sanitary Fairs to be held in several of the larger cities will do an immense service to our soldiers. God prosper them and those who work for them and the great cause which they are intended to subserve.

Late December   *Evert Duyckinck sends M a book for review.*

December 31 *M replies to Evert Duyckinck:*

I return the book, thinking you may want it. I have read it with great interest. As for scribbling anything about it, tho' I would like to please you, I have not spirit enough.

We are going to have Allan & his family here to night, with Mrs [Ellen] Brittain from Pittsfield, & one or two other friends, who will come early, stay socially & go early. If convenient, pray, join us.

.   .   .   .   .   .

M responds to a request from John P. Kennedy, in Baltimore, to contribute a manuscript, to be reproduced in facsimile in a volume entitled Autograph Leaves of our Country's Authors; *he sends a poem:*

Inscription

For the Slain

At Fredericksburgh.

A glory lights an earnest end;
In jubilee the patriot ghosts ascend.
Transfigured at the rapturous height
Of their passionate feat of arms,
Death to the brave's a starry night, —
Strown their vale of death with palms.
                    HERMAN MELVILLE

PARIS   Nouvelle Biographie Générale *is published (edited by Dr. Hoefer) with a biographical sketch of "*MELVILLE (Herman), *romancier américain . . ." (condensed from the* Cyclopædia of American Literature).

*

1864

*

NEW YORK   February 9   *M pays Harper & Bros., on his account, $200.*

GANSEVOORT   Mid-February?   *M comes to visit his sick mother.*

February 29   *Augusta Melville writes to Catherine Gansevoort:*
Herman has been talking of going to Albany on his way home [to

New York] to see Uncle & Aunt Susan & his Cousin Kate, & have a peep at the great Bazaar but he may not be able to make it out.

ALBANY February 29   *Peter Gansevoort's diary:*
My nephew Herman Melville arrived at 9 P M from Gansevoort & reports that his mother is much better —

March 1   It has snowed all day —
   Accompanied Susan to [Erastus Dow] Palmers Studio to see the Arts Exhibition for the Bazaar — Herman Melville joined us — . . . [At home] found Herman Melville, who after a lunch left by the car in time to take the Rail Rd for New York at 4¹⁰

NEW YORK April 7?   From Augusta's last letter we learn that Herman & Allan have gone down to Washington & intend if possible to see you & your camp at Vienna. — *Catherine Gansevoort to her brother, Henry, Apr 21*

WASHINGTON April 8   *M & his brother, Allan, arrive at the Ebbitt House; from there Allan Melville writes to Richard Lathers, in New York:*
   My brother Herman & I arrived here this morning. He is very anxious to go to the front, but it appears that it is difficult to get a pass — It has occurred to me that perhaps you might address a line to Secretary Stanton introducing Herman & stating his wish, as a literary man he might be favored. As such men should have opportunities to see that they may describe.

From the Senate Chamber Charles Sumner writes to the Provost Marshal, requesting a pass to the front for M, "a loyal citizen & my friend." A pass to the front is issued:

War Department,
Washington, D. C., *April 8* 1864
Pass Herman Melville Esq & his brother Allen Melville Esq have permission to visit the Army of the Potomac & return
By order of the Secretary of War:
Edwin M Stanton

NEW YORK April 9
Among the gifts chronicled this morning, was a work entitled "Autograph Leaves of our Country's Authors," the copyright of which had been secured

for the benefit of the Sanitary Commission. (*A Record of the Metropolitan Fair in Aid of the United States Sanitary Commission* . . . , New York, 1867)

WASHINGTON April 10 . . . to our surprise we learned at that *poor place* the Ebbitt House that Allan & Herman had left W[ashington] on Sunday for the *front. — Jane D. Melville to Henry Gansevoort, Apr 13*

Elizabeth Melville's memoir of M:
Herman went to Virginia with Allan in April 1864 Visited various battle-fields & called on Gen. Grant Henry Gansevoort then in service in camp at Vienna Virginia —

VIENNA, VA. April 10? Herman & Allan visited me last week I was at-tending to Ordnance business in Washington. Allan left before I saw him . . . — *Henry Gansevoort to his father, Apr 25*

I enjoyed my visit very much, & would not have missed it on any account, and can only regret that you happened to be away when we arrived. But as when the sun reappears after being hidden; so — &c &c &c. Your imagination and modesty will supply the rest. — *M to Henry Gansevoort, May 10*

BOSTON April 12 *Hope Shaw's diary:*
Mrs Herman Melville & her two daughters left here for New York . . .

NEW YORK April 12 The Spirit of the Fair *announces* Autograph Leaves:
The number of copies is limited, the price is $6 — the day of publication, April 19th.

WASHINGTON April 13 *Jane D. Melville writes to her step-daughter, Florence:*
. . . we arrived here safely, but did not find *Papa.* We learned he had gone with Uncle Herman to the *front* of the Army of the Potomac on Sunday last . . . We hope to see Papa tomorrow — unless the Guerrillas have got Papa & Uncle Herman.

VIENNA April 14? . . . Herman went on a Scout & then spent a day with me. He was well and seemed to enjoy it. — *Henry Gansevoort to his father, Apr 25*

> The sun is gold, and the world is green,
>   Opal the vapors of morning roll;
> The champing horses lightly prance —
> Full of caprice, and the riders too
>   Curving in many a caricole . . .
>
> By the hospital-tent the cripples stand —
>   Bandage, and crutch, and cane, and sling,
> And palely eye the brave array;

The froth of the cup is gone for them
(Caw! caw! the crows through the blueness wing) . . .

How strong they feel on their horses free,
Tingles the tendoned thigh with life;
Their cavalry-jackets make boys of all —
With golden breasts like the oriole;
The chat, the jest, and laugh are rife . . .

The weary troop that wended now —
Hardly it seemed the same that pricked
Forth to the forest from the camp:
Foot-sore horses, jaded men;
Every backbone felt as nicked,
Each eye dim as a sick-room lamp,
All faces stamped with Mosby's stamp.
("The Scout Toward Aldie")

M & Col Gansevoort exchange visits with Brigadier-General Robert O. Tyler, who presents two books to M. (When I read of you at Cold-Harbor, I recalled your hospitality at Fairfax, and the agreeable evening I spent with you there, in company with my cousin, Col. Gansevoort . . . — *M to Tyler, July 21;* Pray, give my respects to [Tyler], & say that I agree with him about "Titan" [by Jean Paul Richter]. The worst thing I can say about it is that it is a little better than "Mardi" The Terence I highly value; indeed both works, as memorial of the hospitality of an accomplished General & jolly Christian. — *M to Henry Gansevoort, May 10*)

NEW YORK Late April? *Allan Melville writes to Catherine [?] Gansevoort.* (Allan gave quite a graphic account of his visit to your camp. Herman M. is suffering from a terrible attack of Neuralgia after his exposure in visiting the front of Our Army of the Potomac. — *Catherine Gansevoort to her brother, Henry, May 3*)

May 10 *M writes to his cousin, Col. Henry Gansevoort:*
I embrace the earliest opportunity afforded by my recovery from an acute attack of neuralgia in the eyes, to thank you for your hospitality at the camp, and make known the fact that I have not forgotten you . . . How is Captain Brewster? Coke on Lyttleton, and Strap on the Shoulder. My friendly regards & best wishes to the Captain & say to him that I hear the neigh of his war-horse in my dreams, likewise that I have a flannel shirt of his in my keeping; which I hope one day to exhibit as the identical shirt worn by that renowned soldier shortly after his entrance into the army. — Edwin Lansing — remember me to him. Tell him I frequently think of him & his tent & there is pleasure in the thought. Tell him to tell Dr Wolf (savage name, but sweet man) that my prayers ascend for him . . . And now, Col. Gansevoort of the 13ᵗʰ N.Y. Cavalry, conceive me to

be standing some paces from you, in an erect attitude and with manly bearing, giving you the military salute. Farewell. May two small but choice constellations of stars alight on your shoulders. May your sword be a Lesson to the despicable foe & your name in after ages be used by Southern Matrons to frighten their children by. And after death (which God long avert, & bring about after great battles, quickly, in a comfortable bed, with wife & children around) may that same name be transferred to heaven — bestowed upon some new planet or cluster of stars of the first magnitude. Farewell, my hero & God bless you . . .

Before May 19   *M writes to his mother.* (I enclose to you Herman's letter thinking you would like to read it. It is the one you forwarded to me. — *Maria Melville to Peter Gansevoort, May 24*)

PLYMOUTH, N. H.   May 19   *Nathaniel Hawthorne dies at the age of sixty.*

GANSEVOORT   May 24   *Maria Melville writes to Peter Gansevoort:*
I was quite shocked to see the sudden death of Nathaniel Hawthorne, in New Hampshire where he was on a visit, & was found dead in his bed, he had left home for the benefit of his health. A few weeks since he visited Philadelphia with his friend W. D. Ticknor, the Boston publisher, who was taken sick & died, Mr Hawthorne never leaving him from the time he was taken sick, & was holding his hand at the moment he was breathing his last. Mr Hawthorne was deeply affected at his death, & not being well; then travelling for his health. It is very probable the sudden shock was too much for him, Herman was much attached to him & will mourn his loss. He staid with him a few days in Liverpool, & I beleive has not seen him since. We have just received a letter from Lizzie, she writes that Herman was much shocked at hearing of Mr Hawthornes sudden death.

NEW YORK   May?   *M composes the first stanza of "Monody":*
> To have known him, to have loved him,
>   After loneness long;
> And then to be estranged in life,
>   And neither in the wrong;
> And now for death to set his seal —
>   Ease me, a little ease, my song!

Elizabeth Melville receives a legacy, from Dr. Hayward's estate, of $3000, which pays off the mortgage on 104 East 26.

COLD HARBOR   June 1   *At the battle of Cold Harbor Brigadier-General Tyler receives a severe wound in the ankle which lames him for life & permanently shatters his constitution.*

NEW YORK   June   *M acquires* The Poems of Elizabeth Barrett Browning

(*2 vols, New York, 1860*); *In "Lady Geraldine's Courtship," M scores*
this passage on p 162:

> There's no room for tears of weakness in the blind eyes of a Phemius:
> Into work the poet kneads them, — and he does not die *till then.*

In "A Vision of Poets," M scores & underscores:

> Lucretius — nobler than his mood:
> Who dropped his plummet down the broad
> Deep universe, and said 'No God,'
>
> Finding no bottom: he denied
> Divinely the Divine, and died
> Chief poet on the Tiber-side . . .

In "Casa Guidi Windows," M scores:

> Through the blue Immense
> Strike out all swimmers! cling not in the way
> Of one another, so to sink; but learn
> The strong man's impulse, catch the fresh'ning spray . . .

ALBANY July 20   *Catherine Gansevoort writes to her brother, Henry:*
Sam¹ returned from "Gansevoort" (where his Cousin lives in Aunt Mel-
ville's Family,) yesterday he reports all well & the place he says looks
"Splendid Elegant."

Cousin Herman & his two boys Mr Hoadley Kate & her children are
there —

GANSEVOORT July 21   *M writes to Brigadier-General Robert O. Tyler:*
When I read of you at Cold-Harbor, I recalled your hospitality at
Fairfax, and the agreeable evening I spent with you there . . .

Though I hope I am patriotic — enthusiastically so — yet I will not
congratulate you, General, upon your wound, but will reserve that for
the scar, which will be equally glorious and not quite so irksome. — I am
glad it is no worse with you, and rejoice to learn that you are in a promising way. I trust that you are in a condition to enjoy your book and your
cigar, also (but this should have gone before) the sweet eyes of the
sympathetic ladies, who, you know, have a natural weakness for heroes.
How they must hover over you — the angels! — and how must your
dreams be mingled of love and glory. I dont know but that I ought to
congratulate you at once, after all.

But methinks I hear somebody say, Dont bore him with too long a
yarn.

NEW YORK August 1 [M's 45th birthday]   *Harper & Bros. sends M*
its 16th account:

> Balance due Harper & Bros. $41.51

GLENS FALLS August 4   Herman, Augusta, & Hermans two boys, Malcolm & Stanwix, also took the cars for Glens Falls to spend the day.
— *Maria Melville to Catherine Gansevoort, this date*

GANSEVOORT August 8 Augusta is at New York, she went down with Herman on Monday the eighth, & will stay until Lizzie & her little girls return home . . . — *Maria Melville to Catherine Gansevoort, Aug 19*

NEW YORK August 20 *Samuel Shaw's diary:*
Elizabeth [Melville] left New York for Gansevoort.

GANSEVOORT September 9 *Maria Melville writes to Catherine Gansevoort:*
Lizzie left us this morning with her two boys & girls, they all look better than when they came, & profess to have passed their time very pleasantly.

The boys Malcolm & Stanwix have been here eight weeks & have been perfectly happy, Lizzie & the little girls three weeks.

We are now all alone & for a novelty shall enjoy it for a few days.

October 4 *Maria Melville writes to Catherine Gansevoort:*
Guert [Gansevoort] has been at Glen's falls for a week or more on a visit, he while there had a letter giving him the choice either to return to his old place on board the "Roanoke" at, or near Fortress Monroe, or take his old position at the Navy Yard in Brooklyn. Guert went to New York yesterday, to take up his old, or new quarters.

ALBANY? October 8 *Leonard Gansevoort dies.*

FALLS CHURCH October? *Col Henry Gansevoort writes to M.* (How is Cousin Herman? My love to him & Cousin Lizzie; I hope to hear from him in answer to my last — *Henry Gansevoort to Allan Melville, Nov 3*)

NEW YORK November 19 *Captain Thomas Melville returns on the Bengal from his seventh & last voyage.*

November 23 Aunt Melville is en route for New York where she is to meet Capt. Tom. Melville & make Cousin Herman a visit . . . Aunt Melville expected to be met at the cars in 26 S^t, by her four Sons, Tom, Herman, Allan & Mr John Hoadley. — *Catherine Gansevoort to her brother, Henry, this date*

November 24 Aunt Melville is to dine with her four sons, two daughters-in-law — & eight grand children Thanksgiving Day — & expects to enjoy the family party. — *Catherine Gansevoort to her brother, Henry, Nov 23*

. . . . . .

LONDON *Publication of* Forty Years of American Life, *by Dr. Thomas L. Nichols:*
I met Herman Melville often, after I read "Typee," both before and subsequent to its publication. He was a simple-hearted, enthusiastic, gentlemanly

sailor, or sailorlike gentleman. His subsequent works have been marked by certain eccentricities, but have, on the whole, sustained the promise of his maiden production.

*

1 8 6 5

*

NEW YORK   Mid-February?
> With burning woods our skies are brass,
>   The pillars of dust are seen;
> The live-long day their cavalry pass —
>   No crossing the road between.
>   We were sore deceived — an awful host!
>   They move like a roaring wind,
>   Have we gamed and lost? but even despair
>   Shall never our hate rescind.

This piece ["The Frenzy in the Wake"] was written while yet the reports were coming North of Sherman's homeward advance from Savannah. It is needless to point out its purely dramatic character (M's note *Battle-Pieces*)

February 24   *Bayard Taylor writes to M:*
  On Monday evening next, the 27th, "The Travellers" meet here, and it would give me great pleasure to see you among the guests of the Club. Many of the members are no doubt old friends of yours — Darley, Church, Bierstadt, Gottschalk, Cyrus Field, Hunt, Bellows and Townsend Harris. We simply meet to talk, winding up our evenings with a cigar and frugal refreshments.

February 27   [?] *M meets the members of "The Travellers."*

March 11   *In the* New-York Times *T. B. Peterson & Brothers, of Philadelphia, advertise:*
> THE REFUGEE,
by Herman Melville, Author of "Typee," "Omoo," "The Two Captains," "The Man of the World," etc. etc.

March?   *M addresses a communication to the Editor of* The World:
  Permit me through your columns to make a disavowal. T. B. Peterson & Brothers, of Philadelphia, include in a late list of their publications "The Refugee; by Herman Melville."
  I have never written any work by that title. In connection with that title Peterson Brothers employ my name without authority, and notwithstanding a remonstrance conveyed to them long ago.

RICHMOND   April 3   *Federal troops enter the Confederate Capital.*

THE FALL OF RICHMOND.
The Tidings Received in the Northern Metropolis.

What mean these peals from every tower,
    And crowds like seas that sway?
The cannon reply; they speak the heart
    Of the People impassioned, and say —
A city in flags for a city in flames,
    Richmond goes Babylon's way —
        Sing and pray . . .

Well that the faith we firmly kept,
    And never our aim forswore
For the Terrors that trooped from each recess
When fainting we fought in the Wilderness,
    And Hell made loud hurrah;
But God is in Heaven, and Grant in the Town,
    And Right through might is Law —
        God's way adore.

NEW YORK   After April 3   *M examines his war-time poems, & begins the composition of a volume of verse:*
    With few exceptions, the Pieces in this volume originated in an impulse imparted by the fall of Richmond. They were composed without reference to collective arrangement, but, being brought together in review, naturally fall into the order assumed. (prefatory note, *Battle-Pieces*)

APPOMATTOX COURT HOUSE   April 9   *General Grant telegraphs Secretary of War Stanton:*
    Gen. Lee surrendered the Army of Northern Va. this afternoon on terms proposed by myself.

THE SURRENDER AT APPOMATTOX.
As billows upon billows roll,
    On victory victory breaks;
Ere yet seven days from Richmond's fall
    And crowning triumph wakes
The loud joy-gun, whose thunders run
    By sea-shore, streams, and lakes.
        The hope and great event agree
        In the sword that Grant received from Lee.

WASHINGTON   April 14   *Abraham Lincoln is assassinated in his box at Ford's Theatre by John Wilkes Booth.*

NEW YORK   April 15?   *M composes:*
THE MARTYR.
Indicative of the Passion of the People on the 15th of April 1865.

Good Friday was the day
    Of the prodigy and crime,
When they killed him in his pity,

> When they killed him in his prime
> Of clemency and calm —
>   When with yearning he was filled
>   To redeem the evil-willed,
> And, though conqueror, be kind;
>   But they killed him in his kindness,
>   In their madness and their blindness,
> And they killed him from behind.
>
>> There is sobbing of the strong,
>> And a pall upon the land;
>> But the People in their weeping
>>   Bare the iron hand:
>> Beware the People weeping
>> When they bare the iron hand.

April   *M attends the National Academy Exhibition; two paintings there suggest poems:*
"The Coming Storm," by R. Swain Gifford
>   No utter surprise can come to him
>   Who reaches Shakspeare's core;
>   That which we seek and shun is there —
>   Man's final lore.

"Jane Jackson, Formerly a Slave," by Elihu Vedder
>   The sufferance of her race is shown,
>   And retrospect of life,
>   Which now too late deliverance dawns upon;
>   Yet is she not at strife.

ALBANY May 3   *Catherine Gansevoort writes to her brother, Henry:*
Tom spent a day with us on his way to Boston — He & Mr Hoadley are deep in the Petroleum Speculation — have purchased quantities of Land in Western Virginia and are making money very rapidly —

NEW YORK May   *M re-reads Hawthorne's Mosses from an Old Manse; in "Monsieur du Miroir" he underscores:*
Will he linger where I have lived, to remind the neglectful world of one who staked much to win a name . . . **X**
M's comment: **X** What a revelation.
He will pass to the dark realm of Nothingness, but will not find me there. **X**
M's comment: **X** This trenches upon the uncertain and the terrible.
In "The Celestial Railroad," M scores & underscores:
There was one strange thing that troubled me; amid the occupations or amusements of the fair, nothing was more common than for a person — whether at a feast, theatres, or church, or trafficking for wealth and honors, or whatever he might be doing, and however unseasonable the interruption — suddenly to vanish like a soap-bubble, and be never more seen of his fellows; and so accustomed were the latter to such little accidents, that they went on with their business, as quietly as if nothing had happened. But it was otherwise with me.

M's comment: **X** Nothing can be finer than this. May 1865

PHILADELPHIA May The Refugee *is noticed in* Godey's Lady's Book and Magazine:
A well-written story of Revolutionary times.

NEW YORK June 29 Augusta driven by dire necessity [for farm help] took on Thursday morning the 29 June the early train of cars, to New York. She arrived there at three ½ Oclock & quite astonished Herman & Lizzie at her unexpected appearance. — *Maria Melville to Catherine Gansevoort, July 5*

GANSEVOORT August 16 I wish you could have been here yesterday, four Sabbath Schools met in your Fathers Grove, a band of music the Cornet band of Fort Edward, thought here to be wonderful performers, they were dressed in long red coats & made a fine appearance, fifteen in number, large fine looking men. Herman, Florence Kitty & Lucy are staying here & all went to the Picnic, had a grand supply of iced cakes, sugar-plums, peaches nuts, biscuit &c, quantities left were given to the poor — Fifteen hundred persons were there at least, enjoying themselves, about three O clock a tremendous wind came up filling the air with sand, the sky became black, & all the picnickers, rushed to the Church or tumbled into their waggons, galloping home, Augusta & her party re-turned blew home for the wind was fair. Shortly after the rain fell in torrents. Some of the younger girls wore white dresses wreaths on the head bare arms & pink cotton bows behind crossing the bust — *Maria Melville to Catherine Gansevoort, Aug 17*

August 17 *Maria Melville writes to Catherine Gansevoort:*
We expect Lizzie with Bessie & Fanny in a few days . . . Herman just came in — he desires me give his love & regards to Uncle & Aunt Susan.

NEW YORK August 18 *M orders, on his Harper's account:*
 1 Sherman's March [*The Story of the Great March,* by Brevet Major George Ward Nichols] 1.17

GANSEVOORT Before September 9 *The Melvilles return home.* (From home, I heard Friday they are alone now, Herman & his family having returned to New York, & Allan's children to Pittsfield . . . Malcolm & Stanwix have also been here [New Bedford] during their vacation. — *Frances Priscilla Melville to Catherine Gansevoort, Sept 12*)

NEW YORK September 26 *Col. Henry Gansevoort writes to his sister, Catherine:*
I am staying here at my friend Brewsters room. Allan Melville I saw yesterday. He came down from Pittsfield to bring his children to school. He thinks of going abroad.

September   *Evert Duyckinck sends to all writers included in his* Cyclo-pædia *(including M?) a form letter announcing that a revised edition is in preparation, & that corrections & additions will be welcomed.*

Before October 7   *M writes to the family at Gansevoort.* (We have just heard from Herman & Lizzie. He has been unusually well ever since his visit here. — *Augusta Melville to Catherine Gansevoort, Oct 7*)

Before October 12   *M writes again (?) to the family at Gansevoort.* (Herman & Tom are urgent that we should come at once, but Augusta wants to close her Sabbath School with the year — & I want to pay Taxes as soon as I can find out what they are to be — *Maria Melville to Catherine Gansevoort, Oct 12*)

October 19   *M orders four bound volumes of* Harper's Weekly, *for Christmas presents. ($18.67)*

November 13   *Harper & Bros. sends its 17th account to M:*
              Balance due Herman Melville, Esq. $43.17

December 21   *Maria Melville reports the New York family activities to Catherine Gansevoort:*
We have been reading aloud, "Faith Gartneys Girlhood," "The Gay-worthys," by the same author [Mrs Adeline Whitney] — Helen brought us "The clever woman of the Family" [by Charlotte Mary Yonge] — which we are now reading in the eve^g aloud —

December 25   *M's Christmas presents:* Harper's Weekly *for 1861 to Malcolm Melville, for 1862 to Stanwix Melville, for 1863 to Bessie Melville, for 1864 to Fanny Melville, for 1865 to Dolly [Elizabeth].*

Malcolm Melville gives his sister, Fanny, a present: Ethel's Story: Illustrating the Advantages of Cheerfulness, by the Child's Friend (*Philadelphia, n.d.*)

·   ·   ·   ·   ·

NEW YORK
Herman Melville was invited to the Twentieth Street house [of Alice & Phoebe Cary] at the time when he was at work on his *Battle Pieces,* and could look back on years of adventure by land and by sea, and on the hardships that had supplied him with the material from which to write so much that was odd and interesting. At one of these Sunday-night receptions, at which Alice Cary introduced him first, Melville told the company, and told it far better than he had ever written anything (at least so one of his hearers has recorded), the story of that life of trial and adventure. He began at the beginning, telling of his boyhood in New York, of his shipping as a common sailor, and of his youthful wanderings in London and Liverpool. In true sailor fashion, and with picturesque detail, he spun the tale of his eighteen months cruise to the sperm fisheries in the Pacific, and held his hearers' close attention while he

related the coarse brutality of his captain, who had forced him to desert at the Marquesas Islands. Then he traced his wanderings with his one companion through the trackless forest of Nukahiva and of his capture by the Typee cannibals. He related how there was little hope in his heart that he could ever escape, but that he still held tight to life and his courage did not desert him; how with the thought of death before him by night and by day he yet hourly studied the strange life about him and garnered those facts and fancies which he afterwards used to such advantage in his successful *Typee*. It was a thrilling tale to listen to . . . (Charles Hemstreet, *Literary New York*, New York, 1903)

In 1865 or later M acquires Modern Painters, *by John Ruskin, 5 vols (First American from the Third London Edition, New York, 1860-62) in which he scores & underscores in Vol V, "Of Vulgarity," p 280:*
. . . to men not of his kind he cannot open himself, though he tried it through an eternity of clear grammatical speech. By the very acuteness of his sympathy he knows how much of himself he can give to anybody . . . Whatever he said, a vulgar man would misinterpret: no words that he could use would bear the same sense to the vulgar man that they do to him . . .

Publication of The Income Record, A List Giving the Taxable Income of Every Resident of New York; *in the 8th district (18th, 20th, 21st wards):*

Melville, H. $851

*

1866

*

ALBANY   Before January 9   *Susan Gansevoort invites M & Elizabeth Melville to a party on January 15.*

NEW YORK   January 9   *Elizabeth Melville writes to Catherine Gansevoort, declining the invitation for herself & M.*

January 11   *M orders a volume of* Harper's Weekly — *4.76.*

Before January 20   *Publication of [M's poem] "The March to the Sea," in* Harper's New Monthly Magazine *(February):*

> For behind they left a wailing,
>   A terror, and a ban,
> And blazing cinders sailing,
>   And houseless households wan,
> Wide zones of counties paling,
>   And towns where maniacs ran.

It was Treason's retribution
(Necessity the plea);
They will long remember Sherman
And his streaming columns free —
They will long remember Sherman
Marching to the sea.

ALBANY January 20 *Catherine Gansevoort writes to her brother, Henry:*
I have been over looking the Harper for Feb^y & find there a piece of Poetry entitled "The March to the Sea" — I think it is written by Herman Melville as Aunt Melville when here told us a piece of Poetry by Herman would appear in that magazine — I never have read any of his poetry before — *This piece* is very inspiring & describes Sherman's Grand March.

NEW YORK January 29 *Thomas Melville writes to Catherine Gansevoort:*
You were right in your idea that Herman was the author of the "March to the Sea" in Harpers of Feb. 1866, do you not think it is good. John [Hoadley] read it aloud in New Bedford the other evening, he thinks it is splendid . . .
I am staying at Hermans 60 East 26 Street & shall probably be here about two weeks.

NEW BEDFORD February 8 *Frances Priscilla Melville writes to Catherine Gansevoort:*
Did you read "The March to the Sea" in the last Harpers? It is thought grand by all.

NEW YORK March [1] *Publication of [M's poem] "The Cumberland," in* Harper's New Monthly Magazine:
. . . She warred and sunk. There's no denying
That she was ended — quelled;
And yet her flag above her fate is flying,
As when it swelled
Unswallowed by the swallowing sea: so grand —
The Cumberland.
Proud a name as ere was sung,
Roundly rolling on the tongue —
Cumberland! Cumberland!

BROOKLINE March 6 *Maria Melville writes to Catherine Gansevoort:*
. . . Mr Hoadley expects to go to New York next week & I shall take the opportunity of accompanying him, & make my visit to Herman & Lizzie.
By the way Malcolm has a fine position in the Great Western Marine

Insurance Co — He is but 17 years old gets a salary of $200 a year. They all have a fine lunch at the office equal to a dinner, & if kept in after six in the Evening have a regular supper Mr Lathers who is President, is an active industrious man — Prompt, energetic, & just the Man for Malcolm or any other boy.

NEW YORK Before March 20 *Maria Melville comes to 26 Street & is taken ill; M writes to his sister Augusta.* (On Tuesday afternoon I received a few lines from Herman saying that Mamma had been quite sick for three days, & although she was then able to sit up, he thought I had better come down as soon as possible. — *Augusta Melville to Catherine Gansevoort, Mar 23*)

March 21 *Augusta Melville comes to New York.* (So I packed up at once & took the morning train on Wednesday. Found Lizzie & Stannie waiting for me at the dépôt who told me that my dear Mother had improved much since Herman had written me. I found her sitting up but looking very pale & feeling very weak. The doctor however says she will be quite well in a few days. — *Augusta Melville to Catherine Gansevoort, Mar 23*)

BOSTON? March 30 *M's aunt, Jean Melvill Knight, dies at the age of 78; at some time before her death she sends M an old broadside:* Speech of Thomas Jefferson . . . delivered at his instalment, March 4, 1801, at the City of Washington; *on it M scores this passage:*
And let us reflect that having banished from our land that religious intolerance, under which mankind so long bled and suffered, we have yet gained little, if we countenance a political intolerance, as despotic, as wicked, and capable of as bitter and bloody persecutions.

NEW YORK April [1] *Publication of [M's poem] "Philip," in* Harper's New Monthly Magazine:
> . . . There is glory for the brave
> Who lead, and nobly save,
> But no knowledge in the grave
> Where the nameless followers sleep.

FORT MONROE April 7 *Col Henry Gansevoort writes to his sister, Catherine:*
Your account of Mrs. Melvilles explorations of the river Nile is particularly interesting. We shall have on her return great pleasure in listening to her adventures with Allan in the East and West.

Happy are they who can enjoy such a luxury as the gratification of curiosity in these days of depreciated currency.

WASHINGTON April *Robert E. Lee testifies before the Reconstruction Committee of Congress:*

His testimony is deeply interesting, both in itself and as coming from him. After various questions had been put and briefly answered, these words were addressed to him: —

"If there be any other matter about which you wish to speak on this occasion, do so freely." Waiving this invitation, he responded by a short personal explanation of some point in a previous answer, and, after a few more brief questions and replies, the interview closed.

In the verse ["Lee in the Capitol"] a poetical liberty has been ventured. Lee is not only represented as responding to the invitation, but also as at last renouncing his cold reserve, doubtless the cloak to feelings more or less poignant. If for such freedom warrant be necessary, the speeches in ancient histories, not to speak of those in Shakspeare's historic plays, may not unfitly perhaps be cited. (M's note, *Battle-Pieces*)

ROME   May 4   *Robert Macpherson sends M a copy of his handbook on* Vatican Sculptures (*London, 1863*).

GANSEVOORT   May 30   *Thomas Melville informs Catherine Gansevoort that he is on his way to New York to stay at 104 East 26 Street.*

NEW YORK   June [1]   *Publication of [M's poem] "Chattanooga," in* Harper's New Monthly Magazine.

LONDON   June 4   *Diary of Benjamin Moran, Secretary of U. S. Legation:*
Mr. Allan Melville, a brother of Herman Melville and of Gansevoort Melville, who died when secretary of Legation here in 1845, brought me a letter from Capt. Hoadley. This is rather a pleasant good looking man, but rather exacting and inconsiderate. He has been in Egypt all winter & altho I was busy wanted to tell me all his adventures.

June 5   Mr. Allan Melville has been here again. He is considerable of a bore.

NEW YORK   June 29   *Allan Melville returns from his tour abroad.*

Late June?   *A[lfred]. H. G[uernsey]., editor of* Harper's Monthly, *writes a memo:*
I think you ought to agree with Mr. Melville what should be paid for these poems for this use in the Magazine, distinct from their use in the Volume.
M notes on this memo: I never got.

July [1]   *Publication of [M's poem] "Gettysburg: — July, 1863," in* Harper's New Monthly Magazine:
   . . . Then the three waves in flashed advance
    Surged, but were met, and back they set:
    Pride was repelled by sterner pride,
    And Right is a strong-hold yet.

> Before our lines it seemed a beach
> Which wild September gales have strown
> With havoc on wreck, and dashed therewith
> Pale crews unknown . . .

July 11   *M orders, from Harpers, a copy of* Thoughts on the Future Civil Policy of America, *by J. W. Draper, M.D.* (*1865*).

Mid-July?   *M composes the Supplement to* Battle-Pieces:
   Patriotism is not baseness, neither is it inhumanity. The mourners who this summer bear flowers to the mounds of the Virginian and Georgian dead are, in their domestic bereavement and proud affection, as sacred in the eye of Heaven as are those who go with similar offerings of tender grief and love into the cemeteries of our Northern martyrs. And yet, in one aspect, how needless to point the contrast.
   Cherishing such sentiments, it will hardly occasion surprise that, in looking over the battle-pieces in the foregoing collection, I have been tempted to withdraw or modify some of them, fearful lest in presenting, though but dramatically and by way of a poetic record, the passions and epithets of civil war, I might be contributing to a bitterness which every sensible American must wish at an end. So, too, with the emotion of victory as reproduced on some pages, and particularly toward the close . . . Zeal is not of necessity religion, neither is it always of the same essence with poetry or patriotism.
   . . . The years of war tried our devotion to the Union; the time of peace may test the sincerity of our faith in democracy.

July 20   *Allan Melville writes to Colonel Henry Gansevoort:*
As yet I have not had time to run up [to Gansevoort] to see my mother. Herman goes up tomorrow morning. Did you see his poem "The March to the Sea" in Harpers monthly for February. It is published in advance of a volume of Poems he has in press shortly to appear.

GANSEVOORT   July 21   Saturday Night, Mr Hoadley & Cousin Herman [arrived here] . . . Cousin Herman, looking thin & miserable I think. Cousin Lizzie is in Boston & Malcolm has gone East during his vacation. — *Catherine Gansevoort to her brother Henry, July 23*

NEW YORK   July 24   *Harper's mails its 18th account to M:*
Balance due H. M. $64.31

GANSEVOORT   August 1   [M's 47ᵗʰ birthday]   *A croquet game in the evening:*
   The hammock is in high favor. I enjoyed a quiet swing last evening while the others were playing croquet. Herman is quite a hand at it. He talks of making you a flying visit on his way to New York, but he may not make it out as he must be in New York on Thursday when Malcolm arrives from Boston. — *Augusta Melville to Catherine Gansevoort, Aug 2*

SARATOGA LAKE   August 2   Herman & Tom have gone to spend the day at Saratoga Lake . . . — *Augusta Melville to Catherine Gansevoort, Aug 2*

ALBANY August 5 *Peter Gansevoort's diary:*
Herman Melville arrived before 2 Oclk to Dinner.

August 6 Herman Melville left after Breakfast at 7AM for N. Y.

NEW YORK August 12 *A note in the* New-York Herald's *column,* "The Book World":
Harper & Bros. announce "Fetridge's Guide Book of European Travel," 5th year; "The Hidden Sin," a novel; "Bound to the Wheel," a novel, by John Saunders; "Battle Pieces and Aspects of the War," by Herman Melville, (for ten years the public has wondered what has become of Melville) . . .

August 17 *Deposited at the Clerk's Office, Southern District of New-York:* Battle-Pieces and Aspects of the War.

August *M sends copies of* Battle-Pieces *to his sister, Mrs Helen Melville Griggs, to his mother, to his mother-in-law, Mrs Hope Shaw, & gives one to his wife.*

September 1 Battle-Pieces *is noticed in the* American Literary Gazette and Publishers' Circular:
Mr. Melville has abundant force and fire. He breathes the enthusiasm of his time and his words will kindle afresh the patriotic flame. But he has written too rapidly to avoid great crudities. His poetry runs into the epileptic. His rhymes are fearful . . .

FORT MONROE September 1 *Col Henry Gansevoort writes to his father:*
Have you seen Herman Melvilles new work "Battle-Pieces." There are some beautiful things in it. Unfortunately he has so much of Emerson & trancendentalism in his writing that it never will really touch the common heart. Still I must say that this work shows him to be a poet of high order & certainly of originality —

BROOKLINE September 2 *Thomas Melville writes to Catherine Gansevoort:*
Have you seen Hermans New book "Battle-Pieces" it is called and what do you think of it. I bought a copy last week in Boston, it is a very p[r]etty volume & I hope will have many readers.

NEW YORK September 3 Battle-Pieces *is reviewed in the* New-York Herald:
A rough time of it the country had during our four years' war, and many of the lines in which Herman Melville, in his new character as a poet, commemorates it are not inappropriately rugged enough . . . But we wish to direct special attention to the "supplement" which Mr. Melville has added, in obedience to a claim overriding all literary scruples — a claim urged by patri-

otism not free from solicitude. So far from spoiling the symmetry of the book, this supplement completes it . . .

September 6   Battle-Pieces *is reviewed in* The Nation, *within an article,* *"More Poetry of the War" [by Charles Eliot Norton?]:*
Unless the poet is as great as his theme, he must submit to be crushed by it, and the literary critic has little to do but to confront the verse and its subject.
   If measured by this standard, Mr. Melville must take his place with the herd of recent versifiers. But his literary reputation gives his volume special claims to notice, and the abilities which he has shown in some of his other works entitle whatever he produces to respectful consideration. It is impossible, in view of what Mr. Melville has done and of his intention in his present book, not to read his "Battle Pieces" with a certain melancholy. Nature did not make him a poet. His pages contain at best little more than the rough ore of poetry . . . [we] cannot refrain from expressing surprise that a man of Mr. Melville's literary experience and cultivation should have mistaken some of these compositions for poetry, or even for verse.

ALBANY   September 17   *Catherine Gansevoort writes to her brother,* *Henry:*
   We have a copy of Herman Melville's "Battle-Pieces" — I must say I cannot get interested in his style of Poetry. It is too deep for my comprehension.

LONDON   October 1   Trübner's American and Oriental Literary Record *lists* Battle-Pieces *for 9s.*

NEW YORK   October 10   Battle-Pieces *is reviewed in* The Evening Post:
   Those who have read Herman Melville's "Omoo," "Typee" and "Pierre," need not be told that a strong vein of poetic feeling pervades passages of these works, expressed sometimes rather wildly and even vaguely, but nevertheless real and unquestionable . . .
   His style in verse is as unfettered by ordinary precedents as in such of his prose works as "Pierre."

ALBANY   November 24   *Catherine Gansevoort writes to her brother,* *Henry:*
   Ask Cousin Herman if he has seen Mr. Streets "Frontenac" & what he thinks of it.

NEW YORK   November 28   *Henry A. Smythe, Collector of Customs,* *writes to the Secretary of the Treasury, nominating M as Inspector at* *$4 per diem.*

WASHINGTON   November 30   *William E. Chandlen, Assistant Secretary* *of the Treasury, writes to Henry A. Smythe, Collector of Customs at* *New York, approving the nomination of M as Inspector at $4 per diem.*

NEW YORK December 5 *M takes the oath of office as Inspector [No. 75] of Customs at New York [& goes to his first post, District Office No. 4, North River, at 207 West Street].*

After December 5
My good friend [James S.] Benedict sent me, one gloomy November [?] forenoon, this curt announcement of a new appointment in Herman Melville: "He seems a good fellow, Dick, and says he knows you, though perhaps he doesn't, but anyhow be kind to him if this infernal weather will let you be to anybody." I bowed to the gentleman who handed the note to me, in whom I recognized a famous writer whom I had met some twenty-five years before; no American writer was more widely known in the late forties and early fifties in his own country and England than Melville . . .
Whether any of Melville's readers understood the real drift of his mind, or whether he understood it himself, has often puzzled me. Next to Emerson he was the American mystic. He was one of our great unrecognized poets . . . (Richard Henry Stoddard, *Recollections Personal and Literary*)

December 7 *William H. Demarest, of Harper & Bros., writes to M:*
According to promise I beg to report that there were printed of the "Battle Pieces," 1260 copies: there have been given to Editors, say in round numbers, 300: There were on hand yesterday 409. So there were sold, or in hands of book-sellers on sale, up to yesterday, say 551 copies.

December 8 *M's poem, "Sheridan at Cedar Creek," is reprinted in the New York* Leader.

December 19 *M presents a copy of* Battle-Pieces *to his colleague in the Custom House, Colonel Henry L. Potter.*

PHILADELPHIA December *Battle-Pieces is noticed in* Godey's Lady's Book and Magazine.

NEW YORK December *R. H. Stoddard asks M for, & receives from him a transcript of "Sheridan at Cedar Creek":*

Philip.

Shoe the steed with silver
That bore him to the fray,
When he heard the guns at dawning,
Miles away —
When he heard them calling, calling,

Mount! nor stay —
Quick, or all is lost,
They're surprised and stormed the fort,
They push your walled host —
Gallop! retrieve the day.

*

1867

*

NEW YORK January [1]   Battle-Pieces *is reviewed in* Harper's New Monthly Magazine:
  Mr. Melville has broken a long silence in a manner hardly to have been expected of the author of "Typee" and "Mardi." Among these poems are some . . . which will stand as among the most stirring lyrics of the war.

January 7   *M & his brother, Thomas, go to the French Theatre to attend "Ristori's Last Night . . . before her departure for the West"; the play is* Elizabeth of England, *by Giacometti.* (*Thomas Melville to Catherine Gansevoort, Jan 8*)

BOSTON February [1]   Battle-Pieces *is reviewed in* The Atlantic Monthly:
  Mr. Melville's work possesses the negative virtues of originality in such degree that it not only reminds you of no poetry you have read, but of no life you have known. Is it possible . . . that there has really been a great war, with battles fought by men and bewailed by women? Or is it only that Mr. Melville's inner consciousness has been perturbed, and filled with the phantasms of enlistments, marches, fights in the air, parenthetic bulletin-boards, and tortured humanity shedding, not words and blood, but words alone?

NEW YORK Early February   . . . we had a quick passage down & I reached Herman's ten minutes to eleven P M, just as Lizzy was shutting up the house, Herman having gone to bed with a bad cold. — *Thomas Melville to Catherine Gansevoort, Feb 9*

February 28   *Maria Melville, her daughters, Frances Priscilla & Augusta, arrive at 26th Street to stay "a few weeks."* (I rec'd a letter from Augusta this morning in which she announces their safe arrival at 60 East 26th

Street. Herman & his family met them on the arrival of the Harlem Train. — *Catherine Gansevoort to her brother, Henry, Mar 2*)

March 11 *Maria Melville writes to Catherine Gansevoort:*
Tom has a bad cold & does not seem to feel well he dined with us yesterday, nobody went to church but Augusta — for it rained all day . . . Herman's health is much better since he has been compelled to go out daily to attend to his business. He is one of the District Officers in the Custom House. He has been in Office about three months.

ALBANY March 19 *Catherine Gansevoort writes to her brother, Henry:*
Aunt Melville sent me a letter last week. She is at Herman's & delighted with the change from the quiet of Gansevoort . . . Gus is with her Mother & devoted to church going — Cousin Herman has a position in the Custom House & is quite well this winter. His intercourse with his fellow creatures seems to have had a beneficial effect he is less of a misanthrope.

ON THE *Liberty* April 19 *Col Henry Gansevoort continues to read* Battle-Pieces:
> "With undulating long-drawn flow
> As rolled Brazilian billows go
> Voluminously o'er the Line"

This is Herman Melvilles description of the wavy folds of the star spangled banner [in "America"]. It is good. — *Henry Gansevoort to his mother, this date*

NEW YORK May 17 *M acquires* Poems from the Portuguese of Luis de Camoens, with Remarks on His Life and Writings . . . *by Lord Viscount Strangford (London, 1824); M scores two passages in Strangford's introduction:*
So true it is, that the decline of public spirit in matters of taste is a certain indication of political decay.
Woman was to him [Camoens] as a ministering angel, and for the little joy which he tasted in life, he was indebted to her.
In Sonnet VI M scores this passage:
> My senses lost, misjudging men declare,
> And Reason banish'd from her mental throne,
> Because I shun the crowd, and dwell alone . . .

GANSEVOORT July 29 *M begins his vacation here.* (I had a letter from Gus Melville this morning — They must have a full house at Gansevoort just now. Mr Hoadley, Cousin Kate — three children & nurse — Malcome & Maria from Pittsfield — Cousin Helen, & Cousin Herman are there — *only ten*, besides their own family — & what a delightful time they have — *Catherine Gansevoort to her brother, Henry, July 30?;* Flory and myself arrived here saftly, last evening at about seven o'clock and found all the good people well and expecting us . . . Grandmama and all your Aunts, Uncles and cousens were real disapointed that you did not come with us . . . We found Papa here, he came up Monday evening; Stan is expected this afternoon; and I can tell you that we shall have a housefull. — *Malcolm Melville to his cousin Maria, July 31*)

August 12?   *M has returned to his job in New York, at District Office No. 4.* (. . . as this has been a very rainy day we have devoted ourselves to the house, & passed the time very pleasantly. Cousin Kate Hoadley, her three children, Cousin Helen, & Stanwix Melville — (Cousin Herman's youngest son —) Fanny, Gus, Aunt Melville, & K.G. form the household here. — *Catherine Gansevoort to her father, Aug 16*)

NEW YORK Before September 10
   But the pistol? How came [Malcolm] by that?
   He had carried it in his pocket and slept with it under his pillow for weeks, as he had told his fellow clerks and his brother Stanwix. Having recently joined a volunteer regiment he had a boy's newly awakened enthusiasm for whatever related in any way to weapons, arms and military equipments. His new uniform received a few days before must be tried on in the evening, to gratify his desire to see himself in the habiliments of a soldier, and to amuse his sisters younger than himself, who teased him with harmless banter on his martial vanity . . .
   He was also a member of a base ball club, and was looking forward with a lively interest to a match game to be played in two or three days from that time. His club had been beaten and he hoped to aid in winning back their lost laurels.
   He possessed to the fullest extent the confidence of his employer, Richard Lathers, esq., president of the Atlantic and Great Western Insurance Company (Marine and inland), and the love and respect of his fellow clerks, who had remonstrated with him for his carelessness in handling his pistol.
   He had been out sometimes pretty late in the evening after joining the military organization already referred to . . . (editorial, signed J. C. H[oadley]., *Boston Weekly Advertiser* [?])

He has also been out late at night recently, so much so that his father took away his night key from him and both his parents have talked very seriously about it but they both say that they believe that there was nothing in his dissipation more than a fondness for social frolicking with his young friends, and acquaintances that he made down town. They know he had *no* vices. — *Samuel S. Shaw to his mother, Sept 12*

September 10   On Tuesday night he was out till 3 o'clock and his mother sat up for him. When he came home he said he had been at an entertainment at Yorkville given by some friends. He showed no signs of having had any liquor. His mother remonstrated with him kindly but she says did not scold him in the least. He kissed her good night and went to bed. — *Samuel S. Shaw to his mother, Sept 12*

September 11   In the morning he was found to be late and one of the girls went up and called him. He answered "yes" but did not come down — Time went on and Herman advised Lizzie to let him sleep, be late at the office & take the consequences as a sort of punishment — and then went himself down to his business [on West Street]. The day went on and though Lizzie tried to wake him by knocking & calling, she did not succeed — a not un[u]sual thing she says — and it was not till Herman got home in the evening unusually late that the door was broken down and Macky found in his night clothes in bed with a pistol shot in his head and apparently several hours dead. Dr. [Augustus Kinsley] Gardner advised that the coroner should be called . . . — *Samuel S. Shaw to his mother, Sept 12*

. . . when Mr. Melville returned in the evening, the door of the room was opened, and young Melville was found dead, lying on the bed, with a single-barrelled pistol firmly grasped in his right hand, and a pistol-shot wound in the right temple. (a New York newspaper, Sept 13)

September 12   *A Coroner's jury holds an inquest at 104 East 26 Street:*
VERDICT.
That the said Child came to his death by Suicide by shooting himself in the head with a pistol at said place while laboring under temporary insanity of Mind.
CHARGES.

Taking Inquest,	5 00
Summoning and Swearing Jury	37½
Subpoenaing and Swearing 3 Witnesses	93¾
Labor,	5 00
	11 31¼

A STRANGE CASE OF SUICIDE. — An inquest was held yesterday by Coroner Wildey at 104 East Twenty-sixth street, over the remains of Malcolm Melville, a native of Massachusetts, 18 years of age, who committed suicide on Wednesday by shooting himself in the head with a pistol. It appears that the deceased was a son of Mr. Herman Melville, well-known in literary circles, and occupied a responsible position in a down-town insurance office . . . The parents of the deceased could not assign any cause for the suicidal act, and the jury came to the conclusion that deceased must have been suffering from a temporary aberration of mind, and they accordingly rendered a verdict to that effect. (a New York newspaper, Sept 13)

Samuel Shaw writes to his mother:
. . . went with Allan & Stanny, whom I found on the train in the afternoon, coming from Pittsfield, straight to Elizabeth's house. The circumstances of Macky's death are very mysterious . . . today they have been subjected to the distressing ordeal of having an inquest . . . Poor Lizzie is much exhausted but has not had time to realize the situation.

September 13   The New-York Times *prints a paragraph:*

Malcolm Melville, a youth of 18 years of age, son of a well-known literary gentleman, committed suicide yesterday by shooting himself with a pistol. *& on the page opposite, a Death notice:*
MELVILLE. — On Wednesday, Sept. 11, Malcolm Melville, son of Herman Melville, aged 18 years.
The relatives and friends of the family are invited to attend the funeral from the residence of his father, No. 104 East 26th, near 4th, on Saturday, the 14th inst., at 8½ o'clock A.M.

September 13? *M writes to John C. Hoadley:*
I wish you could have seen him as he lay in his last attitude, the ease of a gentle nature. Mackie never gave me a disrespectful word in his life, nor in any way ever failed in filialness.

September 14 Well the funeral took place last Saturday morning Dr. Osgood (their Clergyman) read a chapter from the Bible — the 15th Chap. Corinthians the one used in the Episcopal Burial Service, made a short address & a prayer — Then after a pause — the young Volunteer Company to which Malcom belonged & who had asked the privilege of being present & carrying the coffin from the house to the cars — filed in at one door from the hall & out at the other — each pausing for an instant to look at the face of their lost comrade. Cousin Helen says they were all *so young* & it was really a sadly beautiful sight — for the cold limbs of the dead wore the same garments as the strong active ones of the living — Cousin Lizzie — his almost heart broken Mother having dressed her eldest son in the new suit he had taken such pride & pleasure in wearing — Four superb wreaths & crosses of the choicest white flowers were placed on the coffin & it was lifted to the shoulders of six of the company & born down the steps, through the street to the car (on the Harlem R.R. I think) which Allan had secured for special use.
The family, & mourners followed — They left the car at the entrance of the *Woodlawn Cemetery,* & the young bearers carried the coffin to the hearse — others bearing the flowers — What a sad sight — "The stone was rolled from the mouth of the cave — " as the scripture saith " — & the remains placed in the [?] vault. Cousin Herman Lizzie the children, Gus & Allan selected a location & the others wandered through this new cemetery which she says will one day rival Greenwood . . . — *Catherine Gansevoort to her brother, Henry, Sept 19*

September 14? *Augusta Melville writes to her mother.* (Cousin Gus says "Poor Mackies death is a lesson to all who place pistols under their pillows he must have been handling the pistol, for it was found in his hand — His friend George Starr, had remonstrated with him several times, telling him, he would kill himself some day with his carelessness in using fire-arms . . . Cousin Herman she says is quite composed — Cousin Lizzie had not shed a tear but poor little Stanwix seems heart

[*689*]

broken. Cousin Tom, Allen Mrs. A. M., Millie & Gus Peebles, were all at the house . . . — *Catherine Gansevoort to her brother, Henry, Sept 16*)

ALBANY September 15 *Catherine Gansevoort writes to her brother, Henry:*
Last Friday's paper contained a notice of a sad case of suicide. That of *Malcolm Melville* — the eldest son of Herman Melville — I send you a Journal with the notice marked . . . I will however tell you about it for fear the paper may have been mis-carried . . . We have heard nothing from the family at Gansevoort — It will be a sad sad blow for Aunt Melville who thought Malcom a very promising young man — & Henry I believe you at one time saw a great deal of him. What kind of person was he . . . I pity the poor parents — both Cousin Herman & Lizzie are of such nervous temperaments I should fear for *their peace* of *mind*.

GANSEVOORT September 15? *Maria Melville writes to Catherine Gansevoort, enclosing letters from Augusta & Helen Griggs ("both of whom, are at that sad, sad home, 104 26th Street New York City").*
(Aunt Melville speaks of Malcom as a promising boy — good, kind, & gentle, & most aff. to all — & says he was in the habit of carrying a pistol & laying it under his pillow at night, & that she has no doubt he was examining it when it went off — & can never believe he committed suicide — A very natural conclusion for one who loved poor Malcom so dearly — He was her eldest Grandson, & all last winter was so devoted to her, & so kind in his little attentions. — *Catherine Gansevoort to her brother, Henry, Sept 16*)

NEW YORK September 16 The Evening Post *publishes two communications:*
The jurors on the inquest held in regard to the death of the son of Mr. Herman Melville have made the following explanation of their verdict:
"We, the undersigned jurors in the inquest of the death of Malcolm Melville, on the 11th inst., desire to correct any erroneous impressions drawn from their verdict of 'suicide.' We believe that his death was caused by his own hand, but not that the act was by premeditation or consciously done . . ."
[Signed by Dr. Alfred Starr, Charles C. Simpson, James Reed, Jr., William D. Forman, W. L. Childs.]
This goes to clear the reputation of the deceased young man from the imputation of suicide.
We have also received the following from Dr. Osgood:
                                                    New York, September 16, 1867.
"Messrs. Editors: — Will you allow me to say in your columns that I believe that a wrong impression of the cause of the death of young Malcolm Melville has been given by our newspapers, though unintentionally . . .
"I make this statement as the officiating clergyman, quite sure that Dr. Bellows, the regular pastor of the family, would have done the same if present . . .
                                                    "Samuel Osgood."

ALBANY September 16 *Catherine Gansevoort writes to her brother, Henry:*
Enough, of this sad story Henry & do you beware of carelessness with your pistols! — Suicide seems such a cowardly act — I wonder if poor Malcom reallly commited the act or was it an accident? — God only knows — May he spare us all from such a dreadful act . . . Cousin Herman is I think a very strict parent & Cousin Lizzie thoroughly good but inefficient. She feels so thankful she did not scold him or remonstrate as she intended So she cannot blame herself for having induced him from despair at her fault-finding, to put an end to his life.

I sometimes wish we mortals had the power of seeing the heart & feelings of our friends — I believe there would be greater happiness were such the case — We so often distrust & blame where we should not, because we judge wrongly — & mistake the motives of the actions of others . . .

I would write a line to Cousin Herman Henry! He will no doubt feel gratified to know you sympathize with him in the loss of his first born!

BOSTON September *Publication of a lengthy communication, signed J. C. H[oadley]., in the* Boston Weekly Advertiser [?]:
But it is sad to think that his memory should lie under the imputation either of such a crime as suicide or of such a fearful scourge as insanity, against which all the facts of the case revolt.

NEW YORK Before September 20? *M presents a tinted photograph of Malcolm Melville to his Volunteer Company.* (Herman presented it to the company soon after the dear boy's death in Sept. 1867 and I think there is an inscription on the frame to that effect — You would readily recognize it — a colored photograph of the full length figure . . . — *Elizabeth Melville to Catherine Gansevoort, May 6, 1872*)

PITTSFIELD Before September 20 *M & Elizabeth Melville visit the Allan Melvilles at Arrowhead.*

September 20 *Mrs Ellen Brittain gives Elizabeth Melville a copy of Faber's* Hymns (*Northampton, 1867*), *in which the inscription for Malcolm's grave-stone is found:*
> So good, so young,
> So gentle, so sincere,
> So loved, so early lost,
> May claim a tear.

September *M presents a copy of* Battle-Pieces *to "The College Colonel" — Major-General William F. Bartlett.*

NEW YORK September 29 *Thomas Melville writes to Catherine Gansevoort:*

Herman & Lizzy have been at Allan's making a visit & have just returned I think the visit has done them both good they feel poor Mackie's loss deeply.

October 10   *Herman & Elizabeth Melville purchase Lot 656, Catalpa plot, sections 24 & 23, in Woodlawn Cemetery.*

October 12   *M acquires* Poems *by William Cullen Bryant (New York, 1863) & reads it with a pencil; he triple-checks the poem "Earth," & scores these lines:*

> The forgotten graves
> Of the heart-broken utter forth their plaint
> The dust of her who loved and was betrayed,
> And him who died neglected in his age . . .

He checks the poem "The Living Lost," & scores its final lines:

> Grief for your sake is scorn for them
> Whom ye lament and all condemn;
> And o'er the world of spirits lies
> A gloom from which ye turn your eyes.

October 31   *M writes an authorization:*
District Office, No 4 N[orth] R[iver]. Oct 31, 1867 Mr. Henry L. Potter, my associate, is authorised to draw the money on my Pay Roll for the present month.

November 13   *Allan Melville writes to Catherine Gansevoort:*
   Captain Tom, for whose well doing we are all interested, will be urged by his friends here to fill a vacancy just about to happen in the position of Governor of the Sailors Snug Harbour, a place he is well calculated to fill, as is believed by Mr Greenleaf who has been the treasurer of the institution for 30 years and knows well (and none better), what qualities are most desirable in the incumbent, and who has spoken to me in confidence on the subject —

ALBANY   After November 13   *Catherine Gansevoort acts in Thomas Melville's behalf.* (Last week Allan wrote me asking if I could procure letters in Toms favor from Father, Judge Parker &c. I applied to Hon. Robert H. Pruyn who wrote a strong recommendatory letter, to Mayor Hoffman which he signed as also did Father & Judge Parker — I forwarded it as was desired, but could get no one to write to Senator Morgan or Rev. Morgan Dix Rector of Trinity Church. However my one epistle proved of service — Allan presented it in person . . . — *Catherine Gansevoort to her brother, Henry, Nov 21*)

NEW YORK   November 19   *Thomas Melville is elected Governor of Sailors' Snug Harbor.* (You are repaid for your exertions in behalf of Capt Tom, now Governor of the Sailors Snug Harbour to which honorable and desirable position he was unanimously elected by the Trustees of the institution — yesterday as I learned at a late hour last night. — *Allan Melville to Catherine Gansevoort, Nov 20; . . .* Mr Greenleaf an old friend of the family . . . no doubt was of great service in gaining the post for the son of his valued friend (our Aunt Melville). — *Catherine Gansevoort to her brother, Henry, Nov 21*)

Before November 24   *Catherine Gansevoort visits the Melvilles.* (I saw Cousin Herman & Lizzie while in N. Y. They all feel Malcolm's death but the knowledge of its not being a crime mitigates their grief. They sent Papa a carte photograph of Malcom . . . — *Catherine Gansevoort to her brother, Henry, Nov 24*)

ALBANY   November 25   *Catherine Gansevoort writes to her brother, Henry:*
[Thomas Melville] is delighted with this appointment, & will make a home for himself, Mother, & sisters at Staten Island. The Salary is $2000 — per annum, & after May 18th (when the Trustees meet again) it is supposed, it will be doubled —, So Tom has a nice berth . . .

GANSEVOORT   December 9   *Maria Melville writes to Catherine Gansevoort:*
I do not know that I shall leave home at all this winter. I have promised to go to Hermans early in the Spring, & make them a visit. Herman & Lizzie were very earnest to have us shut up the house last month . . . but I have come to think that threescore & ten & over if wise will remain snug at home through the cold winter months.

December 23   *Maria Melville relays to Catherine Gansevoort news from New York:*
Herman has not been well, but is now able to go out, his trouble was a "Kink in his back."

NEW YORK   December?   *The revived* Putnam's *exchanges letters with* M.

.   .   .   .   .   .

In response to a letter & volume sent him by Charles Warren Stoddard, M writes:
I have read with much pleasure the printed verses you sent me, and among others, was quite struck with the little effusion entitled "Cherries and Grapes"
I do not wonder that you found no traces of me in the Hawaiian Islands.

*

1 8 6 8

*

NEW YORK January [1] Putnam's Monthly *is revived as* Putnam's Magazine; *in this first number of the new series Charles F. Briggs publishes a memoir, "The Old and the New. A Retrospect and a Prospect":*

There are others [contributors], who have strangely disappeared from the world of letters, after letting their light shine for a brief while in the pages of the MONTHLY, who, we trust, are still among the living . . . And where, let us ask, is Herman Melville? Has that copious and imaginative author, who contributed so many brilliant articles to the MONTHLY, let fall his pen just where its use might have been so remunerative to himself, and so satisfactory to the public?

In the last pages of the issue:

The publishers have received cordial responses from eminent writers, in reply to their invitation for suggestions and cooperation . . .

Herman Melville, Esq., author of *"Typee."* — "I feel much complimented. * * * You may include me in the list of probable contributors."

January 8 *M acquires* Our Old Home: A Series of English Sketches, *by Nathaniel Hawthorne (Boston, 1863).*

VALPARAISO January *"R.S." sends to the Editor of* The Athenæum, *a report on a trip taken to "Melville's Marquesas" at the end of 1867:*

Melville's account of Typee (they always spoke of him as "Shore") was well known; and we were told that Fa-a-wa and a daughter of Melville's were still living, the former an old woman.

NEW YORK February 13 *Harper's sends M their 19th account, showing a sale of 486 copies of* Battle-Pieces *& a deficit of $338.93.*

March 5 *Elizabeth Melville clips from the* Boston Evening Transcript *of this date a poem entitled: "The Fount of Bitterness."*

March [?] *The Melvilles hear Dickens give a reading.* (So you have been to hear Dickens; we have had letters from New York & Boston, they all mentioned having been to hear Dickens's readings, & their opinions vary. — *Maria Melville to Catherine Gansevoort, Mar 23*)

April 22 *M acquires* Shelley Memorials . . . *(Boston, 1859).*

LONDON April 25 The Athenæum *publishes the letter from "R.S."*

GANSEVOORT May 6 *Maria Melville writes to Catherine Gansevoort:*

[694]

Tom writes me that I must get strong, & Herman & Tom have sent me strengthening cordials.

NEW YORK   May 29   *The Melville clan gathers at 26th Street.* (Aunt Melville & Fan went down to N.Y. last Friday . . . They are staying at Cousin Hermans in 26th St, also Cousin Kate Hoadley & children — *Catherine Gansevoort to her brother, Henry, June 1*)

M sends Catherine Gansevoort "a very sweet invitation" to stay at 26 Street when she attends the wedding of his brother, Thomas:
"Cousin Herman and Cousin Lizzie" will be glad indeed to have you stay with them so long as you please. We shall be a little crowded, but, on these occasions, the more the merrier, you know.
I have just brought Mama on from the H[udson] R[iver] R.R. Depot. She told me about your plans for coming down &c, so I hasten to dispatch this note.

June 4   [On the night of June 4] I stayed at Cousin Herman Melvilles — 104 East 26th St. as they very kindly invited me . . . — *Catherine Gansevoort to her brother, Henry, July 13*

June 5   *Catherine Gansevoort's diary:*
— returned to Cousin Herman's for Dinner . . .

June 6   *Thomas Melville & Catherine Bogart are married; the subsequent festivities are described by Catherine Gansevoort in her diary:*
. . . came home [to 104 East 26 Street] by 11 AM when we took the R.R. to New Rochelle accepting Mr Richard Lathers very kind & hospitable invitation to lunch at his beautiful country seat — carriages met our party — (the whole bridal Party & friends numbering over thirty) at the Station & we drove over to "*Winyah*" a lovely English home — The host & hostess Mr Richard Lathers & his wife née Thurston met us on the Piazza & we went up stairs & refreshed ourselves by a delicious wash — came down stairs & feasted on claret Punch & Cake — Heard the famous *Orchestrian* which contains some 22 Musical instruments — There are only two of the kind in this Country — & it was a rare treat — had [?] with some of the guests — wandered over the house — & looked at the pretty Articles of Vertu picked up in Europe — They gave us a splendid entertainment — bride's cake & all, in honor of Capt. Melville — Madame Melville the Mother was toasted as well & the others of the party — toasts given & we had a merry time — The Long Island party left at 5 P.M. & a number of us remained until the evening train down — We had a splendid train from the Tower The Hudson Palisades were visible & the Country looked lovely. walked over the grounds plucked wild flowers . . . We all enjoyed our day's excursion, Thanks to Mr Lathers warm heartedness.
Our Party consisted of *Dr. S. V. R. Bogart — Madame Melville*

Mr. & Mrs. Allan — Milly & Florence — Cousin Herman & Fanny — Mr John C. Hoadley & Minnie & Lottie & Kate Hoadley — Cousin *Helen Griggs — Fanny Melville Mr Greenleaf*, & *daughter* Tilly Mrs. *Barrington* Miss Effie Bogart & the Brides maids & grooms men E. Y. L[ansing]. & Belle Bogart — Mr Whittemore & Milly Melville Miss Minnie & Mr Osgood Mary Custis & Kate G[ansevoort] our grooms men being absent. &c &c —

SCHENECTADY July 15   *Guert Gansevoort dies.*

GANSEVOORT   August 8?   *M begins his two week vacation here.* (Cousin Herman Melville we expect from "Gansevoort Saratoga Co. to morrow. he is on route to "Arrowhead" where he intends joining Mrs. Herman & their two little girls, Lizzie & Fanny . . . — *Catherine Gansevoort to her brother, Henry, Aug 14*)

ALBANY   August 15   *Catherine Gansevoort's diary:*
Cousin Herman Melville arrived this A.M. from Gansevoort. Mother Carrie McC.L. & I drove out to the *Rural* Cemetery, had a lovely time — Herman is so interesting in conversation.

. . . we again visited this home for our dead, in company with Cousin Herman Melville (who I told you we expected) & Carrie McC.L. Made a long tour & saw all of interest stopped at the Dudley monument & that of Prince John Van Buren — a cross — entwined with Ivy. — *Catherine Gansevoort to her brother, Henry, Aug 19*

August 16   *Catherine Gansevoort's diary:*
This morning Cousin Herman & I went to St Peter's Ch — & afterwards walked up to St Josephs Ch. up 2d St to Swan & down Clinton Avenue. Dined at 103.N.Pearl . . .

Sunday Cousin Herman & I dined at 105 N.P[earl]. In the afternoon A.L[ansing] & the Major escorted "Typee" as Papa calls him to Kenwood Convent, for a view of the City — the Hudson & surrounding country. — *Catherine Gansevoort to her brother, Henry, Aug 19*

August 17   *Catherine Gansevoort's diary:*
Went with Cousin Herman to Genl. Rathbones Garden — It looked lovely . . . Dined at 2 P.M. & Cousin Herman left by the 3.50 train for Pittsfield.

Unhappy that I am, I went off without bidding you good-bye. But my bundles and my luggage, and the catching of the car, with my desire to be "on time" too much engrossed me . . .
I had a very pleasant ride here to Pittsfield, and at the house I found Lizzie and the children, who had arrived a few hours before me, and were well and frisky. Allan's family are all absent for a few days, leaving

only Kate to preside. But Kate, like all the Kates, inherits the good old Dutch talent for housekeeping, and takes good care of us. — *M to Catherine Gansevoort, Aug 18*

PITTSFIELD   August 18   *M writes to Catherine Gansevoort:*
I hope Uncle Peter enjoyed his afternoon ride yesterday, and was the better for it. My respectful and affectionate remembrances to him, and also to Aunt Susan; and say to both that I shall not soon forget my most agreeable visit to Albany, full of diversified pleasure.
The country hereabouts is looking as fresh as — yourself. I was going to say a rose, but chose the more appropriate comparison. However, I must cease this strain, for Lizzie just sat down by me and may catch me at it, and consider that I slightly [as] it may be, exceed the due limits of cousinly compliment.

Before August 24   *M returns to his inspector's desk at the Custom House office [at 62 Harrison?].* (During my two weeks' absence, the apartment underwent a horrible cleaning & setting-to-rights, which means putting things where one can't find 'em. — *M to Catherine Gansevoort, Sept 9*)

NEW YORK   August 25   *M is excused from his job to attend the funeral of George Adler:*
Adler was buried last Tuesday in the forenoon at Trinity Cemetery. I found Dr Houghton at St Michaels with Dr [Thomas M.] Peters and Warved [?] who all took part in the services, where I rode with Dr H to the grave. Herman Melville, [F. W.] Downer with me & two others were at the funeral and Dr. [D. Tilden] Brown of the Asylum in whose face and mien you may read the secret of Adler's regard for him. — *Evert Duyckinck to his son, George, Aug 30*

ALBANY   Before September 9   *Catherine Gansevoort writes to M, & sends him a photograph of a mausoleum[?].* (Thank you for your note. Following it came the photograph. What an imposing mass of masonry. But a critic must needs be fastidious. There appears on the central pediment a sort of dilated sentry-box, which seems to be without due foundation. Look for yourself, and if you agree with me, drop a polite note to the architect, and quote Vitruvius the great classic authority, — though old as our Era, — in architecture, you know. — *M to Catherine Gansevoort, Sept 9*)

NEW YORK   September 9   *M writes to Catherine Gansevoort:*
About the newspaper account of Cousin Guert, I have diligently searched my room, but in vain . . .
Concerning Stanny — tell Uncle Peter that the main reason why he did not stop at Albany was a violent cold, from which he still suffers in a

measure. He sends his love to all. As for Lizzy-Ann and the young ladies, I enjoined upon them not to omit that visit. But Lizzy-Ann is wilful, and I can't make her mind.

BOSTON Mid-September? *Elizabeth brings her daughters to Boston.*

September 14 *Hope Shaw writes to a relative [?]:*
Mrs Helen Griggs called here and I had a full and plain discourse with her about not writing to Mrs Melville, & giving her a sympathy for her distress relating to her husband when all Mrs M asks [is] a little sympathy from her friends.

NEW YORK September 29 *M acquires* The Men of the Time or Sketches of Living Notables (*New York, 1852*), *in which he scores & underscores, on p 136:*
CULLEN, PAUL, Roman catholic archbishop of Armagh, Ireland, and a notable enemy of the Copernican system of the universe . . .

& he acquires The Gulistan, or Rose-Garden; *by Musle-Huddeen Shaik Sâdy, of Sheeraz, translated by Francis Gladwin (London, 1822); he scores & underscores, in Sâdy's preface:*
Whosoever stretcheth out his neck claiming consequence, is beset by enemies from all quarters. Sâdy lies prostrate, freed from worldly desires; no man attempteth to combat with one who is down on the ground.
& scores:
Many a person has slept and hungered without anyone knowing who it was: many a vital spirit has departed, over which no one has wept.
& doubly scores:
In a season of scarcity and drought, inquire not of a distressed Durwaish how he does; unless you mean to apply ointment to his wound by giving him subsistence.

October 10 *M acquires an unidentified book.*

October 23 *Catherine Gansevoort's diary:*
Called on Cousin Lizzie & Herman at 104 East 26th St.

Early November? *Peter Gansevoort visits New York & calls at 26 Street.* (We were very glad that Uncle was so much benefited by his visit to New York — Herman wished me to say how sorry he was that he was not able to see him either of the times he called . . . — *Elizabeth Melville to Catherine Gansevoort, Nov 10*)

November 10 *Elizabeth Melville writes to Catherine Gansevoort:*
We thank your father and mother very much for their kind interest in Stanny, and their cordial invitation to him — but at present he would hardly be able to leave his post — he is Allan's only assistant, and being near the close of the year it is a busy time. We consider this position

for him merely a temporary one, & hope that he will be able to get something more permanent before many months — his hearing we think is improving under the treatment for catarrhal weakness — and as it is, perhaps he had better give it a fair trial before doing anything else — & he seems to feel much encouraged about it himself — Be assured we most fully value and appreciate your father's & mothers kindness & interest — Stanny would take much pleasure in visiting Albany, & I hope he may at some future time — as I much desire that all the children should be acquainted with their father's relatives as far as possible —

Stanwix Melville writes to his uncle, Peter Gansevoort:
I thank you for your very kind invitation, to come and see you and I should like to very much, but I am needed here in Uncle Allan's Office. My deafness has been a great trouble to me lately, but I am glad to say that it is getting better.

December 22   *Maria Melville & her daughters arrive.* (We arrived on Tuesday Eve^g the 22 Dec, Herman & Tom were at the Depot ready to receive us . . . — *Maria Melville to Peter Gansevoort, Jan 4, 1869*)

NEW BRIGHTON   December 25   *Christmas dinner at Thomas Melville's:*
I have seen my thirteen children & Grandchildren they are all well & seemed to enjoy the Christmas & New Years holidays . . .
On Christmas day the whole family dined here, Dr Bogart, wife & three daughters, Dr Edward Bogart wife & child, Herman Lizzie, Stanwix Bessie & Fanny, those five came in the morning & remained until the next day at Noon . . .
This seems to be a very social place little family whist parties, private Billiard tables, or I should say perhaps Billiard tables in private houses — are very general . . . — *Maria Melville to Peter Gansevoort, Jan 4, 1869*

NEW YORK   December 26   *M's family returns from Staten Island in the early afternoon, & in the evening Elizabeth Melville "made a little party for her nephew, Oakes Shaw, who is said to resemble Malcolm so much."* (*Maria Melville to Peter Gansevoort, Jan 4, 1869*)

*

1 8 6 9

*

NEW YORK   January 16   *M acquires* The Rule and Exercises of Holy Dying, &c, *by Jeremy Taylor; among other markings, M scores a passage on p 51:*
He that is no fool, but can consider wisely, if he be in love with this world,

we need not despair, but that a witty man might reconcile him with tortures, and make him think charitably of the rack, and be brought to dwell with vipers and dragons, and entertain his guests with the shrieks of mandrakes, cats, and screech-owls, with the filing of iron and the harshness of rending of silk, or to admire the harmony that is made by a herd of evening wolves, when they miss their draught of blood in their midnight revels. The groans of a man in a fit of the stone are worse than all these; and the distractions of a troubled conscience are worse than those groans; and yet a careless merry sinner is worse than all that.

NEW BRIGHTON February 10 *Maria Melville writes to Catherine Gansevoort:*
Augusta left 26 St — & is now staying here — next month we shall go to New York, & make Herman & Lizzie a visit.

Mid-February Last week we had a pleasant visit from Herman, & Lizzie & the children. Stanwix is full of the desire to go to sea, & see something of this great world. He used to talk to me about it, but I always tried to talk him out of it. But now he seems so bent upon it, that Herman & Lizzie have given their consent, thinking that *one* voyage to China will cure him of the fancy. So he may possibly sail with a Captain who is a friend of Tom's in a few weeks. You may have heard him speak of him Capt. Paul, there are three other boys, gentlemen's sons, who are also going, & they have a room to themselves. — *Augusta Melville to Catherine Gansevoort, Feb 23*

March 5 *M goes over to Staten Island to bring his mother back to the house.* (Augusta & myself with Tom & Herman as escort arrived here [104 East 26 Street] on Friday the 5th. The day was lovely & we enjoyed the water & its views, the ride to Hermans &c . . . — *Maria Melville to Catherine Gansevoort, Mar 13*)

NEW YORK March 12 Yesterday was charming weather. Lizzie invited me to a walk in the morning. In the afternoon Herman tempted me to take a walk to Madison Park. I accepted both invitations & felt better for the effort. We stopt to look at the fat little sparrows hopping about who seem to have feet, but no legs. — *Maria Melville to Catherine Gansevoort, Mar 13*

Madison Square, New York

March 31? *A party of Melvilles visits Stanwix's first ship.* (Yesterday Tom & Katie & quite a party of us went down to the "Yokohama" and made Capt. Paul's acquaintance. I like him much, & so does Lizzie who had a long talk with him. Herman has known him for years I believe. — *Augusta Melville to Catherine Gansevoort, April 1?*)

April 4   *The* Yokohama *sails for Canton.*

ALBANY April 16   *Maria Melville arrives at the Gansevoorts', & Catherine Gansevoort writes to her brother, Henry:*
Aunt Melville is quite rejuvenated by her stay on the Island & prefers it to Hermans home in 26th St. N.Y. City.

NEW BRIGHTON April 30   *Augusta Melville writes to Peter & Susan Gansevoort:*
They are all well at Herman's & Allan's. We saw them all this week.

NEW YORK May 8   *A sermon by Dr Bellows, at All Souls Church, suggests these lines to Elizabeth Melville:*
II Timothy 4th chap. 7th verse
"Hold on," my soul, with courage for the "fight"
"Hold out" my feet, the weary "course" to run
"Hold fast" my faith, bring patience to the "rack" —
    Oh God, thou knowest each hour of need! look down,
Give thine own help for courage, strength and faith,
    Or never may we win the victor's waiting crown.
                                                                E. S. M.

May 13   *M writes (from "Down Town") to Elias Dexter, framer, at 562 Broadway:*
    That mezzotint, The Healing of the Blind [by Rembrandt], which I left at your place — pray, be good enough to cause the Lettering at bottom, when cut off, to be glued upon the back of the frame. — I am glad, by the way, that my chance opinion of that picture receives the confirmation of such a judge as yourself. — Let me thank you for the little print after Murillo.

June 1   *Evert Duyckinck answers an inquiry by William Gilmore Simms:*
    The Melville letter must be a stupid joke of some possessor of the volume. It is not in M's hand writing and of course is not at all like him in any way. I will return it to you presently — though I do not see how I can throw any further light upon it. It is a curious affair even in the light of a stupid hoax.

Before June 4   *Elizabeth Melville writes to her mother-in-law.* (Heard from Lizzie, she is preparing to go to Boston some time this month with

Bessie & Fanny. Herman has to remain in town until some time in August when he will probably come to us [at Gansevoort] for the enjoyment of his short vacation. — *Maria Melville to Peter, Susan & Catherine Gansevoort, June 4*)

GANSEVOORT Before June 9 [*?*] *Maria Melville replies to her daughter-in-law.* (By letter from Gansevoort we heard how much Mama enjoyed her visit in Washington Avenue [Albany]. — *M to Peter Gansevoort, June 9*)

NEW YORK June 9 *M writes to Peter Gansevoort:*
Hearing that Kate thinks of visiting New York, I desire to say, that Lizzie and I will be extremely happy to welcome her to 26ᵗʰ St. We have a vacant room at her service, and expect her to occupy it ere long. All she has to do, is to notify us a day or two beforehand.
. . . The weather here is cool and pleasant, though we have had some sultry and unseasonable days.
My love and Lizzie's to Kate, and tell her to hasten her preparations, and come down before the Dog Star rageth.
His Excellency the Governor of the S.S.H. is, I am happy to state, well and happy. So is his wife.

June 11 *Catherine Gansevoort accepts M's invitation.* (Drove at once to 104 East 26ᵗʰ St. where we [Catherine & Henry Gansevoort] had a hearty welcome from Cousin Herman & Lizzie — The girls Bess, & Fanny had gone to School . . . — *Catherine Gansevoort's diary*)

June 13 [Elizabeth Melville's 47th birthday] *Catherine Gansevoort's diary:*
Went to Ch. with Cousin Lizzie. Heard Dᵣ Belors [Bellows] a famous unitarian preach — Dined at Hermans . . .

ALBANY June 26 *Catherine Gansevoort, returned, writes to her brother, Henry:*
I made a delightful visit at Staten Island & in New York. Cousin Lizzie & Herman Bessie, & Fanny — Kate & Tom M so kind.

STATEN ISLAND June 25 *Allan Melville sends to Evert Duyckinck an invitation from Thomas Melville to the Trustees' annual dinner at Sailors' Snug Harbor.*

June 28 *The Trustees of Sailors' Snug Harbor hold their annual dinner:*
(It will be a pleasant occasion & you will meet some friends Drs [Morgan] *Dix* & [William] *Paxton* are among the Trustees as well as Mr Dodge. Herman, Mr Lathers Mr Wilson G. Hunt will be present — only a few invited. 12 oclock is the best hour to go as all are going by that Boat. — *Allan Melville to Evert Duyckinck, June 25*)

Sailors' Snug Harbor, Staten Island

NEW YORK July 10   *M acquires* Essays in Criticism, *by Matthew Arnold (Boston, 1865), & reads it with a pencil; he first scores & underscores the legend opposite p 1:*

"Our antagonist is our helper. This amicable conflict with difficulty obliges us to an intimate acquaintance with our object, and compels us to consider it in all its relations. It will not suffer us to be superficial."   — Burke.

In the essay on Maurice de Guerin M triply scores on p 93:
But to a nature like his, endued with the passion for perfection, the necessity to produce, to produce constantly, to produce whether in the vein or out of the vein, to produce something good or bad or middling, as it may happen, but at all events *something,* — is the most intolerable of tortures.

& on p 99, he underscores:
In him, as in Keats, and as in . . . David Gray, — the temperament, the talent itself, is deeply influenced by their mysterious malady . . .

M's comment: **X** So is every one influenced — the robust, the weak — all constitutions — by the very fibre of the flesh, & chalk of the bone. We are what we were made.

& on p 102, he scores, underscores & boxes two passages:
"There is more power and beauty," [Maurice de Guerin] writes, "in the well-kept secret of one's self and one's thoughts, than in the display of a whole heaven that one may have inside one . . . The literary career seems to me unreal, both in its essence and in the rewards which one seeks from it, and

therefore fatally marred by a secret absurdity."

M's comment on the latter passage: **X** This is the finest verbal statement of a truth which every one who thinks in these days must have felt.

In the essay on Joubert, he scores & underscores on p 202:
. . . the delicacy of his health will not by itself account for his changeless preference of being to seeming, knowing to showing, <u>studying</u> to publishing . . .

In the essay on Spinoza, he brackets & comments:
". . . There shall no man speak to him, no man write to him, no man show him any kindness, no man stay under the same roof with him, no man come nigh him."

  With these amenities, the current compliments of theological parting, the Jews of the Portuguese synagogue at Amsterdam took in 1656 . . . their leave of their erring brother, Baruch or Benedict Spinoza.

M's comment: **X** These "amenities," are still, (tho not spoken) in vogue and even among the atheists.

In the essay on Marcus Aurelius, he boxes & comments on p 273:
". . . he is like a vine which has produced grapes, and seeks for nothing more after it has once produced its proper fruit . . ."

M's comment: **X** A maxim, and with even the better sort of men, is "Never do a thing without getting the credit of it."

In the essay "On Translating Homer," he marks two quoted lines of Wordsworth (from The Prelude, Book III):
   The marble index of a mind forever
   Voyaging through strange seas of Thought, alone.

August 4 [22nd wedding anniversary] *M purchases* The Poems of Winthrop Mackworth Praed (*2 vols, New York, 1866*).

August 9 *As birthday presents [?], M gives the first volume of Praed's poems to his sister, Augusta, & the second to his sister, Frances Priscilla.*

August 14 *M begins his two week vacation with a week-end at home.*

PITTSFIELD August 16 *Maria G. Melville's "Story of the Summer of 1869":*
. . . Mr. Herman Melville came up from New York at 6.P.M. . . .

August 19 On the 19 was a large Picnic on the Lake at which nearly all Pittsfield was present.

August 23 *Allan Melville writes to Col Henry Gansevoort:*
Herman is now with us.

NEW YORK August 30 *Inspector 75 is back at his desk [at 470 West Street?].*

September 7? *Augusta Melville comes to 26th Street.* (. . . you have heard of my coming to New York to be with Herman & the children until Lizzie was able to leave Boston. — *Augusta Melville to Peter Gansevoort, Sept 29*)

September 28   *His parents receive letters from Stanwix Melville, in Shanghai.* (Yesterday we had our first letters from Stanwix. He is well & happy. — *Augusta Melville to Peter Gansevoort, Sept 29;* Letters have been received from Stanwix Melville dated Shanghai, writes that his deafness has nearly left him, that he had been well, & liked the Sea even better than he had thought he would. — *Maria Melville to Catherine Gansevoort, Oct 8*)

September 29   *Augusta Melville writes to Peter Gansevoort:*
The last letter [from Elizabeth Melville] speaks of her gaining strength daily, so we may look for her return next week. Next Thursday I shall have been a month in the city. On that day October 7ᵗʰ I hope to turn my face homeward as it is high time I should do so.

NEW ROCHELLE   September 30   *Among the guests at Winyah Park, on the occasion of a presentation to Col Richard Lathers, are:*
. . . Capt. Luce of the ill-fated Arctic, Bishop Beckwith of Georgia, Herman Melville . . . (New York *Sun*)

NEW YORK   Mid-October   *Peter, Susan & Catherine Gansevoort visit New York.* (I have been hoping to be able to go and see you, but my persistent neuralgia & weakness have kept me housed since last Thursday — please tell Uncle with my love, that I shall make it my first object when I go out again — I hope you will be in the city for some time yet — The girls were much disappointed when the rain came down last Saturday, and prevented them from accepting your kind invitation . . . — *Elizabeth Melville to Susan Gansevoort, Oct 28*)

October 28   *Elizabeth Melville writes to Susan Gansevoort:*
If you see Herman, please do not tell him that I said he was *not well* — but if you think he looks well, I hope you will tell him so —

October 30   [?] *M takes his daughters to see the Gansevoorts.* (Herman says he will go with them next Saturday morning & take the chance of finding you in, (or they can go alone) but you must not let it interfere with any other engagements you may have — *Elizabeth Melville to Susan Gansevoort, Oct 28*)

Early November   *Catherine Gansevoort writes to Maria Melville.* (I am sorry to hear our dear Lizzie looks so ill, she has not been well since last summer. Her visit to Boston did not seem to restore her strength as she has fondly hoped it would, & always had done before. Every Spring she seems to lose her strength & appetite & with the fresh breath of spring

Flowers every spring she suffers from "Rose cold," which is in its effects a severe influenza lasting from six to eight weeks. Judge Shaw had during his lifetime what is called "The Hay Fever," attacking him in the month of September & continuing its uncomfortable visit for six weeks or more. — *Maria Melville to Catherine Gansevoort, Nov*)

November 25   *Thanksgiving dinner at 26th Street.* (Last week we had letters from all the scattered members of our family giving an account of their Thanksgiving . . . And Lizzie wrote about their splendid turkey sent all the way from Boston. — *Augusta Melville to Catherine Gansevoort, Nov 27*)

December 4   *M sends his photograph to Professor T. Apoleon Cheney.* (I had the great pleasure to be in receipt of your kind favor of Dec. 4th, '69 . . . my sincere thanks for it, together with the complimentary enclosure of your carte-de-visite . . . — *Cheney to M, Dec 7*)

WATKINS   December 7   *Professor T. Apoleon Cheney writes to M:*
  I will try to suggest — in accordance with mention made in your note of Dec. 19, '62 — that if you may now have it at your *convenience* to present our [Georgic] Library with any part of your Works . . . the generous favor would be gratefully appreciated.

1870 VIII 1880

1870: *Jan [?], Melville begins work on a long poem,* Clarel; *May, Melville sits for his portrait by J. O. Eaton; July, Stanwix Melville returns from sea*

1871: *Spring, Col. Henry Gansevoort dies; Stanwix leaves home again, but returns from Kansas by Winter*

1872: *Feb 9, Melville's brother Allan dies; Apr 1, his mother dies; Spring, Stanwix again leaves for Kansas & points South; Fall, the great Boston fire destroys Elizabeth Melville's Boston properties*

1873: *Jan, threat of dismissal from the Custom House is warded off; Stanwix returns home from Nicaragua, only to leave again, for California, by Apr*

1874: *Summer, the marriage of Melville's niece Maria to William Morewood; Fall, Melville's aunt, Susan Gansevoort, dies*

1875: *Spring [?], Melville plans a work of alternating prose & poetry,* Parthenope; *Summer, Stanwix returns from California to his former work as a dentist's assistant; Melville's uncle, Peter Gansevoort, proposes to pay for the publication of* Clarel; *Stanwix leaves again for California*

1876: *Jan, Melville arranges for the publication of* Clarel; *Peter Gansevoort dies; Spring, Melville's sister Augusta dies; June 3,* Clarel *is published*

1877: *Summer, dismissal from Custom House is again threatened, & Melville's working hours are increased*

1878: *Summer, Evert Duyckinck & Mrs Martha Marett die, the latter (Elizabeth Melville's aunt) willing Elizabeth & her children substantial sums of money*

1879: *Spring, the arthritis of Melville's daughter Bessie grows more serious; news comes of the tubercular condition of Stanwix in California*

1880: *Apr 5, Melville's daughter Frances marries Henry B. Thomas*

*

1 8 7 0

*

LONDON January 18? *Stanwix Melville writes to his parents.* (We have not heard from Stanwix since receiving his London letter in February . . . — *M to his mother, May 5; a clipping from a London newspaper, this date, marked "From Stanny"*)

NEW YORK Before January 27 *M & Elizabeth write to the Melvilles at Gansevoort.* (Herman & Lizzie write that they are all well there. They want us to come down next month, but the winter is so mild, Mamma sometimes thinks she will not leave home. — *Augusta Melville to Catherine Gansevoort, Jan 27*)

January 31 *M acquires two books by W. H. Bartlett for his work on* Clarel: Forty Days in the Desert, on The Track of the Israelites; or, a Journey from Cairo, by Wady Feiran, to Mount Sinai and Petra; *he scores, on pp 10 & 11:*
There is a terrible and triumphant power of the sun upon this wide region of sterility and death, like that of a despot over a realm blighted by his destructive sway: no trace of verdure is there but the stunted shrub, which straggles at wide intervals about the sandy bed of some dried watercourse . . .
There is a rapture in pacing alone with such fancies among the drifted sand-heaps, and listening to that wild music, till night has fallen upon the wilderness, over which millions of stars, rising up resplendently from the very edge of the vast horizon, seem quietly brooding. One may hear, as it were, the solemn pulsation of the universe.

& The Nile Boat in which he scores, on p 133:
. . . the system of oriental slavery, which is wanting in the far more cruel and hopeless despotism of the great western republic. [This is followed by correspondence from the *Cincinnati Herald* on a slave auction:]
'You see that man in the crowd,' pointing to one within a few paces of the stand, 'that is Dr. C. He hired that girl last year, and that child is his!' . . . her eyes rested on Dr. C., who instantly averted his face. She gazed one moment, then burst into a torrent of tears. She was knocked off to the Georgian. Thus the fiend saw his child and its mother sold into southern bondage.

ALBANY February 1 *Catherine Gansevoort writes to her brother, Henry:*

[709]

What have you heard of Stanwix Melville from what point did he run away? & where was his place of destination? — Poor Cousin Lizzie She will be almost broken hearted. Such is life & if boys are not boys in their childhood they will run away & explore for themselves when they should be preparing themselves for the duties of life.

NEW YORK Before February 7 *Richard Henry Stoddard & M serve at the Custom House:*
I knew him somewhat more than twenty years ago, when we both sat at the receipt of customs, I at the cold stone building in Wall Street, and he on the river front, but I did not know him as well as I could have wished, for we only met casually and officially and he was as reserved as a man of genius had a right to be. — *Richard Henry Stoddard to Elizabeth Melville, Oct 28, 1891*

Melville's official duty during the last years of my Custom House life confined him to the foot of Gansevoort Street, North River, and on a report that he might be changed to some district on the East River, he asked me to prevent the change, and Benedict said to me, "He shan't be moved," and he was not; and years later, on a second report of the same nature reaching him, I saw Benedict again, who declared with a profane expletive, "He shall stay there." (Stoddard, *Recollections Personal and Literary*)

February 8 *Mrs R. H. Stoddard's diary:*
Stoddard was turned out of the Custom-House yesterday without warning.

March 2 [Frances Melville's fifteenth birthday] *A birthday-party for Frances Melville.* (There was a Birthday party at Hermans the other night. — *Jane Melville to Col Henry Gansevoort, Mar 21*)

M presents a birthday gift to his daughter: The Buried Cities of Campania: or, Pompeii and Herculaneum . . . *by W. H. Davenport Adams (London, 1869).*

ALBANY March 3 *Catherine Gansevoort writes to her brother, Henry:*
If you see any of the Shaw family please ask about Stanwix Melville — if he has been heard from? —

NEW YORK March *Ellen Marett Gifford presents to M two albums of illustrations, by Moritz Retzsch (with explanations), to Schiller's "Pegasus in the Yoke," & "Fridolin, or The Message to the Forge."*

April 4 *M acquires for his work on* Clarel: Sinai and Palestine in Connection with Their History, *by Arthur Penrhyn Stanley (New York, 1863); in the introduction M underscores & comments:*
. . . of all the towns and temples we shall pass there is not one of the slightest historical interest — not the villages in the wilds of Australia and America can be less known or less important than these.

M's comment: **X** How naturally this allusion & illustration occurs here & how just.

ALBANY   May 2   *Maria Melville writes to her son, Herman.* (As you express a wish in your last letter dated the 2nd inst. to hear from me again before you leave Albany, I accordingly write this . . . — *M to his mother, May 5*)

NEW YORK   Before May 5   The other day I visited out of curiosity the Gansevoort Hotel, corner of "Little twelfth Street" and West Street. I bought a paper of tobacco by way of introducing myself: Then I said to the person who served me: "Can you tell me what this word 'Gansevoort' means? is it the name of a man? and if so, who was this Gansevoort?" Thereupon a solemn gentleman at a remote table spoke up: "Sir," said he, putting down his newspaper, "this hotel and the street of the same name are called after a very rich family who in old times owned a great deal of property hereabouts." The dense ignorance of this solemn gentleman, — his knowing nothing of the hero of Fort Stanwix, aroused such an indignation in my breast, that disdaining to enlighten his benighted soul, I left the place without further colloquy. Repairing to the philosophic privacy of the District Office [at 470 West] I then moralized upon the instability of human glory and the evanescence of — many other things. — *M to his mother, May 5*

M begins his sittings for his portrait by Joseph Oriel Eaton. (. . . that you may be satisfied that I have not been dilatory about the portrait, I will say that I have already had two sittings, and it is getting on. — *M to his mother, May 5*) [*See Pl. XIV*]

May 5   *M writes to his mother:*
   We have not heard from Stanwix since receiving his London letter in February, but are daily in expectation of one, tho' boy-like he may not think how anxiously we await it . . .
   Lizzie and the girls are well, and for some time past have devoted themselves to the shrine of Fashion, engaged in getting up the unaccountable phenomina and wonderful circumferential illusions which in these extraordinary days invest the figure of lovely woman. — I am called away and must close.

May 11   *M acquires* The Round Table: A Collection of Essays on Literature, Men, and Manners, *by William Hazlitt (Edinburgh, 1817); in Vol I M scores this passage on p 45:*
. . . there are occasions when it is refreshing to escape from the turmoil and final nothingness of the understanding, and repose upon that contentedness of mediocrity, which seems to have attained its end without the trouble of wisdom.
In Vol II M scores this passage on p 252:

[711]

The arts hold immediate communication with nature, and are only derived from that source. When that original impulse no longer exists, when the inspiration of genius is fled, all the attempts to recal it are no better than the tricks of galvanism to restore the dead to life.

GANSEVOORT June 3 *Maria Melville writes to Peter Gansevoort:*
Hermans Portrait is finished & was quite a success from the first sitting. Mr Hoadley is now in New York, having the portrait framed.

NEW YORK June 4 *M acquires Alexander Gilchrist's* Life of William Blake (*London, 1863*).

June 8 *M acquires* Passages from the American Notebooks *of Nathaniel Hawthorne* (Boston, 1868), *paying $4 for the two volumes.*

STATEN ISLAND Before June 12 *M visits his brother, Thomas, at Sailors' Snug Harbor.* (On a visit to the Harbor the other day, Tom handed me a handsomely framed engraving of the Hero of Fort Stanwix, saying that he was acting upon your request & that I was to regard it as a gift from Uncle Peter. — I write this to offer my acknowledgments for your kindness, and to say how much I prize it. — *M to Peter Gansevoort, June 12*)

NEW YORK June 12 *M writes to Peter Gansevoort:*
[Thomas] told me of the proposed visit of Fanny and Cousin Kate. When do they come? I trust that Tom will not wholly imprison them in his Paradise, but will permit the people of 26ᵗʰ St to have a share of their company.

June 14 Hermans portrait was quite a success. I had a small party on the 14ᵗʰ of June, and had determined, if possible to have Hermans portrait to grace my parlor. So, with Lizzies permission, I took a carriage and brought it home and stood it on the Piano. It was much admired. — *Jane Melville to Col Henry Gansevoort, June 26*

BOSTON July 18 *Hope Shaw's diary:*
Who should arrive today but Stanwix Melville from London.

July 19 You will be glad to hear that Herman's son Stanwix is now in Boston. His ship arrived from England this week. Lizzie came to her mother's the very day after his arrival, not knowing of his unexpected arrival. Bessie writes that he has grown much taller & stouter & looks very well. You can imagine how rejoiced Lizzie was to see him. — *Augusta Melville to Peter Gansevoort, July 30*

NEW YORK July *M acquires a [second?] copy of* The Scarlet Letter *by Hawthorne, & the* Diary, Reminiscences and Correspondence of Henry Crabb Robinson . . . (*Boston, 1869*); *in the latter he double-scores the last letter of Elton Hammond on p 427 of Vol I:*

Gentlemen, — To the charge of self-murder I plead not guilty. For there is no guilt in what I have done. Self-murder is a contradiction in terms. If the king who retires from his throne is guilty of high treason; if the man who takes money out of his own coffers and spends it is a thief; if he who burns his own hayrick is guilty of arson; or he who scourges himself of assault battery, then he who throws up his own life may be guilty of murder, — if not, not.

NORTH CONWAY Late July *M spends part of his vacation here.* (Hermann Melville and his wife have gone to North Conway. — *Margaret Duyckinck to her son, George, of July 25*)

BOSTON July 23 *Col Henry Gansevoort writes to his sister, Catherine:* Cousin Hermans Children are spending a few weeks at Mrs Shaws. Have not yet seen them.

GANSEVOORT Before August 13 *M visits here.*

ALBANY August 13 We had a short visit last evening from Cousin Herman who was on his way from Gansevoort to New York — he is looking remarkably well — & was very cheerful . . . — *Catherine Gansevoort to her brother, Henry, Aug 14?*; Coz Herman Melville was here a week ago Saturday . . . — *Catherine Gansevoort to her brother, Henry, Aug 22*

BOSTON August 20 *Hope Shaw's diary:* Saturday Mr Melville called & went to his sister [Helen] Griggs.

ALBANY August 22 *Catherine Gansevoort writes to her brother, Henry:* Have you seen Stanwix? he is at Gansevoort & Cousin Lizzie has gone off to the sea side with Lemuel Shaw.

August 29 *Stanwix Melville arrives for a two-day visit at the Gansevoorts'.* (Stanwix M. has grown — spread & developed into a manly boy of nineteen, quite a contrast to the boy of two years ago. He thinks of going to Lawrence Mass with his Uncle John Hoadley as he has a decided taste for Machinery. — *Catherine Gansevoort to her brother, Henry, this date*)

EDGARTOWN September 9 *Valentine Pease dies, at the age of 72 years.*

PITTSFIELD September 16 *Journal of Alexander Jackson Davis:* Ride to Pittsfield. Walk with [Allan?] Mellville to South mountain.

NEW YORK September *M sends John C. Hoadley an 1870 facsimile reprint of the original Kilmarnock edition of* Poems, Chiefly in the Scottish Dialect, *by Robert Burns.*

November 1 *M orders from Harper's:*

1 Rob Roy [on the Jordan, Nile, Red Sea, and Gennesareth, &c, . . . by John Macgregor] 1.67

November 2   *Harper's sends their 20th account to M, showing a decrease in the deficit to $187.71.*

PHILADELPHIA   November 2   *Thomas Melville purchases Samuel Johnson's* History of Rasselas *& inscribes it: "J. Bogart was married at West Chester today."*

NEW YORK   Before November 6   Last week I was in the city at Herman's & one evening we were surprised by a call from Mr Hoadley, he had been in town for a few hours on business & was on his way to the cars . . .

Mr Greenleaf & his daughter called to see me while at Herman's, he is looking remarkably bright & well, we are going over to pass a day with them soon . . . — *Frances Priscilla Melville to Catherine Gansevoort, Nov 7*

NEW BRIGHTON   November 17   *Frances Priscilla Melville writes to Catherine Gansevoort:*

I wish you could see Herman's portrait, it is such a grand one, a splendid likeness. Mr Hoadley had it taken for Mamma you know & when we return home [to Gansevoort], we take it with us.

NEW YORK   November 29   *Frances Priscilla Melville visits at 26th Street. (letter to Catherine Gansevoort, Nov 30)*

November   *M acquires* The Conduct of Life *by Ralph Waldo Emerson (London, 1860); in the essay on "Culture" M scores:*
You do not think you will find anything there [in Europe] which you have not seen at home?
M's comment: X Yet possibly, Rome or Athens has something to show or suggest that Chicago has not.
In the essay on "Worship" M scores & checks:
The religion of the early English poets is . . . so devout and so blasphemous, in the same breath. Such is Chaucer's extraordinary confusion of heaven and earth in the picture of Dido: —

> "She was fair,
> So young, so lusty, with her eyen glad,
> That if that God that heaven and earthe made
> Would have a love for beauty and goodness,
> And womanhede, truth, and seemliness,
> Whom should he loven but this lady sweet?
> There n' is no woman to him half so meet."

✔ With these grossnesses, we complacently compare our own taste and decorum.

[714]

M's comment: **X** The idea in the quoted lines is perfect poetry — therefore very far from blasphemous or gross — or so it seems to me.

In the essay, "Considerations by the Way" M scores:
In front of these sinister facts, the first lesson of history is *the good of evil*.
M's comment: **X** He still bethinks himself of his Optimism — he must make that good somehow against the eternal hell itself.

& in the same essay M scores:
By humiliations, by defeats, by loss of sympathy, *by gulfs of disparity*, learn a wider truth and humanity than that of a fine gentleman . . . A rich man was never insulted in his life: but this man must be stung.
M's comment: **X** Nothing can be truer or better said.

In the essay "Illusions" M comments on:
. . . it is the undisciplined will that is whipped with bad thoughts and bad fortunes.
M's comment: **X** Jumps into the pulpit, from off the tripod here.

&:
This reality [of simple virtues] is the foundation of friendship, religion, poetry, and art.
M's comment: **X** True & admirable! Bravo!

December 1   *M acquires Balzac's* Eugénie Grandet, *translated by O. W. Wright & F. B. Goodrich (New York, 1861); M scores & underscores on p 39:*
This sentiment [of pity], which had taken root in Grandet's heart, and was received in perfectly good part by his old servant, had something almost horrible in it. The atrocious miserly feeling of pity, which awakened a thousand agreeable sensations in the old cooper's heart, constituted Nanon's whole source of happiness.
M's comment: **X** What a plunge into that heart!
& scores and checks on p 179:
He had received the horrible education of that society, where, in a single evening, are committed, in thought and in words, more crimes than the law punishes at the Court of Assizes; where a jest or a sneer annihilates the grandest conceptions; where a man is deemed strong only as he sees clearly; and to see clearly there, is to believe in nothing, neither in feelings, nor in men, nor even in events; for they concoct false events.
M's comment: **X** This describes man in his consummate flower of civilization.

December 9   *M acquires Habington's* Castara *(Bristol, 1812); in "The Author" he scores:*
Nothing new is free from detraction, and when princes alter customes even heavie to the subject, best ordinances are interpreted innovations. Had I slept in the silence of my acquaintance, and affected no study beyond that which chase or field allowes, poetry had then beene no scandall upon me, and the love of learning no suspition of ill husbandry. But what malice, begot in the country upon ignorance, or in the city upon criticisme, shall prepare against

me, I am armed to endure . . . I think even these verses will have that proportion in the world's opinion, that Heaven hath allotted me in fortune; not so high, as to be wondred at, nor so low as to be contemned.
p 330:

> Even I, while humble zeale
> Makes fancie a sad truth indite,
> Insensible away doe steale:
> And when I'me lost in death's cold night,
> Who will remember, now I write? **X**

M's comment: **X** *I* remember thee, and more than 200 years after. At the end of the next 200 — I'll not answer for that.

Before December 15?   *M writes to Mrs Ellen Gifford.* (When Henry left here I gave him a note of introduction of Mrs Gifford, a cousin of Lizzie's now spending the winter at Nassau for her health. — *M to Susan Gansevoort, Jan 15, 1871*)

December 15 [Henry Gansevoort's 36th birthday]   *Catherine Gansevoort visits 26th Street.* (. . . the day you left . . . I soon vacated my room [at the Hotel] & went to Cousin Hermans for the night. — *letter to her brother, Henry, Dec 19*)

December 17   *Catherine Gansevoort leaves 26th Street.* (I came over here [to Staten Island] Saturday. Aunt Melville, & Fanny, are staying with Tom & Kate, & Cousin Gus at Hermans . . . — *her letter to her brother, Henry, Dec 19*)

December 25   *A Christmas present for Elizabeth from M:* Walks about the City and Environs of Jerusalem, *by W. H. Bartlett (London, n.d.).*

A Christmas present for his daughter, Bessie: Characteristics of Women, *by Mrs Anna Jameson (London, 1870).*

A Christmas present for his daughter, Frances: The Holy Grail, *by Tennyson (Boston, 1870).*

LONDON   December 25   *Dante Gabriel Rossetti writes to F. S. Ellis:*
I am going to add two to my list of high-class orders which you have already been favoured with: viz: a *Lemprière* and a book called *Pierre, or the Ambiguities*, by Herman Melville, which I believe is not easily met with like others of his, as it has not been republished in England.

NEW YORK   December   *M acquires* The Literary Works of Joshua Reynolds *(London, 1855).*
In Vol II, The Eleventh Discourse, M scores:
If we examine with a critical view the manner of those painters whom we consider as patterns, we shall find that their great fame does not proceed from their works being more highly finished than those of other artists, or from a more minute attention to details, but from that enlarged comprehension which

sees the whole object at once, and that energy of art which gives its characteristic effect by adequate expression.

In The Thirteenth Discourse M scores:

What has been said, may show the Artist how necessary it is, when he looks
about him for the advice and criticism of his friends, to make some distinc-
tion of the character, taste, experience, and observation in this Art, of those,
from whom it is received.

In The Fourteenth Discourse M scores:

However they may appear to superficial observers, painters know very well
that a steady attention to the general effect takes up more time, and is much
more laborious to the mind, than any mode of high finishing, or smoothness,
without such attention.

In The Fifteenth Discourse M triply scores:

He that is sure of the goodness of his ship and tackle puts out fearlessly from
the shore . . .

· · · · ·

NEW YORK

. . . late one night about 1870 [M] was one of a cheerful group of four who
walked up Fourth Avenue from the Century Club, which was then in Fifteenth Street . . . I often recall him as one of the very most agreeable men
I have ever met. (Henry Holt, *Garrulities of an Octogenarian Editor*)

＊

1 8 7 1

＊

January 6   *M acquires* The Snow-Image and Other Twice-Told Tales,
*by Nathaniel Hawthorne (Boston, 1865), & scores two passages in "The
Devil in Manuscript":*

"No," said Oberon, tossing the manuscripts on the table. ". . . My picture,
painted in what seemed the loveliest hues, presents nothing but a faded and
indistinguishable surface. I have been eloquent and poetical and humorous in
a dream — and behold! it is all nonsense, now that I am awake." . . .

"Let me alone!" cried Oberon, his eyes flashing fire. "I will burn them!
Not a scorched syllable shall escape! Would you have me a damned author? —
To undergo sneers, taunts, abuse, and cold neglect, and faint praise, bestowed,
for pity's sake, against the giver's conscience! A hissing and a laughing-stock
to my own traitorous thoughts! An outlaw from the protection of the grave —
one whose ashes every careless foot might spurn, unhonored in life, and remembered scornfully in death! Am I to bear all this, when yonder fire will
insure me from the whole? No! There go the tales! May my hand wither
when it would write another!"

January 7   *Augusta Melville writes to Catherine Gansevoort:*

Lizzie says Herman said at the breakfast table this morning, see that a letter goes to Kate Gansevoort inviting her to come right here."

NASSAU   Before January 15   *Mrs Ellen Gifford writes to M. (M to Susan Gansevoort, Jan 15)*

NEW YORK   January 15   *M writes to Susan Gansevoort, enclosing Mrs Gifford's letter to him:*
I enclose the letter to you. I felt some reluctance in so doing until Allan happened to inform me this evening of Abraham Lansing's leaving here for Havana, and that you had heard no favorable tidings of Henry from some passenger in the last steamer from Nassau.

January 20   *M acquires another edition of Shakespeare's Sonnets (Boston, 1865), checking XV, XVII, XX, XXII, XXV, this passage in XXVI:*
> I may not evermore acknowledge thee,
> Lest my bewailed guilt should do thee shame;
> Nor thou with public kindness honour me,
> Unless thou take that honour from thy name . . .

triple-checking in LXVI:
> Tired with all these, for restful death I cry . . .

& CXXII, & CXXIII.

January 27   *M acquires* In Memoriam [*by Alfred Tennyson*] (*Boston, 1865*), *scoring the last two stanzas of canto LXXIII:*
> Thy leaf has perished in the green,
>   And, while we breathe beneath the sun,
>   The world which credits what is done
> Is cold to all that might have been.
>
> So here shall silence guard thy fame;
>   But somewhere, out of human view,
>   Whate'er thy hands are set to do
> Is wrought with tumult of acclaim.

February 13   *M acquires Matthew Arnold's* New Poems (*Boston, 1867*), *scoring these passages in "Empedocles on Etna":*
> 'T is not the times, 't is not the sophists vex him;
> There is some root of suffering in himself,
> Some secret and unfollowed vein of woe,
> Which makes the time look black and sad to him . . .
>   Couldst thou but once discern
>   Thou hast no *right* to bliss,
> No title from the Gods to welfare and repose . . .

M's erased comment: A Western critic here exclaims — "Where in thunder did the Gods create us for then? If not for bliss, for hate? If so, the devil take the Gods."

> The mass swells more and more
> Of volumes yet to read,
> Of secrets yet to explore.

M's comment: **X** "Damn the volumes," exclaims the Western critic. — "What could a sage of the nineteenth century teach Socrates? Why, nothing more than something about Cyrus Feilds and the ocean telegraph, and the Sewing Machine &c"

March 12   *John C. Hoadley makes M a gift:* The Art Idea: Part Second of Confessions of an Inquirer, *by James Jackson Jarves* (New York, *1864*); *M scores this passage on Egyptian art on pp 31-32:*
Every phase of existence contains within itself its seeds of destruction, or, more strictly speaking, change, by which a higher condition of life is ultimately evolved out of the lower. Ideas and manners go through as natural a process of growth, decay, and renewal in new forms, as does the vegetable creation.
& scores on p 206:
But the artistic fire was too deep within him to be put out even by the aesthetic chill of New England. What a man of the exquisite impressibility of Allston must have felt in this atmosphere can only be conjectured. He, however, nobly stood to his post . . .

Before April 8   *Catherine Gansevoort brings her dying brother, Henry, back from Nassau.*

April 8   *Augusta Melville writes to Susan Gansevoort:*
Herman & Lizzie have just called [on Henry Gansevoort].

April 12   *Colonel Henry Sanford Gansevoort dies on board the* Drew, *on his way home to Albany.*

KANSAS CITY   Before May 17   *Edwin Lansing writes to M about his son, Stanwix. (Elizabeth Melville to Catherine Gansevoort, May 17)*

NEW YORK   May 17   *Elizabeth Melville writes to Catherine Gansevoort:*
Please tell Mama (and I know that you will be interested to hear) that we had another letter from Stanny today, from the interior of Kansas — on the line of the Santa Fe R. R. whither he had gone by advice of Mr Lansing (or Brewster, or both) both of whom he found on his first arrival in Kansas City — They have been exceedingly kind to him, and it is a great relief to me that he has found such good friends — Mr Lansing was kind enough to write to Herman himself, the other day about him —

May 22   [Bessie's 18th birthday]   *M gives his copy of* In Memoriam *to his daughter, Bessie, as a birthday gift.*

May 28 *Elizabeth Melville writes to Catherine Gansevoort:*
Mrs Gifford has been in the city for a week, but I have not seen her
yet, being housed with my lame foot, but Herman and I are going to
try to get there this evening — she is at the New York Hotel.

May *M acquires* Greece, Pictorial, Descriptive, and Historically, *by
Christopher Wordsworth, D.D. (London, 1844), & scores this passage
on p 319:*
[The Temple of Apollo at Bassae] was founded, not in a spot to which the
materials for building could readily be brought, or where it might display to
passing crowds the evidence it afforded of the affluence and skill of those who
erected it; but it stood alone, exposed to winds and storms, on a bleak and
rugged mountain difficult of access, and seeming, by its seclusion and solitude,
to ask for no other notice than that of the Deity to whom it was consecrated.

NORTH CONWAY Summer *M spends his vacation here.* (About not
coming to see you. — I am only allowed two weeks' vacation. This I
take in the summer; and last summer I spent it, for a change, at North
Conway, with Lizzie. Had I gone to Northumberland as usual, I should
not have failed seeing you on the way, going or returning. — *M to Peter
Gansevoort, Dec 26*)

PITTSFIELD October 25 *J. E. A. Smith writes to Allan Melville:*
Many thanks for the volumes of your brother's works rec'd by the
[Berkshire] Athenaeum . . . I wish we could get a copy of [a portrait
of Major Thomas Melvill], and also Mr. Herman Melville's on steel for
our history which will go to press about the first of next June.

LONDON October 25 *Lemuel Shaw writes to his brother, Samuel:*
We are to bring home the Rev. Mr Alger who is hopelessly insane, in a
hospital in Paris . . .

NEW YORK Autumn? *M acquires* The Solitudes of Nature and of Man;
or, The Loneliness of Human Life, *by William Rounseville Alger (Boston, 1867); in it M marks on p 110:*
Even the kindly Emerson illustrates the temptation of the great to scorn the
commonalty, when he speaks of "enormous populations, like moving cheese, —
the more, the worse"; "the guano-races of mankind"; "the worst of charity is,
that the lives you are asked to preserve are not worth preserving"; "masses!
the calamity is the masses . . ."
M's comment: X These expressions attributed to the "kindly Emerson"
are somewhat different from the words of Christ to the multitude on the
Mount [an erasure] — Abhor pride, abhor malignity, but not grief &
poverty and the natural vices these generate.
On p 158 M scores:
Schopenhauer says: "For the most part we have only the choice between
solitude and vulgarity. The most social men are the least intellectual. To say

'He is very unsocial,' is almost equivalent to saying, 'He is a man of great qualities.'"

On p 268 M underscores:

[Beethoven] says, "I was nigh taking my life with my own hands. But Art held me back. I could not leave the world until I had revealed what lay within me."

On p 295 M scores:

A poem published at that time referred to [Byron] thus: —

> Wisely he seeks some yet untrodden shore,
> For those who know him less may prize him more.

On p 394 M scores:

There is one text [by Jesus], however, fit to be the motto of all truly aristocratic souls who writhe back from the stinging wrong and scorn of a misappreciating world . . . "Cast not your pearls before swine, lest they trample them under their feet, and turn again and rend you."

ALBANY Before November 13 *Catherine Gansevoort sends an intaglio ring to M, with this note:*

I send you an intaglio ring which I have chosen for you at the request of my dear Brother Henry S. Gansevoort. He desired that all his blood Cousins should be given rings in his memory — as his gift — I hope you will wear this as a memorial of one who lived a pure & noble life, & was sincerely attached to you & your family.

NEW YORK November 13 *M acknowledges the gift:*

Be assured that I shall sacredly preserve the ring, esteeming it as if it have been given me by the living hand — *his* who now lies so honorably at rest.

[P.S.] Promptitude must atone for brevity

ALBANY Mid-December Augusta tells me that during her late visit in Washington Avenue you kindly enquired after me, asked 'why I did not come to see you, and also expressed a desire that I should write you. — *M to Peter Gansevoort, Dec 26*

NEW YORK December 25 *Christmas presents — from M to his son, Stanwix:* The Words of Wellington (*New York, 1869*); *from M to his daughter, Bessie:* Emblems, Divine and Moral, *by Francis Quarles (London, 1866*).

NEW BRIGHTON December 25 Yesterday (Christmas) we all dined on Staten Island at Tom's, who gave us a bountiful and luxurious banquet. It was a big table, belted round by big appetites and bigger hearts, but the biggest of all the hearts was at the head of the table — being big with satisfaction at seeing us enjoying ourselves. Mamma looked uncommonly well; and Helen, Augusta, Kate (two Kates), Fanny, Minnie, Lottie, Frankie, Bessie, Fanny, Stanny, Mr Hoadley, Mr Griggs, not excluding the present modest writer — we all looked very well indeed.

Among the toasts Uncle Peter was remembered, Aunt Susan & Cousin Kate; nor was Henry forgotten. Tom offered that toast to his memory.

Stanny and I were obliged to leave at an early — or rather early hour, in order to take the last boat for New York. We left them still enjoying themselves in the parlors. — *M to Peter Gansevoort, Dec 26*

Augusta, I believe has written you all about the family gathering at Tom's on Christmas Day — It was a pleasant meeting, though it comes at last that these anniversaries bring as much of sadness as gladness, and the places left vacant by the dear ones who have "gone up higher" seem more empty still — And were it not for the sympathy and interest in the young branches who are able to hail these seasons with delight, I for one would almost be glad to let them pass without outward notice —

I was glad to see Mother Melville looking so well and bright — she is certainly a most remarkable old lady . . . — *Elizabeth Melville to Catherine Gansevoort, Jan 9, 1872*

NEW YORK   December 26   *M reports the Christmas festivities to Peter Gansevoort:*

I write this at my office [470 West Street], so you must excuse the paper; it is the best I happen to have at hand here.

December   *M acquires vols I & II of* The Works of Eminent Masters, in Painting, Sculpture, Architecture, and Decorative Art (*London, 1854*).

*

1 8 7 2

*

LAWRENCE   January 1   *Augusta Melville writes to Peter Gansevoort:*

You will be glad to hear, my dear Uncle, that Mr. Hoadley had engaged Mr. Eaton to paint Mamma's portrait. You will remember he was so very successful in taking Herman's.

He is expected this week to begin with the sittings, while Mamma is looking so well, John says.

NEW YORK   January 9   *Elizabeth Melville writes to Catherine Gansevoort:*

Do you not think, dear Kate that you could come down to the city while so many of the family are here? If you would come and stay with us, we should be most happy to have you, and I would do all in my power to make you comfortable — You know you could not come to a quieter house than this, where you might be at liberty to do just as you liked, and I think a change of scene at times is best for all of us . . .

LAWRENCE February 3 *Augusta Melville passes on to Catherine Gansevoort news from New York:*
We are all so sorry that Mamma's indisposition should have put a stop to the sittings for her portrait, for John [Hoadley] says that Mr Eaton's engagements will prevent his going on with it for some weeks to come. Fanny writes that it is excellent so far.

NEW YORK February 9 *Allan Melville dies.* (*The change* was very sudden & Allan died in great agony his *well lung* having *colapsed* as far as I can judge from what I have heard . . . — *Catherine Gansevoort to her parents, Feb 11*)

February 10 *Catherine Gansevoort arrives to attend Allan Melville's funeral:*
We arrived safely a few moments after 7 P.M. came directly here — (Cousin Herman Melville's — 104 E. 26 St.) found Bessie & Fanny waiting for me & Cousins Lizzie & Herman up at Cousin Allan's house — Abe very kindly took me up to 109 E. 35th St. — & left me — I saw them all — Jennie & the girls — & they are so heart broken at the sudden Death of their Father & of *her loved husband* — the rudder of the household — *Catherine Gansevoort to her parents, Feb 11*

LANSINGBURGH? Before February 11 *Augustus Peebles writes to M.* (Your letter to Herman, Mamma has asked me to answer; he sent it over to us to-day. — *Helen Griggs to Augustus Peebles, Feb 12*)

NEW YORK February 11 *Catherine Gansevoort writes to her parents:*
Aunt Melville is very feeble — & confined to her bed & wants me to come over & see her . . .
Allan looks *so young* & *so fair* — & this is his first Sabbath in the unknown world of spirits . . . The funeral takes place from Zion Church [Feb 12] at 2 P.M. & we are *all* going to *Trinity Cemetery*, near — Carmansville [?] — up the River —

February 14 *Catherine Gansevoort's diary:*
Staid on the [Staten] Island until this afternoon when I returned to Cousin Herman, leaving Aunt Melville very miserable.

NEW BRIGHTON February 17? *Augusta Melville writes to Peter & Susan Gansevoort:*
Kate's visit & affectionate attention to her gave [Aunt Melville] great pleasure. Herman was here this morning, & said she was to leave New York for Albany at 10 O'clock.

February 18   Helen Melville Griggs writes to her brother, M. (Papa had a note from Aunt Helen this afternoon, saying that Grandma was about the same. — *Fanny Melville to Catherine Gansevoort, this date*)

February 20   M visits his mother. (Yesterday [she was] more comfortable again & able to see Herman & the children. — *Augusta Melville to Catherine Gansevoort, Feb 21*)

February 26   Augusta Melville writes to Peter & Susan Gansevoort:
Mamma just called me to her bedside, & said "Augusta, I want you to write to your Uncle & Aunt Susan, & tell them how comfortable I have been to-day, & was yesterday; that that dreadful oppression has left me, & I have no pain nor uneasiness now. That I am in God's hands to restore me to my usual health, or take me to himself. His will be done."
"And tell them that Dr. Irving was here this afternoon & administered to me the Communion That all my children were with me, my four daughters, & Herman & Tom, & John & Katie, & that Mrs Bogart & Evie joined us; & that they sang sweetly that beautiful hymn
"Abide with me
Fast flows the even-tide
The darkness thickens,
Lord with me abide"
I wish you both, & dear Kate, could have heard that lovely chant. Never shall I forget those sweet notes, nor the impressive scene of this afternoon. The western sun shining in so brightly, & that group around the bed, Mamma's perfect composure, & Dr. Irving's solemnity . . .
And now Mama wants me to thank Kate for her beautiful flowers sent by John, & say that they brightened up her room to-day with Herman's, & Tom's & Katie's —

March 11   Helen Melville Griggs leaves to attend the funeral of her uncle, John D'Wolf, age 92.

NEW YORK *March 23   M acquires* Passages from the French and Italian Notebooks *of Nathaniel Hawthorne, in which he scores a passage on p 50 of Vol I:*
My receptive faculty is very limited, and when the utmost of its small capacity is full, I become perfectly miserable, and the more so the better worth seeing are the things I am forced to reject. I do not know a greater misery; to see sights after such repletion, is to the mind what it would be to the body to have dainties forced down the throat long after the appetite was satiated.

NEW BRIGHTON April 1   *Maria Gansevoort Melville dies, at the age of 81.*

NEW YORK April 2   *Catherine Gansevoort, come to attend her aunt's funeral, stays at 26th Street.* (her diary)

April 3   *M gives Abraham Lansing a present:* Memoirs of Samuel Pepys, Esq.

NEW BRIGHTON   April 3   *Catherine Gansevoort's diary:*
Went over [to Staten Island] with Herman, by 12 M. Boat saw Aunt Melville & the girls — all *her children* & sons, & daughters in law were there Aunt Melville looks so naturally — dressed in white Alpaca dress — tulle cap — & just as *she* directed — What a remarkable woman — Dr Thos. E. Vermilyea officiated at the Funeral services which took place at 3 PM. A large number of relatives & friends filled the house — & afterwards left, *the remains*, with us, for the night.

ALBANY   April 4   Tom. Melville & wife, Fanny, Kate, & Mr Hoadley. — Helen, Dr Bogart — Mrs Allan Melville & her *four* daughters — Cousin Herman & Stanwix A. L[ansing] & K.G. met at the Depot 42 St, to convey, by the 10^30 Train the remains of their dear Mother . . . to Albany to be interred in the Vault at the Cemetery. Mother met us at the upper depot — Mr Morange gave us a terrible quick drive to the Cemetery where Dr Clark made *some* remarks & we all returned & had a dinner at 115 Wash[ington] Ave. . . . How many more of those I love must I see buried?

NEW YORK   Before April 22   [*?*] *M writes to Elizabeth.* ([Stanwix] is full of the idea of going West again. Herman, I believe, has written Lizzie about it. — *Augusta Melville to Hope Shaw, Apr 22*)

STATEN ISLAND   April 21   Last evening [M] went with us to hear an eloquent minister at New Brighton. Stannie took care of the house for us. — *Augusta Melville to Hope Shaw, Apr 22*

April 22   *Augusta Melville writes to Hope Shaw:*
   Lizzie's letter to Kate has just been received. We are both very glad to hear that she has been out to drive, & now proposes walking out for the air. We hope that she may soon be able to join Herman here. He & Stannie left us with Tom for New York after our seven O'clock breakfast. He is quite like his old natural self, & seems to take an interest in every thing; & it is very pleasant having him here.

NEW YORK   April 30   *M replies to Samuel Drake's request for information on Major Thomas Melvill:*
Dear Sir: I am sorry that the little that is peculiar in the information I possess with regard to my grandfather the late Major Melville of Boston is but of that familiar sort hardly adapted to historical use.
   Concerning the more interesting event — his connection with the "Tea Party," I think I know nothing that has not already received local mention . . .
   I renew my regret at being forced to send you so barren a response.

[725]

April   *Stanwix Melville leaves, heading for "a small town [Sedgwick] in Kansas."*

May 6   *Elizabeth Melville writes to Catherine Gansevoort:*
If you could get that picture of Macky for me, dear Kate, I should be so happy — it seems as if we might have it, when it is of so much value to us, and so little to anyone else It went to Albany with the effects of Company "B."

Second Reg^t of Infantry
First Brigade First Division
N.Y.S.N.G.

when the regiment was disbanded, or consolidated with others — And I have been told that an application to Adjt. Gen. Townsend will doubtless be all that is necessary to secure it — Herman presented it to the company soon after the dear boy's death in Sept. 1867 . . .

STATEN ISLAND   June 2   *Catherine Gansevoort's diary:*
Cousin Herman & Lizzie are staying here.

NEW YORK   June 12   *Harper's sends its 21st account to M showing a slight increase in the deficit to $210.55, partly due to M's book orders, including on this date:*
    [The Desert of the] Exodus [by E. H. Palmer] $2.10
                Robertson   1.05

STATEN ISLAND   June 17   *The annual dinner of the trustees of Sailors' Snug Harbor. (Elizabeth Melville to Catherine Gansevoort, June 13)*

NEW YORK   Before July 17   *The photograph of Malcolm Melville is traced to the home of Robert Coster on 53 Street, & M calls at that address without finding him home.*

July 17   *M brings a water-color painting to 53 Street, & carries a photograph away.* (. . . we have the much-wished for picture of our dear boy — owing to the excessive heat mainly, Herman has not been able to get it from 53^d st till today — as on his first call Mr. Coster was not in, & he had to find him at his place of business — Herman found the picture occupying a conspicuous position over the mantlepiece in their pretty little parlor (they are a newly married couple) and not wishing to leave the place absolutely vacant, he carried a pretty water-color, handsomely framed, to replace it . . . — *Elizabeth Melville to Catherine Gansevoort, this date*)

Elizabeth Melville writes to Catherine Gansevoort:
Stanny is still in Sedgwick, Harvey Co Kansas — where he went first, & he expects to remain there for the present —

SEDGWICK-NEW ORLEANS   July ?   . . . I thought I could do better South, so I came down through the Indian Nation, & then into Arkansas, I stopped at a number of towns on the Arkansas river till I came to the Mississippi, then down that river to Vicksburgh I staid there a few days, & then took the train to Jackson, from there by Railroad to New Orleans, I found that a lively city, but no work . . . — *Stanwix Melville to his grandmother, Feb 23, 1873*

NEW YORK July ? *M writes to his son, Stanwix, at some point on his itinerary:*
. . . rejoiced that you have . . . of going to New Orleans . . . can not but think . . . to Ellis on the farm . . . Your affectionate father
H. Melville

August 1 [M's fifty-third birthday] *Elizabeth Melville gives her husband a birthday present:* Septimius Felton; or The Elixir of Life, *by Nathaniel Hawthorne (Boston, 1872).*

August 3 *M begins his vacation by taking his wife to Pittsfield.* (Herman and I expect to go to Pittsfield the first week in Aug. on Sat. the 3ᵈ I think, if we find there is an afternoon train — as his vacation will date from Monday — I am impatient to go, for Jenny has kindly invited the girls to be there at the same time, and I so long to see them again . . . — *Elizabeth Melville to Catherine Gansevoort, July 17;* Herman & Lizzie left here yesterday for Pittsfield where they will stay some days & then go to Gansevoort. — *Mr & Mrs Thomas Melville to Catherine Gansevoort, Aug 4)*

PITTSFIELD August 4 [25th wedding anniversary] *M & Elizabeth celebrate their silver wedding anniversary in the company of their daughters, & their late brother's family.*

GANSEVOORT Before August 19 *M comes here before the end of his vacation.* (Since I wrote you last we have had visits from Herman; & Tom; & Lizzie & Samuel Shaw. — *Augusta Melville to Catherine Gansevoort, Aug 31)*

NEW YORK August 19 *M returns to his desk at 470 West Street at the end of his two-week vacation.*

PHILADELPHIA After August *Publication of* A Manual of American Literature *by John S. Hart, including a critical sketch of M's career:*
Melville is the author of several exciting works based upon his adventures . . . His two best works are, perhaps, Typee and Redburn . . . [*Typee*] and its successors attracted great attention at the time of their appearance, and although interest in them has since abated, they are still excellent in point of style. Melville is a writer of forcible and graceful English, although in some of his works he lapses into mysticism.

QUEBEC September 2 *Samuel Shaw reports to his mother on his half-sister, Elizabeth Melville:*
Elizabeth's catarrh is somewhat relieved here but I am sorry to see how generally feeble she is, and prematurely old.

NEW YORK November 5 *Jane Melville writes to Catherine Gansevoort:*
I saw Lizzie yesterday — and shall see her again this evening. She is looking very well indeed. There is considerable excitement here this evening owing to the Election returns —

BOSTON November 9 *The great Boston fire begins, destroying seventy-five millions in property.* (The fire is the all-absorbing topic, and friends on every side have met with losses greater or less — I have plenty to keep me company . . . — *Elizabeth Melville to Catherine Gansevoort, Dec 10;* The loss of $5000. — by the Boston fire, carrying with it an income of $500. — part of the small property left her by her Father, making Mrs. Melville additionally solicitous that Mr. Melville should retain his place. — *John Hoadley to George Boutwell, Jan 9, 1873*)

GANSEVOORT November 20 *Augusta & Frances Priscilla Melville write to their brother, Herman, in regard to the inscription on their mother's tomb.* (. . . & to ask you to hand the enclosed note to Herman. He will tell you if he thinks with us, & approves [of the inscription]. I spoke to Tom, but Herman will enclose his note if he does not see him. — *their letter to Catherine Gansevoort, this date*)

NEW YORK November 30 *M writes to Susan Gansevoort.*

ALBANY Early December? *Catherine Gansevoort sends her cousins a silver soup ladle to commemorate their silver wedding anniversary, & Peter Gansevoort presents M with a gift of money ($500).*

NEW YORK December 6 *Bessie Melville writes to Catherine Gansevoort, on her father's behalf:*
Papa wanted me to write a few lines to thank you for the soup ladle — he would write himself but he has a very bad attack of influenza which keeps him in the house today — He was very much pleased with it, thought it was beautiful —

December 7 *Bessie Melville writes again to Catherine Gansevoort:*
Papa has been, or rather *is* quite sick with a bad influenza so that he can not use his eyes at all, and that is the reason he has not written you to acknowledge the receipt of the soup ladle, but he said it must not be put off any longer, and yesterday asked me to write & thank you for him, which I did . . .

December 8? *M writes to his wife, in Boston, of the gifts received from Catherine & Peter Gansevoort.* (Herman wrote me about the

[728]

beautiful soup ladle that you presented us with . . . I feel so much relieved by your father's kind and generous gift to Herman (removing the
necessity of renting our house or part of it, which I feared) that I can
bear my loss [in the Boston fire] with equanimity — I say *I*, because
Herman from his studious habits and tastes being unfitted for practical
matters, all the *financial* management falls upon me — and one cannot
make bricks without straw — you know — Mother and my brothers feel
much relieved on my account . . . — *Elizabeth Melville to Catherine
Gansevoort, Dec 10*)

December 9   *M finally writes to Catherine Gansevoort himself:*
My Dear Cousin Kate: Do you know much about the Natural History
of Angels? Well, there is one variety known by this: in the place where
they may have tarried for a time they leave behind them a fragrance as
of violets. Another sort, besides bequeathing the fragrance, leave along
with it — what do you think? — Silver soup ladle. — But I must alter
my tone. It is a serious business receiving presents, and calls for serious
acknowledgments. Well then: cordial thanks to you for your memorial
of the
Silver Wedding.
Lizzie and I will ever think of you at our soup; and I shall always pour
out a libation from the tureen to the angelic donor, before helping a
mere vulgar broth-bibbing mortal like myself

And more so for as this is an acknowledgment of your valued gift,
it is the earliest I could make with my own hand and eyes. You knew
I would not be guilty of the Hottentotishness (word just imported by
the Cambria) of a causeless delay.

December 25   Our Christmas time has been a very quiet and sad one —
The losses in our family circle come home forcibly to our hearts at these
anniversary times — as you well can realize — Jenny and the girls dined
together with us — very quietly . . . — *Elizabeth Melville to Catherine
Gansevoort, Dec 29*

We passed quite a pleasant Christmas in New York altogether. In the
morning we all went up to Zion Church which was very handsomely
dressed. Afterwards we went to Aunt Lizzie's where we dined, and also
spent the evening. Maria and I stayed with Mamma at the Gramercy,
while Florence and Lucy stayed at Uncle Herman's. The next day the
great snow storm prevented us from returning to the Island, but on Friday we managed with some difficulty to get to the boat . . . — *Catherine
Gansevoort Melville to Catherine Gansevoort, Jan 2, 1873*

. . . . . .

NEW YORK   *M reads again in his 1673 folio of Davenant's Works; on
p 320 he scores the whole "Song" (The Lark now leaves his watry Nest),
underscoring:*

He takes this Window for the East . . .

M's comment: What a fine Persian tone is here. Hafiz Englished. Ah Will was a trump.

In "The Philosopher and the Lover; to a Mistress dying," M triple-scores & underscores the last stanza:

PHILOSOPHER.

But ask not Bodies doom'd to die,
To what abode they go;
Since Knowledge is but sorrows Spy,
It is not safe to know.

On p 322, "To Mistress E. S. Married to an old Usurer," M scores & checks:

But Wealth has Married Wealth; with Youth Age joyns
His feeble heat, and melts his wither'd Loines,
Not to engender Men but sev'ral Coynes.

Throughout "The Philosophers Disquisition Directed to the Dying Christian," M scores & checks, in stanza 9

For Errors Mist doth bound the Spirits sight
As Clouds (which make Earths arched Roof seem low)
Restraine the Bodies Eyes; and still when light
Growes cleerer upward, Heaven must higher show.

Stanza 11

Wee meerly toyle to find our Studies vaine . . . ✔

Stanza 22

Though life, since finite, has no ill excuse
For being but in finite objects learn'd,
Yet sure the Soul was made for little use,
Unless it be in infinites concern'd.

Stanza 63

And vulgar Reason findes, that none knowes more
Then that which he can make another know.

Stanza 75

Why did not Heav'ns prevention Sin restraine?
Or is not Pow'rs permission a consent?

M's comment: **X** Cogent

*

1 8 7 3

*

LAWRENCE January 9   *John Hoadley writes to George Boutwell:*
There is one person in the employment of the Revenue Service, in whom I take so deep an interest, that I venture a second time to write you about him; — not to solicit promotion, a favor, or indulgence of any

sort, — but to ask you, if you can, to do or say anything in the proper quarter to secure him permanently, or at present, the undisturbed enjoyment of his modest, hard-earned salary, as deputy inspector of the Customs in the City of New York — Herman Melville. — Proud, shy, sensitively honorable, — he had much to overcome, and has much to endure; but he strives earnestly to so perform his duties as to make the slightest censure, reprimand, or even reminder, — impossible from any superior — Surrounded by low venality, he puts it all quietly aside, — quietly declining offers of money for special services, — quietly returning money which has been thrust into his pockets behind his back, avoiding offence alike to the corrupting merchants and their clerks and runners, who think that all men can be bought, and to the corrupt swarms who shamelessly seek their price; — quietly, steadfastly doing his duty, and happy in retaining his own self-respect —

By the rules of any conceivable "civil service," he must be secure against removal. — Advancement or promotion he does not seek, — nor would his friends seek it for him. — The pittance he receives ekes out his slender income and that of his wife, (who is a daughter of the late Lemuel Shaw, C. J. of Mass —) and affords him the quiet, simple livelihood he values — The loss of $5000. — by the Boston fire, carrying with it an income of $500. — part of the small property left her by her Father, making Mrs. Melville additionally solicitous that Mr. Melville should retain his place — I most earnestly wish that representations might be made in the proper quarter so that in the event of any general change in the Custom House in New York, Mr. Melville might find a sheltering arm thrown over him. — Pardon me: my sincere feeling must be my excuse . . .

SAN FRANCISCO January   *A reissue of Mayo's* Kaloolah *is reviewed in* The Overland Monthly:
At the time of its appearance, in 1849, it ran through four editions in four months . . . Its success might have been aided by the desire for graphic and picturesque literature awakened by the advent of Herman Melville's fascinating story of *Typee* . . .

NEW YORK February 11   *Stanwix Melville returns home on the steamer* Henry Chauncey, *Captain A. G. Gray.*

February 23   *Stanwix Melville writes to his grandmother, Hope Shaw:*
   I am glad enough to get home again, & I am going back to my old business in dentistry again in a few weeks as soon as I can get a chance.
   Maybe you would like to hear where I went to when I was away, and how I got along.
   You know I left New York in April & went to a small town in Kansas, I staid there a few weeks, then I thought I could do better South so I came down through the Indian Nation, & then into Arkansas, I stopped at

a number of towns on the Arkansas river till I came to the Mississippi, then down that river to Vicksburgh I staid there a few days, & then took the train to Jackson, from there by Railroad to New Orleans, I found that a lively city, but no work, so I thought I should like a trip to Central America, I went on a steamer to Havana, Cuba & from there to half a dozen or more ports on the Central America coast till I came to Limon Bay in Costa Rica. I walked from there on the beach with two other young fellows to Greytown in Nicarauga, one of the boys died on the beach, & we dug a grave in the sand by the sea, & buried him, & travelled on again, each of us not knowing who would have to bury the other before we got there, as we were both sick with the fever & ague.

I went up the San Juan river to Lake Nicarauga about a hundred miles with a Naval surveying expedition going up to survey for a ship Canal: from Greytown I shipped on a schooner for Aspinwall; after arriving in Aspinwall, I got wrecked there in that heavy gale of wind . . . and I lost all my clothes, & every thing I had, & was taken sick again with the fever, I went into the hospital there, & then came home on the Steamer Henry Chauncey, where I find the cold weather agrees with me much better, than the sun of the tropics.

Now I say New York forever.

March 3   *Stanwix Melville writes to his grandmother, Hope Shaw:*
Patience is indeed a virtue and which, for one, I wish I was the happy possessor of, for as the days roll slowly along, at times I think the year will never draw to a close, so that I will find myself better off than when I started; but I know that if I am steady at the profession I am learning that in a few years I will be independent of any man.

I am happy to announce to you that this morning I went to work for a dentist, a Dr. Read; I went to his office on Saturday, & told him I wanted a place to work & perfect myself in the profession, (it was a dentist I had done a little work for before, when I was with Dr. Starr) he immediately employed me without asking any questions except as to where I lived, & if my father & mother were living. I am to give him all the time he wants, & in return he is to teach me every thing relative to the dental profession, & in the course of a few months will commence to remunerate me for my services.

April 4   *Jane Melville writes to Catherine Gansevoort:*
Do you know that Herman is quite ill?

. . . you heard through Augusta, of his sudden & severe illness . . .
— *Elizabeth Melville to Catherine Gansevoort, May 26*

April 25   *Stanwix Melville writes to his grandmother, Hope Shaw:*
I have encountered a serious obsticle which will prevent me from be-

coming a number one dentist, & that is I am too near sighted; I found it out as quick as I commenced operating in the mouth; heretofore I had been working at the mechanical part of the business. Fate is against me in most of my undertakings.

I am going to sail Wednesday for San Francisco, Calafornia, and shall probably go to Southern Calafornia on a farm or something like that.

I cant find anything in New York. I dont like to be a clerk in an office. This time is going to decide my fortune.

April 30   *Stanwix Melville leaves for California on the* Henry Chauncey, *sailing from Pier No. 42, North River, at noon.* (We all thought he was foolish to give up his place, especially as the Dr. was desirous to keep him, but he seems to be possessed with a demon of *restlessness*, and there is nothing to do but let him go . . . — *Elizabeth Melville to Catherine Gansevoort, May 26*)

May 24   *M receives the wardrobe of the late Henry Sanford Gansevoort.* (The parcel by express came safely to hand on Saturday, and we thank you very much for your thoughtful kindness — The coat fits Herman very well I think, though it is a little snugger than the loose sacks he is accustomed to wear — His figure, and Henry's were very similar — At Boston they constantly noticed how much they were alike in various ways — but *mainly*, in figure and carriage — *Elizabeth Melville to Catherine Gansevoort, May 26*)

May 26   *Elizabeth Melville writes to Catherine Gansevoort:*
We are also very busy here, the girls are getting ready to go to Boston somewhat earlier this year — to be in Cambridge on Class Day — My brother's son graduates, and a "good time" is expected — The pique skirt comes in very opportunely — we are dressmaking with all our might, as usual "on our own hook" — and are independent of dressmakers and their frightful charges with the exception of an occasional "cut and baste" — I do not expect to go away till Herman has his vacation, probably the last of July or August, and we shall be very happy to see you here any day agreeable to yourself . . . Herman is quite well again now . . .

June 13   [Elizabeth Melville's 51st birthday]   *Catherine Gansevoort comes to 26 Street for a visit.*

June 15   *Catherine Gansevoort writes to Abraham Lansing:*
26 Months ago To-day we laid our darling Henry to rest & that all came over me — & with the familiar scenes here — the very streets & stones are all full of memories — Cousin Herman is so like Henry in manner & in appearance & in little trifling ways — It does me good to see him . . .

June 28   *Catherine Gansevoort writes to her parents:*
Cousin Herman & Lizzie are well & anxious to have me remain until the latter part of this week . . .

July 2   *Elizabeth Melville writes to Catherine Gansevoort:*
Accept Herman's and my thanks for the loaf of bread — it was very nice indeed, & we enjoyed it much —
I miss you very much and wish you were here to help me get along with this dreary time without the children — When Herman is gone all day, or the largest part of it, the house seems utterly desolate — it is quite a new sensation for me to have the days seem *long* — We are counting the days for going to Pittsfield and think with longings of the refreshing breezes from the hill-tops . . .
Herman sends his love, and wishes to know if you have succeeded in getting the book you wished — if not to let him know, and he will get it for you —

July 16   *Elizabeth Melville writes to Catherine Gansevoort:*
Herman . . . has gone to the Central Park. — I scribble this hasty line between daylight & dark.

July 26   *The M's leave for Pittsfield.* (. . . the house will be closed for the two weeks that Herman expects to be absent. — *Elizabeth Melville to Catherine Gansevoort, July 20*)

HONOLULU   August 1   [M's 54th birthday]   *Publication by Reverend Samuel C. Damon, in* The Friend, *of:*
A CURIOSITY RELATING TO A LITERARY AUTHOR
Among the papers of the late Isaac Montgomery, Esq., was found the following [Montgomery-Melville contract of June 1, 1843] . . . We would merely add that Mr. Melville now resides in New York, and his brother is now Superintendent of the Sailor's Snug Harbor on Staten Island.

PITTSFIELD   Before August 11   Herman and I had a *delightful* visit in Pittsfield — and — have you heard the news? — it has happened since I left — Maria is engaged to young Mr. Morewood — Willie, as we always call him — we have known him from infancy, and feel sure that his character and standing are such as to make the match a very suitable one —
He is a young man of most excellent principles and a good heart . . . the mutual attachment is based upon a long tried *friendship* which is the best ground for married happiness . . . Herman was there a few days ago *after* I left, (as I wanted to see Bessie *here* [in Boston] before she went home) and Willie took that opportunity to talk with him and have it settled — He approves of it very much . . .
Our visit to Arrowhead did us both much good — and I wish you could go there and see how delightful it is — We spent nearly all the time walking, or driving, or sitting out doors — and it seemed as if we could

not get enough of the reviving air, after being nearly suffocated in the heat and *smell* of New York . . . — *Elizabeth Melville to Catherine Gansevoort, Aug 15*

We had a very pleasant visit from Uncle Herman and Aunt Lizzie, and I think it did them both good . . . Uncle Herman stayed till Monday, for which I was very glad. — *Maria Gansevoort Melville to Catherine Gansevoort, Aug 18*

NEW YORK   August 12   *M returns from his two-week vacation a day late.*

BOSTON   August 15   *Elizabeth Melville writes to Catherine Gansevoort:*
Herman and Bessie are in New York, & she has a young friend to keep her company —

NEW YORK   September 8   *M replies to a note from [?Richard Henry Stoddard, who has added seven poems from* Battle-Pieces *to his new edition of Griswold's* The Poets and Poetry of America], *saying that he has nothing to add to the existing biographical details on him.*

September 23   *Elizabeth Melville writes to Catherine Gansevoort:*
Herman begs me to send his special thanks for the pears . . .

November 14   *Catherine Gansevoort writes to her fiancé, Abraham Lansing:*
Poor fellow, even Cousin Herman says if you are not happy it will be *my fault* — how cruel always to blame we poor women!!!

ALBANY   Before November 23   *Catherine Gansevoort invites the Melvilles to her wedding to Abraham Lansing.*

NEW YORK   November 23   *Elizabeth Melville writes to Catherine Gansevoort, declining the invitation regretfully:*
Herman cannot leave his post at this very pressing time of business — He sends his very best wishes for you, & would like to give them in person if it were possible —

ALBANY   November 25   *Catherine Gansevoort becomes Mrs Abraham Lansing.*

NEW YORK   December 25   *M gives his daughter, Frances:* Pearls of Shakespeare, *illustrated by Kenny Meadows (London, 1873).*

.   .   .   .   .

NEW YORK   *M acquires Shelley's* Essays, Letters from Abroad, Translations and Fragments (*London, 1852*).

M acquires Mitford's copy of Songs from the Dramatists, *edited by*

[735]

Robert Bell (London, 1854) in which he checks this stanza in John Heywood's poem:

> In such things as we cannot flee,
> But needs they must endurèd be,
> Let wise contentment be decree
> Make virtue of necessity;
> > Be merry, friends!

Elizabeth Melville's memoir of M:
Uncle Peter Gansevoort gave Herman $500 as a present in 1873 [December, 1872?] . . .

*
1874
*

LONDON January?   *Publication of* Summer Cruising in the South Seas *(U. S. title:* South-Sea Idylls), *by Charles Warren Stoddard (preface dated December 1873), with several references to M, including that on p 279:*
A moist cloud, far up the mountain [Nouka Hiva], hung above a serene and sacred haunt, and under its shelter was hidden a deep valley, whose secret has been carried to the ends of the earth; for Herman Melville has plucked out the heart of its mystery, and beautiful and barbarous Typee lies naked and forsaken.

I was rather glad we could not get any nearer to it, for fear of dispelling the ideal that has so long charmed me.

NEW YORK March 2 [Frances Melville's 19th birthday]   *M gives his daughter, Frances, a birthday gift:* Old English Wild Flowers, *by J. T. Burgess (London, 1868).*

March 14   *Elizabeth Melville writes to her step-mother:*
We have better news from Stanny — He is on a sheep-ranch in California where George Nourse who has very kindly interested himself for him advised him to go — Today we have a letter from George enclosing one from his employer expressing satisfaction with him and promising to give him 25.00 a month from the time he commenced, as long as he has work for him — George wrote to Stanny encouraging him, and advising him to stick at it till he gets a chance of "taking sheep to keep on shares, and gradually get up a flock of his own — He says that sheep raising is *now* the most profitable business in California — and if Stanny will only *perservere* he will come out all right —
> Stanny's address is

Care of Smith & Chapman
Merced — Merced Co.
Chowchillon   Cal.

I wonder if Sam would not write to him, or send him a paper to let him feel that his friends are interested in him — I suppose it is very hard work, for Stanny, but *every* thing is hard work —

STATEN ISLAND *June 10   Maria Gansevoort Melville & William B. Morewood are married at St. Paul's Memorial Church, Edgewater:*
Yesterday was the Wedding Day of your neice Maria G. Melville, Cousin Jenny A. L[ansing] & I went down to Staten Island by Quarantine Boat . . . The Bridal Party were very late as is usual, but this was 3/4 of an hour — but at length they came Dr Ewer read the service & after those few exercises — The Bride & Groom — & the four groomsmen & Bridesmaids returned to New Brighton — But the rest of the party did not get there until after 2.³⁰ as there was great detention — but a more hungry & tired set of people I never saw, & a good while after our arrival salads & tongue sandwiches Strawberryies & Cream, Champagnes &c — were served to the exhausted guests. Every one looked well as they always do. The Melville Clan was strong powerful & very defensive . . .
All are well in 26th St. — *Catherine Lansing to her parents, June 11*

NEW YORK *June 14-15   Augusta Melville comes in from Staten Island to exchange places with her sister Helen at 26 Street. (Augusta Melville to Peter & Susan Gansevoort, June 16)*

Before June 20   M gives Catherine Lansing a message for her husband, Abraham:
Cousin Herman sends his kindest regards & says he is surprised at your leaving all your *treasures* [to go to an army training camp] . . . — *her letter to her husband, June 20*

June?   After the death of Rachel Turner Pond M writes a memorial poem:

IRIS . . .
But the ravisher has won her
   Who the wooers three did slight;
To his fastness he has borne her
   By the trail that leads through night.
With peace she came, the rainbow,
   And like a bow did pass
The balsam trees exhaling,
   And tear-drops in the grass.

July 25?   M leaves on his two-weeks vacation for the White Mountains.

Before August 10   M returns to his desk at the District Office of the Custom House. (We had letters from Bessie this morning . . . Found Herman at the house looking very well after his fortnight among the mountains . . . — *Augusta & Frances Priscilla Melville to Abraham Lansing, Aug 14;* Herman is quite well & enjoyed the White Mountains. — *Augusta Melville to Catherine Gansevoort, Aug 21*)

September 22   *M acquires* Ballads, *by William Makepeace Thackeray (Boston, 1856).*

September   *M acquires* Three Dramas of Calderon, from the Spanish. Love the Greatest Enchantment, The Sorceries of Sin, and the Devotion of the Cross, *translated by Denis Florence MacCarthy (Dublin, 1870). M subsequently reads the three plays, sometimes marking the parallel columns of the Spanish text, as well as those of the English translation:*
In Love the Greatest Enchantment, *M checks on p 30:*

> Cual era ya racional
> Bruto, de pieles cubierto;
> Cual, de manchas salpicado
> Fiera con entendimiento . . .

In The Sorceries of Sin, *M brackets on p 164:*

> The Man
> Why for ever words of woe
> Speak'st thou, understanding, thus?
> Why for ever shadows throw
> On the path my senses take?
> Dost thou not their nature know,
> That they're human, and require
> Something soothing to console —
> Something sweet to ease the pangs
> That from birth-time they have known?

In The Devotion of the Cross, *he scores on p 229:*

> Lisardo
>   I cannot;
> For already the red river
> Of my life is past all staying,
> And I think the soul but lingers
> To go forth, because it knows not
> Which, 'mid many, is the right door.

& scores on p 265:

> Curcio
> Doth it happen not in sorrow,
> When the heart is full of sadness,
> That one seeketh self-communion
> Rather than confide in any?

& scores on p 273:

> Eusebio
> . . . Love no more impelleth me —
> I some subtler law obey.

BOSTON   October 21   *Publication, by James R. Osgood & Co., of Vol III of* Little Classics: Tragedy, *containing "The Bell Tower" by M.*

ALBANY   October 28   *Susan Gansevoort dies.*

NEW YORK   October 29   *M writes to Peter Gansevoort:*
I write this note to assure you of my own and Lizzie's true sympathies, and how we share in feelings which on such an occasion it is hardly for words to express. — May God keep you, and console you.

M writes to Abraham Lansing:
My recollections of Aunt Susan are of a kind to make me keenly alive to the loss which has befallen Uncle Peter as well as all others united by blood or socially to so true a woman.

Elizabeth writes to Catherine Lansing:
. . . Herman has written [Peter], briefly, but of course cannot express what we all realize so painfully.

ALBANY   November 18   *Catherine Lansing, carrying out her late step-mother's wishes to provide black silk dresses for the Melville girls, instructs her husband:*
The names are *Fanny Melville* & *Elizabeth Melville.* I would have them made out in the girls names, as it will save Cousin Herman the trouble of either endorsing the drafts or going to the Bank.

BOSTON   November 26   *M & Elizabeth spend Thanksgiving at her family's home.* (Family Dinner. All my father's descendants present except Stanwix — Party in the evening — Mother unexpectedly well and bright. — *Samuel Shaw's diary*)

SAN FRANCISCO   December 22   *Stanwix Melville writes to his grandmother Shaw:*
Mama has sent me so many kind messages from you, that I have deemed it my duty to acknowledge them by writing you, although I fear it will give you but little pleasure to hear from one, who has been guilty of so many follies, and deaf to the counsel of older heads. Eighteen months in California! and though I have had more experience seen more of the ways of the world, and learned more about this State since I came here, I am still stationary, and sailing in about the same boat as when I left home; but I hope to retrieve the past, & for better times in the future.

NEW YORK   December 25   *M gives Elizabeth a Christmas present:* The Handbook of Engraved Gems, *by C. W. King, M.A. (London, 1866).*

BOSTON   End of December?   *Hope Shaw writes to Stanwix Melville:*
My very dear Grandson,
The most valuable present sent to me this year has been your *last Letter.* It was written with a beautiful spirit. Never forget the old friends. I am confident the worst is over — You are beginning a new life — Perseverance is my *motto* & never be *discouraged.* Keep on — God rewards noble *endeavors* and generally they are rewarded if you are not successful

in all you wish — Your help will be patience and submission. Trust my dear Stanwix, something you will receive that will reward you for every exertion you make to be that character commands respect, and love. Last Thanksgiving day you were wished with us. You little know how much we think of you. I am delighted that you attend Church — I think the essence of Religion consists in being intimate with our *Heavenly Father* . . .

.   .   .   .   .

LONDON   *In* The National Reformer *James Thomson writes an essay on Walt Whitman:*
I know but one other living author who approaches him in his sympathy with all ordinary life and vulgar occupations, in his feeling of brotherhood for all rough workers, and at the same time in his sense of beauty and grandeur, and in his power of thought; I mean Herman Melville . . . but Melville is sometimes strangely unequal to his better self, and has lavished much strength in desultory doings; while Whitman has concentrated himself from the beginning on one great strenuous endeavour . . .

*

1 8 7 5

*

NEW YORK   January 14   *M acquires & subsequently reads,* Polonius [*by Edward Fitzgerald*] *(London, 1852); he marks the concluding rhymed maxim:*

> For every ill beneath the sun
> There is some remedy, or none.
> Should there be one, resolve to find it;
> If not, submit, and never mind it.

February 12   *Harper's sends its 22nd account to M showing a deficit of $52.38.*

March 9   *Elizabeth Melville writes to her step-mother:*
You ask why I did not tell you about Aunt Susan's present to the girls — Dont you remember it was sent while I was in Boston at Thanksgiving time, and I *told you about it then?* She did not *leave* them anything, only there was a memorandum found of hers, to remind her husband to send for himself one hundred dollars each to Bessie and Fanny "to buy a black silk dress" — probably for a Christmas present — so as soon as he knew of it he sent a check at once to them — Of course it was all owing to her thoughtful kindness that they had it — Be sure I should not omit to tell you such a stroke of good luck as that!! —

. . . Herman is pretty well and very busy — pray do not mention to *any one* that he is writing poetry — you know how such things spread and he would be very angry if he knew I had spoken of it — and of course I have not, except in confidence to you and the family — We have been in much fear lest his pay should be reduced, as so many others have, but it has not been, so far — it is hard enough to get along at all —

Spring?   *M projects a new work of alternating prose & poetry:*

Parthenope

An. ~~Afternoon~~ ~~Evening~~ in Naples

In the time of Bomba:

with

An Introduction

merging into

A Symposium of Old Masters

At ~~Delmonico's~~.

~~Literally~~ rendered from the ideal
of
The Marquis de Grandvin.

[74¹]

June 7   *Elizabeth Melville writes to Catherine Lansing:*
I wanted to tell you that we are expecting Stanny home in a short time — A very favorable opening for his going back to his old business, *mechanical* dentistry offered itself, and since he [had] not got settled at anything in California, and had undergone a very marked change in his ideas and purposes, born of his own experience (which is the best teacher) we thought he would be very glad to come home and settle himself & we sent for him and he will do well now, we have every reason to believe since he feels himself how foolish he has been to give up a good home — His old friend, Fred Starr has succeeded to his father's practice, and he wants just such an assistant as he knows Stanny can be, and will set him at work at once — & put him in a fair way to earn a handsome living — We think he will be home about the 24th of June — He naturally feels some compunctions about coming back no better off in fortunes than when he left, & fears his friends may look coldly on him — but I told him I should say, and I want it to be distinctly understood that *we sent for him* — I wanted also to ask you dear Kate, if you would have any objection to my giving Stanny to wear, the coat that belonged to your dear brother, that you remember you sent Herman some time ago — it did not fit him very well, so it has remained in my woolen chest — If you have, do not be backward to say so to me — I shall well understand it — but if not, please let me know, as I am getting together something for him to wear, as I suppose he will be quite out in the wardrobe way, on his arrival in civilized parts — We shall all be so glad to have him home and satisfied to stay, and he, poor fellow, is overjoyed at the thought of coming —

June 13   [Elizabeth Melville's 53rd birthday]   *M gives Elizabeth a birthday present:* The Wonders of Engraving, *by Georges Duplessis (London, 1871).*

June 24   *Stanwix Melville returns home in the steamer* Acapulco(?).

July 20   *Elizabeth Melville writes to her step-mother:*
Stanny begs me to thank you very much for all your kind wishes — he is very well now (with the exception of a little bowel trouble) and has a good appetite — he looks much better than when he first arrived, and is very happy to be home again — He went into his old place at the Dentists yesterday, though this is the dull season when every one (that can get away) being out of town there is not much to do —

Before July 30   *M writes to his sister, Frances Priscilla [or Augusta?].* (Herman writes, that he will be in Albany next Saturday, & will stop to see Uncle & you & Abe. — *Frances Priscilla Melville to Catherine Lansing, July 30)*

Before August 4   *M writes a "note to Kate"* Lansing.

ALBANY August 4 [28th wedding anniversary] *Abraham Lansing writes to M.* (I have just received your note of yesterday. I thank you for the prospective welcome. But as for meeting me on the wharf — dont mention it. When the Shah of Persia or the Great Khan of Tartary comes to Albany by the night-boat — *him* meet on the wharf and with salvoes of artillery — but not a Custom House Inspector. — *M to Abraham Lansing, Aug 5*)

NEW YORK August 5 *M writes to Abraham Lansing:*
I should have mentioned in my note to Kate that I should not appear upon the scene till some time after breakfast — since on Sunday morning my appetite will be clamorous at an hour too early for any rational household to satisfy. As for my plunder or impedimenta, I shall carry nothing but what I take in my hand.

August 7 *M begins his two-week vacation.* (Herman left yesterday for Gansevoort, for two weeks — *Elizabeth Melville to her step-mother, Aug 8*)

ALBANY August 8 *M arrives here this morning by the night-boat.*

August 9 *M remains here for the day.* (We looked for Herman by the morning train; but as he did not arrive, concluded, that his stay has been made so pleasant by Abe & you, that he will not be here until evening. — *Frances Priscilla Melville to Catherine Lansing, this date*)

Peter Gansevoort hears of M's manuscript poem, Clarel, *& proposes to pay the expenses of its publication.*

GANSEVOORT August 9 *M arrives by the evening train, bringing a gift from the Lansings.* (The macaroons were simply delicious. Herman shall have some this evening. — *Augusta Melville to Catherine Lansing, this date*)

After August 9 *M writes to Catherine Lansing:*
Lounging on the sofa after dinner just now in the parlor which was my mother's, my eye chanced to fall on a photograph of Henry in a gilt frame hanging under my mother's portrait. I took it down & brought it to the window, & looked at it. —
Now let me say, that the engraving you showed me of Henry, meant for the book [a memorial to Henry Gansevoort], is detestable. Also, I have seen other pictures, claiming to be he, which do not look like him, and are a caricature of him. The picture for the book is the one that I referred to at the outset. It is he, and is not bad-looking, and it has character. —
Michael, the angel of truth, inspired me to write this to you on the instant. — Take it for what its worth . . .
— P.S. Since writing the foregoing Fanny tells me that Mr Hoadley

much dislikes the engraving. There's confirmation. — Stop tinkering, and do the right thing, I pray you, and impute to the right motive my outspokenness.

I have written to Abe to thank him for his great kindness in sending us two baskets of peaches. He is too good. Oh, I wish you could have heard all that Herman said about him. I must tell you of one remark he made in speaking of what constituted a *true* gentleman. "There is Abraham Lansing — He is a gentleman, *instinctively* he is the gentleman." — *Augusta Melville to Catherine Lansing, Aug 26*

We had a charming visit from Herman in August. I dont know when I have seen him better. — *Augusta Melville to Hope Shaw, Oct 9*

PITTSFIELD Before August 23? [?] *M concludes his vacation here.* (*Augusta Melville to Catherine Lansing, Aug 26*)

NEW YORK August 23 *M returns to his desk at the Custom House* [*as a weigher?*].

August 25? *M writes to Augusta Melville.* (With your package this morning came letters from Tom, & Jenny Townsend, besides one from Herman I wrote Abe about. — *Augusta Melville to Catherine Lansing, of Aug 26*)

Thomas Melville writes to his sister Augusta. ([Tom & Kate] had been to see Herman & thought him looking very well, & Fannie too after their sojourns at Gansevoort & the Berkshire Hills. — *Augusta Melville to Catherine Lansing, Aug 26*)

NEW YORK August 26 [Frances Priscilla's 48th birthday] *Enclosing a note to Peter Gansevoort, M writes to Abraham Lansing:*
Herewith is a note for my uncle, which you — or Cousin Kate will be kind enough to read to him; or seal and deliver; you know best.

My Dear Uncle Peter:
Last evening I received through a note from Mr. Lansing a check for $1200, which he says you requested him to send me. — I shall at once deposite the money in a Savings Bank, there to remain till needed for the purpose designed.

And now, My Dear Uncle, in receiving this generous gift from you, so much enhanced by the circumstances, I feel the same sentiments which I expressed to you in person at Albany when you so kindly made known your intention. I will not repeat them here; but only pray God to bless you, and have you in His keeping.

With respect and true affection,
Your nephew
Herman Melville

GANSEVOORT August 26 *Augusta Melville writes to Catherine Lansing:*
We have heard from Lizzie & Bessie, who are enjoying the mountain air
at Jefferson. Stanwix has quite recovered from the effects of his illness,
Tom writes he dined with them [on Staten Island] on Sunday.

NEW YORK October 4? *M presents a book to Catherine Lansing:* The
Life of Saint Elizabeth, of Hungary, Duchess of Thuringia. *By the Count
de Montalembert. Translated by Mary Hackett (New York, 1870).*

ALBANY Before October 8 *Catherine Lansing writes to M, acknowledging the gift.* (I am glad you were pleased with that book of the
sainted queen. — *M to Catherine Lansing, Oct 8*)

NEW YORK October 8 *M writes to Catherine Lansing:*
My best love to my sister Kate, and Fanny, and say that they both must
come down & see us before leaving for the East. —

WASHINGTON December 3 *A memorandum is sent from the Treasury
Department to the New York Custom House, ordering its employees'
compensation reduced, including:*
282 Inspectors from $4.00 to $3.60 per diem.

. . . . . .

NEW YORK *Before the end of this year Stanwix Melville leaves again for
San Francisco.*

*M inscribes a book that had been presented to his father by the Rev
Robert Swan:* Anster Fair. A Poem in Six Cantos. With Other Poems,
by William Tennant *(Edinburgh, 1812).*

George Parsons Lathrop & M exchange letters. (. . . when I was making my *Study of Hawthorne* I wrote to him for permission to use two or
three letters, & received his consent given with a sort of gloomy reluctance. — *Lathrop to H. E. Scudder, October 20, 1890*)

The Duyckincks' Cyclopædia of American Literature *appears in a new
edition, "edited to date by M. Laird Simons," with this "information"
added to the biographical sketch of M:*
In 1860 Mr. Melville made another whaling voyage around the world . . .
In 1865 he wrote The Refugee . . . A year later he printed Battle Pieces and
Aspects of The War, a series of disconnected verses . . .

*

1 8 7 6

*

ALBANY   January 3?   *Augusta Melville writes to M of Peter Gansevoort's approaching death.* (M to Abraham Lansing, Jan 4)

NEW YORK   January 4   *M completes arrangements with G. P. Putnam & Sons for the anonymous publication of* Clarel. (*M to Abraham Lansing, this date*)

ALBANY   January 4   *The Hon Peter Gansevoort dies; among the relatives notified by Abraham Lansing, by telegraph, is M.*

NEW YORK   January 4   *M writes to Abraham Lansing:*
   I received the despatch not long since. A letter from Augusta received this morning had prepared me for it. Uncle is released from his suffering. — *In peace.* — The event happened at a time which brings it home to me most sensibly, since, as it happened, only to-day I made arrangements for that publication which he (inspired by the spirit of Aunt Susan) enabled me to effect.

ALBANY   January 8   *M comes to Albany [for the funeral of Peter Gansevoort?].* (I will be up on Saturday, and will have to return that evening. — *M to Abraham Lansing, Jan 4*)

NEW YORK   January 12   *Among the "Literary Notes" of the* New-York Daily Tribune:
   A narrative and descriptive poem on the Holy Land, by Herman Melville, is in press by G. P. Putnam's Sons.

Before January 15   *Catherine Gansevoort Lansing sends copies of the Albany* Evening Journal, *containing a tribute to the late Peter Gansevoort, to members of the family, including M.*

NEW YORK   Before January 15   . . . Lizzie says Herman was so much pleased to secure his [copy of the *Evening Journal's* tribute]. Said it told him many things he did not know. — *Augusta Melville to Catherine Lansing, Jan 14(?)*

Before February 2   *Elizabeth Melville asks her sister-in-law, Augusta, not to visit them.* ([M] was not willing to have even his own sisters here, and I had to write Augusta before she left Albany to that effect — that was the reason she changed her plan, and went to Tom's . . . — *Elizabeth Melville's private letter to Catherine Lansing, Feb 2*)

February 2   *Elizabeth Melville writes two letters to Catherine Lansing:*
I have just received Fanny's letter [suggesting Catherine Lansing's visit] and hasten to reply that I am sorry it so happens just now that we cannot receive any visitor . . . The book is going through the press, and every minute of Herman's time and mine is devoted to it — the mere mechanical work of reading proof &c is so great and absorbing — You know dear Kate, how happy Herman and I always are to have you come here freely, and make yourself perfectly at home . . . Just as soon as the stress is over, I will let you know & then hope you will come down and make us a good visit . . .

Dear Kate,
I have written you a note that Herman could see, as he wished, but want you to know how painful it is for me to write it, and also to have to give the real cause — The fact is, that Herman, poor fellow, is in such a frightfully nervous state, & particularly now with such an added strain on his mind, that I am actually *afraid* to have any one here for fear that he will be upset entirely, & not be able to go on with the printing — He was not willing to have even his own sisters here, and I had to write Augusta before she left Albany to that effect — that was the reason she changed her plan, and went to Tom's — If ever this dreadful *incubus* of a *book* (I call it so because it has undermined all our happiness) gets off Herman's shoulders I do hope he may be in better mental health — but at present I have reason to feel the gravest concern & anxiety about it — to put it in mild phrase — please do not speak of it — you know how such things are exaggerated — & I will tell you more when I see you . . .

NEW BRIGHTON   February 17   *M goes to Staten Island to inquire after his sick sister, Augusta, at Thomas Melville's house.* (Dr. Bogart & the physicians from New York decided after a careful study of all the symptoms, & seeing just how Gus was, that it was an *internal hemorrhage* . . . Herman was here yesterday. — *Frances Priscilla Melville to Catherine Lansing, Feb 18*)

February 26   *M goes to Staten Island.* (Herman was here again on Saturday, & saw Gus for the first time, he was deeply moved, could hardly control his feelings while with her. — *Frances Priscilla Melville to Catherine Lansing, Feb 29*)

March 2   *M gives his daughter, Frances, a birthday gift:* Wills of Their Own, Curious Eccentric and Benevolent, *collated & arranged by William Tegg (London, 1876).*

STATEN ISLAND   April 4   *A death notice:*
MELVILLE — On Tuesday, April 4, at the residence of her brother, Thomas Melville, Sailors' Snug Harbor, Staten Island, Augusta Melville of Gansevoort,

Saratoga Co., N.Y. Relatives and friends are invited to attend the funeral services at the house, Friday (to-day), April 7, at 2 o'clock. Boat leaves Pier 1, East River, at 1:15 P.M. Interment in Albany.

NEW YORK April 7 *The Melvilles' family physician, Dr Augustus Kinsley Gardner, dies.*

ALBANY April 8-9 *M accompanies Augusta's body to Albany & the cemetery.*

NEW YORK April 22 *Elizabeth Melville writes to Catherine Lansing:*
Congratulate us that the book is *at last,* in type, to the last page of Ms. and a few days more will finish up the *plate-printing* and the various little odds and ends of the work — Herman has consented on the *very strong* representations of the publishers, to put his name on the title-page, for which I am very glad — and *therefore* he has changed his mind about having a dedication — Now, he wants me to tell you he is going to inscribe that book in your father's name, as seems most natural and fit — I have been all along in strong hopes that he would, but he seemed averse to having *any* dedication whatever or any name on the title page — I shall be so thankful when it is all finished and off of his mind, and cannot help hoping that his health will improve when he is released from this long continued mental strain —

April 30 *M visits Evert Duyckinck in the evening.*

Early May *Catherine Lansing visits the Melvilles in New York.*

May 14 *Catherine Lansing writes to her husband, Abraham:*
Cousin Herman invites us to stay over Sunday & if you can wants you to come down Friday — He seems very well & is very entertaining — *The Book* will be out by June 1st . . .

May 26 *M visits Evert Duyckinck.*

May 30 *M visits Evert Duyckinck on the morning of Decoration Day.*

June 3 Clarel *is published.* (Congratulate us, for the *book* was published yesterday after a series of the most vexatious delays . . . — *Elizabeth Melville to Catherine Lansing, June 4; advertisement in the* New-York Daily Tribune, *this date*)

If during the period in which this work has remained unpublished, though not undivulged, any of its properties have by a natural process exhaled; it yet retains, I trust, enough of original life to redeem it at least from vapidity. Be that as it may, I here dismiss the book — content beforehand with whatever future awaits it. (*Clarel,* facing first page of text)

June 4 *Elizabeth Melville writes to Catherine Lansing:*

. . . Herman will write you and *I hope*, send you a copy — (or perhaps he will by-and-by if he does not now) for I know you would value it —

His ring came from Tiffany's — all nicely marked, and he wears it frequently . . .

Mr & Mrs Thomas Melville dine at 104 East 26 Street. (M to Catherine Lansing, June 5)

ALBANY   June 4?   *Catherine Lansing writes to M.* (You repeat, and with added emphasis, what you verbally said to me at the depot here last April, as to carrying out your father's intention . . . — *M to Catherine Lansing, June 5*)

NEW YORK   June 5   *M writes to Catherine Lansing:*

Aside from your special object in writing it, you do not know how deeply I felt the sincere tone of your note to me, Cousin Kate.

. . . I appreciate your fidelity, my cousin. — But though the matter is not yet developed into a clear statement rendered; I think now, as before, that nothing more is necessary . . .

. . . And now — with my heart upbraiding me for writing so cold a response to so cousinly a note as yours — I hasten to end the sheet — and let it be with a benediction: — God bless you!

June 6   *M gives Elizabeth her copy of* Clarel *with this inscription:*

> This copy is specially
> presented to my wife, without
> whose assistance in manifold ways
> I hardly know how I could have
> got the book (under the circumstances)
> into shape, and finally through
> the press.
>   Herman Melville
> June 6, 1876
>   New York.
> 104 E. 26 St.

ALBANY   June 6   *Catherine Lansing presents a copy of* Clarel *to Judge & Mrs [Amasa J.] Parker.*

June 9   *Catherine Lansing gives her husband a copy of* Clarel.

NEW YORK   June 12   *M visits Evert Duyckinck in the evening.*

ALBANY   June 15   *Catherine Lansing lends* Clarel *to Asa W. Twitchell. (Catherine Lansing to her husband, Abraham, June 17 [?])*

NEW YORK   June 16   Clarel *is reviewed [by Edmund Clarence Stedman?] in the* New-York Daily Tribune:

After a long silence, Mr. Herman Melville speaks again to the world. No more a narrator of marvelous stories of tropical life and adventure, no more a weird and half-fascinating, half-provoking writer of romances, but now a poet with a single work, in four parts, and about 17,000 lines in length. We knew already that Mr. Melville's genius has a distinctly poetical side; we remember still his stirring lines on Sheridan's Ride . . . But the present venture is no less hazardous than ambitious . . . "Clarel," we must frankly confess, is something of a puzzle, both in design and execution . . .

There is thus no plot in the work; but neither do the theological doubts, questions, and disputations indulged in by the characters, and those whom they meet, have any logical course or lead to any distinct conclusions. The reader soon becomes hopelessly bewildered, and fatigues himself vainly in the effort to give personality to speakers who constantly evade it, and connection to scenes which perversely hold themselves separate from each other. The verse, frequently flowing for a few lines with a smooth, agreeable current, seems to foam and chafe against unmanageable words like a brook in a stony glen: there are fragments of fresh, musical lyrics, suggestive both of Hafiz and of William Blake; there are passages so rough, distorted, and commonplace withal, that the reader impatiently shuts the book. It is, in this respect, a medley such as we have rarely perused, — a mixture of skill and awkwardness, thought and aimless fancy, plan shattered by whim and melody broken by discords . . .

. . . Some may suspect a graver enigma hidden in the characters of the story . . . There is a vein of earnestness in Mr. Melville's poem, singularly at variance with the carelessness of the execution . . .

June 21   *Elizabeth Melville writes to Catherine Lansing:*
. . . Bessie & Fanny and I are to go to the mountains, 1st Aug. through my good brother Lem's kind provision — and I am trying to arrange for comfortable quarters for Herman during our absence, so as to shut up the house — I think the change will benefit him also — take him out of himself —

June 25   *M visits Evert Duyckinck in the evening.*

June 26   Clarel *is reviewed [by Richard Henry Stoddard?] in* The World:

The reader who undertakes to read a poem of 600 pages in length, thirty-five lines to the page, is more than apt to receive the reward given by Jupiter to the man whom he caused to seek a grain of wheat in a bushel of chaff – to wit, the chaff. Good lines there must be, but they and their effect will alike be lost in the overwhelming tide of mediocrity . . .

[There is] no plot to sustain the interest of the reader, but there is a constant opportunity, fatal to such a facile writer as Mr. Melville, for digression, discussion, and, above all, description . . . Not being in his confidence we cannot of course say why he wrote the book, and what he intended it to mean . . .

The philosophizing of the book is its least agreeable part . . . Its best passages, as a rule, are the descriptive ones, which, notwithstanding frequent turgidness and affectation, are frequently bold, clear, and judicious. On the whole, however, it is hardly a book to be commended, for a work of art it is not in any sense or measure . . .

STATEN ISLAND June 30 *Thomas Melville writes to Catherine Lansing:*
Have you seen Hermans Book yet & what do you think of it –

LAWRENCE July 8 *John Hoadley writes to Abraham Lansing:*
– Thanks for your appreciative allusion to "Clarel." I saw the criticism, – if such it can be called even by courtesy, – in "The World" –
It [is] very flippant and foolish in the extreme.

"Clarel" is not easy reading. It requires determined study, and every attention must be at it furnished [?], to relish it until after several perusals.

But it will grow on thoughtful reading, and will give Her[man] Melville a firm footing on a higher plane than anything he has before written.

I wish it might make him at once rich, famous and happy! – Noble Fellow! [?] to be all three! –

NEW YORK July 10 Clarel *is reviewed in* The New-York Times:
The appearance of a poem in two volumes of three hundred pages each from a writer of Mr. Herman Melville's undoubted talent cannot fail to be a matter of interest to a wide circle of readers . . . *Clarel* is not without signs of power such as we should have expected from Mr. Melville. Here and there we have delicate and vigorous pieces of description. But of the poem as a whole we do not think we can be far wrong when we say that it should have been written in prose. The author's genius is evidently not of the kind which must express itself in numbers. Nor has he that minor gift of facile verse which constitutes him one of the "mob of gentlemen who write with ease." . . .

Such merit as Mr. Melville's poem has is in its descriptions and in the Oriental atmosphere which he has given in an honest and sincere style, but verse is certainly not the author's forte.

STATEN ISLAND July 20
The well-known yacht Mohawk owned by Vice Commodore William T.

Garner was capsized in a squall in the upper bay, off Stapleton; Staten Island, yesterday afternoon about 4:30 o'clock, and Commodore Garner, his wife, Mrs. Garner, and Miss Adele Hunter . . . were drowned . . . Three of the crew were also drowned, making a total loss of six lives, caused by the carelessness or incompetency of the sailing master, Rawlings, who acted in a cowardly manner when the disaster occurred. The Commodore made a gallant effort to save his wife, and failing in the attempt perished with her. (*The New-York Times*, July 21)

After July 20   Lizzie and I went to see Tom at the island the other day (starting in 5 P.M. boat, & returning in 9 P.M. Quarantine) Found Tom & Kate well. — How tragical a thing that oversetting of the yacht [*Mohawk*]. We passed the wreck in the boat — the two masts projecting from the water. — *M to Catherine Lansing, July 25*

NEW YORK   July 25   *M writes to Catherine Lansing:*
You have made such earnest assurances to me in reference to that book of mine, and in connection with what, you tell me, were your father's expressed wishes, that I can not doubt your sincerity. And so I make the following statement to you:
As it turned out, the 1200 covered the printing expenses, with a fraction to spare. But the supplementary charges — not long ago brought to my attention — against the account of the book — advertising &c, and customary copies distributed for advertising purposes — will make a difference with me in any receipts to come, of about one hundred dollars.
Whether this comes within the scope of Uncle Peter's design or not, I do not venture to determine . . .
. . . And now, accept this note in testimony that as regards your cousinly interest in me I am neither insensible nor incredulous.

ALBANY   July 31   *Catherine Lansing writes to M:*
Herewith I send you a check [for $100] to meet the balance due for Clarel's publication.
I beg you to receive it, as a contribution of my father's to that object. He desired it, & for that reason I am the more earnest in having his wishes fulfilled.

NEW YORK   August 1   [M's 57th birthday]   *Harper's sends M its 23rd account, showing a deficit of $84.12.*

August 2   *M writes to Catherine Lansing:*
The postman has just handed me yours of July 31, enclosing check for the $100; and, while the first impulse stirs me, I square round to my desk to tell you — however briefly — how deeply I feel the frank and affectionate spirit which penetrates it. I wont say anything more — only this: that I heartily reciprocate your wish that we may always be true and sincere friends. Amen!

ALBANY August 2 *Paul F. Cooper acknowledges a gift from Catherine Lansing:*

Many thanks to you for the copy of Mr Melville's poem. I expect to derive much pleasure from reading it; for I was always a great admirer of Mr M.'s writings.

NEW YORK August 12? *M leaves to spend his two-week vacation in the White Mountains with Elizabeth & his daughters.*

CLEVELAND August 15 *The Revd William B. Thomas acknowledges the gift of* Clarel, *sent to him by Catherine Lansing.*

BROOKLINE Before August 27 *M visits his sister & brother-in-law, Helen & George Griggs, before the end of his vacation.*

BOSTON August 26 [Frances Priscilla's 49th birthday] *M leaves, for New York, on the Fall River Route. (his letter to Catherine Lansing, Aug 27) He boards at the Hartnetts' house.*

NEW YORK August 27 *M writes to Catherine & Abraham Lansing:*

Passing thro' Nassau St. to-day I chanced upon a good set of the poet [Chaucer], at a very moderate price — ($4.) and, as these things are fugitive, I snapped it up immediately, and ordered it to be sent by express to 115 Wash. Ave. Albany. — What with his other volumes Chaucerian, Abraham will now have quite a variorum library of the old poet who did'nt know how to spell, as Artemus Ward said.

I arrived in N.Y. this morning . . . on my way from White Mountains. Lizzie & the girls are jolly . . . I myself am ever hilarious, & pray sincerely that you & your Abraham may likewise ever be so . . .

To Abraham: I have been thinking of what you said about changing the name of the Hotel. — I think that *"The Fort Stanwix Hotel"* is the right thing. You need a change. Besides, "Stanwix Hall" is indefinite . . .

Final P.S. — *"Fort Stanwix Hotel."* That is genuine, historic, natural, and purely American. It avoids the snobbish imitation of English names to our N.Y. Hotels. It sets a good example. It is the thing.

August Clarel *is reviewed in* The Library Table:

The verse is flowing and musical, the hero and his companions meet with the customary adventures, see the customary sights, and, during their journeyings, chance upon much that surprises and interests them and that furnishes abundant food for thought. The poem is a long one, and it seems to us might judiciously be somewhat curtailed, but we doubt not it will meet with some readers who will not object to linger with the author by the way and who will think it none too long.

Clarel *is reviewed [by Arthur C. Stedman?] in* The Galaxy:

We confess that we are puzzled by the title of Mr. Herman Melville's last volume — "Clarel: a Poem and Pilgrimage in the Holy Land." How a book can be a poem in the Holy Land, or a pilgrimage in the Holy Land, or a pilgrimage at all, or how it can be both a poem and a pilgrimage, we really cannot discover. The fact of the matter, set forth in simple English is, that "Clarel" is a poem which narrates and comments upon a pilgrimage in the Holy Land. We are by no means in a captious, or a dissenting, or even a fastidious mood, but we cannot praise Mr. Melville's poem or pilgrimage, or poem-pilgrimage. It is sadly uninteresting. It is not given even to the gods to be dull; and Mr. Melville is not one of the gods.

September 2   *M visits Evert Duyckinck in the evening.*

JEFFERSON, N. H.   September 6   *Elizabeth Melville writes to her step-mother:*
We have heard again from Stanny — he is much better and has got to work again — I feel very anxious about him but hope to hear better news soon — I want to send him all the clothing that Sam has to spare for him when I go to Boston —

NEW YORK   September 7   Your note reached me yesterday in the midst of a jumping tooth-ache . . . — *M to Catherine Lansing, Sept 8*

September 8   *From his office at 507 West Street M writes to Catherine Lansing:*
. . . with one hand to my "jole," with the other I indite this note . . . I will keep a look out for a fair copy at the Nassau St prices . . . Should I not succeed in lighting on a copy . . . before your visit to us in October — then we three — yourself, Abraham & your humble servant — will take council together touching the matter, and doubtless hit upon some wise decision. — . . . Lizzie & the girls have been greatly benefited by the mountain air — entirely excepting the annual ["rose"] cold, &c.

September 12   Last night (Tuesday) the first [plums] arrived all right in 25th St, giving great pleasure to the Misses Hartnett, and furnishing to me an added example of your cousinly good feeling. Edwin [Lansing], with Mr Brewster dined with us (at the Misses Hartnett's) last evening, and spent the remainder of it with me in my room at 26th St. I was well pleased to see him again, & looking so well. — *M to Catherine Lansing, Sept 13*

September 13   *M writes to Catherine Lansing, enclosing a receipt from the New York Society for the Relief of the Ruptured & Crippled, to which he has turned over the $100 that Mrs Lansing had sent him to cover the extra expenses of Clarel:*
I have upon consideration determined that as touching the provision for the publication of "Clarel," it is best to restrict myself to what Uncle Peter so kindly presented me with in person, as I may say. By your subsequent supplemental act you faithfully carried out what, as you averred, was your father's directions or wishes: you are irreproachable

there; and anything that I can do or have now done, does not and can not revoke that affectionate act of yours, while yet *my* action operates in a way favorable to the unembarrassed freedom of mutual good will. (Rather *"tall writing,"* that last clause.) . . . Let us therefore, my Dear Cousin, congratulate ourselves all round — you, me, and the poor cripples, and say no more about it. —

By the way — your rainy Sunday was also experienced by me, alone here as it chanced, to chew the cud of sweet and bitter fancies. I doubt not there was no lack of others — a plentiful sprinkling of them all over the world. — *M to Catherine Lansing, Sept 26*

September 17   *M visits Evert Duyckinck.*

ALBANY September 17   *Catherine Lansing replies to M:*
. . . I thank you for the gift you have bestowed on me, in giving me, the credit for your own "sweet charity" to the destitute & suffering.

NEW YORK September 21   *Elizabeth Melville writes to Catherine Lansing:*
Herman tells me that you and Cousin Abe think of going to the Centennial [in Philadelphia] before long and that he has asked you to stop on your way, and make us a visit — We all "second that motion" and hope you will.

September 26   *M hears from his sisters, Frances Priscilla & Helen, & writes to Helen & Catherine Lansing. (M to Catherine Lansing, this date)*

WASHINGTON September 28   *Lot M. Morrill, Secretary of Treasury, writes to General C. A. Arthur, Collector of Customs at New York, informing him that the reduction in salaries that took effect on December 1, 1875, has been reconsidered & that, dating from October 1, 1876, the employees' prior compensation ($4 per diem) is to be paid them.*

PHILADELPHIA September   Clarel *is reviewed in* Lippincott's Magazine:
If Mr. Melville has written anything since the three captivating books *Omoo, Typee* and *Mardi,* which were the delight of our early youth, we do not know it. If we should hereafter discover that he has done so, we shall feel our loss to be great . . . for it would be of no use to read them now . . . After an interval of twenty-five years or more it was rather startling to see his pleasant name of happy memories on the back of a new book, and surprise changed to dismay on finding that this book of two stout volumes was a poem . . . There are a few striking descriptions . . . But generally there is a want of point and distinctness, whether it be in the figures of speech, word-painting or dialogue; it produces a confusion of ideas and clumsiness of outline, arising not from obscurity of thought, but of expression, and that arises originally from Mr. Melville's imperfect command of metre and rhythm. He gives evidence of wide though desultory and superficial information, presenting rather than anything new a great quantity of things one has heard before.

The book is neither dull, stupid, nor heavy, and it is full of prettiness: it conveys an impression that the author is bright and genial, yet it is almost unreadable because of its length and the dead average commonplace level along which it stretches. There is nothing in it which could not have been said as well or better in prose . . .

October 11 *M visits the Centennial Exhibition.* (By the way, I was there yesterday — went & returned same day; you will be much impressed with it; it is immense — a sort of tremendous Vanity Fair. — *M to Catherine Lansing, Oct 12*)

[?] *While in Philadelphia M visits the book-shop of Moses Polock & proposes some publication to him.*

NEW YORK October 12   *M writes to Catherine Lansing:*
In response to yours of the 1st: The Chaucer is in eight vols. — good print — same edition as mine — [Robert] Bell's — but it is perfect . . .
I was very much pleased with Mr Street's little poem. It is admirable in its fidelity to nature and happy ensemble.

November 14   *Catherine Lansing writes to her husband:*
Priscilla & your Kate arrived at Cousin Hermans about 4 P.M. . . .
Cousin Lizzie — Herman Bessie & Fanny gave us a warm welcome — & it seems very natural here —

November 22   *Catherine Lansing writes to her husband:*
Cousin Herman invites you to spend Sunday with him. It is his free day —

ALBANY December 6   *Peter Gansevoort's will is proved, awarding M a bequest of $500.*

NEW YORK December 25   *For Christmas M sends Abraham Lansing his copy of* The Songs of Béranger, *& receives from him a Christmas Story [?] & an almanac for 1877:*
I liked that Christmas Story you sent me, especially in the opening portion — the good old Dutch Saint's lamentation over these "degenerate days" which we account such an "advance." . . .
By the way, — the almanac — I should have been sorry to have forgotten it — That venerable almanac, which bears witness to the old times when some imagination yet lingered in this sort of publication. I relish looking over it mightily. It has set me to getting from Boston a similar almanac which still continues to be published there. (*M to Abraham Lansing, Jan 2*)

M gives his daughter, Fanny, a copy of Goldsmith's Deserted Village.

SAN FRANCISCO December 29   *Stanwix Melville writes to his uncle, Lemuel Shaw, Jr:*

I obtained a situation in S.F. about a month ago, as clerk in a wholesale house, at a pretty fair salary to commence with; and from what one of the partners told me I expected to get a steady situation & a larger salary after this work of dissolving partnership was over. The salesman told me privately that this man's word was not to be relied upon; and so it proved, I was discharged after getting through the work of taking stock. The other partner asked for my address &c. & said he might want me again in the store, & would let me know by mail, after waiting a week, I went around to his office this morning, & he told me that he was going to bring his son into his store & he thought he would not need me.

That was the last straw that completely upset me, for I thought to obtain a respectable & steady situation here, but was disappointed.

The reason that I write to you is this. I want to obtain $60. at the least I dont ask you to loan it to me for my note, payable at any specified time, because I do not know whether I can meet it.

I have borrowed money here in San Francisco on the strength of a speculation & lost, & I am now reduced to desperate circumstances. I relied on this situation to see me through all right.

There is a party of five or six of us that are going to start for the Black Hills country about the middle or last of January two of them who were there before & were doing well until driven away by the Indians, & I am going with them if I can get this money, I put it at the smallest amount possible to do me any good, if I do not get it, I shall start now as quick as I receive an answer to this, on my own account and foot it till I get there, if it takes all winter. I have made up my mind, this is a chance, & I may be lucky there, at any rate I can get miners wages which is more than I can make here; and I am going this winter if I die of starvation or get frozen to death on the road.

. . . do not let any one know of my intentions to go to the Black Hills

.   .   .   .   .

SPRINGFIELD *Publication of* The History of Pittsfield (Berkshire County), Mass., from the Year 1800 to the Year 1876, *by Joseph E. A. Smith; including an anonymous contribution by M, a memoir of his uncle, Thomas Melvill, Jr. Smith thus introduces the memoir in his biographical sketch:*

He finally experienced pecuniary misfortunes, and, says a relative, "living in the plainest way, became a simple husbandman; though of broad acres, whereof many lay fallow, or in lake and pasture" . . . The relative from whom we have before quoted writes as follows . . .

*
1877
*

NEW YORK   January 2   *M writes to Abraham Lansing:*
I was glad to get your note, and to know that you were pleased with Beranger — *the volume:* a shabby looking little cask it is, but then, the contents! —

Elizabeth Melville sends tardy news to her brother, Lemuel Shaw, Jr:
We have a letter from Stanny this morning — he is employed in an "iron & steel firm" at present, engaged in settling matters previous to dissolving partnership — he has 2.50 a day, and a *prospect* of a steady engagement with the partner who goes on with the business — I earnestly hope he will be able to make it sure —

January 4   *M writes to Catherine Lansing:*
. . . let me acknowledge your note, with enclosure. — What shall I say? — Well, so be it. Yet, in the repetition, how can I otherwise than accept it in the spirit in which it is proffered, and as coming thro' you from Uncle Peter in the carrying out of his kindly purpose.

January 6   *M sees Evert Duyckinck in the evening.*

SAN FRANCISCO   January 21   *Stanwix Melville writes to his uncle, Lemuel Shaw, Jr:*
Your letter enclosing the check for $75. I received yesterday afternoon
I do not know how to thank you for your kindness in suitable terms; I can only say that I am very grateful.
I go [to] this mining country to take my chances with hundreds of others, & I am satisfied that something will come of it I start in a few days.
You shall hear from me in a few months

LAWRENCE   January 31   *Helen Griggs writes to her brother, M; & to Abraham Lansing, about the Hoadley girls:*
I have just been writing to Herman, and among other interesting items, "wished he could have seen the blackbirds," as he calls them, last evening, as they left us arrayed for conquest, with their two attendant cavaliers.
They went to an assembly, and returned "among the sma' hours," with their eyes as bright, and their cheeks as rosy, as when they started; all rapturous with having each "danced *every* dance," and displaying their well filled tablets, to attest the truth of the statement.

As I commented, to Herman — "ah me! what a thing it is to be young, to be sure!" To be able to enjoy such protracted weary fatigue, as we in our more sober years would think it, and come home, all agog for just such another delightful time, despite of tired feet, and the loss of a night's natural rest in sleep!

NEW YORK   February 25   *Elizabeth Melville writes to Catherine Lansing:*
. . . I want you *always* to mention Herman's name in your letters, especially if it is to say anything about coming down — *I* know your feeling is always right to him, and so does everyone else, but he is *morbidly* sensitive, poor fellow, and I always try (though I can't succeed to my sorrow) to smooth the fancied rough edges to him wherever I can — so I know you will understand why I mention it —

March 6   Now about President Hayes? I chanced to turn over a file of your Albany Argus yesterday, and was all but blown off the stool by the tremendous fulminations of that indignant sheet. — But what's the use? life is short, and Hayes' term is four years, each of 365 days. — *M to Catherine Lansing, Mar* 7

March 7   *M writes to Catherine Lansing:*
I was disappointed by your not dropping in upon us during your last trip to town . . . I have had something to say to you which I did not want formally to annoy you about in a letter . . .
It was this: You should have let that matter of the $100 rest where it was left for a finality last summer. Your subsequent letter — not very long ago [before January 4] — re-inclosing the money, made such an appeal to me, and placed the matter on such grounds as to make declination difficult without an appearance of obstinacy and rudeness. But I repented my assent. — And I revoke it. Be prepared therefore, sooner or later I beg you, to receive the money back without comment. Should you return it, some Charity will receive it, and down goes your name again for the Lady Bountiful of Albany. —
Now, my dear Kin, my cousinly disposition towards you may not be worth much to you; still, if you desire me to retain it unimpaired, you must uncomplainingly indulge me in my whim, for such you may call it, if you like. Indeed, you are welcome to almost any opinion, except that I am prompted by the remotest thought of wounding you, or any absurd idea of setting up for myself a spurious dignity. —

March 24
Arrived . . . Brig Carolus, (Ital.) Muro, Catania 110 ds., with sulphur to order — vessel to master. (*The New-York Times,* Mar 25)

By the way I have a ship on my District from Girgenti — Where's that? Why, in Sicily — The ancient Agrigentum. Ships arrive from there in this port, bringing sulphur; but this is the first one I have happened to have officially to do with. I have not succeeded in seeing the captain [Muro] yet — have only seen the mate — but hear that he has in possession some stones from those magnificent Grecian ruins, and I am going to try to get a fragment, however small, if possible, which I will divide with you. — *M to John Hoadley, Mar 31*

LAWRENCE March 25 *John C. Hoadley writes to M, sending him a poem "Foundation Stones," on a legend of Samarcand told by Marco Polo, & "He Wins Who Highest Aims," a condensed paraphrase from Virgil. (M to John Hoadley, Mar 31)*

GOWANDA March 25 *Edward Sanford writes to Catherine Lansing:* I have been reading 22 chapter of 2ᵈ part of "Clarel — Concerning Hebrews — I like the book very much, how did Friend Melville know so much about the Jews —

NEW YORK March 31 *M writes to his brother-in-law, John C. Hoadley:*
My Dear Fellow:
   I propose buying a hair-shirt and a scourge, and putting them to use for a week or so, as a penalty for my remissness in allowing your most friendly note of the 25 ult. to remain unanswered so long. — And yet I might say something in palliation of my incivility. You are young; but I am verging upon three-score, and at times a certain lassitude steals over one — in fact, a disinclination for doing anything except the indispensable. At such moments the problem of the universe seems a humbug, and epistolary obligations mere moonshine, and the — well, nepenthe seems all-in-all.
   Your legend from Marco Polo I had never previously met with. How full of significance it is! And beauty too. These legends of the Old Faith are really wonderful both from their multiplicity and their poetry. They far surpass the stories in the Greek mythologies. Dont you think so? See, for example, the loss of St Elizabeth of Hungary . . .
   In return for your M.S. favors I send you something I found the other day [the 1862(?) version of "The Age of the Antonines"] — came across it in a lot of papers. I remember that the lines were suggested by a passage in Gibbon (Decline & Fall) Have you a copy? Turn to *"Antonine"* &c in index. What the deuce the thing means I dont know; but here it is . . .
   Just looked over the accompanying letter which I wrote this morning. It is a queer sort of an absurd scribble, but if it evidences good-fellowship and good feeling, it serves the purpose. You are young (as I said before) but I aint; and at my years, and with my disposition, or rather constitution, one gets to care less and less for everything except downright good feeling. Life is so short, and so ridiculous and irrational (from a certain

point of view) that one knows not what to make of it, unless — well, finish the sentence for yourself.

Thine

do these inexplicable fleshly bonds

H. M.

N. B. I aint crazy.

BATH   April 7   *Dr Amos Nourse, M's uncle by marriage, dies.*

NEW YORK   April 8?   *Lizzie writes to Dr Nourse's widow, and M adds a note:*
My Dear Aunt Lucy:
   Lizzie has written you above; and I hardly know what I can add unless it be to assure you, with my own hand, of my sincerest sympathy and affectionate remembrance.

H. Melville

STATEN ISLAND   April 12   *M visits his brother, Thomas.* (Last evening I went down to the Island and anchored for the night in the
"Snug Harbor," . . .
   Tom was greatly pleased with your proposed gift to the Institution, and charged me to express to you as much — and more . . .
   We visited the new wing, and selected a good place for the Prints [of the Battle of the Nile], where the old Salts can look up at them from off their dominoes — a favorite game with them. — *M to Evert Duyckinck, Apr 13*)

NEW YORK   April 13   *M returns from Staten Island "in an early boat," & at noontime writes to Evert Duyckinck on the back of a customs form (the Discharging of Vessels):*
All you have next to do, is to provide for an annual Lecture, to be delivered before the old veterans in the big hall of the Institution [of Sailors' Snug Harbor], on the Battle of the Nile, the pictures serving to illustrate the matter . . . (not abounding in note-paper in this shanty of an office [at 507 West], I write on the best substitute at hand.)

STATEN ISLAND   April 15   *Thomas Melville writes to Evert Duyckinck:*
Hearing from Herman that [the pictures] are ready for delivery, I will send the Express men for them on Tuesday the 18ᵗʰ.

NEW YORK   May 9   *Catherine Lansing writes to her husband, Abraham:*
I did go to the "Dog Show" . . . I hope to go [again] for a few moments this Eveᵍ with Cousin Herman —

The great dog-show is astonishing its promoters with its success . . . All day long yesterday the Hippodrome was crowded to excess with elegantly-dressed ladies and gentlemen. (*The New-York Times*, May 10)

May 10   *Catherine Lansing writes to her husband:*
I hope Cousin Herman will come up [to Albany] & bring Cousin Lizzie [?] the following Monday May 22ᵈ.

May 22   [Bessie's 24ᵗʰ birthday]   *M gives a birthday present to his daughter, Bessie:* A Book of Reference to Remarkable Passages in Shakespeare, *by Susanna Beever (London, 1870).*

ALBANY   June 1   *Abraham Lansing sends M his share of Peter Gansevoort's estate ($500).*

NEW YORK   June 4   *M acknowledges Abraham Lansing's communication.*

June 5   *Elizabeth Melville writes to Catherine Lansing:*
Today probably Cousin Abe has acknowledgment from Herman of his missive recᵈ yesterday — I need not say that the kindly remembrance from your dear father gave him great pleasure — and I hope it will make him really happier to have something to call his own — poor fellow he has so much mental suffering to undergo (and oh how *all* unnecessary) I am rejoiced when anything comes into his life to give him even a moment's relief —

June 7   *A news item in the* New-York Daily Tribune:
CUSTOM-HOUSE PRUNING
SELECTING THE VICTIMS . . .
Collector Arthur has appointed the committee to make the selection of persons to be dismissed from the Custom-house in conformity with the recommendations of the Investigation Commission. The committee consists of Samuel G. Ogden, Auditor of the Custom-house; William H. McMahon, Chief Clerk of the Fifth Division; and Richard Grant White, who is in charge of the Revenue Cutter Bureau.

June 17   *Catherine Lansing comes to visit the Melvilles, & writes to her husband:*

Cousin Herman wants you to go with him & in to the Lenox Library. It is closed after this month & is well worth seeing for its superb building & its valuable endowment fund . . .

June 19 *Elizabeth Melville writes to her brother, Lemuel Shaw:*
. . . both myself and the girls thank you most heartily for your kindness — I suppose you could not do any act from which *more* comfort might be derived than to put it in our power to go to Jefferson — both on account of the release, for the time for me, and entirely for Bessie from the dreadful hay-fever, and for the general relaxation from care & anxiety, and the real benefit which we all experience . . . *hope* we shall be able to compass a six weeks absence from New York — the only doubt of which is the being able to leave Herman alone so long, in his state of mental health, with a free conscience — I shall try to bring about some suitable arrangement and he will have two weeks vacation out of it which he will probably pass at Gansevoort.

June 23 *Catherine Lansing writes a memo on M's letter of Mar 7:*
Cousin Herman gave me the 100-Dollars which he in this note said he would refund to me. Given to me at his house 104 E. 26th St N.Y. City . . .

ALBANY Before June 28 *Catherine Lansing sends to M, Peter Gansevoort's "sleeve-buttons" & a note, acknowledging the receipt of the $100.*

NEW YORK June 28 *Elizabeth Melville writes to Catherine Lansing:*
Herman sends love and was much pleased with his letter.

June 30 *After nearly being dismissed from the Customs service, M's working hours are increased.*

LAWRENCE July 2 *Frances Priscilla Melville writes to Catherine Lansing:*
Herman is going to spend half of his vacation with us at Gansevoort, & the other with [Lizzie & the girls] at Jefferson —

NEW YORK July 12 *M writes to Catherine Lansing:*
I heartily thank you for the sleeve-buttons which — it is all but needless to say — I shall always preserve as a lasting memorial of one whom I have more than one reason to remember with love . . .
. . . as regards all that dreadful trouble you lament you give on your travels, I really know nothing about it; and, in fact, have only to say *anent* it, what indeed you are already aware of — namely — that your visits, long or short, are always welcome to all of us. If I, for one, have any fault to find it is that

Abraham

dont come along with you.

Early August   *M writes to Catherine Lansing referring to the Lansings as "people of leisure." (M to Catherine Lansing, Sept 5)*

ALBANY August 9   *Catherine Lansing replies to M's letter, "disclaiming the thing." (M to Catherine Lansing, Sept 5)*

NEW YORK August 10   *M leaves for Albany, beginning his two-week vacation.*

ALBANY August 11   *M spends the day & evening with the Lansings, who take him for the evening to the home of Judge Elisha P. Hurlbut. (M to Mr & Mrs Abraham Lansing, Aug 14)*

SARATOGA SPRINGS August 12   *M stops here before going to Gansevoort.* (I staid over about three hours or so at the Springs. I lunched at a neat little restaurant I found there, and visited the hotels, presenting no doubt a distinguished appearance in my duster, and finally took up a commanding position on the piazza of the Great Union, and surveyed at my leisure the moving spectacle of fashion and — in some instances — folly. A New York paper also of the day helped to occupy the time.

I found Kate and Fanny and Frankie here [at Gansevoort] — all well and warm in welcome. — *M to Mr & Mrs Abraham Lansing, Aug 14)*

GANSEVOORT August 14   *M writes to Mr & Mrs Abraham Lansing:*
To-day is faultless weather and I shall dedicate it to leisure and the piazza . . .
P.S. — I go off visiting so seldom, that, really, I omit to do some things I ought to do, and would take pleasure in doing; they, simply, do not occur to me at the time, but reproachfully molest me afterwards in the omission. — Well, I did not call to pay my respects to Miss Lansing and Miss Anna [in Albany]. But apologies are awkward, and incredulity is but natural in some circumstances. Pray, Abraham, do the fitting thing for me, and redeem me in the good opinion of the ladies.
N.B. I will subject myself to any penance the ladies may be pleased to assign.
Final P.S. — Having, at Fanny's request, left this letter open . . . I am tempted to say one word more — namely: I have just been reading in a copy of Frank Leslie's Illustrated paper [of August 18] *The Old Garden* by Mr. [Alfred B.] Street. How beautiful, and poetically true to nature it is! It is like a flower-and-fruit piece by some mellow old Fleming. — There, I wont bore you any more. — H.M.

August 15   *M leaves Gansevoort to join Elizabeth & the girls at Jefferson, in the White Mountains.*

NEW YORK August 27   *M returns to his desk at 507 West Street, &*

subsequently sends a set of Chaucer to the Lansings, for which Catherine Lansing repays him.

September 5 *M replies to Catherine Lansing's note of Aug 9:*
I have just looked over the note again. — So it appears that I used in my letter to you [of early August] the expression *"people of Leisure."* If I did, it was a faulty expression — as applied in that case. I doubtless meant people the disposition of whose time is not subject to another. But it amused me — your disclaiming the thing, as if there was any merit in *not* being a person of leisure. Whoever is not in the possession of leisure can hardly be said to possess independence. They talk of the *dignity of work*. Bosh. True Work is the *necessity* of poor humanity's earthly condition. The dignity is in leisure. Besides, 99 hundredths of all the *work* done in the world is either foolish and unnecessary, or harmful and wicked. But bless my heart! I am scribbling here at a pretty rate. I will stop at once; and promise never to do so again.

Bessie & the girls are doing well at the White Mountains, and will remain there yet for a time. Their absence makes it decidedly lonely often in the house. But I take my meals at the Hartnetts', who are all that one can wish as hostesses. There are more agreeable people there too whom I meet.

My kindest regards to Abraham. Tell him not to be rash now, and sit up all night reading Chaucer, and comparing his variorum editions &c.

October 9 *Elizabeth Melville writes to Catherine Lansing:*
. . . we are now all upside down with painters — for *wonderful* to say, we are making some much needed renovation of some parts of the house — and getting some new furniture in the bed rooms, to replace the shabbiness which has so long prevailed there . . .
I don't believe Herman will go to the Saratoga Cen[tennial] he cannot get away, even if he care to — he is well . . .

BOSTON October 24 *Samuel Shaw's diary:*
Mrs. Lucy M. Nourse [M's aunt] died at Bath Me. at 4 A.M.

NEW YORK November 13 *Evert Duyckinck's blotter:*
Evening Melville, Drowne, [Alexander Jackson] Davis

November 17 *M sees Evert Duyckinck.*

November 27? *Elizabeth leaves, to spend Thanksgiving with the Shaws.*

December 3 *Evert Duyckinck places M first on a list for calendars, & sees him in the evening.*

December 11 [this year?] *M replies to an invitation from Rossiter Johnson to participate in the editing of his* Library of American Literature *[?]*:

Yours of the 9th is received, — Your friendly proposition I must decline. And this — in part at least — from a sense of incompetence. For I am unpracticed in a kind of writing that exacts so much of heedfulness — heedfulness, I mean, of a sort not demanded in some other departments.

BOSTON Before December 12 *Publication of* Péhe Nú-e, The Tiger Whale of the Pacific, *by Captain Barnacle [C. M. Newell], another telling of the hunt for "Timor Tom," "Mocha Dick, or, as rendered by some authors, Moby Dick."*

NEW YORK Before December 25 *M sends the members of the Hoadley family inscribed engravings of English architectural monuments.*

STATEN ISLAND December 25 *The Melvilles go to Sailors' Snug Harbor for Christmas dinner.* (We had a very pleasant Christmas gathering at Tom's and the nieces, all, spent the rest of the week there, and the baby [Morewood] . . . on this occasion he sat up at the table for an hour or more as straight and good as any one . . . — *Elizabeth Melville to Catherine Lansing, Dec 31*)

NEW YORK December 28 *Evert Duyckinck's blotter:*
Evg. C C Moreau wife & son — Herman Melville

ALBANY December *Catherine Lansing sends a copy of J. C. Hoadley's* Memorial of Henry Sanford Gansevoort *to: Mr & Mrs Herman Melville*

.   .   .   .   .

NEW YORK *M's office as inspector is listed at 6 State Street in the new Directory.*

LONDON *Publication of a selection by W. J. Linton,* Poetry of America *. . . from 1776 to 1876, including two poems by M: "Sheridan at Cedar Creek" & "Shiloh, A Requiem."*

*

1 8 7 8

*

NEW YORK January 26 *M acknowledges Catherine Lansing's gift of the memorial biography of her brother, Colonel Henry Sanford Gansevoort:*

Though, of course, neither Lizzie nor I have as yet had opportunity and time to give the book a thorough and deliberate examination; yet, from glimpses here and there, added to previous acquaintance with portions of the sheets, I can not but again praise the taste which it evinces, and also the literary skill and good judgement of Mr Hoadley the editor.

January 30   *Evert Duyckinck's blotter:*
Herman Melville   Mr Davis

February 9   *Harper's sends its 24th account to M, showing a sum of $64.38 due him, owing to these sales, since Aug 1, 1876:*

    33 Omoo
    35 Redburn
    58 White-Jacket
    66 Moby-Dick

February 23   *Evert Duyckinck's blotter:*
Evg. [John Bell] Bouton Robinson and Herman Melville

March 24   *Catherine Lansing writes to her husband, Abraham:*
    Fanny P[riscilla] sends love as do Cousin Herman (to who I last Eve^g gave the Oriskany & Schuylerville Centennial Volumes —) . . .

March 31   *Catherine Lansing writes to her husband, Abraham:*
    Cousin Herman wished for you at dinner & drank to you —

April 15   *M sees Evert Duyckinck in the evening.*

LAWRENCE April 27   *Frances Priscilla Melville writes to her cousin, Catherine Lansing:*
    Did Lizzie's letter, telling you of Fannie's engagement to Mr Harry Thomas, take you by surprise, or did you, with me, rather expect it, after our meeting him at Herman's, when we were there last month? . . .
    Lizzie writes that they all give their hearty approval to Fannie's choice . . .

NEW YORK May 7   *M sees Evert Duyckinck.*

Frances Melville writes to Catherine Lansing:
Last Saturday evening, Uncle Tom and Aunt Kate, Florence Kitty & Lucy were all here to meet the "gentleman from Philadelphia" [Henry Thomas] and the girls spent Sunday with us. You can imagine that with all those girls in the house and Bessie, I did not get much peace . . . I suppose they will get tired of teasing me after a while.

Before May 25   *M writes to John C. Hoadley.* (Last week Mr Hoadley had a short note from Herman, much to my relief, for it proved that he could again use his right hand. His left is improving. — *Frances Priscilla Melville to Catherine Lansing, May 28*)

June 4 *M sees Evert Duyckinck.*

June 13? [Elizabeth Melville's 56th birthday] *M writes to his sister, Frances Priscilla.* (I heard from Herman yesterday, his left hand has not yet, he tells me, entirely recovered — Speaking of Mr Charles Thurston's sudden death — he says, "whose end by the way may hardly be thought unhappy — the manner of it I mean — since he died in saneness and suddenly, and in the open air, and in a garden." — *Frances Priscilla Melville to Catherine Lansing, June 15*)

STATEN ISLAND July 4 [?] *The Melvilles celebrate the holiday at Sailors' Snug Harbor.* (Herman & family had been invited for to-day, so I suppose they have had a merry time. — *Frances Priscilla Melville to Catherine Lansing, this date.*)

LAWRENCE July 28 *Frances Priscilla Melville writes to her cousin, Catherine Lansing:*
Lizzie goes to Boston to-morrow with Fannie. Bessie was to leave Pittsfield yesterday & on the 7th they start for the Mountains . . .
Herman will spend his vacation there also. I have just been writing asking him to take Lawrence on his way, so we can see him — as Gansevoort is not open.

NEW YORK August 1 [M's 59th birthday] *M writes to Catherine Lansing, agreeing to act as her "agent in presenting to the Lenox Library a copy of Henry's Memorial."*

STATEN ISLAND August 1 *M takes Henry B. Thomas over to see his brother, Thomas.* (*Frances Priscilla Melville to Catherine Lansing, Aug 10*)

NEW YORK August 6 *Notified by Catherine Lansing that she has mailed the copy to the Adams Express office at 23 Street near Fifth Avenue, M stops there for it on his way to work, & later reports to her:*
. . . this morning on my way to my far uptown "District" [76 Street & East River?], I took the Memorial Volume to the Lenox Library, hoping to see there Mr Moore the librarian, whom I have met two or three times. Unfortunately he was not there; and the library it seems, is closed for the season. I got in, however, and left the Book with the janitor in perfect security, leaving a brief note for Mr Moore, in which I said I should take an early opportunity to call again & say something to him especially about the gift. — By the way, it is a beautiful copy; and upon my first opening the parcel in the janitor's presence, he exclaimed admiringly at the binding.
About the invitation to stay over with you Saturday & Sunday next — thank you for your kindness. Yes, I will come with pleasure. I will leave here Thursday night on the boat, & will probably be at 115 Wash[ington] Ave. at breakfast time . . .

Before August 8? *M writes to his sister, Frances Priscilla.* (Heard from Herman this week. — *Frances Priscilla Melville to Catherine Lansing, Aug 10*)

August 8 *M leaves for his Albany week-end.*

ALBANY August 9-11 *M stays with the Lansings.* (I enjoyed myself very much while with you — in fact, *so* much, that upon returning to this solitary house the loneliness is enhanced. I dont know that I shall visit you & Abraham again, if the eventual result is but an augmentation of the blues. — Howsomedever, every one manages to rub along . . . — *M to Catherine Lansing, Aug 12*)

COPPS HILL Before August 11 *Henry B. Thomas writes to M.* (Upon unlocking the front door — two letters awaited me . . . one from Lizzie & one from a young gentleman by the name of Thomas. The latter dated his note from Copps Hill. Curious coincidence — Fanny is there. — *M to Catherine Lansing, Aug 12*)

NEW YORK August 11 *M returns from Albany to 104 East 26 Street.* (After two prodigious bumpers of coffee at the depot (from the effect of which I have hardly yet recovered) off we started for New York where we arrived about ½ past 10. — *M to Catherine Lansing, Aug 12*)

August 12 *M writes to Catherine Lansing:*
. . . and so, Cousin Kate, with love to yourself and kindliest remembers to him whom you only a thousandeth part appreciate.

August 13 *Evert Duyckinck dies.*

August 16 [?] *M attends the funeral of Evert Duyckinck.*

Before August 26 *M writes to his sister, Frances Priscilla.* (With your kind letter came one from Herman, saying how much he enjoyed his little visit in Albany. I do not know any one he thinks more highly of than he does of you. It is quite refreshing to ones soul to hear one gentleman speak of another as he does of you, Abe. — *Frances Priscilla Melville to Abraham Lansing, Aug 26*)

NEW HAVEN August *Mrs Martha Bird Marett dies.*

GANSEVOORT September 13 *Frances Priscilla Melville writes to Catherine Lansing:*
We are all rejoicing over Lizzies great fortune & I write to tell you, knowing well how glad Abe & you will be to hear, that *she* has been left $10,000. Stanwix $4,000. Bessie & Fanny *each* $3000 a piece, by the will of her Aunt Mrs Marett who died this month — your friend Mrs. Gifford's mother — as the children would say, is it not splendid!

NEW YORK Before October 16   *M writes to his sister at Gansevoort.*
(We have had letters from Fannie, Lizzie, Tom Katie Lottie & Herman,
within a day or two . . . — *Frances Priscilla Melville to Catherine Lansing, Oct 16*)

November 6   *Elizabeth Melville writes to Catherine Lansing:*
The carpet came safely yesterday afternoon, and Herman has given me
a long message to send you — He thinks it a very handsome one, and
thanks you very much for your kindness in thinking of it for his room,
and sending it, and hopes you will not think he does not appreciate it,
if he hands it over to Bessie for her room . . .
    As to Herman's room he is so enamored of a *floor* without a "stuffy
carpet" that he does not want to have it covered at all but only have a
mat here & there — I fear it will be cold for him in the winter, but as all
the cracks have been filled up, he thinks not . . .
    We have been *very* busy and are now nearly at rights again — I have
been spending Aunt Lucy's [Nourse] special legacy to me ($100.00) on
our back parlor . . .
    I have been writing to Stanny — he is in Quincy Cal. where he has
occupation, and is quite well — but he has been sick poor fellow, and had
to go in the hospital at Sacramento for some time — he has seen some
very hard times, and deserves much credit for his pluck and patience
under difficulties and disappointments —

ALBANY November 25   *Catherine Lansing & Frances Priscilla Melville write to M, inviting him to bring the girls to the Lansings for
Thanksgiving (while Elizabeth goes to Boston & the Shaws).*

NEW YORK November 26   *M replies to Catherine Lansing:*
. . . I write forthwith as to your kind invitation, regretting for myself,
Bessie & Fanny, that we shall not be able to accept it, seeing that it is arranged already that we are to have a little Thanksgiving affair here, of
which "the young man" [Henry Thomas] will of course be the central
figure.

November 28   *"A little Thanksgiving affair," at which Henry Thomas
is present.*

December 5   *Catherine Lansing, visiting the Melvilles, writes to her
husband:*
    I gave your kind messages to Cousin Herman.

STATEN ISLAND December 19   *Frances Priscilla Melville writes to Catherine Lansing:*
    I have just returned from spending two days at Herman's. Lizzie ar-
rived at home this morning, coming by boat. She looks well & has had
a pleasant time, in her dear Boston.

NEW YORK December 27? *Catherine Lansing visits the Melvilles. (her letter to her husband, Dec 27)*

Catherine Lansing gives M a "Photograph of the Old Revolutionary Flag presented to Genl. Peter Gansevoort Col. of the 3ᵈ N.Y. Regt. at the surrender of Lord Cornwallis."

*

1 8 7 9

*

LAWRENCE January 3 *John C. Hoadley writes to Abraham Lansing:*
I came home from New York to-day at noon, and receive by this evening's mail the superb cards of invitation to the New Capitol Reception, for which I am happy to feel myself indebted to your kind courtesy . . .
. . . Tom and Dr. Bogert intend to go, I believe, and to induce Herman to go if possible.

NEW YORK February 9 *Catherine Lansing, visiting New York, records in her diary:*
Took walk on 5th Avenue Meet Cousin Herman & Fanny. we went to 104 E. 26ᵗʰ St made a call — Took tea there.

February 17? When in N.Y. last week Herman & I went up to the Lenox Library, were there several hours, & I was sorry enough to come away, hope to go again. — *Frances Priscilla Melville to Catherine Lansing, Feb 25*

February 28 Friday I spent at Herman's . . .
Lizzie was not very well had one of her "run down" turns, as she calls them. — *Frances Priscilla Melville to Catherine Lansing, Mar 2*

March 4 Tuesday evening, *Tom* gives a party, has invited about fifty of his gentlemen friends to be with him from "8 to 11."
Herman is coming, & no doubt, but will enjoy the affair — *Frances Priscilla Melville to Catherine Lansing, Mar 2*

March 7 *Elizabeth Melville writes to Catherine Lansing:*
Your letter to Bessie I am going to try to write a few lines in answer to — though I am sick myself with one of my prostrated turns — and hardly able to guide my pencil — but I want to express my thanks to you for all your kindness to the girls while they were on their visit to you — they enjoyed themselves very much — and more especially for

your interest so generously shown in Bessie's poor hands — You will be glad to hear, I am sure, that she began the binding up her fingers in splints at once with a *very marked* favorable effect towards straightening out though it is hardly a week yet . . . only one thing [Dr Cox] ought to know & that is her *extreme delicacy* of constitution, and want of vital force — how little strain on her strength she can bear & how anxious we feel about her generally . . . she says she did not tell him anything about her general health — his suggestion about straightening her fingers at once, *by force,* if carried out I believe would kill her — You . . . can hardly appreciate what it is to be in the weak and prostrated condition that Bessie and I suffer from more or less nearly all the time and which in my case drags me down at intervals as now when I cannot walk across the room without staggering —

March 13   Please say to Aunt Fanny that Bessie was not able to go up to the depot yesterday & as papa wanted to see her before she went, he offerred to take the box, and got there just too late, so he sent the box by express . . . — *Frances Melville to Catherine Lansing, Mar 14*

ALBANY   April 14   *Catherine Lansing writes to M.*

SAN FRANCISCO   April   *A listing in the current* San Francisco Directory:
Melville Stanislaus, canvasser, r. 418 Broadway

NEW YORK   Before June 2   [?] *M writes to his sister, Frances Priscilla.* (Herman is much better, has been to Elizabeth [N. J.] to see his new niece, Miss Agnes [Morewood]. — *Frances Priscilla Melville to Catherine Lansing, June 2*)

June 2   *Catherine Lansing's diary:*
Took tea at Cousin Hermans . . .

August 10   *Edwin Lansing writes to his brother, Abraham:*
On leaving the wharf I went down town and while there called at the Custom House to endeavor to find Herman Melville as agreed upon, but ascertaining that I would have to go as far up town as 76th St. and East river to see him I concluded to leave your message of farewell [with] Mr Brewster, whom I afterwards met, who agreed to deliver it soon.

Before August 13   *M writes to his sister, Frances Priscilla.* (Herman writes me that Lizzie & the girls are enjoying themselves very much at the "Overlook" Catskill, & that he will soon join them there — *Frances Priscilla Melville to Catherine Lansing, Aug 13*)

BOSTON   August 13   *Mrs Hope Savage Shaw dies.*

August 16   *Samuel Shaw's diary:*

Mothers Funeral. Mr. [James Freeman] Clark officiated in absence of Mr Tilden. Service at the house at 12 M. Rainy day —

NEW YORK   August 29?   Herman & Mr Thomas were to go to Catskills yesterday — *Frances Priscilla Melville to Abraham Lansing, Aug 30*

GANSEVOORT   August 30   *Frances Priscilla Melville writes to Abraham Lansing, in London:*
Herman met your brother Edwin in the street, & heard of Kate & you having gone abroad, from him — Too bad that your [farewell] note turned up in London & not, at 104 East 26 Street

WOODSTOCK   September 12   *Samuel Shaw's diary:*
To the Overlook Mt. House in the Catskills . . . Lizzie and Bessy there

NEW YORK   September 15   *M returns to his office at 76th Street, on the East River.*

ALBANY   November 15   *Abraham Lansing sends invitations for Christmas dinner to "Cousin Herman Lizzie Bessie Fany P M Thomas."*

NEW YORK   November 17   *M replies to Abraham Lansing's invitation:*
We are all very much obliged to you for your Christmas invitation, but upon consideration, hardly think we shall be able to accept it. The truth is Lizzie is not very robust — and the journey northward at midwinter — why, she rather dreads it.

November 18   *Catherine Lansing arrives at the Melvilles' in a heavy rain, receives a warm welcome, & writes in her diary:* All well at 104.

NEW HAVEN   November 18   *Mrs Ellen Marett Gifford writes her will, giving Elizabeth Melville $10,000, & to each of her three children, $3,000, &:*
Article Second — I give, as a token of remembrance to Herman Melville — the sum of Eight thousand dollars (8,000$) and my share or right in the New York Society Library — without assessments on the share — should he desire it —

At some later date, Mrs Gifford adds, in a codicil:
4ᵗʰ I give to Mrs. Herman Melville . . . $5,000 — in addition to what I gave her in my will —

NEW YORK   November 19   *Catherine Lansing's diary:*
Dined at Cousin Hermans.

November 23   In the Eveg took Carriage & went to the Grand Hotel — took room   Expecting A. L[ansing]. in the morning —
My last visit to 104   I never will be so awkwardly situated at the mercy of the politeness of friends —

December 4   *Frances Priscilla Melville writes to Catherine Lansing:*
I was at "Perks" with Herman on Thursday, & there met Mrs Sandford . . .

NEW BRIGHTON December 15   *Frances Priscilla Melville writes to Catherine Lansing:*
The contents of your envelope was full of interest. The remarks on The Arms of the State," I sent to Herman to read —

December 25   *Frances Priscilla Melville gives M a photograph of "General Gansevoort's Phaeton, still to be seen in the carriage house at Gansevoort, N. Y. . . ."*

.   .   .   .   .

STOCKHOLM   *Publication of No. 11 in Bonnier's Familje-bibliotek:*
Teipi. En berättelse om fyra månaders vistelse bland infödingarne på en af Marquesasöarne.

*

1 8 8 0
*

NEW YORK   January 14   *Frances Priscilla Melville writes to Catherine Lansing:*
Kate H[oadley] & I are here at Herman's, return to Tom's to-morrow — Saturday.

ALBANY   Before January 20   *Catherine Lansing sends M a gift of tobacco.*

NEW YORK   January 20   *Elizabeth Melville writes to Catherine Lansing:*
Herman was going to add a note to this to thank you for the tobacco, but as he is hurried this morning I will not let this wait.

February 18   *M orders [for Stanwix?], on his Harper's account, a copy of* Sporting Adventures in the Far West, *by John Mortimer Murphy.*

February 28   *Harper's sends its 25ᵗʰ account to M, with a check for the amount due him: $68.62.*

April 5   *An invitation:*
Mʳ & Mʳˢ Herman Melville | request your presence | at the marriage of their daughter | Frances, | to | Henry B. Thomas, | Monday, April fifth, at one o'clock, | All Souls Church | Fourth Avenue & 20th Street. | New York.

Even on the occasion of the 5th I was not at perfect liberty for the day.
— *M to Catherine Lansing, Apr 15*

ALBANY April 14   *Catherine Lansing writes to M, notifying him of the death of John Thomas Lansing this day.*

NEW YORK April 15   *M writes to Catherine Lansing:*
How sudden the event. Express to Abraham the true sympathies of all of us. — Though I met Mr. John Lansing but two or three times, yet each time I was most agreeably impressed with his intelligence and social disposition. —
I am sorry that my being at the funeral is hardly possible.

October 10   *Elizabeth Melville writes to Catherine Lansing:*
. . . Herman is well as usual . . . Herman and I are going out [to visit Fanny in Orange] this week.

November 7   *Catherine Lansing's diary:*
. . . after church . . . I went to Cousin Hermans
   They were at dinner . . .

November ?   *M attends Sarah Bernhardt's repertoire twice.*

December 1   *Frances Priscilla Melville writes to Catherine Lansing:*
The weather being bright, we have been out a good deal with Herman & by ourselves. Lizzie is enjoying herself in Boston.

December 4   I was about two weeks at Herman's, had a pleasant time there. Saturday, Fannie came back from Philadelphia & *she* & *Harry* are to stay *there* [at 104 East 26 St] until Lizzie's return from Boston.
— *Frances Priscilla Melville to Catherine Lansing, Dec 6*

ALBANY Before December 8   *Abraham Lansing invites the Melvilles to come up for a reception by the Fort Orange Club on Jan 19, 1881.*

NEW YORK December 8   *M writes to Abraham Lansing, declining the invitation:*
Thanks in behalf of the family, I mean, myself included. But Lizzie is in Boston & Bessie is keeping house, and I am an — old fogy; so none of us can comply, much as we regret it.

1881 **IX** 1891

1882: *Feb 24, Melville's first grandchild, Eleanor Thomas, is born; Fall, Melville declines to assist in founding the Authors Club*

1884: *Mar 5, Melville's brother Thomas dies; Fall, Melville begins a correspondence with an English admirer, James Billson*

1885: *May 17, Melville's poem, "The Admiral of the White" (an early version of "The Haglets") is published in both a New York & a Boston newspaper; July 9, Melville's sister Frances Priscilla dies; Dec 31, Melville resigns his post as Customs Inspector*

1886: *Feb 23, Stanwix Melville dies in San Francisco; Oct 21, Melville's brother-in-law, John C. Hoadley, dies in Lawrence*

1888: *Feb, Melville makes his last voyage, to Bermuda, returning via Florida; June 11, he writes his will; Sept 7, the private, limited printing of* John Marr and Other Sailors; *Nov 16, begins the composition of* Billy Budd

1890: *Feb 13, Melville compiles a volume of verse,* As They Fell, *& puts it aside; Apr, he experiences a second attack of erysipelas*

1891: *Apr, Melville completes* Billy Budd *& turns over a volume of verse,* Timoleon, *for private printing; Sept 28, Herman Melville dies*

ALBANY January 1 *Catherine Lansing sends Munsells Almanac to a
list of relatives, including:* Mr & Mrs Herman Melville —

NEW YORK May 15 *Catherine Lansing's diary:*
. . . came home [from church] dined at 4³⁰ & afterwards called upon
Mrs Allan Melville & at Cousin Hermans 104 E. 26ᵗʰ St.

DAVENPORT July 20 *A death notice:*
MELVILLE — In this city, Thursday, July 20, Capt. Robert Melville, in his
65th year, of paralysis of the heart.

ALBANY August *Catherine Lansing sends to Stanwix Melville, in San
Francisco, a draft for $110.*

THE PACIFIC Summer *Robert Taylor Prichett, in the* Wanderer, *at
Tahiti, prepares illustrations for* Omoo.

NEW YORK December 25 *M receives a Christmas present from his
sister, Catherine Hoadley — a vase.*

December 28? *M thanks Catherine Hoadley:*

My dear Kate:

    Dont be alarmed by these beautiful flourishes of mine; I have been
recently improving my penmanship by lessons from a High Dutch professor who teaches all the stylish flourishes imaginable. —
    But my object in dropping you this line is to thank you, My dear
Kate, for your little vase. It is now on my mantle, and contributes much
to the embellishment thereof, and I value it as your gift.
    We are all as usual — that is to say, jolly; and trusting that you too
are in the same happy case, — with kind regards to John & love to the
girls . . .

*

1 8 8 2

*

ORANGE February 24 *To Frances & Henry Thomas is born their first child, a daughter [Eleanor], & M's first grandchild.*

BROOKLINE February 27 *Frances Priscilla Melville writes to Catherine Lansing:*
I send you a San Francisco paper, which Herman sent to us, the curious specimen of Japanese Dictionary English is for Abe with my love. —

Before April 12 Maria Hoadley writes to M. (Just received a note from Minnie, — for the which, pray, give her my affectionate acknowledgments — Wherein among other interesting matters, she says — what she previously had heard distant rumors of — or did she read it under the head of *"Personal"* in the newspaper? — I say, she says that you and John propose a visit to these parts some time next week. — *M to his sister, Catherine Hoadley, Apr 12*)

NEW YORK April 12 *M writes to his sister, Catherine Hoadley:*
Well: I write at once to say that, altho', I suppose, you will spend some days with Tom, you must not fail — you & John — to spend a portion of the time with us . . . Lizzie — who at present is at Orange helping Fanny to break in the "babby" [Eleanor] to going without its nurse — would cheerfully unite with me in the invitation, were she here. Indeed, she was talking with me about making the invitation some days ago.
Lizzie & I rec^d letters from Helen & Fanny (jointly to & from) which I acknowledged by paper; & will ere long be happy to reciprocate by letter. With love to them and yourself & all, I remain — *No, I don't,* for I forgot to say we had a pleasant visit from the Lieutenant [?], who went with Bessie to the Zoo & shook hands with Mr Barnum. — How he has grown!

May 17 *Catherine Lansing's diary:*
Up town called on Mrs Allan Melville & at Cousin Hermans

BOSTON June 27 *Lemuel Shaw, Jr writes his will.*

NEW YORK August 1 [M's sixty-third birthday] *Elizabeth gives to M for his birthday, Volume 13 of* Little Classics *edited by Rossiter Johnson:* Poems Narrative (*Boston, 1881*).

Before August 28 M writes to his sisters at Gansevoort. (Helen has just brought the mail, letters from Tom, Lottie & Herman . . . Herman writes, that he hoped to get away for a week's vacation soon, to join Lizzie at the Overlook [Mountain House, in Woodstock] — *Helen M. Griggs & Frances Priscilla Melville to Catherine Lansing, Aug 28*)

WOODSTOCK September 8 *Elizabeth Melville writes to Catherine Lansing:*
We hear constantly from Stanny — I wish I could say he is materially better — but he keeps about the same, & cannot yet get rid of his cough — I feel very anxious about him — that it holds so long.

NEW YORK? October 27 *M gives his autograph to someone.*

October? Rather to my surprise Herman Melville the elusive accepted the original invitation [from the founders of the Authors Club], but, as he soon wrote, he had become too much of a hermit, saying his nerves could no longer stand large gatherings and begged to rescind his acceptance. — *reminiscences of the Authors Club, by Charles De Kay*

ALBANY November 13 *M, in Albany, writes to (?).*

GALENA December 18 *George R. Melvill writes to Lemuel Shaw, Jr:*
My brother Robert left a Wife and two sons, as follows.
Susan R. Melvill   Davenport Iowa
Robert T.   "   do
Julien H.   "   I dont know his address . . .
My brother A. C. M. left a Wife two daughters and one son
Florinda D Melvill Wife   Galena Ill.
Jessie D   "   "   "
Lucy   "   "   "
Charles Allen   "   "   "
Mrs Dean left two sons
Melvill Dean and Kenneth Dean . . .
My Mother is very well for one of her age: she goes to church once a month . . .

ALBANY December 31 *Catherine Lansing's diary:*
Send Almanacs to . . . Herman Melville . . .

.   .   .   .

NEW YORK *Publication of* Life in Hawaii, an Autobiographical Sketch of Mission Life & Labors (1835-1881), *by Titus Coan, in which this passage appears on pp 199-200:*
From this bay [Taiohai], in 1842, the gifted Herman Melville, with his friend Toby, absconded to the hills . . . Melville lost his reckoning of distances as well as his track. The enchanted valley of Taipi, Melville's "Typee," is only four hours climb by the trail from Taiohai . . . During all his four months

of romantic captivity, the gifted author of "Typee" and "Omoo" was only four or five miles distant from the harbor whence he had fled.

EDINBURGH *Publication of* American Literature, *by John Nichol, with comment about M's books "among minor works worthy of note."*

*

1 8 8 3

*

January 1 *M gives his daughter, Bessie, a New Year's present:* Sir Roger De Coverley, *reimprinted from* The Spectator . . .

March 31 *Robert Barry Coffin presents to M copies of his works:* My Married Life at Hillside; Matrimonial Infelicities, with an Occasional Felicity, by Way of Contrast . . . ; Out of Town: A Rural Episode; Castles in the Air, and Other Phantasies.

In exchange, M gives Coffin a copy of Omoo.

Spring *Julian Hawthorne visits M.*
In 1883, when I was writing a biography of my father, I called on [M] in a quiet side-street in New York, where he was living almost alone. He greeted me kindly, with a low voice and restrained manner; he seemed nervous, and every few minutes would rise to open and then to shut again the window opening on the courtyard. At first he was disinclined to talk; but finally he said several interesting things, among which the most remarkable was that he was convinced Hawthorne had all his life concealed some great secret, which would, were it known, explain all the mysteries of his career. ("Hawthorne at Lenox," *Booklover's Weekly,* Dec 30, 1901)

. . . I met him, looking pale, sombre, nervous, but little touched by age . . . He conceived the highest admiration for my father's genius, and a deep affection for him personally; but he told me, during our talk, that he was convinced that there was some secret in my father's life which had never been revealed, and which accounted for the gloomy passages in his books. It was characteristic in him to imagine so; there were many secrets untold in his own career. (*Hawthorne and His Circle*)

He seems to have pondered much over his brief intercourse with Hawthorne, conjecturing some baffling problem in his life . . . When I visited him in 1883 to ask whether he had letters from my father, in reply to those he had written him, he said, with a melancholy gesture, that they had all been destroyed long since, as if implying that the less said or preserved, the better! ("When Herman Melville was 'Mr. Omoo'," *Literary Digest International Book Review,* Aug, 1926)

. . . Mr. Melville recently informed the present writer that it [the Agatha story] was a tragic story, and that Hawthorne had not seemed to take to it. (*Hawthorne and His Circle*)

. . . I talked with him in his house in New York; he was then more than sixty years old [64], and a melancholy and pale wraith of what he had been in his prime.

During the incoherent talk between us on that occasion he let fall several hints as to his interpretation of the source of Hawthorne's insight into the human soul. It was a sad interview; he seemed partly to shrink from the idea that obsessed him, and partly to reach out for companionship in the dark region into which his mind was sinking. I . . . had applied to him for any letters that Hawthorne might have written to him in reply to several of his own during the 1850's. But he said, with agitation, that he had kept nothing; if any such letters had existed, he had scrupulously destroyed them . . .

I knew that he had once proposed to Hawthorne to join [?] him in some literary work . . . I spoke of this project to Melville but he made no intelligible response. His words were vague and indeterminate; and again and again he would get up from his chair and open or close a window with a stick having a hook at the end, which he kept by him seemingly for that purpose. When I tried to revive memories in him of the red-cottage days — red-letter days too for him — he merely shook his head. ("Herman Melville," *The Dearborn Independent*, Sept 24, 1922)

May   *Mrs Downer gives M a reprint of a sketch of Major Thomas Melvill's life, originally printed in the* Columbian Centinel, *Oct 30, 1832.*

August 10   *M writes to Julian Hawthorne.*

August 31?   *M leaves on his two-week vacation.*

RICHFIELD SPRINGS   Before September 14   *M writes to his sister at Gansevoort.* (He writes that he has enjoyed the beauty of the country all about exceedingly, has passed his vacation very pleasantly. — *Frances Priscilla Melville to Catherine Lansing, Sept 14*)

GANSEVOORT   September 14   *Frances Priscilla Melville writes to Catherine Lansing:*
    We are expecting Herman to-morrow, coming to spend Sunday with us, on his way home from Richfield Springs . . .
    Lizzie & Bessie are to stay on [at Richfield Springs], as their coming to Gansevoort will be later.

September 15-16?   *M visits at Gansevoort.*

NEW YORK   September 17   *M returns to his desk at 76th Street & the East River.*

ORANGE December 3   *To Frances & Henry Thomas is born their second daughter [Frances Cuthbert], M's second grandchild.*

ALBANY Mid-December   *Catherine Lansing sends Christmas cards to:* Mr & Mrs Herman Melville . . .

·   ·   ·   ·   ·

From its earliest meetings the Authors Club justified the hopes of its founders; and for the first time in the history of New York the members of the writing craft were able to get acquainted with each other . . . authors who survived their earlier fame were called back to mingle with their younger successors. Once or twice the shy and elusive Herman Melville dropped in for an hour or two. (Brander Matthews, *These Many Years* [New York, 1917])

To one of these earlier gatherings [of the Authors Club] we made bold to invite all the men of letters residing in or near New York, and to this meeting, probably in 1883 or 1884, came Herman Melville. Apparently he did not greatly care for our society; he did not apply for membership and I believe that he was never with us again. I recall that I heard some one say to me, "There's Herman Melville!" The name meant little to me then, and I gave him only a casual glance. All that I can now recover is a faded impression of an unobtrusive personality, with a vague air of being somehow out of place in our changing and chattering groups. (Brander Matthews, *New York Times* book review, Dec 25, 1921)

M acquires DeFoe's History of the Plague, Great Fire of London, etc. (*London, 1881*).

In a chat column, New-York Herald:
   In Washington the other day I met A. A. Hayes, a well-known writer of short stories for the magazines. He showed me a letter from W. Clark Russell, the Englishman, whose sea stories are having such a run. ". . . I feel that the best sea stories ever written are those by Henry Melville and Richard H. Dana, jr. If you know that fine writer, Melville, why not write his life? Why not let the world know as much as can be gathered of his seafaring experiences and personal story of the greatest genius your country has produced — leagues ahead of Longfellow and Bryant as a poet . . ."

*

1 8 8 4

*

STATEN ISLAND March 5   Captain Thomas Melville, Governor of Sailors' Snug Harbor . . . died suddenly of heart disease, at his residence, late in the evening of March 5th, in the fifty-fifth year of his age. (*obituary by John C. Hoadley*)

March 8   *Catherine Lansing's diary:*
The funeral *services* were *private* Rev. W. W. Clark officiating. The Casket & families were in the living room — & it was a sad sad sight —

March 10   Nearly ten oclock this morning the funeral left this pleasant hospitable home & carried its dear Master Capt. Thomas Melville to the gate . . . lined with the old sailors with bared heads, & tearful eyes saying farewell to their devoted friend & Governor —
  We carried him to the Moravian Cemetery at *New Dorp* on the other side of the Island . . .

NEW YORK   March 11   Last Eve^g went to see Cousin Lizzie — Cousin Herman not well enough to see me — he has a kind of Rheumatic gout —

BOSTON   May 6   *Samuel Shaw's diary:*
My brother Lemuel died of an attack of apoplexy at 11.45 PM at the Union Club, Park St.

GALENA   July 30   *M's aunt Mary Anne Melvill dies.*

NEW YORK   August 1   [M's 65th birthday]   *Elizabeth Melville gives M a birthday present:* A Book about Roses, *by Samuel R. Hole* . . . (*New York, 1883*).

LEICESTER, ENGLAND   August 21   *James Billson writes to M:*
  I have to thank you for an immense deal of good I have derived from reading your works & can assure you that in Leicester your books are in great request. We have had a great deal of trouble in getting them . . . My object in writing was a more practical one — to ask if you would kindly give me the names of any other works you may have written besides those I mention below — which are what we have succeeded in unearthing . . .
  I have liked the Mardi best although not feeling quite sure I have perceived all the meaning of the allegory.

NEW YORK   September 23   *Harper's sends its 26th account to M, with a check for the amount due him, $223.72.*

LONDON   September   The Contemporary Review *publishes a critical article by W. Clark Russell, "Sea Stories":*
Who are the poets of the deep? Their names may be counted upon the fingers of one hand: they are Herman Melville, and I rank him first; Michael Scott; Dana, the author of "Two Years before the Mast," and Captain Cupples, the author of "The Green Hand." . . .
  Whoever has read the writings of Melville must I think feel disposed to consider "Moby Dick" as his finest work . . .
  Melville takes this vessel, fills her full of strange men, and starts her on her insane quest, that he may have the ocean under and around him to muse upon,

as though he were in a spacious burial-ground, with the alternations of sun-light and moonlight and deep starless darkness to set his thoughts to. "Moby Dick" is not a sea-story — one could not read it as such — it is a medley of noble impassioned thoughts born of the deep, pervaded by a grotesque human interest, owing to the contrast it suggests between the rough realities of the cabin and the forecastle, and the phantasms of men conversing in rich poetry, and strangely moving and acting in that dim weather-worn Nantucket whaler . . . As we read we do not need to be told that seamen don't talk as those men do; probabilities are not thought of in this story. It is like a drawing by William Blake, if you please; or, better yet, it is of the "Ancient Mariner" pattern, madly fantastic in places, full of extraordinary thoughts, yet glori-ously coherent . . . In "Typee," and "Omoo," and "Redburn," he takes other ground, and writes — always with the finest fancy — in a straight-headed way.

NEW YORK October 10 *M replies to James Billson's letter of Aug 21:* I can not but thank you for the kind expressions in it, and really wish that the books you have so patiently disinterred better merited what you say of them. — You ask me to give you the names of any *other* books of mine, with the names of the publishers. The following occur to me: —

"White Jacket" published in London by Bentley.

"Battle Pieces," in verse, published in New York by Harper & Broth-ers.

"Clarel," published by George P. Putnam's Sons, New York — a met-rical affair, a pilgrimage or what not, of several thousand lines, eminently adapted for unpopularity. — The notification to you here is ambidexter, as it were: it may intimidate or allure.

LEICESTER October 28 *James Billson writes to M* (I thank you for yours of Oct. 28th, and its kindly expressions. — *M to Billson, Dec 1*), *& sends to him a volume,* Vane's Story, Weddah and Om-el-Bonain, and Other Poems, *by James Thomson* (*London, 1881*).

BROOKLINE November 25 *Frances Priscilla Melville passes on to Cath-erine Lansing news from New York:* Bessie has had a severe attack of "muscular rheumatism," & has suf-fered greatly, but the doctor assures Lizzie, that the worst is over. The strain of night & day attendance was too much for her mother, & they have a nurse from the training school, which is a great aid & comfort.

NEW YORK December 1 *M replies to James Billson's letter of Oct 28:* I would have acknowledged it ere now but for reasons which it suffices to say — since you will believe it — are adequate.

I owe you sincere thanks also for the volume of poems you were so good as to mail me. The "Weddah and Om-el-Bonain" gave me more pleasure than anything of modern poetry that I have seen in a long while. The fable and the verse are alike supremely beautiful. It is exactly that kind of a *gem* which some of Keats' pieces are; and what can one say more? — You should be happy to think that you personally knew the author of such a poem. —

You say something about my photograph. I should be happy to oblige you but really, there is none that at present I can lay hold of. However, should I have one taken again, I will take pleasure in causing one to be mailed to you. —

December 7   *Catherine Lansing's diary:*
Went up to see Cousin Lizzie — & hear how Bessie is getting along

December 14   After ch[urch] — called on Mrs. Allan Melville & at Cousin Hermans.

.   .   .   .   .

NEW YORK   *On the receipt of her half-brother Lemuel's legacy, Elizabeth puts $25 monthly in M's pocket, to spend on books & prints.*

When I went to America, my very first inquiry was concerning [M] . . . There was some slight evidence that he was 'alive,' and I heard from Mr. E. C. Stedman, who seemed much astonished at my interest in the subject, that Melville was dwelling 'somewhere in New York,' having resolved, on account of the public neglect of his works, never to write another line. Conceive this Titan silenced, and the bookstalls flooded with the illustrated magazines! (Robert Buchanan, note to "Imperial Cockneydom," *The Universal Review*, May 15, 1889)

. . . when a visiting British author a few years ago inquired at a gathering in New-York of distinctly literary Americans what had become of HERMAN MELVILLE, not only was there not one who was able to tell him, but there was scarcely one among them who had ever heard of the man concerning whom he inquired, albeit that man was then living within a half mile of the place of the conversation. (Memorial editorial, *New-York Times*, Oct 2, 1891)

Mid-1880's?
I visited him repeatedly in New York, and had the most interesting talks with him. What stores of reading, what reaches of philosophy, were his! He took the attitude of absolute independence toward the world. He said, "My books will speak for themselves, and all the better if I avoid the rattling egotism by which so many win a certain vogue for a certain time." (Titus Munson Coan, *The* [Boston] *Literary World*, Dec 19, 1891)

. . . he was contented to be forgotten, and among his cherished books he passed his life. With the few who were permitted to know him he was the man of culture, the congenial companion, and the honestest and manliest of all earthly friends. I once asked the loan of some of his books, which early in life had given me such pleasure, and was surprised when he said that he didn't own a single copy of them . . .

This little incident tells a story of his own indifference to the children of his brain. I had before noticed that, though eloquent in discussing general literature, he was dumb when the subject of his own writings was broached. (O. G. H[illard], communication headed "The Late Henry Melville" to the *New-York Times*, Oct 6, 1891)

*

1 8 8 5

*

LEICESTER   January   *James Billson writes to M, & sends him another volume of James Thomson's poems,* The City of Dreadful Night and Other Poems (*London, 1880*).

BROOKLINE   January 7   *Helen Griggs & Frances Priscilla Melville report to Catherine Lansing:*
A note from Lizzie on Monday is more encouraging about Bessie but — her long beautiful hair has been all cut off! Is not that a loss?

January 15   *Frances Priscilla Melville writes to Catherine Lansing:*
Bessie will be in Boston to-day, is coming to make her friend Miss Wells a visit who lives at Cambridge. When she was staying at Herman's, about two years ago, I met her there, & she & Lizzie spent a day at Tom's. She is very bright & pleasant.

LONDON   January 16   The Daily Telegraph *publishes an article [by James Billson?] on the South Sea islands:*
It is to the early navigators, but more particularly to that delightful and original American sailor-writer, Herman Melville, that we owe those fancies of beauty, of peace, of waftings of aromatic sunlit air which possess the mind when the islands of the Pacific are named. There have been scores of books written about the South Seas, since "Typee" and "Omoo" were given to the world, but nothing has been expressed by pen or pencil that does not send the mind hastening back to the lovely imaginations which the very name of Herman Melville arouses . . .

NEW YORK   January 19   *Catherine Lansing's diary:*
Went to see Cousin Lizzie — Bessie Melville improving has had her hair cut & her head shaved [?] —

January 22   *M writes to James Billson & mails him a copy of* Clarel:
I am grateful for the last volume you kindly sent me, received yesterday. — "*Sunday up the River*," contrasting with the "*City of Dreadful Night*," is like a Cuban humming-bird, beautiful in fairy tints, flying against the tropic thunder-cloud. Your friend was a starling poet, if ever one sang. As to his pessimism, altho' neither pessimist nor optomist myself, nevertheless I relish it in the verse if for nothing else than as a

counterpoise to the exorbitant hopefulness, juvenile and shallow, that makes such a bluster in these days — at least, in some quarters.

— In a former note you mentioned that altho' you had unearthed several of my buried books, yet there was one — "Clarel" — that your spade had not succeeded in getting at. Fearing that you never will get at it by yourself, I have disinterred a copy for you of which I ask your acceptance and mail it with this note.

It is the sole [?] presentation-copy of the issue.

BOSTON February [1] *In* The Atlantic Monthly *Thomas Wentworth Higginson reviews* Nathaniel Hawthorne and His Wife, *by Julian Hawthorne:*
The letters, published in full, of his few American correspondents betray habitually the tone of secondary minds, not of men meeting him on high ground . . . In some cases the letters are given so fully as to give an impression of "padding," as where we have nine consecutive pages of not very interesting epistles from Herman Melville (i. 398).

LIVERPOOL February 10 *The Liverpool* Daily Post *publishes an article [by James Billson], "James Thomson: Poet, Essayist, and Critic," which Billson sends to M.*

LEICESTER February 18 *James Billson writes to M.* (Believe me, its friendly proffer of good offices, should occasion occur, this I was, and remain, grateful for. — *M to Billson, Sept 5*)

BROOKLINE April 8 *Helen Griggs writes to Catherine Lansing:*
I do so sorrow at having to give up my post of nurse; dear Fanny is so sweet and patient; but I promised Herman & Lizzie, and others of the family, who have been urging our having a nurse . . .

May 5 *Helen Griggs writes to Catherine Lansing:*
A box of superb flowers has just come from Herman [for Frances Priscilla].

NEW YORK May 11 *Lucy Melville dies at Bloomingdale Asylum.*

BROOKLINE May 14 *Helen Griggs writes to Catherine Lansing:*
This letter is to ask you if you had heard of Lucy Melville's death . . . Dear little Lucy. A short career, & not a happy one. But had she lived, her future was so deeply overshadowed, we can but look on her peaceful, painless death, as a blessed boon.

Her case, mentally, was considered a hopeless one . . .

NEW YORK May 17 *The Sunday edition of the* New-York Daily Tribune *publishes a condensation (30 stanzas) of M's final version of* "The Haglets," *entitled:*

THE ADMIRAL OF THE WHITE.

BY THE AUTHOR OF "OMOO," "TYPEE," "MOBY DICK," ETC.

Copyright, 1885.

By chapel bare, with walls sea-beat,
The lichened urns in wilds are lost
About a carved memorial stone
That shows, decayed and coral-mossed,
A form recumbent, swords at feet,
Trophies at head, and kelp for a winding sheet.

BOSTON May 17 *"The Admiral of the White" is printed in* The Boston Herald.

NEW YORK May 22 [Bessie's 32nd birthday] *Elizabeth Melville gives her daughter, Bessie:* The Quiver of Love (*London, 1876*).

PHILADELPHIA June 21 *W. Clark Russell's article "Sea Stories" is reprinted in* The Times *as "Poets of the Deep."*

LANSINGBURGH June 29 *Mary Louise Peebles writes to Abraham Lansing:*

How are you getting on with the Whale? I have been reading Hawthorne's life [by Julian Hawthorne] and find it very entertaining, principally because it is so indiscreet. It does not chloroform the poor little literary butterflies in its collection, but just sticks a pin through them, and calls you to look. I wonder if Herman Melville was consulted about the appearance of his name? I should think some of the allusions would be very trying to a person of his sensitive nature.

NEW YORK June *Elizabeth gives M a copy of* Nathaniel Hawthorne and His Wife, *by Julian Hawthorne.*

FIRE ISLAND July 3-6 Herman came down on Friday & staid till Monday morning, and seemed to enjoy it very much — I am sure it will benefit him. — *Elizabeth Melville to Catherine Lansing, July 7*

July 7 *Elizabeth Melville writes to Catherine Lansing:*
Bessie and I expect to go to Jefferson N.H. where we are *sure* to escape the enemy [hay fever] . . . but meantime, as Herman does not care to spend his vacation in Jefferson, we have it under consideration to take it early in Aug. and go somewhere, perhaps only on short excursions together, for a couple of weeks — or just whenever he wishes —

I am so fortunate this year as to have an excellent woman to leave in the house which makes Herman much more comfortable in my absence; and relieves me of much anxiety on his account — and though he protested against it vehemently at first, he feels the benefit of it, and is now glad to have her . . .

I am feeling a good deal worried about Stanny's health — his pulmonary troubles have been worse of late, and he has been ordered to San Rafael, where he was relieved before by the dryer air — & I hope it may prove so this time —

BROOKLINE   July 9   *Frances Priscilla Melville dies at the age of 68.*

ALBANY   July 14   *Catherine Lansing sends copies of the* Albany Argus *to:* Herman Melvilles . . .

July 27   *Abraham Lansing writes to M:*
   Will it meet your approval, if steps shall be taken at once for the probate of Fanny's will . . .

NEW YORK   July 29   *Elizabeth Melville writes to Catherine Lansing:*
   Herman's position in the Custom House is in the Surveyor's Department — a *district inspector* — his work is all on the uptown piers nearby to Harlem — and he has held office since Dec. 1866 — Of course there have been removals, and he may be removed any day, for which I should be very sorry as apart from every thing else the *occupation* is a great thing for him — and he could not take any other post that required head work, & sitting at a desk — If Cousin Abe has an opportunity to say anything for him, I should be glad, but *do not let* Herman know that the subject has been mentioned between us — He *did* receive "The Argus" and sent you *a paper* in response.

August 1   [M's sixty-sixth birthday]   *Elizabeth gives M a birthday present,* Balzac, *by Edgar Evertson Saltus (Boston, 1884), in which M subsequently reads & scores one of a collection, compiled by Saltus, of Balzac's reflections:*
   To forget is the great secret of strong and creative lives, — to forget utterly, after the manner of Nature, who knows no past, and who each hour recommences the mysteries of her indefatigable parturitions. It is the weak who live with grief, and who, instead of changing it into apothegms of existence, toy and saturate themselves therewith, and retrograde each day to consummated misfortunes.

PITTSFIELD   Early August?
His last visit to Pittsfield was in 1885 when he was for some days a guest at the Homestead Inn, the Pomeroy homestead on East street, which was for a short time converted into a fashionable hotel . . . He did not evince the slightest aversion to society but appeared to enjoy the hearty welcome which it gave him; time having enhanced instead of diminishing the local pride in and regard for him. Perhaps his manner was a little more quiet than in the old time; but in general society it had always been quiet . . .
   In this last visit to Pittsfield Mr. Melville bore nothing of the appearance of a man disappointed in life, but rather had an air of perfect contentment, and his conversation had much of his jovial, let-the-world-go-as-it-will spirit. (Smith, *Biographical Sketch*)

[?] M writes a poem in Pittsfield:

INSCRIPTION

For a boulder near the spot where
the last hardhack was laid low
by the new proprietor of the
Hill of Arrowhead.

A weed grew here. Exempt from use,
Weeds turn no wheel, nor run;
Radiance pure or redolence
Some have, but this had none,
And yet heaven gave it leave to live
And idle it in the sun.

LONDON August 15 *Publication, in* The Academy, *of a poem by Robert Buchanan:*

SOCRATES IN CAMDEN, WITH A LOOK ROUND . . .

Meantime my sun-like music-maker [Whitman],
   Shines solitary and apart;
Meantime the brave sword-carrying Quaker
   Broods in the peace of his great heart, —
While Melville,† sea-compelling man,
Before whose wand Leviathan
Rose hoary white upon the Deep,
With awful sounds that stirred its sleep,
Melville, whose magic drew Typee,
Radiant as Venus, from the sea,
Sits all forgotten or ignored,
While haberdashers are adored!
He, ignorant of the drapers' trade,
   Indifferent to the art of dress,
Pictured the glorious South-sea maid
   Almost in mother nakedness —
Without a hat, or boot, or stocking,
A want of dress to most so shocking,
With just one chemisette to dress her
She *lives*, — and still shall live, God bless her!
Long as the sea rolls deep and blue,
   While heaven repeats the thunder of it,
Long as the White Whale ploughs it through,
The shape my sea-magician drew
   Shall still endure, or I'm no prophet!

† Hermann Melville, author of *Typee*, *The White Whale*, &c. I sought everywhere for this Triton, who is still living somewhere in New York. No one seemed to know anything of the one great imaginative writer fit to stand shoulder to shoulder with Whitman on that continent.

NEW YORK August 17? *M returns from his last vacation to his desk at 76th Street & the East River.*

ALBANY August 19   *Abraham Lansing writes to M, sending him the will of Frances Priscilla, & a waiver to sign.*

NEW YORK August 21   *M returns the signed waiver to Abraham Lansing.*

September 5   *M writes to James Billson:*
I have to thank you for two papers received some months ago, one containing an article by your hand on the poet Thomson, the other referring to the South Sea Islands (and was this too written by yourself?) both interesting to me: the first because my interest in the author of the "City of Dreadful Night" was measurably gratified by it . . .
But yet further to bring up arrears, my acknowledgments are due for a copy of "The Academy" received the other day containing a poem by Robert Buchanan — "Socrates in Camden." For more than one reason, this Piece could not but give me pleasure. Aside from its poetic quality, there is implied in it the fact, that the writer has intimately penetrated beneath the surface of certain matters here. It is the insight of genius and the fresh mind. The tribute to Walt Whitman has the ring of strong sincerity. As to the incidental allusion to my humble self, it is overpraise, to be sure; but I can't help that, tho' I am alive to the spirit that dictated it.
But a letter on almost any theme, is but an inadequate vehicle, so I will say no more.

ALBANY September 9   *Abraham Lansing writes to M:*
The tenant of Fanny's farm [at Gansevoort] writes for an extension of his lease, so as to sow with a prospect of being able to reap next harvest. His ground has been ploughed.
It seems to be a good plan to extend the lease for a year. If you agree with it, will you please sign & return to me the enclosed power of attorney.

BROOKLYN September 14   The Brooklyn Eagle *reprints the London* Daily Telegraph *article,* "*The South Sea*" [sent to the Melvilles by C. F. Kane].

NEW YORK Early October?   *M has his photograph taken at Rockwood's. [See Pl. XV]*

October 5   *M writes to Mrs Ellen Marett Gifford, enclosing his new photograph:*
It is now quite a time since you first asked me for my photo: — Well, here it is at last, the veritable face (at least, so says the Sun that never lied in his life) of your now venerable friend — venerable in years. — What the deuse makes him look so serious, I wonder. I thought he was of a gay and frolicsome nature, judging from a little rhyme of his about

a Kitten ["Montaigne & His Kitten"], which you once showed me. But is this the same man? Pray, explain the inconsistency, or I shall begin to suspect your venerable friend of being a two-faced old fellow and not to be trusted . . .

P.S. You see the rose-leaves have not yet given out. I shall always try and have a rose-leaf reserved for you, be the season what it may.

LEICESTER October 7 *James Billson sends to M a copy of* Essays and Phantasies, *by James Thomson (London, 1881), which M subsequently reads; in the essay, "Bumble, Bumbledom, Bumbleism," M scores:*

How many English writers of repute, earning good incomes by their writings, would have the courage, however pure and lofty their intent, to treat with the same freedom the same subjects we find treated in a work of Balzac or Heine?

In "Indolence: A Moral Essay," M scores:

. . . they are like certain men of genius who remain always obscure because they are all genius, having no vulgar profitable talents.

NEW YORK November 26 *Catherine Lansing's diary:*

Cousin Helen went to dine at Cousin Hermans with Fanny & Mr Thomas & the children —

BOSTON November 28 *In "our New York letter" (signed "Stylus") of* The Literary World:

Dropping into a bookstore the other day, my attention was attracted by an old gentleman with white hair, but whose eyes are still bright and his movements quick. Upon inquiry I discovered that the old gentleman was no less a person than Herman Melville, whose Omoo, White Jacket, Moby Dick, and other romances of the South Sea delighted my youthful imagination more than twenty years ago. Had he possessed as much literary skill as wild imagination his works might have secured for him a permanent place in American Literature.

At the New York bookshop of Francis P. & Lathrop C. Harper, in the Astor House, Barclay Street, opened this year:

". . . a customer whom they later learned to be Herman Melville used to drop in, look over the books, and occasionally buy an unimportant title for which he paid cash without leaving his name. Therefore no records were kept of these transactions. He was a very quiet man and seldom if ever entered into conversation. If he talked at all it was never about his own writing, or about authors or literature at all. He must have visited the shop many times before Mr. Harper learned his name." — Douglas G. Parsonage to Merton M. Sealts, Jr, 26 Dec 1947 (printed in the *Harvard Library Bulletin,* Spring 1948)

NEW YORK Before November 30 I had a safe passage here [Brick Church], Herman being our most polite escort — We, that is, Fanny & myself, nurse, two babies, four bags, and his cane, were transported by two separate lines of horse-cars, a ferry-boat, a steam-car, and a carriage, to "the haven where we would be."

Herman put us on board the steam cars, and then returned to New York . . . — *Helen Griggs to Catherine Lansing, Nov 30*

December 20   *M writes to James Billson:*

Do not think me indifferent or ungrateful if your last friendly note and gift remain unacknowledged till now. — There are natures that after receiving a certain impression as to another, that *other* need therefore hardly ever enter into intricate explanations, happen what may. — This may perhaps be a little obscure to some, but you will understand.

For the two books I thank you much. It is long since I have been so interested in a volume as in that of the "Essays & Phantasies." — "Bumble" — "Indolence" — "The Poet" &c, each is so admirably honest and original and informed throughout with the spirit of the noblest natures, that it would have been wonderful indeed had they hit the popular taste. They would have been painstakingly diluted for that — diluted with that prudential worldly element, wherewithall Mr Arnold has conciliated the conventionalists while at the same time showing the absurdity of Bumble.

But for your admirable friend this would have been too much like trimming — if trimming in fact it be. The motions of his mind in the best of his Essays are utterly untramelled and independent, and yet falling naturally into grace and poetry. It is good for me to think of such a mind — to know that such a brave intelligence has been — and may yet be, for aught anyone can *demonstrate* to the contrary. — As to his not achieving "fame" — what of that? He is not the less, but so much the more. And it must have occurred to you as it has to me, that the further our civilization advances upon its present lines so much the cheaper sort of thing does "fame" become, especially of the literary sort. This species of "fame" a waggish acquaintance says can be manufactured to order, and sometimes is so manufactured thro the agency of a certain house that has a correspondent in every one of the almost innumerable journals that enlighten our millions from the Lakes to the Gulf & from the Atlantic to the Pacific. — But this "vanity of vanities" has been inimitably touched upon by your friend in one of his Essays. — "Satires & Profanities" are of course written for another plane than that to which the "Essays" are levelled. But many touches are diverting enough. "The Devil in the Church of England," for instance. But I must close. — You asked me for my photograph, but I had none to send you. Now that I *have*, I forward it to you, conditional however upon your reciprocating with your own, and this, permit me to insist on.

December 25   *In the weekly* Harper's Handy Series *is published* In the Middle Watch, *a collection of sea stories by W. Clark Russell, including an expansion of his essay, "Sea Stories," originally published in* The Contemporary Review (*Sept 1884*).

Before December 31 *Elizabeth Melville's memoir of M:*
His last Custom house office was at Simonson's Lumber yard, foot of
79th st on East River.

December 31 *M resigns his post of Inspector.*

*

1 8 8 6

*

January 10 *Elizabeth Melville writes to Catherine Lansing:*
   You and Cousin Abe have so kindly interested yourselves in Herman's
retaining his Custom House post, that I want to tell you among the first
that he has resigned, for very good and sufficient reasons — For a year
or so past he has found the duties too onerous for a man of his years,
and at times of exhaustion, both mental and physical, he has been on the
point of giving it up, but recovering a little, has held on, very naturally
anxious to do so, for many reasons — This month was a good turning-
point, completing 19 years of faithful service, during which there has
not been a single complaint against him — So he retires honorably of his
own accord — He has a great deal unfinished work at his desk which
will give him occupation, which together with his love of books will
prevent time from hanging heavy on his hands — and I hope he will get
into a more quiet frame of mind, exempt from the daily invitation of
over work —

January 14 *A paragraph in the* New York Commercial Advertiser
("*Echoes of the Hour*"):
   Herman Melville exemplifies the transiency of literary reputation. Before
the civil war he enjoyed wide fame, and his very clever books were much admired. To-day, his name would not be recognized by the rising generation.
Still, he is not very old — sixty-five — and his rather heavy, thick-set figure
and warm complexion betoken health and vigor . . . of late years he has
done nothing in literature. For a long while he has been in the custom house
as inspector, and is dependent on his salary. Although his early works are still
popular, the author is generally supposed to be dead. He has, indeed, been
buried in a government office . . . He is a genial, pleasant fellow, who, after
all his wanderings, loves to stay at home — his house is in Twenty-sixth street
— and indulge in reverie and reminiscence.

January 15
   At the New York College of Archaeology and Aesthetics, last Friday evening, Professor J. W. Henry Canoll read the sketch relating to Herman Melville, which on Thursday appeared in this paper. He warmly commended "the

practically archaeologic spirit shown in these columns concerning Manhattan and the Manhattanese," and after giving some additional facts improvised the following poem . . .

MELVILLE

He rests, whose feet have trod all continents;
Whose song has been of Nature's heart and Man's; . . .
The ocean monarch's friend and kindly scribe,
He loved each grain of earth, each drop of sea,
Where his keen microscope of mind discerned
Or home or tomb of Nature's sentient motes. . . .

He rests: though diverse climes beguiled, enthralled,
The western stars were sacred light and beacon,
That guided to the hallowed fires of home.
No cortege waited there, no coarse ovation;
His footsteps ever modest fell and peaceful
As blessed foot whose prints he traced at Saba.
In mart or park, at rest or bent by toil —
The nation's rights he ever toiling guarded —
He still was true — to every man a neighbor,
Though rude Presumption dare not grasp his hand.
His palm was friendly, kind his eye of blue
While rending mask of Vice or piercing Pride.
(*New York Commercial Advertiser*, Jan 18)

January 18   *The* New York Commercial Advertiser's *report of Professor Canoll's evening is headed:* A "BURIED" AUTHOR.

January 23   *J. W. Henry Canoll writes to M.*

January 25?   *M drafts a reply to J. W. Henry Canoll:*
I have just received yours of the 23^d, and beg leave to thank you for it. — When my attention was directed to your Lines in the Comm[ercial] Ad[vertiser] and I had read . . . Your [effaced: Lines — Poem] verse was inspired by the best of feelings [effaced: and executed —], and it gave me true pleasure to recognize the gracious spirit that animates man. — Nor does it at all abate this pleasant feeling that you gave publication to them, though the wisdom of this — from one point of view at least — might admit of a doubt.
For what can one do — the Press. Retaliate? Should it ever publish the rejoinder, they can . . .

Early February?   *M writes to his son, Stanwix, enclosing a power of attorney for M to collect Stanwix's share of the estate of Frances Priscilla Melville, signing his letter:*
Good bye, & God bless you
Your affectionate Father
H. Melville.

SAN FRANCISCO February 14 *Stanwix Melville signs the power of attorney & returns it to his father.*

LEICESTER February 15 *James Billson sends M a "semi-manuscript" copy of Fitzgerald's translation of the* Rubaiyat, *& John W. Barrs sends to M a volume of further poems by James Thomson,* A Voice from the Nile and Other Poems (*London, 1884), with this inscription:*
> To Herman Melville from J. W. Barrs
> as a small tribute of admiration to Typee and Omoo.

NEW YORK February 22? *Elizabeth Melville writes to Helen Griggs.* (I had a letter from Lizzie yesterday. Poor Stannie is very ill again. *— Helen Griggs to Catherine Lansing, Feb 24*)

SAN FRANCISCO February 23 *A death notice:*
MELVILLE — At [German Hospital] San Francisco, Cal., 23^d inst., Stanwix, son of Herman and Elizabeth S. Melville, in the 35th year of his age.

BROOKLINE March 16 *Helen Griggs writes to Catherine Lansing:*
I am so sorry for Lizzie! It is sad indeed to have had Stannie die away from home. But it seems he had a friend, who did all he could to make him comfortable, and there was money enough to procure all that was necessary for his comfort. It is sad enough; but it might have been worse, since there is so much consolation for his poor mother.
Ah! me. The sorrows that lie round our paths as we grow older!

NEW YORK March *M reads* A Voice from the Nile; *in the introduction he underscores:*
I think we must forgive the Americans a good deal of vulgarity and arrogance for some generations yet.
& among other poems he checks this passage in "A Happy Poet":
> Driven by mysterious care and restless pain
> The world rolls round me full of noise and strife,
> Racking what is not loss to dubious gain:
> I live apart my self-fulfilling life,
> Serenely happy, breathing golden air
> Unvext by these dark storms of pain and care.

NEW YORK April 2 *M writes to James Billson:*
If I am late in acknowledging your last kind note and the receipt of the welcome gifts it announced, it is from any cause but indifference . . .
For the semi-manuscript "Omar" — the text, coming in that unique form to me, imparted yet added significance to that sublime old infidel. —
— The discussion about the 100 best books in the Pall Mall [Budget] is perhaps more curious and diverting than profoundly instructive.
— For the "Voice from the Nile" containing the added poems of Thom-

son the memoir and the portrait, give my best thanks to Mr. Barrs. The Pieces having a peculiar interest for that gentleman are extremely pleasing — especially two of them. And yet, if one consider the poet's career, one could heave a big sigh for the fatality investing so genial a spirit. But perhaps the gods may make it all up to him wherever he now may sojourn. If they do not, the shabby fellows ought to be ashamed of themselves.

— It pleases me to learn from you that Thomson was interested in Wᵐ Blake.

April?   *Peter Toft meets M.*
I accidentally discovered him some years ago during my stay in New York, and, having much in common, we became good friends. Though a delightful talker when in the mood, he was abnormal, as most geniuses are, and had to be handled with care. He seemed to hold his work in small esteem, and discouraged my attempts to discuss them. "You know," he would say, "more about them than I do. I have forgotten them." He would give me no information about the old whaling tradition of the fiendish White-Whale ("Moby Dick,") which was said to haunt the sea about the Chiloe Islands, south of Valparaiso, and was almost offended when I inquired so curiously about his falling from the maintopgallant yard of the frigate — ("White Jacket") — a tour de force of writing, in my opinion. (his letter, *New York Times*, Mar 17, 1900)

April 7   *Peter Toft gives M two water-colors:* Flamboro' Head [scene of the battle between the *Bon Homme Richard* and the *Serapis* — painted in July, 1883]; Redondo Rock [*inscribed:* With the Kind Regards to the Author of "The Encantadas." 1886].

After April 7   *M writes to W. Clark Russell a letter to be delivered by Peter Toft; the letter endorses Russell's praise of Richard Henry Dana, Jr.*
Praise when merited is not a boon; yet to a generous nature, is it pleasant to utter it. This pleasure have you doubtlessly taken in some minor contributions, citing certain marine authors of the past, one or two of them, I think, still surviving. Nor, have you beckoned in an instance that comes a little near to me. You; you have regarded as an authoritative marine doctrine and offered a warm tribute none the less just, to R. H. D. —

(Your letter which Mr Toft has been good enough to convey to me has given me a very great and singular pleasure . . . Dana is indeed great. There is nothing in literature more remarkable than the impression produced by Dana's portraiture of the homely inner life of a little brig's forecastle. — *Russell to M, July 21*)

Mr. Melville, I know, greatly admired the genius of Dana. His praise of "Two Years Before the Mast" half fills a letter I possess. (foot-note, W. Clark

Russell, "A Claim for American Literature," *The North American Review*, Feb 1892)

BROOKLINE May 5   *Helen Griggs writes to Catherine Lansing:*
Lizzie is in Mt. Vernon Street, and I saw her yesterday . . . She is in great trouble; and seems unable to find solace for her grief — it was *so* hard, — the sickness and death so far away! . . .
Oh! about the big side-board [at Gansevoort]. It was left to Herman; but neither his house, nor Fanny's Lizzie says, can find sufficient space for it . . .

NEW ORLEANS Spring?   *Lafcadio Hearn writes to Charles Warren Stoddard:*
I can scarcely credit that the letter I have just received is from one whose book [*South-Sea Idylls*, 1874] not only bewitched me before I had heard of Melville and before Viaud had begun to teach the new Gnosticism of nature-feeling and nature-religion in a series of startling studies . . .

NEW YORK Early June   *M writes to his sister, Helen Griggs.* (Herman writes me, that if the sideboard can be accommodated, in the back parlor of their house, he would be very thankful to recieve it under his roof. And the old clock, (which Uncle Herman gave him) is to go to Fanny's at Orange, and will be sent to some *horologist* in New York, on its way to her. — *Helen Griggs to Catherine Lansing, June 7*)

June 13   [Elizabeth's sixty-fourth birthday]   *M gives Elizabeth a birthday present, a set of four satires published in London, 1847 — the year of their marriage:*
> The Natural History of the Ballet-Girl, *by Albert Smith*
> The Natural History of the Gent, *by Albert Smith*
> The Natural History of the "Hawk" Tribe, *by J. W. Carleton*
> London on the Thames . . . , *by Angus B. Reach*

June 22   *M replies to Leonard G. Sanford's inquiry:*
No, I did not go [on] a voyage round the world in 1863. — The Cyclopedias are not infallible, no more than the Pope.
I am glad to know that you like some of the books.
I beg leave to congratulate you upon the honor of having been a whale-hunter in your time . . .

Late June?   *M writes to Helen Griggs.* (Herman wrote directions about his packing, and I shall send his things [from Gansevoort] off first . . . — *Helen Griggs to Catherine Lansing, late June;* Herman wrote me, when I asked how *his* furniture should be forwarded, "that the packers could proportion what each person's charge of material & time should be and the account should be sent to each." *Which I have done. — Helen Griggs to Catherine Lansing, July 15*)

RAMSGATE, ENGLAND   July 21   *W. Clark Russell replies to M's letter:* Your delightful books carry the imagination into a maritime period so remote that often as you have been in my mind I could never satisfy myself that you were still amongst the living. I am glad indeed to learn from Mr Toft that you are still hale and hearty and I do most heartily wish you many years yet of health and vigour . . .

. . . Your reputation here is very great. It is hard to meet a man whose opinion as a reader is worth having who does not speak of your works in such terms as he might hesitate to employ with all his patriotism, towards many renowned English writers . . .

I beg that you will accept my thanks for the kindly spirit in which you have read my books.

SYRACUSE   August 1   [M's 67th birthday]   *Anne Barton writes to M:* As my father, Joseph Barton, is at present out of town, he wished me to write to you and see if you were the same Herman Melville with whom, many years ago, he took a voyage around Cape Horn in the Frigate United States.

MENDHAM   August 7   *Eleanor Melville Thomas, age 4, dictates to her mother a letter to M:* My dear Grandpa,

Frances and I have got a new doll, my dolly's name is Dinah and Frances' dolly's name is Susie and you haven't seen them. When I was just getting into bed, I saw a 'ittle fly in the water, and I took him out with my hand and put him on the floor. We went out to take a walk with Mamma and we saw the biggest rooster he ever saw in his life. And we saw the pigs and they were going to sleep, and we gave them some grass to eat. And we saw a picture of a circus, and a horse was sitting up at a table with a bib on eating his dinner and two waitress. And there was a horse going on a bicycle. And we are having a very, very nice time up here, and we got very nice picture books up here. There is a 'ittle girl called Eloise, and she's got two hammocks at her house. Frances and me got sick eating green apples, but we are all well now. Mamma lets me have corn for dinner if I eat my meat. We had 'ittle tiny kitties and they runned away. I send a kiss to Grandpa. Goodbye

                                              from Eleanor M. Thomas.
This is accompanied by a letter from Frances M. Thomas to M: My dear Papa,

I hope you will find this letter entertaining I wrote just what Eleanor told me. They are having a good time here . . . Harry left yesterday on his bicycle, he expected to meet a friend in New York and take a little trip through Berkshire Co. with him . . .

ALBANY August 19 *Abraham Lansing writes to M, enclosing a check for $3019.50, in payment of the legacy left him by the will of his sister, Frances Priscilla.*

September 28 *Abraham Lansing writes to M, sending him checks for Elizabeth & Bessie Melville's legacies bequeathed to them by Frances Priscilla Melville.*

NEW YORK October 12 *M returns to Abraham Lansing the signed receipts for the two legacies, with instructions for the payment of Stanwix's legacy to M.*

ALBANY October 15 *Abraham Lansing writes to M:*
I send herewith my check as adm^r &c for $96.49/100 in payment of the legacy to Stanwix less the legacy tax, & with interest.

In the absence of testamentary disposition & of claims of creditors you are entitled to the legacy as next of kin. I therefore make the payment to you assuming these facts without the form of administration.

LAWRENCE October 21
DIED.
HOADLEY — At "The Warren," Boston, Mass., Thursday afternoon, Oct. 21, 1886, John C. Hoadley.

Interment at the Albany Rural cemetery Monday afternoon on the arrival of 2:50 train from Boston. Carriages will be waiting at the depot.

NEW YORK November *Elizabeth gives M:* Tea Leaves: Being a Collection of Letters and Documents Relating to the Shipment of Tea to the American Colonies in the Year 1773 . . . [*edited*] *by Francis S. Drake* (*Boston, 1884*).

Elizabeth Melville acquires Na Motu: or, Reef-Rovings in the South Seas, *by Edward T. Perkins* (*New York, 1854*).

December 11 *The Critic reprints an article from the* St. Louis Globe Democrat, *"Writers Who Lack College Training":*
Herman Melville, once renowned as an author, though seldom mentioned of late, published more than forty years ago, 'Typee' and 'Omoo' . . . He wrote other clever books, but none of them won so much reputation as his two first. He had no academic training . . . His writings show a thorough understanding of the force and delicacy of the English language, which he seems to have learned instinctively. He has published nothing for twenty years, having been much of that time buried in a department of the New York Custom House.

December 25 *Christmas presents from M:*
to Elizabeth — Childhood a Hundred Years Ago, *by Sarah Tytler* [*Henrietta Keddie*], *with six chromos after paintings by Sir Joshua Reynolds* (*London, 1877*)

to Bessie — Gems of Home Scenery: Views in Scotland . . . (*London, 1875*)

.   .   .   .   .   .

OAKLAND 1886?
"Taipi," the chart spelled it, and spelled it correctly, but I prefer "Typee" . . . When I was a little boy I read a book spelled in that manner — Herman Melville's *Typee;* and many long hours I dreamed over its pages. Nor was it all dreaming. I resolved there and then, mightily, come what would, that when I had gained strength and years I, too, would voyage to Typee. For the wonder of the world was penetrating to my tiny consciousness — the wonder that was to lead me to many lands, and that still leads and never palls. The years passed, but Typee was not forgotten. (Jack London, "Typee," *Pacific Monthly,* Mar 1910)

LONDON Before 1887 I once read to Philip Bourke Marston the chapter [in *Mardi*] Lombardo & his Costanza to his great delight and altho Marston was perhaps not more than one of our best minor poets he was a true critic. He was so interested that he obtained for reading all your books accessible to him & some time after an American writer of some magazine popularity, Mrs [Louise] Chandler Moulton, and a great friend of Marstons, coming over to London he made enquiries of her concerning you but she only possessed the vaguest impressions of either yourself or y^r books; a lack of patriotism & information which when Marston told me of it certainly did not prepossess me in M^{rs}. Moultons favour from a literary point of view. — *J. W. Barrs to M, Jan 13, 1890*

*

1887
*

NEW YORK March 4 *Harper's sends its 27th & last account to M, with a check for the balance: $50.02.*

March 27 *Catherine Lansing's diary:*
After lunch . . . I [went] to call on Cousin Lizzie & Bessie . . .

May 22 [Bessie's thirty-fourth birthday] *M gives his daughter, Bessie, another volume of* Gems of Home Scenery: Views in the English Lake District . . . (*London, 1875*).

STOCKBRIDGE June? *A social item sent to a Boston newspaper:*
  At Edwards Hall . . . are staying for the summer the daughters of Herman Melville, the friend of Hawthorne and the author himself of some very ex-

citing sea stories extensively read about a quarter of a century ago. Mr. Melville, now a man of sixty odd, is staying at Fire Island.

FIRE ISLAND July 16 *Harriet L. Parker writes to Catherine Lansing:*
. . . your cousin, Mrs. Herman Melville has been here three or four weeks — but leaves next Monday. She has been expecting her husband — but fears, he will not come now. She looks sad & lonely & not in good health.

GLENS FALLS Summer *A boy, Ferris Greenslet, sees M in a barber shop & listens to his tall talk.*

NEW YORK October *An engraving of "A Sunny Day," from a painting by Cuyp at Dulwich is given to M:* From L[izzie?] Oct. 1887

December 4 *M completes his poem, "Bridegroom Dick":*
    Sunning ourselves in October on a day
    Balmy as spring, though the year was in decay,
    I lading my pipe, she stirring her tea,
    My old woman she says to me,
    'Feel ye, old man, how the season mellows?'
    And why should I not, blessed heart alive,
    Here mellowing myself, past sixty-five,
    To think o' the May-time o' pennoned young fellows
    This stripped old hulk here for years may survive . . .

.   .   .   .   .

[M] Took Frances to Madison Square Garden — came home having forgot her — Went back found her. Frances aetat 4 (*Weaver notes on information from Mrs Thomas*)

PHILADELPHIA *Lippincott publishes* Half Hours with the Best American Authors, *edited by Charles Morris, including in Vol IV:* "The Death of the Whale," *by H. Melville, & a paragraph biography of M.*

*

1 8 8 8

*

January 20 *Edmund Clarence Stedman writes to M, asking for "one of your best known shorter poems, in your own handwriting" & an engraved portrait — for an extra-illustrated copy of his* Poets of America. The present writer lived for some time within a short distance of [M's] house, but found no opportunity to meet him until it became necessary to obtain his portrait for an anthology in course of publication. The interview was brief, and the interviewer could not help feeling, although treated with pleasant courtesy, that more important matters were in hand than the perpetuation of a romancer's countenance to future generations . . . (Arthur Stedman, Introduction to *Typee*, 1892)

January 24   *E. C. Stedman, as an editor of* A Library of American Literature, *writes to M:*
We ask your kind permission to use, for the purpose of this work, some extracts from your prose romances, and selections from your poems.
   The Messrs. Harper have given their consent.

January 27   *M replies to Stedman's official request, permitting the publication of whatever extracts the editors desire:*
[P.S.] HM was born in New York City Aug 1, 1819

January 29   *M replies to Stedman's personal request of January 20, with "a short Piece" [from* Clarel *III:iv]:*

Ditty of Aristippus

Noble gods at the board
Where lord unto lord
Light pushes the care-killing wine:
Urbane in their pleasure,
Superb in their leisure —
   Lax ease —
Lax ease after labor divine!

February 1   *E. C. Stedman sends M books by Richard Henry Horne & George Walter Thornbury, along with a manuscript, & a letter:*
Here are three vols. of our old Orion's works — some of the Contents, including "The Death of Marlowe," possibly will be new to you. I had the "Tragedies" bound up together.
   In one I insert the "Petition" of which I spoke, & also his portrait.
   Do glance at Walter Thornbury's Ballads [London, 1851]. The book is one which I doubt if you have seen, as I never have been able to procure another copy. The Cavalier Songs, (Browningesque, with a difference), are my perennial delight.

Moreover, as you said so much of Whitman, I will run the risk of showing you my chapter on him — not that it is of any great importance.

February? *M embarks on his last sea voyage — to Bermuda.*

BERMUDA March 15 *M sends Elizabeth a wooden book-rack.*

March 26? [?] *M leaves Bermuda on the S.S.* Trinidad, *1390 tons:* H Melville [age!] 37 [Male] Merchant [U.S.] 3 [pieces of baggage]

THE ATLANTIC Before March 29 [On the way from] Florida St. Augustine Rough passage home during blizzard Got around on hands & knees.

NEW YORK March 29 *M acknowledges gifts from James Billson:*
Some time ago I received a paper from you containing matter interesting to me: and now thro' the post I get a volume [Marcus Clark's *For the Term of His Natural Life*] which I must needs think comes from the same kind quarter.

I promise myself much pleasure in its perusal, since it opens in a manner to arrest one's attention.

Late March? *M writes to W. Clark Russell, asking his permission to dedicate his next volume of poems to him.*

April 7 *M replies to a note from James Billson:*
Time, just now, hardly admits of my responding to your inquiries as fully as I should like. But let me say that you have all my published books except the "Piazza Tales" now out of print. As for the "Two Captains" and "Man of the World" they are books of the air — I know of none such. The names appear, tho', on the title-page of a book of mine — "Israel Potter" which was republished by a Philadelphia house some time ago [1865] under the unwarrantable altered title of "The Refugee." A letter to the publisher arrested the publication [?].

I thank you for the very friendly tone of your note, and appreciate it; and I hope that some egg in the "Birds Nest Farm" may hatch the Bird of Paradise for you — happiness.

RAMSGATE April 10 [Catherine Lansing's 49th birthday] *W. Clark Russell replies to M's letter:*
I can fully sympathise with your dislike to letter writing more particularly when as I fear your general health is not as I should wish to know it to be. It gratifies me immensely to think that my humble testimony to your genius was expressed long before I had the honour of hearing from you; at a time indeed when I really did not know whether you were living or dead. Quite recently I have been reading your "Redburn" for the third or fourth time and have closed it more deeply impressed even

than heretofore with the descriptive power that vitalises every page, especially with your marvellous creation of the man Jackson whose character I know to be absolutely true to forecastle life. Much indeed should I have enjoyed a visit to the Bermudas in your company . . .

I shall await your volume with real anxiety and expectation. The honour you propose to do me must always prove a memorable one in my professional career.

NEW YORK April 19 The Voyage of the Fleetwing, *by C. M. Newell, is reviewed in* The Nation:
Here is abundant material — the adventures of an old-fashioned whaling cruise; but the author has told his story in a manner which does it great injustice. Similar scenes are described with wonderful power and felicity in Herman Melville's 'Moby Dick,' the classic story of whaling adventure; and it is with work like this that Captain Newell's present story (as well as an earlier one covering similar ground, and called 'Pehe Nui') must challenge comparison.

May [1] The American Magazine *publishes an article by Lieut. H. D. Smith, "The Mutiny on the 'Somers.'"*

BROOKLINE May 8 *Samuel Shaw's diary:*
George Griggs died at about 8 A.M.

May 11 [?] *M attends the funeral of his brother-in-law, George Griggs.*

NEW YORK May? *M composes the "Inscription Epistolary to W. C[lark] R[ussell]," for* John Marr:
Well . . . with what conscientious satisfaction did I but just now, in the heading of this inscription, salute you, W. C. R., by running up your colors at my fore. Would that the craft thus embravened were one of some tonnage, so that the flag might be carried on a loftier spar, commanding an ampler horizon of your recognising friends.

June 11 *M writes his will:*
I, Herman Melville, declare this to be my will. Any property, of whatever kind, I may die possessed of, including money in banks, and my share in the as yet undivided real estate at Gansevoort, I bequeathe to my wife. I do this because I have confidence that through her our children and grand-children will get their proportion of any benefit that may accrue. — I appoint my wife executrix of this will. — In witness whereof I have hereunto set my hand and seal this 11th day of June 1888.
[Witnessed by H. Minturn Smith,
S. N. Robinson, & Henry B. Thomas.]

SAN FRANCISCO Before June 26 *Charles Warren Stoddard gives Robert Louis Stevenson a copy of* Omoo, *which Stevenson later reads on the yacht* Casco.

It was in such talks . . . that I first heard the names — first fell under the spell — of the islands; and it was from one of the first of them that I returned (a happy man) with *Omoo* under one arm, and my friend's own adventures under the other. (Stevenson, *The Wrecker*)

FIRE ISLAND   Before July 10   *M comes to Fire Island.* ([Mrs Melville] says her husband & children have been down to see her since she has been here. — *Harriet Parker to Abraham Lansing, July 12*)

Fire Island Beach.

July 12   *Harriet L. Parker writes to Abraham Lansing:*
Mrs. Melville was here when we arrived & had many inquiries to make about Kate & you. I am happy to say, that her health is greatly improved since last summer. . . . She left on Tuesday morning.

TAIOHAE BAY August 13   *Mrs Margaret Stevenson writes to Jane Whyte Balfour:*
. . . try to get Typee and Omua, two books about the Pacific, for they are very amusing and interesting, and very true, in the main, of life in these islands.

GANSEVOORT   September 1
Executor's Sale by Auction of a Fine Country Seat! at Gansevoort, Saratoga Co., N.Y. J. H. Simmons & Son, auctioneers, will sell on Saturday, Sept. 1, 1888; at 11:30 A.M. . . . Sale by order of Abraham Lansing, Executor for the Estate of Priscilla F. Melville, deceased.

Catherine Lansing's diary:
. . . went to *Gansevoort* . . . attended the sale of the *Old Homestead Auctioned* by Mr Simmons for $4000 —

THE PACIFIC September 6   *Robert Louis Stevenson writes to Charles Baxter:*

I shall have a fine book of travels. I feel sure; and will tell you more of the South Seas after very few months than any other writer has done — except Herman Melville perhaps, who is a howling cheese.

WASHINGTON September 7 *The title of:*

John Marr

and

Other Sailors

with

Some Sea - Pieces

is deposited at the Library of Congress by Theodore L. De Vinne & Co.

DEAL, ENGLAND September 18 *W. Clark Russell writes to M:*
I have received "John Marr" and have read the little volume with the liveliest interest and pleasure. How to thank you for the sentiments to which you give exquisite expression in your dedication I do not know. The closing sentences I read with emotion. Suffer me to regret that your name is not upon the title page. I must confess that I should like the world to know that my books were thought worthy of commendation by the author of "Omoo," "Typee" and "Moby Dick." My father Mr Henry Russell happened to be with me when your little volume arrived. You will probably remember him as the composer of numerous popular songs such as "To the West," "A Life on the Ocean Wave," "Woodman Spare that Tree" and scores more. I read aloud to him the little poem "The Figure Head," the gem of the collection as I think, a brilliant, delicious fancy and of a class of thought peculiar to yourself. He exclaimed "If I were ten years younger I should put those words to music." But at the age of seventy five a man has little melody left in him. "Tom Deadlight" is profoundly good. The line: —
"The black scud a'flying; but, by God's blessing, dam' me"
is profoundly maritime. I was infinitely amused last night on being asked by the author of several boys' books, a Mr Charles St Johnstone whether I had ever read the noblest sea book ever written called "Moby Dick." I smiled and handed him "John Marr." "Is Herman Melville alive?" he shouted. He took down your address and I expect you will hear from him.

[*809*]

CHICAGO September 27 *In* America, A Journal of To-day, *Julian Haw-thorne devotes his literary column to an essay, "Man-Books":*
Herman Melville, in his "Typee" and "Omoo," and in his "Moby Dick" and "White-Jacket," wrote books that were certainly not meant for women; but they were not exactly man-books, either, if we except "Moby Dick"; they were books of adventure — boys' books; and, therefore, admirable though they were, and unequaled since, they did not quite fill the bill. "Moby Dick" was published, I think, in 1854.

NEW YORK October 20 *M returns the books lent by E. C. Stedman, on February 1, with a letter:*
I have been interested in all of them. And your own book in many of its views has proved either corroborative or suggestive to me. I have not by any means so many external demands upon my evenings as you probably have. I am the one most likely to be at home in the evening. Pray remember this, and give me the pleasure of dropping in again here when you feel like it.

October? *M acquires* The Life of Nelson, *by Robert Southey (New York, 1855), in which M makes these notes on the back fly-leaves:*

    110 Mutiny &c

        94 & 60 hate a Frenchman 193
        80 Ca Ira Sans-Culottes

        104 Jervis' victory *Feb.* 1797
            Nelson Rear Admiral

        107 Westminster Abbey or victory.

    The Agememnon in fight — 81

    Dukedom & domain of Bronte 188

    Marines cut down 231

    making a gunner 264
   [*Opposite page:*]
    "Our Nel" — 260
    Sir W. H. Perpetual fluctuation 257

On pp 256-257 M has scored & underscored this passage:
Sir William Hamilton . . . thus, in a letter, described his own philosophy: — "My study of antiquities," he says, "has kept me in constant thought of the perpetual fluctuation of every thing. The whole art is really to live all the days of our life; and not with anxious care disturb the sweetest hour that life affords, — which is the present. Admire the Creator, and all his works to us incomprehensible; and do all the good you can upon earth: and take the chance of eternity without dismay."

November 5 *M gives a copy of* John Marr *"To Lizzie."*

Mid-November? *M gives a copy of* John Marr *to Richard Henry Stoddard.*

November 16   *A date on the manuscript of* Billy Budd:
                Friday Nov. 16. 1888. Began.

November ?   John Marr *is reviewed [by Richard Henry Stoddard] in
an unidentified newspaper* [The World?]:
Familiar from boyhood with such eminent writers of sea stories as Smollett
and Marryatt, he adventured into strange seas in "Omoo" and "Typee," which
were speedily followed by "Mardi," a not very skillful allegory, and "Moby
Dick," which is probably his greatest work. He was the peer of Hawthorne
in popular estimation, and was by many considered his superior. His later
writings were not up to the same high level. With all his defects, however,
Mr. Melville is a man of unquestionable talent, and of considerable genius. He
is a poet also, but his verse is marked by the same untrained imagination which
distinguishes his prose. He is the author of the second best cavalry poem in
the English language ["Sheridan at Cedar Creek"], the first being Browning's
"How They Brought the Good News from Ghent to Aix." . . . Nothing
finer than his unrhymed poems exist outside of the sea lyrics of Campbell.
The present text of these observations is to be found in the little volume, "John
Marr, and Other Sailors," . . . which contains about twenty poems of varying
degrees of merit . . .

LEICESTER December 4   *James Billson sends to M:* Shelley, a poem:
with other writings relating to Shelley, by the late James Thomson
('B.V.'): added an essay on the poems of William Blake, by the same
author (*London, 1884*).

NEW YORK   December 13   *M writes to his niece Minnie, Mrs William
H. Mackintosh, at Roxbury.*

ROXBURY December 14   *Samuel Shaw's diary:*
Mrs Helen Melville Griggs widow of George Griggs died at the Williams
Mansion kept as a boarding house by Mrs Maloy at 5.30 P.M.

Since writing to you last I have been to Boston on a sad errand — the
funeral of my much-loved sister Helen — who died on the 14th Dec. after
many long years of suffering from something like internal cancer in the
stomach & liver — It is a blessed release for her, but it is a great grief to
us all to part with so faithful a friend. — *Elizabeth Melville to Ellen
Marett Gifford, Jan 4, 1889*

ALBANY December 17   *Helen Melville Griggs is buried in the family
lot.*

NEW YORK   December 31   *M writes to James Billson:*
I have your letter, and thank you for it, and not less for the book
accompanying it. You could hardly have sent me anything more welcome.
All the contents are highly interesting; but I agree with you in thinking
the Essay on Blake the most so. I learned much from it. — But "The City

of Dreadful Night," one can hardly overestimate it, massive and mighty as it is, — its gloom is its sublimity. The confronting Sphinx and Angel, where shall we go to match them? — Thomson's criticisms in general are very refreshing in their total ignoring of the conventional in criticism. — But I must rein up. My eyes have been annoying me for some days past; and I know of hardly anything more disconcerting. But let me think of those lines [by Thomson] on Patti, and forget that.

You did well in giving your superfluous volume of "John Marr" to Mr Barrs, to whom I am indebted for "A Voice from the Nile" &c — an appreciated gift.

[P.S.] I inclose a slip that will interest you & other appreciators of Thomson, something my wife came across in her newspaper reading.

H.M.

•　　•　　•　　•　　•

NEW YORK   *In working on* Billy Budd, *M refers to* White-Jacket, *marking, in the back cover of a copy of the Bentley edition:*

192
214 Flogging

M scores a passage in Chapter XXXIII, beginning:

At a sign from the Captain, John, with a shameless leer, advanced, and stood passively upon the grating . . .

A paragraph in an unidentified newspaper:

How many men to whom "Omoo" and "Typee" were delights in their younger days realize that Herman Melville is still in the land of the living, though he writes no more? He dwells in New York, near the University club, and is a handsome and vigorous, if elderly man.

Publication of American Literature, *by Charles F. Richardson; in the chapter, "The Lesser Novelists":*

Reflective or imaginative sentimentalism was presently to yield, in part, to the wide-spread wish for some new thing . . . Another response [to this wish] was made by Herman Melville in his brisk and stirring tales of the sea or sketches of travel, in which fact or fancy were mingled by the nervously impatient author, in the proportion desired by his immediate public . . . the personal narrative or fiction of "Typee," "Omoo," and "Moby Dick" . . . represented the restless facility which has always been an American trait, and which occasionally develops into some enduring literary success.

. . . That [Mayo's] "Kaloolah" has barely outlived Melville's sprightly but now forgotten improvisations in literature is due to the combination . . . of the improbably romantic and the obviously satirical. Melville made some essays in the same direction, but failed completely for lack of a firm thought and a steady hand.

*
1 8 8 9
*

NEW YORK   January 4   *Elizabeth Melville writes to Ellen Marett Gifford of the death of Helen Melville Griggs:*
You must remember her as a girl when she used to spend winters with me, on my first coming into society, now nearly half a century ago! — and she retained the same bright sunny disposition to the last — I shall miss her affectionate letters & her ever-ready sympathy in me and mine, most sorely. So "friend after friend departs" — and now I have but few of those of my youth left —

CHICAGO   January   America *publishes an article by W. Clark Russell,* "The Honor of the Flag":
In Herman Melville's works, too, you meet with an exquisite fidelity of sea portraiture when that writer approaches the marine character. The poetry and passion and sentiment inwoven in the fabric of Melville's narratives are wanting in Dana. I know not if the works of the author of "Omoo," and "Typee," and "Redburn" are much read and esteemed in the United States, but I am sure there is no name in American letters that deserves to stand higher for beauty of imagination, for accuracy of reproduction, for originality of conception, and for a quality of imagination that in "Moby Dick," for instance, lifts some of his utterances to such a height of bold and swelling fancy as one must search the pages of the Elizabethan dramatists to parallel.

DEAL   February 10   *W. Clark Russell writes to M:*
I have done myself the honour to dedicate to you a novel I have recently completed entitled "An Ocean Tragedy." It will be published in the newspapers and then take volume form.
Did you happen to come across an article of mine . . . in a Chicago weekly called "America?" I should have liked to hear your opinion on that contribution. At all events the writing of it gratified me with an opportunity of publicly stating how amongst your warmest admirers is, my dear Mʳ Melville, Yours always sincerely . . .

NEW YORK   March 2   *A note on the manuscript of* Billy Budd:
Revise — began March 2 1889

ALBANY   March 14   *Abraham Lansing writes to M:*
I send herewith my cheque as admʳ &c of Fannys will, for $1216 89/100 being for the share belonging to you on the distribution of her estate as per decree of Surrogate

March 15   *Abraham Lansing sends M a telegram & a letter, advising him that a mistake in calculating the estate reduces M's share to $1123.79.*

NEW YORK   March 16   *M acknowledges Abraham Lansing's three messages & sends him a signed receipt:*
   Received New York, March 16, 1889 from Abraham Lansing as administrator with the will annexed of the will of Priscilla F. Melville deceased Eleven hundred & twenty three & 79/100 dollars — being my portion under said will of the remainder of the estate of said Priscilla F. Melville . . .

March 18   *Harper & Brothers writes to M:*
   We have in course of preparation a new *Fifth Reader* containing selections from the works of American authors, and should be pleased to include in the volume an extract of a few pages from *Moby-Dick* including the passage describing the capture of the whale.

LONDON   May 15   *In* The Universal Review *Robert Buchanan publishes an essay, "Imperial Cockneydom":*
   In New York, and as far away as Chicago, Cockneydom spreads its propaganda; so effectually, indeed, that young men have given no ear to the 'barbaric yawp' of Whitman, know not even the name of Herman Melville . . .

NEW YORK   May?   *M sends to Harper & Brothers his permission to print extracts from* Moby Dick.

June   The Cosmopolitan *begins a three-part serial by Gail Hamilton [Abigail R. Dodge], entitled "The Murder of Philip Spencer":*

"I LEARN, MR. SPENCER, THAT YOU ASPIRE TO THE
COMMAND OF THE *Somers.*"

[*814*]

FIRE ISLAND June 15 *M, Elizabeth, Bessie, Fanny & Fanny's children register at the Surf Hotel.* (Herman came down with me on the 15ᵗʰ and staid a few days . . . — *Elizabeth Melville to Catherine Lansing, June 30*)

NEW YORK June 19 *Harper & Brothers acknowledges M's permission, "received several weeks ago."*

FIRE ISLAND June 30 *Elizabeth Melville writes to Catherine Lansing:* . . . since that [after June 15], Bessie, Fanny & children have spent a week here, all enjoying it very much — I expect to be here all this week, & part of next . . .

NEW YORK August 1 [M's 70th birthday] *Elizabeth gives M a birthday present:* The Correspondence of Honoré de Balzac . . . *translated by C. Lamb Kenney (2 vols, London, 1878), in which M subsequently reads.*
In Vol I, in a letter to Madame Surville, of 1822, M scores:
There are torrents that make a terrible rush, and yet their beds are quite dry a few days after; but there are waters which flow sluggishly, but flow for ever.
In a letter to Madame de Girardin, of 1834, M scores:
Do not accuse me of littleness; for I think I am too great to be offended by anyone in the world. But there are certain sentiments which I give or withhold; I cannot be false, I cannot play a part. Your *salon* was almost the only one where I found myself on a footing of friendship. You will hardly perceive my absence; and I remain alone.
In a letter to Madame Carraud, of 1834, M scores & underscores:
In literature, in painting, in music, in sculpture, ten years' labour is needed before a man can understand the synthesis of an art as well as its material analysis . . . It would be better for him to struggle for two years with light and shade in a corner, like Rembrandt, who never left his own house, than to run about America, and to come back cruelly disenchanted, as he surely would be, in his political ideas.

In Vol II, in a letter to Madame Hanska, Oct 1836, M scores:
I can understand how the absolute asceticism of Pascal, and his immense labours, brought him to the pass that he saw constantly an abyss on both sides of him, and was obliged to have two chairs on each side of the one in which he sat.
In the letters to Louise, of 1836-1837, M scores:
What good there may lie latent in me is stifled under the outside circumstances of the man who is always at his labour. My necessities are not me, any more than is the harsh exterior to which necessity constrains me; everything in me is a contrast, because all that is around me is contrariety.
In a letter to Madame Hanska, Jan 20, 1838, M scores:
Putting aside the question of feeling, let me tell you the secret of this apparent contradiction. Whilst my strength and faculties are night and day at their full stretch to invent, to write, to execute, to recollect, to describe — whilst with slow and painful, often wounded wings, I am traversing the moral fields

of literary creation, how can I at the same time be occupied with material things? When Napoleon was at Essling, he was not in Spain. In order never to be deceived in life, in love, in friendship, in business, in relations of all kinds, dear Countess, recluse and solitary, it would be necessary to attend to nothing else, to be purely and simply a man of the world, a man of business, a financier. For the matter of that, I can see quite well when I am being deceived, and when I am about to be over-reached, that such or such a man does or will betray me, or will disappear after shearing off some of my wool; but even at the very moment when I foresee or know all this, I am obliged to go and fight elsewhere; I see it while I am being carried away by the necessity of the moment, by pressing work, by some labour which would be lost if not finished. I often finish a cottage by the light of my house, which is burning down. I have neither friends nor servants, everyone flies from me — I know not why, or rather I know but too well, because no one either loves or serves a man who works night and day, and who does not lay himself out for the advantage or amusement of others; who stays at home, and who must be visited if he is to be seen; whose genius, if genius he has, will not bear fruit under twenty years; it is because this man has identified his personality with his own works, and because all personality is odious, when it is not accompanied by power to give or bestow.

In a letter to Madame Hanska, Mar 26, 1838, M scores:
. . . I reply, that every man has only a certain amount of strength, of blood, of courage, of hope, and my store of all these is exhausted.

In a letter to Madame Hanska, Feb 5, 1844, M scores:
My revenge is, to write 'Les Petits Bourgeois' in the 'Débats'. It is thus that I make my enemies say with rage, 'At the moment when people thought he had written himself out, he publishes a master-piece!'

In a letter to Madame Hanska, Mar 1, 1844, M scores:
. . . before I fall into that long sleep where one rests from all things at last, *and especially from oneself* . . .

August 8   *Publication, in* The Evening Post, *of a review of* Letters and Literary Remains of Edward Fitzgerald; *M clips this & inserts it in one of his copies of the* Rubaiyat.

NEW HAVEN   September 7   *Mrs Ellen Marett Gifford dies.*

BOSTON   September 8?   *A column, "Here in Boston," is published in the* Boston Post[?]:
I recall with a certain impression of unreality the recent report that Herman Melville, "who more than forty years ago charmed all lovers of the wild and picturesque in writing," is still living in New York . . .
If I am not mistaken, Melville in his later years has been free from the drudgery of the custom house, but with him, as with many other literary men, pecuniary independence came too late to enable him to revive his powers of invention and description . . .
"Moby Dick," which followed "Omoo" and "Typee," did not come up to the high standard established by these delightful books . . . It seems to me that in the revival of the taste for our earlier literature which has been shown

in the republication of the works of almost forgotten authors, some of our enterprising publishers would find it for their interest to reprint "Omoo," and "Typee," and I do not see why the author's life should not find a place in the American Men of Letters series. I am glad at all events to hear that Herman Melville is still alive, and although he may not be able to charm the readers of today as he did those of a past generation, it would please me much to have him try the experiment.

NEW HAVEN September 23   *The will of Ellen Marett Gifford is admitted to probate.*

NEW YORK September 25   *Harper & Bros. sends a note to M, together with "a copy of our new Fifth Reader, published today . . ."*

NEW HAVEN Before October 8   *Simeon Baldwin sends Elizabeth Melville a "box of old letters and papers," containing all of M's letters to Ellen Marett Gifford [except that of Oct 5, 1885].*

NEW YORK November 20   *M acquires a new membership in the New York Society Library (by transfer from the Executors of Ellen Marett Gifford's estate), free from all annual payments.*

HALIFAX, NOVA SCOTIA November 21   *Professor Archibald MacMechan writes to M:*
   Although a stranger, I take the liberty of addressing you on the ground of my ardent admiration for your works. For a number of years I have read and re-read "Moby-Dick" with increasing pleasure on every perusal: and with this study, the conviction has grown up that the unique merits of that book have never received due recognition . . . I am anxious to set the merits of your books before the public and to that end, I beg the honour of correspondence with you. It would be of great assistance to me, if I could gather some particulars of your life and *literary methods* from you, other than given in such books as Duyckinck's dictionary. In the matter of style, apart from the matter altogether, I consider your books, especially the earlier ones, the most thoroughly New World product in all American literature.
   Hoping that I am not asking too much, I remain . . .

[?] November 26   *Ben W. Austin writes to M, asking for autographs of Lemuel Shaw & members of the Gansevoort family.*

EDINBURGH November   *The Scottish Art Review publishes an article by H. S. Salt, "Herman Melville." Following a biographical sketch, based on* Redburn, *& appreciation of* Typee, Omoo, *&* White-Jacket:
   Melville's later works must be considered as phantasies rather than a relation of sober facts. He was affected, like so many of his countrymen, by the transcendental tendency of the age, and the result in his case was a strange blending of the practical and the metaphysical, his stories of what purported

to be plain matter-of-fact life being gradually absorbed and swallowed up in the wildest mystical speculations. This process was already discernible in *Mardi* . . . the first volume of which is worthy to rank with the very finest achievements of its author, while the rest had far better have remained altogether unwritten . . .

Moby Dick; or, The White Whale (1851) is perhaps more successful as a whole than *Mardi*, since its very extravagances, great as they are, work in more harmoniously with the outline of the plot . . .

It may seem strange that so vigorous a genius, from which stronger and stronger work might reasonably have been expected, should have reached its limit at so early a date . . . Whether the transcendental obscurities in which he latterly ran riot were the cause or the consequence of the failure of his artistic powers is a point which it would be difficult to determine with precision . . .

. . . it is a cause for regret that [M] should have fallen to a great extent out of notice, and should be familiar only to a small circle of admirers, instead of enjoying the wide reputation to which his undoubted genius entitles him.

Some weeks ago I promised my friend M^r H S Salt that I w^d forward to you the Scottish Art Review . . .

What you may think of Salts contribution to the S A R of course I can only guess; but I confess I was somewhat disappointed with it & wish instead of slightly passing in review half a dozen volumes he had more or less exhaustively reviewed one say Mardi or Moby Dick, but after all he may be the best judge of the kind of notice likely to reawaken interest in yr writings. Then again I have a very deeprooted fondness for Babbalanja & consequently resented the way Salt dealt with the 2nd & 3rd volumes of Mardi; & much as I admire the first volume I'd rather have Babbalanja and Yoomy slight though the sketch of the latter may be thought to be

. . . "Pierre" I have always liked & don't think Salt does it anything like justice & Israel Potter ought not to have been passed over, although Salt may not have read it. — *J. W. Barrs to M, Jan 13, 1890*

NEW YORK December 5 *M replies to Professor MacMechan:*
I beg you to overlook my delay in acknowledging yours of the 12th [?] ult. It was unavoidable.

Your note gave me pleasure, as how should it not, written in such a spirit.

But you do not know, perhaps, that I have entered my eighth decade. After twenty years nearly, as an outdoor Customs House officer, I have latterly come into possession of unobstructed leisure, but only just as, in the course of nature, my vigor sensibly declines. What little of it is left I husband for certain matters as yet incomplete, and which indeed may never be completed.

I appreciate, quite as much as you would have me, your friendly good will and shrink from any appearance to the contrary.

Trusting that you will take all this, and what it implies, in the same spirit that prompts it . . .

M replies to Ben W. Austin, sending him an autograph of Lemuel Shaw & referring him to Mrs Abraham Lansing for the others.

HALIFAX December 23   *Professor MacMechan writes again to M:*
I was very much gratified to receive your cordial letter of the 5th. I was aware of your advanced age and should have been more thoughtful perhaps in making my vague proposals to you which at the same time would draw heavily upon your time . . . It *is* too much to ask you to correspond but I hope to do myself the pleasure of calling on you in New York in the spring months, and making your acquaintance. I have enjoyed your books so much and, having had at least one adventure like "Redburn," I feel certain we should be at once on common ground.

LONDON December?   *H. S. Salt writes to M, proposing a new edition of* Typee *in the Camelot Series.*
I was brought into touch with Herman Melville through my biography of the pessimist poet James Thomson. He was a great admirer of Melville; and Melville in his turn highly valued *The City of Dreadful Night.* Knowing this, I had [?] sent him a copy of my book, and in consequence received from him two or three letters . . . (Henry S. Salt, *Company I Have Kept*)

The Pall Mall *publishes an interview with W. Clark Russell.*
Singularly enough almost directly afterwards [following the publication of Salt's article in the *Scottish Art Review*], in reporting an interview with the author of the Wreck of the Grosvenor, the Pall Mall also contained more than the customary passing reference to yr books & quoted some lines from the John Marr. So you see notwithstanding the inadequacy of the recognition of your books, on this side, they are not without warm admirers. — *J. W. Barrs to M, Jan 13, 1890*

.   .   .   .   .   .

NEW YORK   *A new edition of* A Library of American Literature from the Earliest Settlement to the Present Time, *compiled & edited by Edmund Clarence Stedman & Ellen Mackay Hutchinson (11 vols), includes (in Vol. VII):* "The Bell-Tower," *& a group of poems from* Battle-Pieces *("The Stone Fleet," "Sheridan at Cedar Creek," & "In the Prison Pen"); Arthur Stedman's biographical sketch in the final volume concludes:*
Mr. Melville voyages around the world in 1860, and on his return held for some time a position in the custom-house of New York, in which city he afterward led a retired life.

*

1 8 9 0

*

DEAL January 5 *W. Clark Russell writes to M:*

I have asked my English publishers to send you a copy of "An Ocean Tragedy." . . . You are, I sincerely hope, well, and I trust that the New Year which has dawned may prove a happy and a healthy one for you and yours. I have lately had some correspondence with Peter Toft, and believe that he returns to America this month. I wish the beastly rheumatism would let me accompany him. I asked Monsignor [Robert] Seton of New Jersey City to call upon you and give you a handshake from me if he happened to be in your city.

January 9 *W. Clark Russell sends M a proof of his dedication with a note:*

The printers have just sent me this at my request. The English edition will not be published, the publishers tell me, till *March*. God bless you. [*Proof:*]
My dear Herman Melville,

In words of beauty and of kindness you lately wished me health and content. Health, alas! you cannot give me; but content you have filled me with. My books have done more than ever I had dared dream, by winning for me, the friendship and approval of the Author of 'Typee,' 'Omoo,' 'Moby-Dick,' 'Redburn,' and other productions which top the list of sea literature in the English tongue. I beg you to accept this dedication as a further public avowal of my hearty admiration of your genius.

NEW YORK January 12 *M replies to H. S. Salt's inquiry:*

Illness has prevented an earlier reply to your note. — The proposition to reprint "Typee" somewhat embarrasses me, since the circumstances are such, that I can not feel myself at liberty to entertain it without first seeking light from Mr. Murray.

. . . Yes, "B.V." interests me much. I shall try and procure here that "Life" which you have written. The "*City of Dreadful Night*" is the modern Book of Job, under an original poem duskily looming with the same aboriginal verities. Much more might be said; but enough . . .

M writes to John Murray:

I have received a note from a gentleman writing for the Editor of the *Camelot Series*, asking me whether I would have any objection to the reprinting of "*Typee*" in that Series. To which note I have written to the effect, that I do not feel myself at liberty to entertain such a proposition without first communicating with you.

I have no exact knowledge as to the bearing at this present time of the Copyright Law on the matter. But even if that set the book free, I should, under the circumstances, still feel myself bound to write you this note, and say that my consent to the proposition in question must be contingent upon yours.

LEICESTER January 13 *J. W. Barrs writes to M:*
Whilst writing of Israel Potter I am reminded of the John Marr you so kindly sent me through Mr Billson & for which I take this chance of thanking you. The prose story reminds me of Israels latter days. Am I right in feeling a similarity? Ned Bunn, among the verse is my favorite, and I have written out the lines for Salt. They recall delightfully the atmosphere of Omoo & Typee. Pierre Loti a quite recent French writer & an officer in the French Navy has published a volume on a twelve months experience of his in one of the South Pacific Isles . . . I hope shortly to get the volume when, if it interests me, I will post it to you . . .

In Brownings death we lose our first poet although the popularity of his verse was almost a cipher compared with that of Tennyson or your Longfellow. The "public" like more sugar than Browning cared to put into his poems & hence, notwithstanding his power, he had — & will have — but a few readers . . .

Do you know Walt Whitman? One cannot write or speak of the Poet of Democracy as "Mister." . . . Do you not think he is your most characteristic poet? I know of no poet with whom one feels such a sense of camaraderie or who voiced the democratic aspirations so nobly & yet with such calm confidence in their realisation & recognition of the dangers to be met & overcome before the democratic ideal is attained . . .
P.S. It wd interest me much to learn which among yr literary progeny is yr favorite child — excluding Omoo & Typee from the selection.

LONDON January ? *Sir John Murray replies to M's inquiry.* (Three or four years ago Mr. Walter Scott wished to bring out shilling editions of "Typee" and "Omoo" and Mr. Murray at that time wrote Mr. Melville that he would not permit them and Mr. Scott dropped the matter. — *Arthur Stedman to the United States Book Company, Oct 24, 1892*)

February 2 *Henry S. Salt sends M a biography:* The Life of James Thomson ("B.V.") . . . by H. S. Salt (*London, 1889*) *in which M subsequently reads; he triple-scores & checks this reference to Thomson's essay, "Bumbleism":*
Thomson saw clearly that true democracy must be rid of other things besides political inequalities; since religious intolerance, backed up by plutocratic influence, is absolutely fatal to the existence of a free community. "Imperialism imposes fines, imprisonment, banishment; Bumble simply imposes death by starvation."

BOSTON February 10   *Lee & Shepard, publishers, write to M, asking for his address & his publications since 1870.*

NEW YORK February 13   *M arranges a volume of verse:*
As They Fell

Part 1ˢᵗ A Rose or Two
From Beads for a Rosary
The Rose Entombed
[The] New Rosecrucians
Hearth Roses
[The] Vial of Attar
The Ambuscade
Under the Snow
Amoroso
Ch[ancel?] Rose ["The Accepted Time"?]
[The] Rose Window
The Devotion of the Flowers to their Lady
Roses of Damascus [alternate title: "The Rose Farmer"]
L'Envoi

Part 2ᵈ Weeds & Wildings (Wild Things)
Murder will out [title altered to: "Time's Betrayal"]
[The] Old Ship[master and His Crazy Barn]
Vine & Goat
Old Rainbow
Profundity & Levity
Inscription for Rip Van Winkle
Lonie [title altered by Elizabeth Melville to: "Shadow
The Cuban Pirate   at the Feast"]
Madcap's Ditty [former title: "Wild-Strawberry Hunters"]
The Avatar
[The] American Aloe [on Exhibition]
Iris [MS dated by Elizabeth Melville: 1874]
A Ground Vine [intercedes with the Queen of Flowers for
                           the merited Recognition of Clover]

M replies to Lee & Shepard's inquiry of Feb 10, claiming to have published nothing but Clarel *since 1870*

ON SS. *Lübeck* February   *Robert Louis Stevenson writes to E. L. Burlingame:*
Our admirable friend Herman Melville, of whom, since I could judge, I have thought more than ever, had no ear for languages whatever: his Hapar tribe should be Hapaa, etc.

NEW YORK February 25   *M writes to H. S. Salt:*
Concerning "Typee" — As I engaged to do, I wrote to Mr Murray. The

information contained in the reply is such, and the manner of conveying it is such, that I consider myself bound, by considerations both of right & courtesy, not to sanction any English issue of the book — (during my lifetime) other than that of the original purchaser and publisher.

NEW HAVEN February 28 *Simeon E. Baldwin writes to all beneficiaries of Ellen Marett Gifford's will that the decree of the Probate Court "was passed today, and we are ready to begin paying the legacies left by Mrs Gifford . . ."*

NEW YORK March 5 *M sends receipt for $8,000 to executors of the estate of Ellen M. Gifford (as well as receipts from Elizabeth, his daughters, & his dead son, Stanwix).*

March 23 *A note on a folder of poems, labelled:*
Greece
Looked over March 23 '90

March 30 *A telegram [from M?] to Catherine Lansing:*
Mrs. Allan Melville died this morning funeral probably Tuesday.

April [1] *In the April number of* Harper's *an article by Henry Clay Lukens, "American Literary Comedians," mentions M.*

April 1 *M withdraws the first volumes on his new share in the New York Society Library:* [Edward] Fitzgeralds Works 1.2. [Boston, 1887]

April 9 *E. C. Stedman writes to Charles Henry Phelps on a meeting of the Authors' Club:*
Here is the guest-roll. It is surprising to me that I never yet have been able to get the members to take an interest in Melville — one of the strongest geniuses, & most impressive *personalities* that New York has ever harbored. *He* ought to be an honorary member. He is a sort of recluse now, but we might perhaps tempt him out.

April 18 *M returns the Fitzgerald volumes & withdraws:* Political Essays; with Sketches of Public Characters, *by William Hazlitt (London, 1819).*

Spring *Eleanor & her grandfather:*
Setting forth on a bright spring afternoon for a trip to Central Park, the Mecca of most of our pilgrimages, he made a brave and striking figure as he walked erect, head thrown back, cane in hand, inconspicuously dressed in a dark blue suit and a soft felt hat. For myself, I skipped gaily beside him, anticipating the long jogging ride in the horse cars . . . the broad walks of the park, where the joy of all existence was best expressed by running down the hills, head back, skirts flying in the wind. He would follow more slowly and call "Look out, or the 'cop' may catch you!" I always thought he used

funny words: "cop" was surely a jollier word than "policeman."

We never came in from a trip of this kind, nor indeed from any walk, but we stopped in the front hall under a coloured engraving of the Bay of Naples, its still blue dotted with tiny white sails. He would point to them with his cane and say, "See the little boats sailing hither and thither." "Hither and thither" — more funny words, thought I, at the same time a little awed by something far away in the tone of voice.

I remember mornings when even sugar on the oatmeal was not enough to tempt me to finish the last mouthful. It would be spring in the back yard too . . . He would say in a warning whisper, "Jack Smoke will come down the chimney and take what you leave!" That was another matter. The oatmeal was laughingly finished and the yard gained. Across the back parlour and main hall upstairs ran a narrow iron-trimmed porch, furnished with Windsor and folding canvas chairs. There he would sit with a pipe and his most constant companion — his cane, and watch my busy activity below. Against the wall of the porch hung a match holder, more for ornament than utility, it seems. It was a gay red and blue china butterfly. Invariably he looked to see if it had flown away since we were there last.

Once in a long while his interest in his grandchildren led him to cross the river and take the suburban train to East Orange, where we lived . . .

His own room [at 26th Street] was a place of mystery and awe to me; there I never ventured unless invited by him. It looked bleakly north. The great mahogany desk, heavily bearing up four shelves of dull gilt and leather books; the high dim book-case, topped by strange plaster heads that peered along the ceiling level, or bent down . . . ; the small black iron bed, covered with dark cretonne; the narrow iron grate; the wide table in the alcove, piled with papers I would not dream of touching . . . Yet lo, the paper-piled table also held a little bag of figs, and one of the pieces of sweet stickiness was for me. "Tittery-Eye" he called me, and awe melted into glee, as I skipped away to my grandmother's room, which adjoined.

That was a very different place — sunny, comfortable and familiar, with a sewing machine and a *white* bed like other peoples'. In the corner stood a big arm chair, where he always sat when he left the recesses of his own dark privacy. I used to climb on his knee, while he told me wild tales of cannibals and tropic isles . . . We came nearest intimacy at these times, and part of the fun was to put my hands in his thick beard and squeeze it hard . . .

Sad it is that he felt his grandchildren would turn against him as they grew older. He used to forebode as much. (recollections of Mrs Eleanor Metcalf; quoted in Weaver, *Herman Melville; Mariner and Mystic*)

April   *Elizabeth Melville's memoir of M:*
Herman had two attacks of erysipelas, the last in April 1890 — both of which weakened him greatly.

May 23   *M sends to Catherine Lansing his share of expenses in the lot in Albany Cemetery:*
   Agreeably to Lottie's [Charlotte Hoadley's] request, in note received the other day, I send you in form of a P. O. order [for $134] my apportioned quota toward defraying certain expences.

For the interest you have shown in overseeing the work — an interest whereof Kate (my sister) and Lottie (at present both here in N.Y.) have told me, I, for one, am by no means unappreciative.

May 31   *M borrows from the New York Society Library:* The Mutiny at the Nore, A Nautical Drama *by Douglas Jerrold;* A Hazard of New Fortunes, *by William Dean Howells.*

June 13   *The Jerrold play & the Howells novel are returned to the New York Society Library; two Scott novels,* Peveril of the Peak *&* Quentin Durward, *are borrowed.*

REDHILL, ENGLAND   July 19   *On the letter-head of The Contemporary Science Series, Havelock Ellis writes to M:*
I am making some investigations into the ancestry of distinguished English & American poets and imaginative writers, with reference to the question of race. Will you kindly tell me to what races you trace yourself back on fathers & on mothers side, & what (if any) recent strains of foreign blood you lay claim to?
I was very sorry to hear that the project of reprinting one of your works in the Camelot Series had fallen through. At present your books are, practically, not before the public at all in this country, and a very large number of people are thus deprived of the delight which they would certainly derive from them, if they were accessible.

[?]Before August 10   I have been away from town, a wanderer hardly reachable for a time . . . — *M to Havelock Ellis, Aug 10*

NEW YORK   August 10   *M replies to Havelock Ellis's inquiry:*
My great grandfather on the paternal side was a native of Scotland. On the maternal side, and in the same remove, my progenitor was a native of Holland; and, on that side, the wives were all of like ancestry.
As to any strain of other blood, I am ignorant, except that my paternal grandfather's wife was of Irish Protestant stock.

BOSTON   September 6?   *Publication in the* Transcript *of correspondence from Paris, "Balzac's Burial," including the text of Victor Hugo's oration; M clips this & inserts it in his copy of the* Correspondence of Balzac.

THE PACIFIC   October 2   *John La Farge writes to his son, Bancel:*
On Sunday morning we shall be dropped into a boat off Tutuila, some sixty miles from the Samoa to which we go. How long we stay as I told you, I do not know, but we think of Tahiti later, and even other places, that I dare not think of, for I must return some day. But before that day, I wish to have seen a Fayaway sail her boat in some other Typee.

BOSTON October 14 *Horace Elisha Scudder, editor of the* Atlantic
Monthly, *writes to George Parsons Lathrop, with suggestions for a
"miniature American men of Letters" series:*
There are two subjects, either of which I should think you might be interested to take up — Fitz-Greene Halleck & Hermann Melville, especially the latter. I believe he is still living, but he must be very much
in retirement. He is not over seventy I think, but I take it that his
writing days are over.

NEW YORK October 20 *Lathrop replies to Scudder:*
Melville, I believe, is alive still, clinging like a weary but tenacious
barnacle to the N.Y. Custom House & very much averse to publicity.
He is an excellent subject, however. I don't know of any unpublished
material that I can get, relating to him. If I could find time I might go
down to the Custom House & unearth him, & perhaps get at something
. . . A capital article could be made about him, even without any new
material. There is enough in the *Study [of Hawthorne]* & references of
Hawthorne's, to suggest a picture of their friendship in Berkshire; a
picture nowhere I think very clearly outlined. But I mean that Melville
himself, any way, would furnish forth a good & interesting article . . .
He produced a curious book of war poems which I have read. It is very
little known, I think, but contains some good stuff.

BOSTON October 22 *From the* Atlantic Monthly *Scudder writes to
Lathrop:*
When I mentioned Melville, I had a notion that you would know something of his South sea life; the Lenox portion would be a good chapter.
I can't help thinking that there must be some good material in the subject, though probably it would be better still if Melville would only let
go of life. So much more frankness of speech can be used when a fellow
is apparently out of hearing. What you say of his aversion to publicity
makes me pause. I hate the whole business of making papers on living
men, when the appeal is not to the interest in the men as writers, or
artists, or publicists or what not, but to a petty interest in personal details.
    On second thought therefore, I believe we had better wait for our shot
at Melville, when his personality can be more freely handled.

October 31 *An item in an auction sale of autograph letters & documents sold by C. F. Libbie & Co.:*
    778 Melville, Herman, Author, a.l.s. 2 pages 8°

NEW YORK Fall *M visits the bookshop of John Anderson, Jr at 99
Nassau Street.*
    It was the beginning of a brief but pleasant friendship between [M & Ander-
son]. Until a short time before his death . . . Melville was a frequent visitor

at the Anderson shop . . . It was my own good fortune several times in those months to be the bearer of bundles of books to the Melville house — some of them were copies of his own sea tales, of which, oddly enough, he seemed to have had virtually no copies until Mr. Anderson supplied him. When the author was at home I was certain to receive a modest but welcome tip . . . (Oscar Wegelin, in *The Colophon*, Summer 1935)

November? *A paragraph in Edward Bok's syndicated newspaper column, "Literary Leaves":*
There are more people to-day who believe Herman Melville dead than there are those who know he is living. And yet if one choose to walk along East Eighteenth Street, New York City, any morning about 9 o'clock, he would see the famous writer of sea stories — stories which have never been equalled perhaps in their special line. Mr. Melville is now an old man, but still vigorous. He is an employé of the Customs Revenue Service, and thus still lingers around the atmosphere which permeated his books. Forty-four years ago, when his most famous tale, "Typee," appeared, there was not a better known author than he, and he commanded his own prices. Publishers sought him, and editors considered themselves fortunate to secure his name as a literary star. And to-day? Busy New York has no idea he is even alive, and one of the best informed literary men in this country laughed recently at my statement that Herman Melville was his neighbor by only two city blocks. "Nonsense," said he. "Why, Melville is dead these many years!" Talk about literary fame? There's a sample of it!

November 19 *Edward Bok's paragraph is reprinted in* The Publishers' Weekly.

BOSTON November 19 *A column in the Boston* Post:
I was struck with the difference between Boston and New York in regard to appreciation of literary men in a newspaper statement that Herman Melville, whom more people are said to think dead than those who know he is living, is really defunct so far as knowledge of his existence in the metropolis is concerned . . . Now such a state of things would be impossible here in Boston . . . To be sure, Melville is in one sense unfortunate in being in the New York Custom House, but other literary men have submitted to such trials without losing their hold on public interest . . .
It is hard to think of Herman Melville as an old man; there is an atmosphere of youth in his books which it would seem must always surround him . . . Yet their author is now in his seventy-second year, but I am glad to hear that he has been spared the infirmities which are apt to afflict persons of that time of life. I suppose most readers associate Herman Melville only with those adventures which his early life as a sailor made the means of his literature; but . . . he wrote such stories as "The Confidence Man," a volume of poems about the Civil War and two volumes on a pilgrimage to the Holy Land . . . he could hardly expect to find scope in the life of the islanders of the Pacific for any extended work in authorship. However, he has a satisfaction in knowing that his best work is unsurpassed in its way in English literature.

December 6   *Edward Bok's paragraph is reprinted in* The Literary World.

NEW YORK   December 13   *An item in* The Critic:
The friends of Mr. Herman Melville have been annoyed by the publication of a paragraph in which it is intimated that practically no one knows of the existence of that veteran romancer, whose "Typee" had a deserved success here and in England over forty years ago. Mr. Melville, it is true, has gone out very little since the death of his son, some two years ago; but in literary circles in New York it is by no means unknown that he is a resident of this city, and an employee of the Customs Revenue Service.

ORANGE   December 14   *Samuel Shaw's diary:*
Fanny Thomas' 3ᵈ daughter [Katherine Gansevoort] born at 6.30.P.M.

NEW YORK   December 17   *Elizabeth Melville writes to Catherine Lansing:*
  Fanny has asked me to write you and tell you the good news — of the safe arrival of a little daughter on Sunday evening — it came somewhat earlier than was expected, but it was a well formed and healthy baby, and as "plump as a partridge."

Late December?
His tall, stalwart figure, until recently, could be seen almost daily tramping through the Fort George district or Central Park, his roving inclination leading him to obtain as much outdoor life as possible. His evenings were spent at home with his books, his pictures and his family, and usually with them alone. (O. G. H[illard], *The New-York Times*, Oct 6, 1891)

He has not been very well all winter & has had a bad cough . . . he has enjoyed this clear weather going out every day & taking long walks — the day before he was taken sick he walked 3/4 of a mile in a bitter cold air — I think it was too much for him . . . — *Elizabeth Melville to Catherine Lansing, Jan 8, 1891*

·   ·   ·   ·   ·   ·

NEW YORK   *In 1890 or earlier M acquires or uses these works in the preparation of* Billy Budd: Battles of the British Navy, *by Joseph Allen;* Horatio. Nelson and the Naval Supremacy of England, *by W. Clark Russell;* The Life of Nelson, *by Robert Southey.*

Before 1891 M buys, either as a set or in the individually issued volumes, a new translation of Balzac's works by Katherine Prescott Wormley (Boston).
In the Preface to Père Goriot (*1885*), *M scores:*
. . . I may add that the writer who cannot stand the fire of criticism is no more fit to start upon the career of authorship than a traveller is fit to undertake a journey if he prepared only for fine weather.

In The Duchesse de Langeais *(1885),* M *scores:*
Men will permit us to rise above them, but they will not forgive him who refuses to descend as low as they. Thus the feelings they bestow on noble characters are never without the elements of hatred and fear. To be worthy of high honor is for them a tacit censure, which they forgive neither to the living nor to the dead.

In Cousin Pons *(1886),* M *scores:*
Poverty, divine stepmother, did for the two young men what their own mothers had been unable to do: she taught them economy, the world, and life; she gave them the high and stern education which she drives like a spur into great men, who are all unhappy in their youth.

In The Two Brothers *(1887),* M *scores & checks several passages in the first chapters:*
Philippe, the elder of the two sons, was strikingly like his mother. Though a blond lad, with blue eyes, he had the daring look which is readily taken for intrepidity and courage . . .

Agathe believed that the purely physical resemblance which Philippe bore to her carried with it a moral likeness; and she confidently expected him to show at a future day her own delicacy of feeling, heightened by the vigor of manhood . . . Joseph, three years younger, was like his father, but only on the defective side. In the first place, his thick black hair was always in disorder, no matter what pains were taken with it; while Philippe's, notwithstanding his vivacity, was invariably neat. Then, by some mysterious fatality Joseph could not keep his clothes clean; dress him in new clothes, and he immediately made them look like old ones. The elder, on the other hand, took care of his things out of mere vanity. Unconsciously, the mother acquired a habit of scolding Joseph and holding up his brother as an example to him. Agathe did not treat the two children alike . . .

. . . [Joseph's] distressful face, whose originality was thought ugliness by those who had no eye for the moral value of a countenance, wore rather a sullen expression during his childhood.

. . . Philippe, a captain at nineteen and decorated . . . flattered the mother's vanity immensely. Coarse, blustering, and without real merit beyond the vulgar bravery of a cavalry officer, he was to her mind a man of genius; whereas Joseph, puny and sickly, with unkempt hair and absent mind, seeking peace, loving quiet, and dreaming of an artist's glory, would only bring her, she thought, worries and anxieties.

[Following M's *reading of this novel, "Timoleon" is composed:*

III

Timophanes was his mother's pride —
Her pride, her pet, even all to her
Who slackly on Timoleon looked:
Scarce he (she mused) may proud affection stir . . .
    When boys they were I helped the bent;
I made the junior feel his place,
Subserve the senior, love him, too;
And sooth he does, and that's his saving grace,
    But me the meek one never can serve,

Not he, he lacks the quality keen
To make the mother through the son
An envied dame of power, a social queen.
 But thou, my first-born, thou art I
In sex translated; joyed, I scan
My features, mine, expressed in thee;
Thou art what I would be were I a man.
 My brave Timophanes, 'tis thou
Who yet the world's forefront shalt win,
For thine the urgent resolute way,
Self pushing panoplied self through thick and thin.

A stanza for Part VI of "Timoleon" is drafted in pencil:
 But, courted therein, his mood elects
 Self exile & secluded place
 For years a hermit, he but meets
 In streets his playfellow's reproachful face]

M scores & checks a passage on p 45 of The Two Brothers:
. . . New York, — a place where speculation and individualism are carried to the highest pitch, where the brutality of self-interest attains to cynicism, where man, essentially isolated, is compelled to push his way for himself and by himself . . .

In Bureaucracy or a Civil Service Reformer (*1889*), *M scores:*
Bixiou. Fleury is right. Serving the State in these days is no longer serving a prince who knew how to punish and reward. The State now is *everybody.* Everybody of course cares for nobody. Serve everybody and you serve nobody. Nobody is interested in nobody; the government clerk lives between the two negations. The world has neither pity nor respect, neither heart nor head; everybody forgets tomorrow the service of yesterday.

In Seraphita (*1889*), *M scores, checks, & underscores several passages:*
. . . doubts, be it said, which modern research and scientific progress have strengthened instead of diminishing.

How came it that Evil, king of the earth, was born of a God supremely good in His essence and in His faculties, who can produce nothing that is not made in His own image?

When the happy day arrives in which you set your feet upon the Path and begin your pilgrimage, the world will know nothing of it; earth no longer understands you; you no longer understand each other . . . your destiny is a secret between yourself and God . . .

Take me, that I no longer be myself!

In Fame and Sorrow (with other Scenes from Private Life) (*1890*), *M scores a passage (scoring later erased) in "The Atheist's Mass":*
"Ah! my dear lad, you have talent enough to be soon plunged into the horrible strife, the incessant warfare which mediocrity wages against superior men . . . Have a headache, and they'll say you are insane. Get angry, and they'll call you a Timon . . . Slip, and you are down!"

Shortly before [M's] death the magnanimous poet-critic, Edmund Clarence Stedman, managed a complimentary dinner for him and with difficulty got him to attend it. It was about the only public recognition he ever received. (Frank Jewett Mather, Jr, in *The Review*, Aug 19, 1919)

*

1 8 9 1

*

January 8 *Elizabeth Melville writes to Catherine Lansing:*
I have been thinking for some days of writing you — because I dont want you to hear in any other or exaggerated way that Herman has been pretty ill for the last week or so — when he had a turn of dizziness or vertigo in the night — which the Dr feared might eventuate in a serious way — but now I am glad to say that his strength which seemed to leave him in one night has gradually returned and he is improving every day — he has not been out yet or even down stairs, but the Dr says there seems to be no reason why he should not entirely recover and be as well as before . . . I have been so much absorbed with Herman who requires a good deal of attention —

January 10 *Cranch's* The Girl and The Bell *[borrowed Jan 8] is returned to the New York Society Library, &* Christs Folk *[in the Apennine, by Francesca Alexander] is borrowed, on M's share.*

January 19 *Borrowed from the New York Society Library:* The Lion's Cub; with Other Verse, *by Richard Henry Stoddard; the book is returned two days later.*

THE PACIFIC After January 27 *John La Farge writes to his son, Bancel:*
We have had days of hard winds and grey weather, and all the more do I make pictures within my mind. For the Otaheite to which we are bound has a meaning, a classical record, a story of adventure, and historical importance, fuller than the Typee of Melville, which we may never see. The name recalls so many associations of ideas, so much romance of reading . . . There are many boyish recollections behind the charm of Melville's "Omoo" and of Stoddard's Idylls, or even the mixed pleasure of Loti's "Marriage."

NEW YORK February 5 *M borrows from the New York Society Library:*
Counsels & Maxims [by Arthur Schopenhauer (London, 1890)]

PAPEITE   February 6   *Henry Adams writes to Elizabeth Cameron:*

Tahiti! does the word mean anything to you? To me it has a perfume of its own, made up of utterly inconsequent associations; essence of the South Seas mixed with imaginations of at least forty years ago; Herman Melville and Captain Cook head and heels with the French opera and Pierre Loti.

NEW YORK   February 12   *M returns the Schopenhauer volume to the New York Society Library; now or later he purchases a copy of his own, as well as other Schopenhauer volumes, in which he reads;*
In The World as Will and Idea, *Vol III. Fourth Book, Chapter XLVI. "The Vanity and Suffering of Life" M scores:*
. . . the insight to which [Voltaire] attained in three respects, and which prove the greater depth of his thinking: (1) the recognition of the preponderating magnitude of the evil and misery of existence with which he is deeply penetrated; (2) that of the strict necessity of the acts of will; (3) that of the truth of Locke's principle, that what thinks may also be material . . .
In the Preface to the Third Edition, M scores:

What is true and genuine would more easily gain room in the world if it were not that those who are incapable of producing it are also sworn to prevent it from succeeding.

M acquires & reads Studies in Pessimism, *by Arthur Schopenhauer (London, 1891); on p 14 M scores:*

He who lives to see two or three generations is like a man who sits some time in the conjurer's booth at a fair, and witnesses the performance twice or thrice in succession. The tricks were meant to be seen only once; and when they are no longer a novelty and cease to deceive, their effect is gone.
On p 28 M scores:
. . . if he is a man of genius, he will occasionally feel like some noble prisoner of state, condemned to work in the galleys with common criminals; and he will follow his example and try to isolate himself.
On p 84 M scores:
Myson, the misanthropist, was once surprised by one of these people as he was laughing to himself. *Why do you laugh?* he asked; *there is no one with you. That is just why I am laughing,* said Myson.

M acquires & reads The Wisdom of Life . . . *by Arthur Schopenhauer (London, 1891); on p 2 of the Introduction M scores:*
In general, indeed, the wise in all ages have always said the same thing, and the fools, who at all times form the immense majority, have in their way too acted alike, and done just the opposite; and so it will continue. For, as Voltaire says, *we shall leave this world as foolish and as wicked as we found it on our arrival.*
On p 120 M scores:
. . . the more a man belongs to posterity, in other words, to humanity in general, the more of an alien he is to his contemporaries; since his work is not

meant for them as such, but only for them in so far as they form part of mankind at large; there is none of that familiar local colour about his productions which would appeal to them; and so what he does, fails of recognition because it is strange. People are more likely to appreciate the man who serves the circumstances of his own brief hour, or the temper of the moment, — belonging to it, and living and dying with it.

TAHITI   February 13?   *John La Farge writes to his son, Bancel:*
In the evening, with some remnant of energy, we walk still further than our house upon the beach . . . We try to find, by the little river that ends our walk, on this side of the old French fort, the calaboose where Melville was shut up. There is no one to help us in our search; no one remembers anything. Buildings occupy the spaces of woodland that Melville saw about him. Nothing remains but the charm of light and air which he, like all others, has tried to describe and to bring back home in words. But the beach is still as beautiful as if composed by Claude Lorraine.

NEW YORK   February 23   *Catherine Lansing's diary:*
[In the morning] made a call on Bessie Melville — Cousin Lizzie & Herman were out —

February 24   *M gives his grand-daughter, Eleanor, a present on her ninth birthday:* Landseer's Dogs and Their Stories, *by Sarah Tytler [Henrietta Keddie] (London, 1877).*

LONDON   February 28   *Publication, in* Black and White, *of* The South Seas: A Record of Three Cruises, *by Robert Louis Stevenson; "IV. — Death":*
Or take the valley of Hapaa, known to readers of Herman Melville under the grotesque misspelling of Hapar. There are but two writers who have touched the South Seas with any genius, both Americans: Melville and Charles Warren Stoddard; and at the christening of the first and greatest, some influential fairy must have been neglected: "He shall be able to see," "He shall be able to tell," "He shall be able to charm," said the friendly godmothers; "But he shall not be able to hear," exclaimed the last.

TAHITI   March?   *John La Farge writes to his son, Bancel:*
. . . I think that a mere dreamer like myself can be excused for turning to more scientific and accurate arrangements of men's history.
These words come to me more distinctly suggested by the place in which I am, not because I am thinking of the ancient ways that I touch, but because I remember how Melville passed from those records of exterior life and scenery to a dwelling within his mind — a following out of metaphysical ideas, and a scheming of possible evolution in the future of man.

NEW YORK April 19 *The last page of* Billy Budd:
    Fathoms down, fathoms down, how I'll dream fast asleep.
    I feel it stealing now, Sentry, are you there?
    Just ease this darbies at the wrist,
    Ease it, and roll me over fair,
    I am sleepy, and the oozy weeds about me twist.

[handwritten manuscript reproduction:]

Fathoms down, how I'll dream
          fast asleep.
I feel it stealing now, Sentry, are
          you there?
Just ease this iron at the wrist,
Ease it, and roll me over fair,
I am drowsy, and the oozy weeds
          about me twist.

——— // ———

End of Book April 19th 1891

Early May? *M turns over a volume of verse to the Caxton Press:*

Timoleon
And Other Ventures
in
Minor Verse.

[*dedicated*] To my countryman, Elihu Vedder

[*834*]

WASHINGTON   May 15   *A title is deposited at the Library of Congress:*
Timoleon
(Etc)

NEW YORK   May 28   *Elizabeth Melville writes to Catherine Lansing:*
I was very glad to hear from you and have been trying for the
few days past to get from Herman what he might chance to know of
Uncle Herman [Gansevoort] by leading the conversation that way —
He says that Uncle went to G[ansevoort] at an early age to take charge
of the lumbering interests there for his father — to whom he thinks,
but is not sure that a large wooded tract of land was granted to him for
his military services — the land in question having belonged to a tory
and was confiscated — there was also a saw mill to put the timber into
marketable shape — On one of his first visits to New York he met and
married Catherine Quackenboss who cheerfully went to this wilderness
and lived the rest of her life — She was a very eccentric character as no
doubt you have heard . . .
His military career was only that of the State militia as far as H[er-
man] knows — and he has never seen any printed notice . . .
I hope you are quite well — Herman is tolerably well but not strong —
Fanny's children have been having the measles — Eleanor, just in the
midst of moving — Frances was sick here — both mild attacks — and all
well now — but Harry has been laid up with them, and is not out yet —
We expect to go to Fire Island in June — Herman also, as he is not well
enough to be left alone — I suppose he will get very impatient but I have
to go there for rose cold

June 13? [Elizabeth Melville's 69th birthday]   *M composes a dedica-*
tion for Timoleon:
To Her — without whose assistance both manual and literary Timoleon
&c could not have passed through the press — with her name I gratefully and affectionately inscribe this volume.
New York   Herman Melville
June 1891

WASHINGTON   June 16   *A copy of* Timoleon *is deposited, for copy-*
right, at the Library of Congress.

NEW YORK   July   *Dr Everett S. Warner begins his final attendance on*
M.

After August 4   *M sets the arrangement of his volume of lyric poems,*
alters its title to: Weeds and Wildings Chiefly: with a Rose or Two,
& composes a dedication to "Winnefred" [Elizabeth]:
Neither have we, jointly or severally, so frequently lighted upon that rare
four-leaved variety [of clover] accounted of happy augury to the finder;

though, to be sure, on my part, I yearly remind you of the coincidence in my chancing on such a specimen by the wayside on the early forenoon of the fourth day of a certain bridal month, now four years more than four times ten years ago . . .

Well, and to whom but to thee, Madonna of the Trefoil, should I now dedicate these 'Weeds and Wildings,' thriftless children of quite another and yet later spontaneous aftergrowth, and bearing indications, too apparent it may be, of the terminating season on which the offerer verges. But take them.

August-September? M occupies himself with *"readings in the 'Mermaid Series' of old plays, in which he took much pleasure."* (*Arthur Stedman, Introduction to* Typee, *1892*)

September 28 Everett S. Warner, M.D., *signs M's death certificate:* . . . and I further certify that I attended the deceased from July 1891 to Sept. 28, 1891 that I last saw him alive on the 27th day of Sept. 1891 that death occurred on the date stated above at 12/30 A.M. that the cause of death was as follows:

Cardiac dilatation, Mitral regurgitation . . . Contributory Asthenia.

Elizabeth Melville's memoir of M:
He died Sept. 28ᵗʰ 1891 after two years of failing health, induced partly by severe attacks of erysipelas terminating finally in enlargement of the heart.

Elizabeth Melville [?] sends telegrams to the family, informing them of M's death.

ROXBURY *September 28* Maria Gansevoort Mackintosh *writes to Catherine Lansing:*
You have doubtless learned of Uncle Herman's death at an early hour this morning. The poor man is out of his suffering, and we can not but rejoice for him. Poor Aunt Lizzie must be about worn out with her long and constant care of him.

Mama & I will leave for New York on Wednesday morning, and may perhaps meet you there.

NEW YORK *September 29* An item in The Press:
DEATH OF A ONCE POPULAR AUTHOR.
There died yesterday at his quiet home in this city a man who, although he had done almost no literary work during the past sixteen years, was once one of the most popular writers in the United States.

Herman Melville probably reached the height of his fame about 1852, his first novel having been printed about 1847 . . . Of late years Mr. Melville — probably because he had ceased his literary activity — has fallen into a literary decline, as the result of which his books are now little known.

Probably, if the truth were known, even his own generation has long thought him dead, so quiet have been the later years of his life.

An obituary notice in the New-York Daily Tribune:
He won considerable fame as an author by the publication of a book in 1847 entitled "Typee" . . . This was his best work, although he has since written a number of other stories, which were published more for private than public circulation . . . During the ten years subsequent to the publication of this book he was employed at the New-York Custom House.

The World:

Death of Herman Melville.
Author of Several Volumes of Poems and of Romances.

Herman Melville, formerly a well-known author, died at his residence . . .

Arthur Stedman hears more about M:
Meeting with Mr. Charles Henry Webb ("John Paul") the day after Mr. Melville's death, I asked him if he were not familiar with that author's writings. He replied that "Moby Dick" was responsible for his three years of life before the mast when a lad, and added that while "gamming" on board another vessel he had once fallen in with a member of the boat's crew which rescued Melville from his friendly imprisonment among the Typees. (Stedman, Introduction to *Typee*)

ALBANY September 29 *Catherine Lansing's diary:*
I went down town & had notices of Cousin Herman Melville in "Ev'g Journal," "Argus," & "Press & Knickerbocker" . . .

September 30   Up by 5 o'ck. Packed own bag & after a hurried breakfast left Albany by the 6 A.M. Train for N.Y.

NEW YORK   September 30   Arrived on Time . . . went up 104 E. 26th Saw Cousin Herman in his last sleep —

HERMAN MELVILLE'S FUNERAL.

The funeral of the late Herman Melville was held at the family residence . . . yesterday afternoon, the Rev. Theodore C. Williams, of All Souls' Church, delivering a short address. Among the relatives and friends present, beside the widow and daughter[s?] of the deceased, were Mrs. Thomas Melville, widow of the late governor of the Sailors' Snug Harbor; the Misses Melville, daughters of the late Allan Melville; Samuel Shaw, of Boston; W. B. Morewood, George Brewster, Mrs. Griggs [Hoadley], Miss Lathers, Dr. Titus Munson Coan, Arthur Stedman and George Dillaway. (*New-York Daily Tribune*, Oct 1)

*

THE SOURCES

*

THE ENDLESS STUDY

*

The Sources

HCL-C Correspondence of George William Curtis, Harvard College Library

HCL-D Correspondence of J. H. Dix, Harvard College Library

HCL-E Papers of the Emerson family, Harvard College Library

HCL-Fe Fearing Marine Library, Harvard College Library

HCL-Fi Collection of W. B. O. Field, Harvard College Library

HCL-M Papers & library of the Melville family, Harvard College Library

HCL-S Correspondence of Charles Sumner, Harvard College Library

HCL-T Correspondence of Bayard Taylor, Harvard College Library

HCL-W Papers of the Ward family, Harvard College Library

HENNESEY Formerly in the collection of Mrs Ella D. Hennesey, Brooklyn, N. Y.

HL Collections of the Henry E. Huntington Library, San Marino, Calif.

HOWE Collection of Parkman D. Howe, Boston, Mass.

HSP-BUCHANAN Correspondence of James Buchanan, Historical Society of Pennsylvania, Philadelphia

HSP-DREER Collection of Ferdinand Julius Dreer, Historical Society of Pennsylvania

HSP-GRATZ Collection of Simon Gratz, Historical Society of Pennsylvania

HU-BL Collections of the Baker Library, Harvard University, Cambridge, Mass.

HUNLEY Collection of Maxwell Hunley, Beverly Hills, Calif.

LC Collections of the Library of Congress, Washington, D. C.

LC-CURTIS Papers of Benjamin R. Curtis, Library of Congress

LC-CUSHING Correspondence of Caleb Cushing, Library of Congress

LC-LATHERS Correspondence of Richard Lathers, Library of Congress

LC-POLK Papers of James K. Polk, Library of Congress

LC-RB Collections of the Rare Books Division, Library of Congress

LILLY Collection of Josiah K. Lilly, Jr, Indianapolis, Ind.

LORING Collection of Augustus P. Loring, Jr, Boston, Mass.

MARTIN Collection of H. Bradley Martin, Jr, New York

MATTHIESSEN Collection of the late F. O. Matthiessen, Boston, Mass.

MELVILL Archive of Charles A. Melvill, La Grange Park, Ill.

METCALF Archive of Mrs Henry K. Metcalf, Cambridge, Mass.

METROPOLITAN Collections of the Metropolitan Museum of Art, New York

MHS-D Papers of the Dana family, deposited at the Massachusetts Historical Society, Boston, Mass.

MHS-E Letterbooks of Edward Everett, Massachusetts Historical Society

MHS-P Correspondence of Francis Parkman, Massachusetts Historical Society

MHS-S Papers of the Shaw family, Massachusetts Historical Society

MHS-W Papers of the Ward family, Massachusetts Historical Society

MiL Collections of the Mitchell Library, Sydney, Australia

MoL Collections of the Morgan Library, New York

MOREWOOD Archive of the Morewood family, Pittsfield, Mass.

MURRAY Collection of Dr Henry A. Murray, Topsfield, Mass.

MURRAY V Archive of Sir John Murray V, London [consulted through the courtesy of the Harvard College Library]

NA-A Archives of the Department of Agriculture, National Archives, Washington, D. C.

NA-C Archives of the Department of Commerce, National Archives

NA-N Archives of the Navy Department, National Archives

NA-S Archives of the State Department, National Archives

NA-SEN Archives of the U. S. Senate, National Archives

NA-T Archives of the Treasury Department, National Archives

NBFPL Collections of the New Bedford Free Public Library, New Bedford, Mass.

ND Archives of the Navy Department, Washington, D. C.

NHA Collections of the Nantucket Historical Association, Nantucket, Mass.

NICHOLSON Collection of Paul C. Nicholson, Providence, R. I.

N-TR Town Records, Nantucket, Mass.

NY-HR Hall of Records, New York

NYHS Collections of the New-York Historical Society, New York

NYHS-G Correspondence of Albert Gallatin, New-York Historical Society

NYPL Collections of the Manuscript Division, New York Public Library, New York

NYPL-A The Arentz Tobacco Collection, New York Public Library

NYPL-B The Henry W. & Albert A. Berg Collection, New York Public Library

NYPL-D Papers of the Duyckinck family, New York Public Library

NYPL-F The Gordon Lester Ford Collection, New York Public Library

NYPL-G Collections of the Genealogical Room, New York Public Library

NYPL-GL Papers & library of the Gansevoort & Lansing families, New York Public Library

NYPL-GLF Materials purchased through the Gansevoort-Lansing fund, New York Public Library

NYPL-O Library of Mrs A. D. Osborne, Edgartown, Martha's Vineyard, Mass., presented to the New York Public Library

NYPL-P Papers of George Palmer Putnam, New York Public Library

NYPL-PC Prints in the Picture Collection, New York Public Library

NYPL-RB Collections of the Rare Book Room, New York Public Library

NYPL-T Papers of the Townsend family, New York Public Library

NYSoL Records of the New York Society Library, New York

NYStL Collections of the New York State Library, Albany, N. Y.

ODHS Collections of the Old Dartmouth Historical Society, New Bedford, Mass.

PCH Town Records, Pittsfield, Mass.

PEABODY Collections of the Peabody Museum, Salem, Mass.

J PEARSON Collection of John C. Pearson, Cleveland, O.

N PEARSON Collection of Norman H. Pearson, New Haven, Conn.

PEIRSON Archive of Miss Alice Peirson, Pittsfield, Mass.

PLEADWELL Collection of Captain F. L. Pleadwell, Honolulu, Hawaii

PTR Collections in the Treasure Room, Princeton University Library

PUTNAM Archive of Palmer C. Putnam, Boston, Mass.

RHODEBECK Collection of Dr Edmund J. Rhodebeck, New York

ROSENBACH Collection of Dr A. S. W. Rosenbach, Philadelphia

RRL Collections of the Rhush Rees Library, Rochester, N. Y.

RUL Collections of the Rutgers University Library, New Brunswick, N. J.

SC-PR Probate Records of Suffolk County, Boston, Mass.

SCRIBNER Rare Book Department, Charles Scribner's Sons, New York

SEALTS Collection of Merton M. Sealts, Appleton, Wis.

SEDGWICK Papers of the Sedgwick family, Stockbridge, Mass. [papers at present in process of transfer to the Massachusetts Historical Society]

SHSW Collections of the State Historical Society of Wisconsin, Madison, Wis.

STRALEM Collection of Donald Stralem, New York

SUKEL Collection of Samuel Sukel, Pittsfield, Mass.

THS Collections of the Tennessee Historical Society, Nashville, Tenn.

UVL Collections of the University of Virginia Library, Charlottesville, Va.

VIETOR Collection of Alexander O. Vietor, New Haven, Conn.

WEAVER Collection of the late Raymond M. Weaver, New York

WHEELOCK Archive of Mrs John Hall Wheelock, New York

WILLETS Archive of Mrs C. R. E. Willets, Halifax, Nova Scotia

WOODLAWN Records of the Woodlawn Cemetery, New York

YUL-A Aldis Collection, Yale University Library, New Haven, Conn.

YUL-B Papers of the Baldwin family, Yale University Library

YUL-V Gift of Alexander O. Vietor to the Yale University Library

YUL-VV Gift of Carl Van Vechten to the Yale University Library

LOCATIONS OF MANUSCRIPTS, ILLUSTRATIONS, MEMORABILIA

1. 1819-1829

1819 AUGUST: 2, NYPL-GL; 13, Morewood; 14, letter-book, NYPL-GL; letter-book, NYPL-GL; NYPL-GL; receipted bill, NYPL-GL; 19 [facsimile], Bible Record, NYPL-GL. SEPTEMBER: 14, NYPL-GL. NOVEMBER: diary, HCL-M; 19, NYPL-GL

1820 [24 May 1866, NYPL-GL] JANUARY: 12, NYPL-GL. APRIL: 8, letter-book, NYPL-GL. MAY: accounts, NYPL-GL. JUNE: 12, Morewood; diary, HCL-M. JULY: 14, transcript [by Allan Melville, Jr?], Morewood. AUGUST: 8, MHS-S; 15, Morewood. SEPTEMBER: 18, HCL-M; 26, HCL-M. OCTOBER: 7, HCL-M

1821 JANUARY: 10, NYPL-GL. MARCH: accounts, NYPL-GL. APRIL: 23, Bible Record, Melvill. MAY: 12, MHS-S; 26, NYPL-GL. JUNE: 15, letter-book, NYPL-GL. JULY: 7, MHS-S. AUGUST: 18, MHS-S; Bible Record, NYPL-GL. NOVEMBER: 3, NYPL-GL

1822 MARCH: 11, NYPL-GL; diary, HCL-M. APRIL: 16, NYPL-GL. MAY: 25, MHS-S; 29, NYPL-GL. JUNE: 13, Bible Record, MHS-S. AUGUST: diary, HCL-M; 29, Morewood. OCTOBER: diary, HCL-M; diary, NYPL-GL; diary, HCL-M. DECEMBER: 9, MHS-S; 24, Morewood

1823 JANUARY: 11, MHS-S; 22, NYPL-GL. MARCH: 11, NYPL-GL; 29, NYPL-GL. APRIL: 7, Bible Record, NYPL-GL; 8, NYPL-GL; 26, Morewood; MHS-S.

MAY: 13, MHS-S; HCL-M; 16, Bible Record, NYPL-GL. JUNE: 10, NYPL-GL; 26, NYPL-GL. JULY: 7, NYPL-GL. AUGUST: 9, NYPL-GL; diary, HCL-M. OCTOBER: 4, HCL-M; 14, NYPL-GL; engraving (from a drawing by C. Burton), NYHS; 22, NYPL-GL; NYPL-GL. NOVEMBER: 21, NYPL-GL. DECEMBER: NYPL-GL

1824 MARCH: 11, HCL-M. APRIL: 1, HCL-M; 20, NYPL-GL. MAY: 4, NYPL-GL; 17, MHS-S; 20, HCL-M. JUNE: diary, HCL-M; 12, NYPL-GL; 30, NYPL-GL. JULY: 23, carriage bill, NYPL-GL. AUGUST: 9, NYPL-GL. SEPTEMBER: 3, NYPL-GL; 28, NYPL-GL. OCTOBER: 27, NYPL-GL. NOVEMBER: 4, letter-book, NYPL-GL; 12, letter-book, NYPL-GL. DECEMBER: 17, carriage bill, NYPL-GL; 29, HCL-M

1825 FEBRUARY: 14, NYPL-GL. MARCH: 30, HCL-M. APRIL: NYPL-GL. MAY: 19, MHS-S. JUNE: 8, Bible Record, NYPL-GL; 15, NYPL-GL; 18, NYPL-GL. AUGUST: 2, NYPL-GL; 29, NYPL-GL. OCTOBER: 22, NYPL-GL; 29, receipted bill, MHS-S

1826 JANUARY: 13, NYPL-GL; 31, NYPL-GL. FEBRUARY: 20, NYPL-GL. APRIL: 8, Morewood; 15, Morewood; 18, NYPL-GL; 19, NYPL-GL. MAY: 20, NYPL-GL; 6, NYPL-GL; diary, HCL-M; 20, NYPL-GL; NYPL-GL. AUGUST:

9, HCL-M; 10, HCL-M; 15, MHS-S; 25, NYPL-GL; 28, Melvill. SEPTEMBER: 2, Morewood; 12, HCL-M; 14, HCL-M; 17, HCL-M; 26, Morewood. OCTOBER: 6, NYPL-GL; 14, Morewood. NOVEMBER: 7, NYPL-GL. DECEMBER: 5, NYPL-GL; 8, NYPL-GL

1827 FEBRUARY: 10, NYPL-GL; 14, MHS-S; 20, NYPL-GL. MARCH: 2, NYPL-GL; 30, NYPL-GL; 31, NYPL-GL. MAY: 1, NYPL-GL. JULY: 28, HCL-M. AUGUST: 26, Bible Record, NYPL-GL; 29, Bible Record, MHS-S; 30, HCL-M. SEPTEMBER: 22, NYPL-GL

1828 FEBRUARY: 15, NYPL-GL; 22, NYPL-GL; 23, NYPL-GL; 28, HCL-M;

NYPL-GL. MARCH: 10, NYPL-GL; 27, MHS-S. MAY: 10, NYPL-GL; 23, NYPL-GL; NYPL-GL. JULY: diary, HCL-M. AUGUST: 7, NYPL-GL; MHS-S; 20, NYPL-GL. OCTOBER: 11 [facsimile], HCL-M; 21, NYPL-GL; 27, NYPL-GL. DECEMBER: 7, NYPL-GL; diary, HCL-M; 31, NYPL-GL

1829 FEBRUARY: will, SC-PR. APRIL: 20, HCL-M. MAY: 6, NYPL-GL. JUNE: 18, receipted bill, NYPL-GL; [Oct 6, NYPL-GL] will, NYPL-GL. JULY: diary, HCL-M; 15, NYPL-GL; 25, NYPL-GL. AUGUST: 31, NYPL-GL. SEPTEMBER: 10, NYPL-GL; 12, HCL-M; 26, NYPL-GL

II. 1830-1839

1830 JANUARY: 24, Bible Record, NYPL-GL. MAY: 6, carriage bill, NYPL-GL; 20, NYPL-GL. JUNE: will, NYPL-GL; accounts, NYPL-GL. JULY: 27, NYPL-GL. AUGUST: 3, NYPL-GL; 11, NYPL-GL. SEPTEMBER: 4, NYPL-GL; 22, NYPL-GL; 30, NYPL-GL. OCTOBER: diary, HCL-M; *English Reader*, NYPL-GL. DECEMBER: 4, HCL-M; ms *Red Rover* review, NYPL-D

1831 MARCH: 13, NYPL-GL. APRIL: 15, HCL-M. JULY: receipted bill, MHS-S. AUGUST: *London Carcanet*, YUL-V; diary, HCL-M; ms transcript, NYPL-GL; diary, HCL-M; 17, NYPL-GL; engraving, *Albany Citizens' Advertiser*, 1834-5. SEPTEMBER: 23, NA-N. OCTOBER: 8, Bible Record, NYPL-GL; accounts, NYPL-GL. NOVEMBER: 15, AAAL; diary, HCL-M. DECEMBER: diary, HCL-M; 18, NYPL-GL; 22, HCL-M

1832 JANUARY: Bible, NYPL-GL; 8, NYHS; 10, NYPL-GL; 15, HCL-M; 27, HCL-M; ledger, NYPL-GL. MARCH: certificate, NYPL-GL. APRIL: minutes, FRD; 27, MHS-S; 30, NA-N. MAY: 1, MHS-S; 22, NYPL-GL. JUNE: certificate, HCL-M. JULY: 14, NYPL-GL; 17, NYPL-GL; 24, NYPL-GL; NYPL-GL. AUGUST: 2, NYPL-GL; 7, NYPL-GL. SEPTEMBER: *Firemen's Advocate* clipping, NYPL-GL; 23, MHS-S; 24, NYPL-GL. OCTOBER: Webster speech, in *Writings*

and Speeches; 15, NYPL-GL. NOVEMBER: affidavit, MHS-S; 8, MHS-S; 15, MHS-S

1833 FEBRUARY: 20, NYPL-GL; Bible Record, Melvill. MAY: 25, NYPL-GL. JUNE: 20, HCL-M. SEPTEMBER: 2, MHS-S. NOVEMBER: bill in equity, NYPL-GL

1834 JANUARY: journal, Morewood. FEBRUARY: 12, NYPL-GL; 19, HCL-E. MARCH: journal, Morewood. MAY: 14, MHS-S; 29, MHS-S; NA-N. JUNE: 16, MHS-S; ms transcript of memoir, NYPL-GL. SEPTEMBER: 9, MHS-S; ms transcript, NYPL-GL

1835 JANUARY: minutes & cash-book, APL. OCTOBER: 24, MHS-S; register, NA-C. DECEMBER: cash-book, APL

1836 JANUARY: receipted bill, NYPL-T; minutes, APL. MAY: 5, MHS-S. JUNE: miniature, NYPL-GL; 17, ACR. JULY: 8, cash-book, APL. AUGUST: *Tales of a Grandfather*, Morewood. SEPTEMBER: cash-book, APL; 16, NYPL-GL. OCTOBER: composition, NYPL-GL; mortgage, A-CC. NOVEMBER: 8, HCL-M; 29, NYPL-GL. DECEMBER: 31, ACR

1837 JANUARY: 5, cash-book, APL; composition, NYPL-GL. MARCH: 14, MHS-S; 16, records, PCH. APRIL: 15, NYPL-GL; 17, PCH; 26, minutes, APL; bond, NYPL-GL. MAY: 16, MHS-S. JUNE: 3, MHS-S; journal, Morewood. JULY: records, FRD.

SEPTEMBER: diary, MHS-S; fragment transcribed in *Albany Microscope*, 31 March 1838. NOVEMBER: 1, NYPL-GL; *Self-Teacher* [unlocated, Forsythe notes]; 28, NYPL-GL. DECEMBER: 30, NYPL-GL

1838 MAY: journal, Morewood. JUNE: 9, NYPL-GL; 12, draft, NYPL-GL; 16, NYPL-GL; 20, draft, NYPL-GL. AUGUST: 2, NYPL-GL; 20, Morewood; Bible Record, Melvill. OCTOBER: records, FRD; 30, NYPL-GL. NOVEMBER: 1, MHS-S; 10, Morewood. DECEMBER: 17, MHS-S; 27, NYPL-GL

1839 JANUARY: 9, MHS-S. FEBRUARY: check, NYPL-GL; *Student's Manual*,

Morewood. APRIL: 4, draft, NYPL-GL; 20, receipt, NYPL-GL. MAY: 23, NYPL-GL; 24, Morewood; journal, Morewood; note on *Democratic Press*, HCL-M; *London Carcanet* [facsimiles], YUL-V. JUNE: 1, NYPL-GL; transcribed crew-list, NA-T; [July 9, MHS-S] journal, Morewood. JULY: consular return, NA-S; Duyckinck journal, NYPL-D. AUGUST: crew-list, NA-T. SEPTEMBER: 25, Morewood; crew-list, NA-T. OCTOBER: 4, Morewood; draft, NYPL-GL; 18, draft & receipt, NYPL-GL. DECEMBER: 7, Morewood; 14, NYPL-GL; 16, NYPL-GL; 18, draft, NYPL-GL; 24, NYPL-GL; receipted bill, MHS-S

III. 1840-1844

1840 JANUARY: 9, MHS-S; 21, Morewood. FEBRUARY: 5, Morewood. MARCH: Morewood. APRIL: 3, Morewood. MAY: 16, NYPL-GL; *Amazon* log, Nicholson; information from Mary Parmelee's granddaughter, Mrs Frances Wickes. JUNE: 2, NYPL-GL; receipt [facsimile], HCL-M; 26, MHS-S. JULY: ms transcript, NYPL-GL; 7, N-TR; *Confidence-Man* fragment, HCL-M. AUGUST: 11, NYPL-GL; 29, MHS-S. SEPTEMBER: ms "Trophies of Peace," HCL-M. OCTOBER: 15, NYPL-GL. NOVEMBER: 3, NA-N; *Amazon* log, Nicholson; 7, NA-N; 26, Morewood. DECEMBER: 16, register, NA-C; 21, Morewood; 26 [facsimile], NBFPL; register, NA-C; *Acushnet* plan, Weeks journal, HCL-Fe; crew-list, NA-T & ODHS

1841 JANUARY: crew-list, NA-T; 11, HCL-M; 31, MHS-S. MARCH: Chase memoir, Brown; ms Browne review, NYPL-D; consular return, NA-S. APRIL: *Acushnet* abstract, NA-A; 5, NYPL-GL; *Acushnet* abstract, NA-A. MAY: *Wm Wirt* log, HU-BL; *Acushnet* abstract, NA-A. JUNE: 30, certificate on crew-list, ODHS. JULY: [July 22, 1842, MHS-S] *Acushnet* abstract, NA-A; *Wm Wirt* log, HU-BL; *Lima* log, NHA; Chase memoir, Brown. AUGUST: *Acushnet* abstract, NA-A; 11, Morewood; *Lima* log, NHA. SEPTEMBER: 4, MHS-S; [Nov 18 & Aug 26, 1844, MHS-S] *Wm Wirt* log, HU-BL. OCTOBER: *Acushnet* abstract, NA-A; *Joseph Maxwell* log, Vietor; bark *United*

States log, ODHS. NOVEMBER: *Rousseau* log, NBFPL; *Columbus* log, Gardner; *Acushnet* abstract, NA-A. DECEMBER: *Roman* abstract, NA-A; 22, diary, MHS-S; *Acushnet* abstract, NA-A; Chase memoir, Brown

1842 JANUARY: *Acushnet* abstract, NA-A; 10-12, diary, MHS-S; 25, MHS-S. FEBRUARY: *Acushnet* abstract, NA-A; 20, MHS-S. MARCH: diary, MHS-S. APRIL: *Acushnet* abstract, NA-A. MAY: Smith journal, Nicholson; 28, memorandum, HCL-M. JUNE: Smith journal, Nicholson; *Acushnet* abstract, NA-A; 7, German & Ventom affidavits, MiL; Chase memoir, Brown; *Acushnet* abstract, NA-A. JULY: crew-list, ODHS; *Acushnet* abstract, NA-A; sketch of *Acushnet* in *Wm Thompson* log, NBFPL; 13, MHS-S; 27, MHS-S. AUGUST: Byrne affidavit, MiL; Wilson notes, MiL, crew-list, MiL; Ventom affidavit, MiL. SEPTEMBER: 5, MHS-S; Ventom affidavit, MiL; [facsimile] round-robin ms (for *Omoo*), Howe; affidavits, MiL; 22, MiL; affidavits, MiL; 23, MiL; affidavits, MiL; *Reine Blanche* log, AN; 25, MiL; Wilson notes, MiL; affidavit, MiL; engraving courtesy of J. W. Earnshaw, Sydney; Wilson notes, MiL; affidavit, MiL. OCTOBER: 4, draft & reply, MiL; 5, MiL; affidavit, MiL; 14-15-19, transcript in ms of Wise's *Los Gringos*, NA-N; [Nov 19, draft, MiL] 21, MHS-S; 26, MiL; 27, NA-S. NOVEMBER: 2, Armstrong; 19, draft, MiL; bill, MiL.

DECEMBER: 24, draft, NYPL-GL; 31, transcript, NYPL-GL

1843 JANUARY: 2, NYPL-GL; 7, NYPL-GL; Dana journal, MHS-D; 25, NYPL-GL; 28, draft, NYPL-GL; 29, NYPL-GL. FEBRUARY: 18, NYPL-GL; Lowell Smith journal printed in *Lowell and Abigail*, by Mary Dillingham Frear (New Haven, 1934). MARCH: 10, HCL-AB. APRIL: *Lalla Rookh* log, Nicholson. MAY: 2, NA-S; Reynolds journal, Peabody; 18, NA-S; *Acushnet* abstract, NA-A; crew-list, ODHS, 29, Statement of Cases of Relief etc., NA-S; crew-list, NA-T; engraving by Butler, from *Narrative of the U. S. Exploring Expedition during the Years 1838-1842*, Vol 4, by Charles Wilkes (Philadelphia, 1845). JUNE: indenture printed in *The Friend*, Aug 1873; 2, certificate, ODHS; 5, consular return, NA-S; Reynolds journal, Peabody; 20, MHS-S; Reynolds journal, Peabody. JULY: 21, HCL-AB; Lowell Smith journal in *Lowell and Abigail*; Reynolds journal, Peabody; Lowell Smith journal in *Lowell and Abigail*. AUGUST: Reynolds journal, Peabody; muster roll of the *United States*, NA-N; Sharp journal, NA-N; Reynolds journal, Peabody; 19, NA-N. SEPTEMBER: *United States* log, NA-N; *United States* abstract, NA-N. OCTOBER: *United States* abstract, NA-N; diary, MHS-S; *United States* abstract, NA-N

1844 JANUARY: *United States* log, NA-N; 16, NYPL-GL; *United States* abstract, NA-N. FEBRUARY: diary, MHS-S; *United States* abstract, NA-N. MARCH: 22, NYPL-GL; *United States* abstract, NA-N. APRIL-JUNE: *United States* log, NA-N; *United States* abstract, NA-N. JULY: diary, MHS-S; Sharp journal, NA-N; *United States* abstract, NA-N. AUGUST: *United States* abstract, NA-N; 22, THS; *United States* abstract, NA-N; 26, MHS-S; 30, Morewood. SEPTEMBER: 4, Morewood; 13, Morewood; 17, Morewood; 16, LC-Polk; 24, LC-Polk; 29, Morewood. OCTOBER: 3, NA-N; LC-Polk; [facsimile] NYPL-GL; *United States* log, NA-N; pay-roll of the *United States*, NA-N; 17, LC-Polk; Morewood; 22, LC-Polk; 26, LC-Polk; diary, MHS-S. NOVEMBER: 4, LC-Polk; 7, NYPL-GL. DECEMBER: 17, LC-Polk; Tennyson's *Poems*, Metcalf; [facsimile] page of *Typee* draft, NYPL-GL

IV. 1845-1849

1845 JANUARY: 20, NYPL-GL; 25, NYPL-GL. FEBRUARY: assignment, NYPL-GL. MARCH: *Memoirs of the Literary Ladies*, NYPL-GL. APRIL: 2, NA-S; NA-S; draft, NYPL-GL; 3, NA-S; 4, NA-S; 5, NA-S; NA-S; 7, NA-S; Dana journal, MHS-D; 24, NYPL-GL. MAY: 7, LC-Polk; diary, MHS-S; Saunders recollections, NYPL. JUNE: 13, MHS-S. JULY: 16, NA-S; 30, MHS-S. AUGUST: 5, MHS-S; 17, register, NA-C; 24, MHS-S. SEPTEMBER: 1, MHS-S; 16, NYPL-GL; 18, HSP-Buchanan; 26, NYPL-GL. OCTOBER: 10, LC-Polk; 21, Murray V. NOVEMBER: 3, NYPL-GL; HSP-Buchanan; 18, NYPL-GL. DECEMBER: 3, NYPL-GL; *Philosophy of Mystery*, Morewood; diary, MHS-S; 4, Murray V; 6, Murray V; 13, letter-book, LC; 20, Murray V

1846 JANUARY: diary, NYPL-GL; 13, transcript, HCL-M; diary, NYPL-GL; 14, copy, HCL-M; diary, NYPL-GL. FEBRUARY: 3, copy, HCL-M; diary, NYPL-GL; 26, registration, HCL-M; diary, NYPL-GL. MARCH: diary, NYPL-GL; *Narrative* to Maria Melville, Barrett; to Mrs Bancroft, NYPL-RB; 4, diary, MHS-S; diary, NYPL-GL; *Sketches of Bunker Hill*, HCL-M; books charged, BoA; 12, diary, MHS-S; NYPL-GL; 13, letter-book, NYPL-D; crew-list, NA-T; *Typee* to Mrs Tomlinson, Martin; 19, HCL-M; *Typee* to Shaw, Metcalf; to Susan Gansevoort, NYPL-RB; to Maria Peebles, Stralem; 20, NYPL-B; 27, postmarked envelope, NYPL-GL; NYPL-D. APRIL: 3, HCL-M [including facsimile]; 14, transcript, NYPL-D; 15, NYPL-D; 18, notation in *Typee*, LC-RB. MAY: 4, HSP-Buchanan; 14, copy, NA-S; 18, NA-S; 23, BPL; 27, diary, LC-Polk; 29, Morewood. JUNE: 5, NA-S; 6, NA-S; Doheny; letter-book, NA-S; 7, NYPL-GL; 9, letter-book, NA-S; 13, NYPL-GL;

22, in sale of the *Library of the Late Adrian H. Joline* (New York, 1914); diary, NYPL-GL. JULY: 3, NYPL-D; 8?, NYPL-D; lock of Toby's hair, HCL-M; 11, accounts, HCL-M; 15, Murray V; 22, NYPL-D; 23, journal, Craigie-L; 24, transcript in Dauber & Pine Catalogue No. 100; journal, Craigie-L; 28, NYPL-D; journal, Craigie-L; 30, Murray V; 31, HCL-AB. AUGUST: 15, NYPL-B; accounts, HCL-M. SEPTEMBER: 2, Murray V; 4, HCL-M; accounts, HCL-M. OCTOBER: 7, HCL-M; diary, MHS-S. NOVEMBER: 1, MHS-S; diary, MHS-S. DECEMBER: books charged, BoA; diary, MHS-S; 8, NYPL-D; 9, *Journals of Bronson Alcott*, ed., Odell Shepard (Boston, 1938); 10, NYPL-D; accounts, HCL-M; 15, NYPL-D; Saunders recollections, NYPL; agreement, Harpers & HCL-M; 30, Martin; Murray V; accounts, HCL-M; lecture account, clipping, BeA; *New Testament*, HCL-M; *Cyclopædia*, title-page fragment, Metcalf; Twitchell portrait, Metcalf

1847 JANUARY: *Mardi* draft, Howe; 15, NYPL-D; 19, HSP-Gratz; 21, NYPL-D; 29, Murray V; 30, registration, HCL-M; power of attorney, Martin. FEBRUARY: 1, NYPL-D; bill of lading, HCL-M; 3, NYPL-GL; 6, Morewood; draft, NYPL-GL; accounts, HCL-M; 18, diary, RUL; draft, Martin; diary, RUL; 26, Martin; diary, RUL. MARCH: 1, Martin; 6, ms, NYPL-D; diary, MHS-S; books charged, BoA; 12, NYPL-GL; 19, BoA; NYPL-D; diary, RUL; 31, Martin; Murray V. APRIL: 2?, unlocated; 3, diary, RUL; 10, Burton, HCL-M; accounts, HCL-M; 19, diary, RUL; 21, NYPL-D; 23?, NYPL-F; 26, Barrett; *Omoo* to Herman Gansevoort, Rosenbach. MAY: NYPL-GL; 4, journal, NYPL-D; 7, accounts, HCL-M; *Vicar of Wakefield*, Morewood; 10, HCL-E; 14, NYPL-D; 23, diary, MHS-W; 25, deposit, HCL-M; 29, German *Typee* to M, HCL-M. JUNE: diary, MHS-S; 7, *Omoo* to Hope Shaw, Rosenbach; 11, Fields; Fields; diary, NYPL-D; 16, HCL-M. JULY: 8, MHS-D; 10?, NYPL-D; diary, NYPL-D; 11, NYPL-GL; 14/15, NYPL-D; 19, accounts, HCL-M; remembrancer, NYPL-GL; journal, Craigie-L; remembrancer, NYPL-GL; 23,

HCL-M; engraving by Read, *Yankee Doodle*, July 24; diary, NYPL-D; gossip column, clipping, HCL-M. AUGUST: accounts, HCL-M; diary, MHS-S; 2, LC-Curtis; 3?, journal, MHS-D; 4, ms dedication, HCL-M; Bible to Elizabeth Melville, Metcalf; diary, MHS-S; 6, HCL-M; diary, MHS-S; 21, HCL-M; 28, HCL-M; Summer, *Walden* ms, HL. SEPTEMBER: 23, NYPL-D; 26, NYPL-GL; 30, MHS-S; NYPL-D. OCTOBER: diary, NYPL-D; 5, NYPL-D; diary, NYPL-D; clipping & engraving, NYHS; 10, HCL-M; diary, NYPL-D; 29, Murray V. NOVEMBER: 15, NYPL-D; accounts, HCL-M; letter-book, MHS-E; diary, MHS-S; transcript in Paston [Symonds], *At John Murray's* (London, 1932). DECEMBER: accounts, HCL-M; 3, transcript in Symonds; 23, HCL-M; Weeks journal, HCL-FE; memoir in pocket diary (May 1861), Metcalf

1848 JANUARY: 1, Murray V; accounts, HCL-M; 17, right & charge, NYSoL; accounts, HCL-M; 29, HCL-T; 30, MHS-S; *Old Wine*, Scribner; Books Lent, NYPL-D. FEBRUARY: accounts, HCL-M; 4, HCL-M; accounts, HCL-M; 12, HCL-M; 13, HCL-T; 23, HCL-T; books charged, NYSoL. MARCH: Books Lent, NYPL-D; 8, NYPL-D; 9, NYPL-D; 18, NYPL-D; 25, Murray V. MAY: 4, receipt, NYPL-D; 5, HCL-M; 15, NYPL-D. JUNE: 4, MHS-S; 6, HCL-M; 13, NYPL-D; diary; MHS-S; 19, Murray V; accounts, HCL-M; *An Inquiry*, HCL-M. JULY: 4, NYPL-GL; 7, diary, RUL; 12, diary, MHS-S; 13, MHS-D; diary, MHS-S; 14, Craigie-D; 18, MHS-D; 22, NYPL-D; 23-28, Craigie-L. AUGUST: Books Lent, NYPL-D; accounts, HCL-M; NYPL-D; accounts, HCL-M; 14, NYHS-G; 19, HCL-M. SEPTEMBER: accounts, HCL-M; 11, right, NYSoL; *Letters of James Russell Lowell*, ed., C. E. Norton (New York, 1894). NOVEMBER: Wise journal, NA-N; 11, HCL-M; 13, HCL-M; NYPL-D; 14, NYPL-D; 15, Harpers & HCL-M; accounts, HCL-M. DECEMBER: accounts, HCL-M; 7, NYPL-GL; accounts, HCL-M; deed, NYPL-GL; memoir, Metcalf; MHS-S; *Morals*, NYPL-GL; *Workes*, Haverlin; *Fingal*, PTR

1849 JANUARY: diary, MHS-S; 14, *Correspondence of James Fenimore Cooper*, ed., J. F. Cooper (1922); books charged, BoA; 27, HCL-M; 28, Murray V; diary, MHS-S. FEBRUARY: 5, deposit, HCL-M; 6, Murray V; *Typee* rights, HCL-M; diary, MHS-S; accounts, HCL-M; 21, Craigie-L; 23, diary, RUL; 24, NYPL-D; Shakespeare volumes, HCL-M; charge, BoA; diary, RUL; 26, NYPL-GL. MARCH: diary, RUL; 3, NYPL-D; agreement, HCL-M; 5, HCL-M; accounts, HCL-M; charge, BoA; 18, MHS-D; accounts, HCL-M; 28, NYPL-D; MHS-S; 29, NYPL-D; accounts, HCL-M; charge, BoA; 31, ms, NYPL-D. APRIL: accounts, HCL-M; 3, YUL-A; 5, NYPL-D; *Mardi* to Hope Shaw, Rosenbach; 11, NYPL-GL; NYPL-D; deposit, LC-RB; Books Lent, NYPL-D; 16, MHS-D; 17, HCL-M; 19, HCL-M; NYPL-D; 23, HCL-M; accounts, HCL-M; 27, *Mardi* to Cozzens, Scribner; 28, agreement, Harpers & HCL-M; ms, NYPL-D; 30, HCL-M. MAY: 8, *Macready's Reminiscences and Selections from His Diaries and Letters*, ed., W. F. Pollock (London, 1876); 10, *Correspondence of James Fenimore Cooper;* 19, Sedgwick; 24, NYPL-D; accounts, HCL-M; deposit, HCL-M. JUNE: 1, diary, RUL; 5, Martin; 20, unlocated; 28, Bible Record, NYPL-GL; *Mardi* to Powell, HCL-M. JULY: 2, agreement, Harpers & HCL-M; 20, Martin; Books Lent, NYPL-D; accounts, HCL-M. AU-GUST: 18, deposit, HCL-M; 18?, Martin. SEPTEMBER: NYPL-D; 3, letter-book, MHS-E; 5, NYPL-D; MHS-D; HCL-S; 7, Craigie-D; 10, MHS-S; accounts, HCL-M; 12, NYPL-B; NYPL-D; 13, agreement, Harpers & HCL-M; 27 (including facsimile), HCL-M; Craigie-D; 28, NYPL-D; 30, Bible Record, NYPL-GL. OCTOBER: 2?, NYPL-D; 5, NYPL-D; 6, MHS-S; MHS-D; draft preface, corrected transcript, HCL-M; Schiller *Poems,* NYPL-O; 10, NYPL-D; 12, clipping, HCL-M; 18, NYPL-D; journal, HCL-M; 30, HCL-S; journal, HCL-M; journal, HCL-M. NOVEMBER: 8, inscribed *Redburn,* Barrett; journal, HCL-M; 10, NYPL-D; journal, HCL-M; broadside, Binnian; journal, HCL-M; 14, NYPL-D; journal, HCL-M; 20, Scribner; journal, HCL-M; 22, diary, MHS-S; journal, HCL-M; 23, deposit, LC-RB; journal, HCL-M. DECEMBER: 2, NYPL-D; MHS-D; journal, HCL-M; 10, NYPL-D; journal, HCL-M; 14, transcript in *The Home Journal,* 12 Jan 1850; NYPL-D; journal, HCL-M; 17, agreement, HCL-M; journal, HCL-M; Chatterton, NYPL-B; journal, HCL-M; 19, HCL-M; engraving, *Illustrated London News,* 5 Jan 1856; journal, HCL-M; 24, NYPL-D; 21, accounts, HCL-M; journal, HCL-M; 24, NYPL-D; journal, HCL-M; 25, Goethe *Auto-Biography,* Murray; journal, HCL-M; *Redburn* to Herman Gansevoort, NYPL-RB; *Mardi* to Rowe, HL

v. 1850-1854

1850 JANUARY: Beaumont & Fletcher folio, HCL-M; Davenant folio, Rhodebeck; 9, deposit, HCL-M; 13, Sedgwick; 15, receipt, MHS-S; NYPL-D; 18, MHS-S; journal, HCL-M; *Final Memorials,* PTR; Chatterton, NYPL-B. FEBRUARY: 2, *Mardi* to Allan Melville, NYPL-A; *Mardi* to Evert Duyckinck, NYPL-RB; *Hudibras,* NYPL-RB; *Picture of London,* NYPL-G; 4?, Essex; 10?, HCL-M; 16, NYPL-D; accounts, HCL-M; [March 1, NYPL-D] Books Lent, NYPL-D. MARCH: 6, NYPL-D; 7, NYPL-D; 13, NYPL-GL; 16, ms, NYPL-D; 23, Bible, NYPL-O; 26, deposit, HCL-M; NYPL-D; NYPL-D. APRIL: 17, membership, NYSoL; 21, journal, Craigie-L; certificate, NYSoL; *Typee* & *Omoo* to Elizabeth Melville, HCL-M; 29, charge & Scoresby, NYSoL; 30, HCL-M. MAY: 1, MHS-D; 14, NYPL-D; shares, NYSoL; *White-Jacket* to Langhorne, Vincent; 21, accounts, HCL-M; 28, HCL-W. JUNE: 27, Martin; Books Lent, NYPL-D. JULY: 8, NYPL-D; 10, Beale, Brown; *Constitution* log, NA-N; *History of the County of Berkshire,* Morewood; *Mosses,* HCL-M; *History,* Morewood; 20, NYPL-D; *Mosses,* HCL-M; *Summary View,* UVL; Selfridge ms, NA-N. AUGUST: 2, NYPL-D; 3, NYPL-D; 4, NYPL-D; 5, journal, MoL; 6, NYPL-D; 7, NYPL-D; 8,

NYPL-D; journal, MoL; 9, NYPL-D; Craigie-L; G. H. Putnam, *A Memoir of George Palmer Putnam* (New York, 1903); 10, MHS-S; ms, NYPL-D; 13, NYPL-D; 15, NYPL-D; Browning ms, HCL-M; 16, NYPL-D; 17, ms, NYPL-D; copy-book, BCL; 18, BCL; *Mosses*, HCL-M; 24, NYPL-D; HL; 29, NYPL-D; NYPL-D; transcript by Rose Hawthorne Lathrop, in *Memories of Hawthorne* (Boston, 1897). SEPTEMBER: 1, unlocated; NYPL-D; transcript by Julian Hawthorne, in *Hawthorne and His Wife* (Boston, 1888); 3, NYPL-B; engraving of the Hawthornes' Lenox cottage, *Harper's Magazine*, Nov 1871; 4, NYPL-B; journal, MoL; 9, NYPL-D; 10-13, diary, MHS-S; 14, note in expense-account, HCL-M; diary, MHS-S; 27, Marie Hansen Taylor & H. E. Scudder, *The Life and Letters of Bayard Taylor* (1884); 23, NYPL-D; accounts, HCL-M; Books Lent, NYPL-D; indenture, HCL-M; *Book of Common Prayer*, HCL-M; 30, NYPL-D. OCTOBER: 1, NYPL-D; 6, NYPL-D; 7, transfer, NYSoL; 17, MHS-S. NOVEMBER: memorandum, HCL-M; diary, MHS-S. DECEMBER: 30, charge, BoA; clipping, scrapbook, Craigie-L

1851 JANUARY: *Animal Kingdom*, BeA; 7, MHS-S; *Iphigenia*, unlocated; diary, NYPL-B; *Twice-Told Tales*, HCL-M; diary, NYPL-B; 27, NYPL-B; transcript in American Art Association Catalogue of Sale on April 28-29, 1924. FEBRUARY: accounts, HCL-M; 3, diary, NYPL-B; 12, NYPL-D; *Mariner's Chronicle*, HCL-FI; Brown; *Globe*, Rosenbach; *New England Primer*, HCL-M; diary, NYPL-B; 14, NYPL-D; *Mariner's Chronicle*, HCL-Fi; diary, NYPL-GL; 26, NYPL-D. APRIL: Chase, Brown; *Globe*, Rosenbach; 9, HCL-C; diary, NYPL-B; *House of the Seven Gables*, HCL-M; 16?, transcripts by G. P. Lathrop, in *Study of Hawthorne* (1876), & by Julian Hawthorne, in *Hawthorne and His Wife;* 27, NYPL-D; 29, N Pearson; 30, HCL-M. MAY: 1, note in expense-account, HCL-M; petition, NA-SEN; memoir, Metcalf. JUNE: 1?, transcript by Julian Hawthorne, in *Hawthorne and His Wife;* diary, NYPL-GL; 14, charge, NYSoL; 29, ms transcript by Julian Hawthorne; 30, HCL-M. JULY:

3-7, diary, MHS-S; 4, Hoadley ms, NYPL-GL; 7, Burton, HCL-M; 20, Martin; 22, transcript in HCL-M; diary, MHS-S; diary, MHS-D; 28, NYPL-D; 29, diary, MHS-S; agreement, HCL-M; MHS-S; valuation book, PCH. AUGUST: journal, MoL; *Continental Annual*, unlocated; *Complete Horse-Man*, Scribner; 3, HCL-M; journal, MoL; 7, NYPL-D; 8, NYPL-D; journal, MoL; NYPL-D; journal, MoL; 9, journal, MoL; 11, NYPL-D; 13, agreement, HCL-M; NYPL-D; 29, NYPL-D. SEPTEMBER: [facsimile] HCL-M; Murray; draft, HCL-M; 12, agreement, Harpers & HCL-M; diary, MHS-S; 19, unlocated; 25, HCL-M; 30, accounts, HCL-M. OCTOBER: 8, NYPL-D; deposit, HCL-M; engraving from Goodrich, *Man upon the Sea . . .* (Philadelphia, 1858); 22, HCL-M; certificate transcript, PCH; 27, NYPL-D. NOVEMBER: 7?, NYPL-D; *Wonder Book*, HCL-M; NYPL-D; 10, accounts, HCL-M; diary, MHS-S; journal, Craigie-L; 21, NYPL-D; 17?, transcript by Rose Hawthorne Lathrop, in *Memories of Hawthorne;* deposit, HCL-M; NYPL-D; presented engraving, Metcalf; journal, MoL; 22, NYPL-D; accounts, HCL-M; 28, NYPL-D. DECEMBER: 1, NYPL-D; 3, receipt, MHS-S; 11, NYPL-D; 19, HSP-Gratz; 22, MHS-P; 24, NYPL-D; 28, NYPL-D; *Slovenly Peter*, HCL-M; *White-Jacket* to Robertson, Lilly

1852 JANUARY: 4, NYPL-D; NYPL-D; 8, Martin; 9?, NYPL-D; diary, MHS-S; 21, letterpress copy, HCL-M; *Redburn* to Maria Melville, NYPL-B; *Whale* to Lemuel Shaw, Rosenbach. FEBRUARY: accounts, HCL-M; 8, NYPL-B; 9, accounts, HCL-M; diary, MHS-S; 14, NYPL-D; 18, MHS-S; 20, agreement, Harpers & HCL-M. MARCH: 1, MHS-S; 4, statement, Martin (cut courtesy of *The Colophon*); 15, printed in *The Pioneer*, April 1855; 19, charge, NYSoL. APRIL: charge, BoA; 16, Martin. MAY: 2, MHS-S; 20, MHS-S; 30, MHS-S; [Oct 4, 1892, YUL-V]. JUNE: 7, MHS-S; militia roll, PCH. JULY: date-book, Metcalf; diary, MHS-S; *History of Nantucket*, Chambliss; 7, YUL-A; memoir in Chase, Brown; 13, register, Forbes; 14, HCL-M; deposit, HCL-M; diary, MHS-S; 17, N Pearson; 19, original petitions,

NA-Sen; 28, HCL-M; valuation book, PCH. August: 9-11, deposits, LC-RB; 10, MHS-S; *Pierre* to the Hawthornes, Rosenbach; HCL-M; 17, MHS-S; 29, MHS-S; 31, MHS-S; transcript in *Memories of Hawthorne*. September: 27, MHS-S; diary, MHS-S; [Oct 4, MHS-S] diary, MHS-S. October: 6, NYPL-GL; 9, draft, NYPL-GL; 25, NYPL-B. November: 15, accounts, HCL-M; 22, MHS-S; transcript in *Hawthorne and His Wife;* charge, BoA; 14, MHS-S

1853 January: 7, MHS-S; 10, sold by Mary Benjamin, 1950. February: 1, Scribner; 14, HCL-M. March: accounts, HCL-M; *Illustrated Magazine of Art*, NYPL-O. April: journal, Craigie-L; 20, NYPL-GL; NA-S; 21, draft, NYPL-GL; NA-S; 22, NA-S; NA-S; draft, NYPL-GL; 25, NYPL-GL; 26, NA-S; 29, LC-Cushing; 30, LC-Cushing. May: 3, LC-Cushing; 4, NYPL-GL; NA-S; NA-S; 5, NA-S; 10, draft, MHS-D; HCL-M; MHS-S; 24, MHS-S; HCL-M; NA-S; 25, MHS-S; will, MHS-S. June: 3, MHS-S; Irving's works, HCL-M; 11, list, NYPL-GL; diary, NYPL-GL; HCL-M; 14, diary, MHS-W; LC-Cushing; 16, MHS-S; 28, militia roll, PCH; 29, NYPL-GL. July: [Oct 9, draft, NYPL-GL] 11, NYHS; 25, *Chapel of the Hermits*,

NYPL-RB; MHS-S. August: valuation book, PCH; 10, HCL-M; paper-knife, Peirson; 26, HCL-M; *Light of Nature Pursued*, unlocated. September: 23, NYPL-GL. October: 10, NYPL-D. November: 8, ledger, Putnam; 19, MHS-S. December: 6, ledger, Putnam

1854 January: *Pilgrims of the Rhine*, NYPL-O; *Tanglewood Tales*, HCL-M; *Whale* to Hoadley, NYPL-B; Chatterton, NYPL-B; 7, note in expense-account, HCL-M; 25, NYPL-D; *Seneca's Morals*, NYPL-GL. February: 6, noted in *History of the Great Western Sanitary Fair* (Cincinnati, 1864); 20, Rosenbach. March: ledger, Putnam; 27, MHS-S; 29, ledger, PCH. April: ledger, Putnam; accounts, HCL-M. May: ledger, Putnam; 12, HCL-M; 13, HCL-M. June: 7, transcript by G. H. Putnam, in *A Memoir of George Palmer Putnam* (New York, 1903); militia roll, PCH. July: *Modern Housewife's Receipt Book*, HCL-M; ledger, Putnam; charge, BoA; valuation book, PCH. August: ledger, Putnam. September: ledger, Putnam. October: blotter, NYPL-D; 2, MHS-S; accounts, HCL-M. November: ledger, Putnam; 3, noted in sale of Joline Library; 28, NYPL-GL. December: ledger, Putnam; journal, MoL

vi. 1855-1859

1855 January: ledger, Putnam; 23, ledger, PCH. February: ledger, Putnam; memoir, Metcalf. March: ledger, Putnam; 8, MHS-S; 9, transcript, HCL-C; deposit, LC-RB; Byron's works, Morewood. April: 12, accounts, HCL-M; HCL-D; 17, HCL-D; 19, *Israel Potter* to Herman Gansevoort, NYPL-RB; HCL-D; 20, HCL-D; clipping, scrapbook, NYPL-GL. June: 16, diary, NYPL-GL; 18, HCL-D; 19, HCL-D; 25, NYPL-GL; memoir, Metcalf. July: 4, diary, NYPL-GL; 31, HCL-D. August: valuation book, PCH; 10, NYPL-GLF; 21, HSP-Dreer; Jones journal, NYPL; 28, accounts, HCL-M. September: 7, NYPL-P; HCL-D; 14, HCL-D; diary, MHS-S; 17, MHS-S; 18, NYPL-GL; *Don Quixote*, HCL-M. October: accounts, HCL-M; 24, MHS-S; 27-29, remembrancer, NYPL-GL

1856 January: 2, HCL-D; 7, HCL-D. February: 16, YUL-A; 20, contract, HCL-M. March: 6, NA-N; accounts, HCL-M; agreement, HCL-M; 24, NYPL-GLF. April: 1, MHS-S; 5, HCL-M; Dana journal, MHS-D. May: 12, ledger, PCH; registry, LC-RB; 30, NYPL-GL. June: 16, HCL-M; valuation book, PCH. July: 12, HCL-M; 15, MHS-S; ms fragment, HCL-M. August: remembrancer, NYPL-GL; *Piazza Tales* to Herman Gansevoort, Morewood; 4, MHS-S; remembrancer, NYPL-GL; 8, HCL-AB; remembrancer, NYPL-GL; diary, NYPL-GL; 30, HCL-M. September: 1, MHS-S; 2, HCL-AB; 5, letter-book, HCL-AB; 18, NA-N; *Piazza Tales* to Augusta Melville, NYPL-RB; remembrancer, NYPL-GL. October: diary, NYPL-D; 6, NYPL-D; 7, NYPL-GL; passport, Metcalf; 8, NYPL-D;

diary, NYPL-D; 9, draft, NYPL-GL; 10-11, agreement, HCL-M; memoir, Metcalf; diary, NYPL-D; 19, HCL-M; journal, HCL-M [Nov 11, NYPL-GL]; journal, HCL-M; 25, MHS-S; journal, HCL-M; [Nov 23, MHS-S] journal, HCL-M; agreement, HCL-M; erased note, journal, HCL-M. NOVEMBER: journal, HCL-M; business card, NYPL-GL; journal, HCL-M; Hawthorne journal, MoL; journal, HCL-M; Hawthorne journal, MoL; 11, NYPL-GL; journal, HCL-M; engraving, *Illustrated London News*, Oct 4, 1856; Hawthorne journal, MoL; journal, HCL-M; passport, Metcalf; journal, HCL-M; Hawthorne journal, MoL; journal, HCL-M; Hawthorne journal, MoL; journal, HCL-M; Hawthorne journal, MoL; journal, HCL-M; 18, NYPL-D; journal, HCL-M; 26, NYPL-GL; journal, HCL-M; 27, draft, NYPL-GL; journal, HCL-M; 28, NYPL-GL; journal, HCL-M; 30, NYPL-B. DECEMBER: journal, HCL-M; 7, HCL-M; journal, HCL-M; 15, contract, HCL-M; journal, HCL-M; 25-27, HCL-M; journal, HCL-M; 29, HCL-M; journal, HCL-M

1857 JANUARY: journal, HCL-M; passport, Metcalf; journal, HCL-M; engraving Dead Sea, NYPL-PC; passport, Metcalf; journal, HCL-M; passport, Metcalf; 29, NA-N. FEBRUARY: journal, HCL-M; passport, Metcalf; journal, HCL-M; passport, Metcalf; journal, HCL-M; passport, Metcalf; journal, HCL-M; engraving of Guido's portrait of Beatrice Cenci, Sukel; journal, HCL-M. MARCH: journal, HCL-M; 3, MHS-S; journal, HCL-M; passport, Metcalf; journal, HCL-M; 20, agreement, HCL-M; 24, MHS-S; passport, Metcalf; journal, HCL-M; Valery, NYPL-O; journal, HCL-M; passport, Metcalf; journal, HCL-M; 30, Valery, NYPL-O; passport, Metcalf; journal, HCL-M; 31, NYPL-D. APRIL: Valery, NYPL-O; journal, HCL-M; 7, NYPL-GL; journal, HCL-M; 9, draft, NYPL-GL; journal, HCL-M; 15, NYPL-GL; journal, HCL-M; 17, draft, NYPL-GL; draft, NYPL-GL; MHS-S; journal, HCL-M; passport, Metcalf; journal, HCL-M; 21, MHS-S; journal, HCL-M. MAY: 1, MHS-S; journal, HCL-M; 2, deposit, LC-RB; journal, HCL-M; Valery, NYPL-O; journal,

HCL-M; 11, MHS-S; 13, HCL-M; memoir, Metcalf; diary, NYPL-GL. JUNE: 2, MHS-S; 22, NYPL-GL; [July 9, NYPL-GL] valuation book, PCH; accounts, HCL-M. AUGUST: 19, transcript in *Atlantic Monthly*, Nov 1907; 31, ledger, PCH. SEPTEMBER: 4, Morewood; 9, NYPL-GL; 10, Morewood; 12, diary, MHS-S; 15, Fields; 29, ledger, PCH; clipping, HCL-M. OCTOBER: 12, HCL-M; 31, MHS-S. NOVEMBER: 19, NYPL-GL; diary, MHS-S; 23, NYPL-GL; 27, BM; copy in G Gansevoort's letter to Peter Gansevoort, Apr 9, 1858, NYPL-GL. DECEMBER: 9, expense-account, HCL-M; NYPL-GL; 11, expense-account, HCL-M; 17, NYPL-GL; expense-account, HCL-M; diary, NYPL-GL

1858 JANUARY: expense-account, HCL-M; 9, HCL-M; [Nov 14, 1892, HCL-M] 12, Cash Book, DPL; 21, accounts, HCL-M; expense-account, HCL-M; information from Lesley Frost. FEBRUARY: expense-account, HCL-M; 20, draft, NYPL-GL; charge, BoA. MARCH: memoir, Metcalf. APRIL: 9, NYPL-GL. JUNE: accounts, HCL-M. JULY: 5, NYPL-D; 7, transcript, NYPL-D; 15, NYPL-D; valuation book, PCH; 26, transcript, NYPL-D. AUGUST: 14, diary, MHS-S; 24, NYPL-D; diary, MHS-S. SEPTEMBER: 14, NYPL-D; 17, transcript, NYPL-D; 19, MHS-S. OCTOBER: 4, transcript, NYPL-D. NOVEMBER: Chapman's Homer, HCL-M; 6, NYPL-D; 8, draft, HCL-M. DECEMBER: 8, 13, NYPL-D; 29, transcript, NYPL-D

1859 JANUARY: 30, NYPL-D; 31, transcript, NYPL-D. FEBRUARY: 1, HCL-M; 4, HCL-M; 7, NYPL-GL; 8, clipping, BeA; NYPL-GL; 12, ledger, PCH; Fields; 13, Morewood; 18, diary, NYPL-GL; 25, minutes, SHSW; 26, diary, NYPL-GL; clipping, HCL-M. MARCH: 2, diary, in *Collections of the Illinois State Historical Library*, XX; 26, account, HCL-M. APRIL: 15, deeds, BRD; 20, journal, Gulick, transcript by Mentor Williams; Coan letter printed in Boston *Literary World*, Dec 19, 1891; 23, deed, BRD. MAY: 18, NYPL-GLF; 23, NYPL-GL. JUNE: 18-20, accounts, HCL-M; 23, diary, NYPL-D. JULY: 6, ms, Metcalf; 30, NYPL-D; Emerson's *Poems*, Scrib-

ner. AUGUST: accounts, HCL-M. SEP-
TEMBER: 6, NYPL-D; accounts, HCL-M;
13, NYPL-D; *Hesperides*, HCL-M; *Ballads*, HCL-M. OCTOBER: 7-13, accounts,

HCL-M; [Jan 4, 1860, NYPL-GL]. No-
VEMBER: Books Lent, NYPL-D; 21,
NYPL-D; 30, HCL. DECEMBER: 14,
NYPL-D; 29, MHS-S

VII. 1860-1869

1860 JANUARY: diary, NYPL-D; Books
Lent, NYPL-D. FEBRUARY: Marvell,
HCL-M. APRIL: 9, HCL-M; NYPL-D;
18, Bible Record, NYPL-GL; *Bible in the
Family*, Morewood; 30, ledger, PCH.
MAY: 15, transcript [by Samuel Shaw],
HCL-M; conveyances, MHS-S; 21,
NYPL-D; 22, transcript [by Elizabeth
Melville], NYPL-D; ms "Reasonable
Constitution," HCL-M; *Marble Faun*,
HCL-M; 27, NYPL-D; ambrotype, Met-
calf; 28, NYPL-D; journal, HCL-M.
JUNE: 1, NYPL-D; 4, NYPL-D; journal,
HCL-M; valuation book, PCH; journal,
HCL-M; 19, NYPL-D; 23, NYPL-D;
journal, HCL-M; *Sketches of Life*,
NYPL-GLF. JULY: journal, HCL-M;
Marble Faun, HCL-M; journal, HCL-M.
AUGUST: journal, HCL-M; ms "Admiral
of the White," HCL-M. SEPTEMBER: 1,
HCL-M; 2, HCL-M; Béranger, NYPL-
GL; 16, HCL-M; 19, Schiller, NYPL-O;
22, Elizabeth Melville's note on envelope
postmarked Oct 19, HCL-M. OCTOBER:
Chapman's Homer, HCL-M; *New Testa-
ment*, HCL-M; drawing & note [on re-
verse], unlocated; *English Songs*, HCL-
M; 16, HCL-M; 19, postmarked envelope,
HCL-M. NOVEMBER: passenger-list,
NA-T; engraving *North Star*, *Frank Les-
lie's Popular Monthly*; 5, NYPL-GL; 8,
Schiller, HCL-M; 23, NYPL-D; 24,
HCL-M; 25, ms "To Tom," HCL-M

1861 JANUARY: 1, Poe *Works*, unlocated;
4, HCL-M; 14, HCL-M; 16, HCL-M; 17,
NYPL-D; 24, Morewood. FEBRUARY:
diaries, NYPL-GL; 13, HCL-M; 16, receipt, MHS-S; 20, Morewood; Morewood; 28, NA-S. MARCH: 11, NA-S; 12,
NYPL-GL; 14, NA-S; 15, NYPL-GL;
diary, NYPL-GL; 19, NA-S; NA-S;
NA-S; 20, MHS-D; RRL; NYPL-GL;
HCL-S; NYPL-D; [Apr 18, NYPL-GL]
21, NA-S; NA-S; HCL-S; HCL-S; 23,
draft, NYPL-GL; 24-25, HCL-M; 25,
NA-S; 28, NA-S; NA-S; 30, journal, tran-

script by Frederic Hathaway Chase, in
Lemuel Shaw (Boston, 1918). APRIL: 8,
HCL-M; 9, Shelley, unlocated, noted by
R. Weaver; Spenser, Morewood. JUNE: 3,
SC-PR; *Bijou*, HCL-M; militia roll, PCH;
28, NYPL-D. JULY: diary, NYPL-D;
Thomson, unlocated, noted by R.
Weaver; diary, NYPL-D; 5, transcript,
NYPL-D; 6, accounts, HCL-M; 11,
HCL-M; 13, NYPL-GL; valuation book,
PCH. AUGUST: 10, NYPL-GL; Tenny-
son *Works*, NYPL-GL; 15, NYPL-GL;
19, ledger, PCH. SEPTEMBER: 5, NYPL-
GL; 17, NYPL-GL; 26, ledger, PCH.
DECEMBER: 12, NYPL-D; diary, NYPL-
GL; 26, NYPL-GL; *Voyage to the North
Pacific*, HCL-M

1862 JANUARY: 6, NYPL-GL; diary,
MHS-S. FEBRUARY: 1, NYPL-D; Hood,
NYPL-O; Moore, HCL-M; Mangan,
HCL-M; Fergusson, NYPL-O; Disraeli,
NYPL-O; *Germany*, HCL-M; Heine,
NYPL-O; 18, NYPL-GL; NYPL-GL; 20,
NYPL-GL; Emerson *Essays*, HCL-M; 31,
accounts, HCL-M. APRIL: White, HCL-
M; 5, NYPL-GL; Arnold *Poems*, Mur-
ray; Collins, unlocated, noted by R.
Weaver; Churchill, HCL-M; 15, NYPL-
GL; 26, NYPL-D; *Germany*, HCL-M.
MAY: diary, MHS-S; Spenser, More-
wood; 19, NYPL-GL; 25, HCL-M. JUNE:
militia roll, PCH; ms "Immolated," HCL-
M. AUGUST: valuation book, PCH; 8,
memorandum by Peter Gansevoort,
NYPL-GL; 20, ledger, PCH; diary,
MHS-S. SEPTEMBER: diary, NYPL-GL;
estate, SC-PR; *La Bruyère*, YUL-V. Oc-
TOBER: Moore, HCL-M. NOVEMBER: 11,
NYPL-GL. DECEMBER: 10, HCL-M; Mrs
Hemans, HCL-M

1863 JANUARY: 21, NYPL-GL. FEBRU-
ARY: 8, NYPL-GL; 13, NYPL-GL;
NYPL-GL; 17, NYPL-GL; diary, MHS-
S. MARCH: 6, BPL; 16, accounts, HCL-M.
JUNE: 12, draft, NYPL-GL; 27, diary,
NYPL-GL. JULY: militia roll, PCH;

diaries, MHS-S. AUGUST: diary, MHS-S; valuation book, PCH; accounts, HCL-M; 17, ledger, PCH. SEPTEMBER: 13, NYPL-D; Bible Record, NYPL-O. OCTOBER: 6, accounts, HCL-M; memoir, Metcalf; memorandum, Metcalf; 20, HCL-M. DECEMBER: 10, Pleadwell; 15, transcript in *History of the Great Western Sanitary Fair;* 31, NYPL-D

1864 FEBRUARY: accounts, HCL-M; 29, NYPL-GL; diary, NYPL-GL. APRIL: 21, NYPL-GL; 8, LC-Lathers; Morewood; pass [facsimile], Morewood; 13, NYPL-GL; memoir, Metcalf; 25, NYPL-GL; 12, diary, MHS-S; 13, Morewood. MAY: 3, NYPL-GL; 10, NYPL-GL; 24, NYPL-GL; ms "Monody," HCL-M. JUNE: Mrs Browning, NYPL-O. JULY: 20, NYPL-GL; 21, NYPL-B. AUGUST: accounts, HCL-M; 4, NYPL-GL; 19, NYPL-GL; diary, MHS-S. SEPTEMBER: 9, NYPL-GL. OCTOBER: 4, NYPL-GL. NOVEMBER: 3, NYPL-GL; 23, NYPL-GL

1865 FEBRUARY: 24, HCL-M. APRIL: 9, Rosenbach. MAY: 3, NYPL-GL; *Mosses,* HCL-M. JULY: 5, NYPL-GL. AUGUST: 17, NYPL-GL; 18, accounts, HCL-M. SEPTEMBER: 12, NYPL-GL; 26, NYPL-GL. OCTOBER: 7, NYPL-GL; 12, NYPL-GL; 19, accounts, HCL-M. NOVEMBER: accounts, HCL-M. DECEMBER: 21, NYPL-GL; *Harper's Weekly* volumes, Chapin; *Ethel's Story,* Binnian; Ruskin, NYPL-O

1866 JANUARY: 9, NYPL-GL; 11, accounts, HCL-M; 20, NYPL-GL; 29, NYPL-GL. FEBRUARY: 8, NYPL-GL. MARCH: 6, NYPL-GL; 23, NYPL-GL; Jefferson broadside, Binnian. APRIL: 7, NYPL-GL. MAY: *Vatican Sculptures,* HCL-M; 30, NYPL-GL. JUNE: diary, LC; memo, HCL-M. JULY: accounts, HCL-M; 20, NYPL-GL; 23, NYPL-GL; accounts, HCL-M. AUGUST: 2, NYPL-GL; diary, NYPL-GL; 17, deposit, LC-RB; *Battle-Pieces* to Helen Griggs, NYPL-B; to Maria Melville, Hunley; to Hope Shaw, HCL-M; to Elizabeth Melville, Metcalf. SEPTEMBER: 1, NYPL-GL; 2, NYPL-GL; 17, NYPL-GL. NOVEMBER: 24, NYPL-GL; 28, NA-T. DECEMBER: 5, NA-T; 7, HCL-M; *Battle-Pieces* to

Potter, Barrett; "Philip" transcript, NYPL

1867 JANUARY: 8, NYPL-GL. FEBRUARY: 9, NYPL-GL. MARCH: 2, NYPL-GL; 11, NYPL-GL; 19, NYPL-GL. APRIL: 19, NYPL-GL. MAY: Camoens, Matthiessen. JULY: 30, NYPL-GL; 31, Morewood. AUGUST: 16, NYPL-GL. SEPTEMBER: 12, NY-HR; MHS-S; 13, transcribed fragment by Hoadley, in *Boston Weekly Advertiser*[?], clipping, NYPL-GL; 19, NYPL-GL; 15, NYPL-GL; 16, NYPL-GL; Faber's *Hymns,* HCL-M; *Battle-Pieces* to Bartlett, Francis; 29, NYPL-GL. OCTOBER: 10, Woodlawn; 12, Bryant *Poems,* NYPL-O; 31, authorization, YUL-A. NOVEMBER: 13, NYPL-GL; 20, NYPL-GL; 21, NYPL-GL; 24, NYPL-GL; 25, NYPL-GL. DECEMBER: 9, NYPL-GL; 23, NYPL-GL; transcript in Goodspeed catalogue #387, June 1945

1868 JANUARY: *Our Old Home,* HCL-M. FEBRUARY: accounts, HCL-M. MARCH: 5, clipping, Metcalf; 23, NYPL-GL. APRIL: 22, *Shelley Memorials,* HCL-M. MAY: 6, NYPL-GL; [June 1, NYPL-GL] 29, NYPL-GL. JUNE: [July 13, NYPL-GL] diary, NYPL-GL. AUGUST: 14, NYPL-GL; diary, NYPL-GL; 19, NYPL-GL; diary, NYPL-GL; 18, NYPL-GL; 30, NYPL-D. SEPTEMBER: 9, NYPL-GL; 14, fragment, HCL-M; *Men of the Time,* Sealts; *Gulistan,* YUL-V. OCTOBER: 10, inscription, NYPL-RB; diary, NYPL-GL. NOVEMBER: 10, NYPL-GL; NYPL-GL. DECEMBER: [Jan 4, 1869, NYPL-GL]

1869 JANUARY: *Rule and Exercises,* Hennesey. FEBRUARY: 10, NYPL-GL; 23, NYPL-GL. MARCH: 13, NYPL-GL; engraving of Madison Square, NYPL-PC. APRIL: 1, NYPL-GL; 16, NYPL-GL; 30, NYPL-GL. MAY: 8, ms, Metcalf; 13, Murray. JUNE: 1, Columbia; 4, NYPL-GL; 9, NYPL-GL; diary, NYPL-GL; 26, NYPL-GL; 25, NYPL-D; engraving of Sailors' Snug Harbor, NYPL-PC. JULY: *Essays in Criticism,* HCL-M. AUGUST: 4-9, Praed, NYPL-GL; 16-19, Morewood; 23, NYPL-GL. SEPTEMBER: 29, NYPL-GL. OCTOBER: 8, NYPL-GL; 28, NYPL-GL. NOVEMBER: NYPL-GL; 27, NYPL-GL. DECEMBER: 7, HCL-M

VIII. 1870-1880

1870 JANUARY: 18, clipping, HCL-M; 27, NYPL-GL; 31, NYPL-GLF. FEBRUARY: 1, NYPL-GL; [Oct 28, 1891, HCL-M] 8, diary in Stoddard's *Recollections*. MARCH: 21, NYPL-GL; *Buried Cities*, Metcalf; 3, NYPL-GL; Schiller albums, Metcalf. APRIL: *Sinai and Palestine*, NYPL-O. MAY: 5, transcript [by Hoadley], NYPL-GL; *Round Table*, YUL-V. JUNE: 3, NYPL-GL; Gilchrist's *Blake*, unlocated, described by J. H. Birss in *Notes and Queries*, 5 May 1934; 8, *American Notebooks*, HCL-M; 12, NYPL-GL; 26, NYPL-GL. JULY: diary, MHS-S; 30, NYPL-GL; *Scarlet Letter* & Robinson, HCL-M; 25, NYPL-D; 23, NYPL-GL. AUGUST: 14, NYPL-GL; diary, MHS-S; 22, NYPL-GL; 29, NYPL-GL. SEPTEMBER: Davis journal, Metropolitan; Burns *Poems*, Morewood. NOVEMBER: accounts, HCL-M; *Rasselas*, NYPL-O; 7, NYPL-GL; 17, NYPL-GL; *Conduct of Life*, HCL-M. DECEMBER: *Eugénie Grandet*, NYPL-O; *Castara*, PTR; 19, NYPL-GL; 25, *Walks about the City*, NYPL-GLF; *Characteristics* & *Holy Grail*, HCL-M; 25, *The Letters of Dante Gabriel Rossetti to His Publisher, F. S. Ellis* (London, 1928); Reynolds, NYPL-O

1871 JANUARY: *Snow-Image*, HCL-M; 7, NYPL-GL; 15, NYPL-GL; 20, *Sonnets*, HCL-M; *In Memoriam*, NYPL-O. FEBRUARY: Arnold *New Poems*, HCL-M. MARCH: *Art Idea*, NYPL-GLF. APRIL: 8, NYPL-GL. MAY: 17, NYPL-GL; 22, *In Memoriam*, NYPL-O; 28, NYPL-GL; *Greece*, HCL-M. OCTOBER: 25, Morewood; MHS-S; Alger, HCL-M. NOVEMBER: draft, NYPL-GL; 13, NYPL-GL. DECEMBER: 25, Wellington & Quarles, HCL-M; 26, NYPL-GL; *Works of Eminent Masters*, HCL-M

1872 JANUARY: 1, NYPL-GL; 9, NYPL-GL. FEBRUARY: 3, NYPL-GL; 12, NYPL-GL; 11, NYPL-GL; diary, NYPL-GL; 17?, NYPL-GL; 18, NYPL-GL; 21, NYPL-GL; 26, NYPL-GL. MARCH: 23, *French and Italian Notebooks*, HCL-M. APRIL: diary, NYPL-GL; 3, Pepys, NYPL-GL; diary, NYPL-GL; 22, HCL-M; 30, J Pearson. MAY: 6, NYPL-GL.

JUNE: diary, NYPL-GL; accounts, HCL-M; 13, NYPL-GL. JULY: 17, NYPL-GL; fragment, Metcalf. AUGUST: 1, *Septimius Felton*, HCL-M; 4, NYPL-GL; 31, NYPL-GL. SEPTEMBER: 2, HCL-M. NOVEMBER: 5, NYPL-GL; 20, NYPL-GL; 30, fragment, NYPL-GL. DECEMBER: 6, NYPL-GL; 7, NYPL-GL; 10, NYPL-GL; 9, NYPL-GL; 29, NYPL-GL; [Jan. 2, 1873, NYPL-GL] Davenant, Rhodebeck

1873 JANUARY: 9, NA-T. FEBRUARY: 23, HCL-M. MARCH: 3, HCL-M. APRIL: 4, NYPL-GL; 25, HCL-M. MAY: 26, NYPL-GL. JUNE: 15, NYPL-GL; 28, NYPL-GL. JULY: 2, NYPL-GL; 16, NYPL-GL; 20, NYPL-GL. AUGUST: 18, NYPL-GL; 15, NYPL-GL. SEPTEMBER: 8, YUL-A; 23, NYPL-GL. NOVEMBER: 14, NYPL-GL; 23, NYPL-GL. DECEMBER: *Pearls*, HCL-M; Shelley *Essays*, HCL-M; *Songs from the Dramatists*, NYPL-O

1874 MARCH: Burgess, NYPL-O; 14 HCL-M. JUNE: 11, NYPL-GL; 16, NYPL-GL; 20, NYPL-GL; ms "Iris," HCL-M. AUGUST: 14, NYPL-GL; 21, NYPL-GL. SEPTEMBER: *Ballads*, HCL-M; Calderon, NYPL-O. OCTOBER: 29, NYPL-GL; NYPL-GL; NYPL-GL. NOVEMBER: 18, NYPL-GL; diary, MHS-S. DECEMBER: 22, HCL-M; *Handbook of Engraved Gems*, NYPL-GLF; HCL-M

1875 JANUARY: *Polonius*, HCL-M. FEBRUARY: accounts, HCL-M. MARCH: 9, HCL-M; ms, HCL-M. JUNE: 7, NYPL-GL; *Wonders of Engraving*, HCL-M. JULY: 20, HCL-M; 30, NYPL-GL. AUGUST: 5, NYPL-GL; 8, HCL-M; 9, NYPL-GL; NYPL-GL; NYPL-GL; [Oct 9, HCL-M] 26, NYPL-GL; NYPL-GL; NYPL-GL. OCTOBER: *Saint Elizabeth*, NYPL-GL; 8, NYPL-GL. DECEMBER: 3, NA-T; Tennant, unlocated

1876 JANUARY: 4, NYPL-GL; 14?, NYPL-GL. FEBRUARY: 2, NYPL-GL; NYPL-GL; 18, NYPL-GL; 29, NYPL-GL. MARCH: *Wills of Their Own*, HCL-M. APRIL: 22, NYPL-GL; 30, blotter, NYPL-D. MAY: 14, NYPL-GL; 26, blotter, NYPL-D; 30, blotter, NYPL-D.

JUNE: 4, NYPL-GL; 5, NYPL-GL; 6, *Clarel* to Elizabeth Melville [& facsimile], Metcalf; *Clarel* to the Parkers, NYStL; *Clarel* to Abraham Lansing, NYPL-RB; 12, blotter, NYPL-D; 17?, NYPL-GL; 21, NYPL-GL; 25, blotter, NYPL-D; 30, NYPL-GL. JULY: 8, NYPL-GL; 25, NYPL-GL; 31, draft?, NYPL-GL. AUGUST: accounts, HCL-M; 2, NYPL-GL; NYPL-GL; 15, NYPL-GL; 27, NYPL-GL. SEPTEMBER: 2, blotter, NYPL-D; 6, HCL-M; 8, NYPL-GL; 13, NYPL-GL; 17, blotter, NYPL-D; copy, NYPL-GL; 21, NYPL-GL; 26, NYPL-GL; 28, NA-T. OCTOBER: 12, NYPL-GL. NOVEMBER: 14, NYPL-GL; 22, NYPL-GL. DECEMBER: 25, Béranger, NYPL-GL; *Deserted Village*, Binnian; 29, HCL-M

1877 JANUARY: 2, NYPL-GL; HCL-M; 4, NYPL-GL; 6, blotter, NYPL-D; 21, HCL-M; 31, NYPL-GL. FEBRUARY: 25, NYPL-GL. MARCH: 7, NYPL-GL; 25, Hoadley mss, NYPL-GL; NYPL-GL; 31, NYPL-GL. APRIL: 8?, HCL-M; 13, NYPL-D; 15, NYPL-D. MAY: 9, NYPL-GL; 10, NYPL-GL; Beever, NYPL-O. JUNE: 4, NYPL-GL; 5, NYPL-GL; 17, NYPL-GL; 19, HCL-M; 28, NYPL-GL. JULY: 2, NYPL-GL; 12, NYPL-GL. AUGUST: 14, NYPL-GL. SEPTEMBER: 5, NYPL-GL. OCTOBER: 9, NYPL-GL; 24, diary, MHS-S. NOVEMBER: 13-17, blotter, NYPL-D. DECEMBER: 3, blotter, NYPL-D; 11, Doheny; inscribed engravings, Morewood; 31, NYPL-GL; 28, blotter, NYPL-D; *Memorial*, HCL-M

1878 JANUARY: 26, NYPL-GL; 30, blotter, NYPL-D. FEBRUARY: 9, accounts, HCL-M; 23, blotter, NYPL-D. MARCH: 24, NYPL-GL; 31, NYPL-GL. APRIL: 15, blotter, NYPL-D; 27, NYPL-GL. MAY: 7, blotter, NYPL-D; NYPL-GL; 28, NYPL-GL. JUNE: 4, blotter, NYPL-D; 15, NYPL-GL. JULY: 4, NYPL-GL; 28, NYPL-GL. AUGUST: 1, NYPL-GL; 10, NYPL-GL; 6, NYPL-GL; 12, NYPL-GL; 26, NYPL-GL. SEPTEMBER: 13, NYPL-GL. OCTOBER: 16, NYPL-GL. NOVEMBER: 6, NYPL-GL; 26, NYPL-GL. DECEMBER: 5, NYPL-GL; 19, NYPL-GL; 27, NYPL-GL; photograph, Binnian

1879 JANUARY: 3, NYPL-GL. FEBRUARY: 9, NYPL-GL; 25, NYPL-GL. MARCH: 2, NYPL-GL; 7, NYPL-GL; 14, NYPL-GL. APRIL: letter list, diary, NYPL-GL. JUNE: 2, NYPL-GL; diary, NYPL-GL. AUGUST: 10, NYPL-GL; 13, NYPL-GL; diary, MHS-S; 30, NYPL-GL. SEPTEMBER: diary, MHS-S. NOVEMBER: 15, letter list, Catherine Lansing's diary, NYPL-GL; 17, NYPL-GL; 18, diary, NYPL-GL; will, MHS-S; 19, diary, NYPL-GL. DECEMBER: 4, NYPL-GL; 15, NYPL-GL; 25, photograph, Binnian

1880 JANUARY: 14, NYPL-GL; 20, NYPL-GL. FEBRUARY: accounts, HCL-M. APRIL: invitation, Metcalf; 14, letter list, diary, NYPL-GL; 15, NYPL-GL. OCTOBER: 10, NYPL-GL. NOVEMBER: diary, NYPL-GL; memo on Bernhardt, Metcalf. DECEMBER: 1, NYPL-GL; 6, NYPL-GL; 8, NYPL-GL

IX. 1881-1891

1881 JANUARY: list in diary, NYPL-GL. MAY: diary, NYPL-GL. SUMMER: Prichett's *Omoo*, Scribner. DECEMBER: 28?, NYPL-GL

1882 FEBRUARY: 27, NYPL-GL. APRIL: NYPL-GL. MAY: diary, NYPL-GL. AUGUST: *Little Classics*, HCL-M; 28, NYPL-GL. SEPTEMBER: 8, NYPL-GL. OCTOBER: 27, autograph, pasted in *Clarel*, NYPL-RB; De Kay reminiscences, Wheelock. NOVEMBER: 13, fragment, NYPL-GL. DECEMBER: 18, MHS-S; diary, NYPL-GL

1883 JANUARY: *Sir Roger*, HCL-M. MARCH: Coffin volumes, HCL-M; *Omoo*

to Coffin, unlocated. MAY: *Centinel* reprint, HCL-M. AUGUST: 10, unlocated. SEPTEMBER: 14, NYPL-GL. DECEMBER: diary, NYPL-GL; *History of the Plague*, described in Dauber & Pine Catalogue 7, 1926; *Herald* clipping, HCL-M

1884 MARCH: obituary, Morewood; diary, NYPL-GL. MAY: diary, MHS-S. AUGUST: 1, *Book about Roses*, NYPL-O; 21, HCL-M. SEPTEMBER: accounts, HCL-M. OCTOBER: 10, Martin; 28, *Vane's Story*, unlocated. NOVEMBER: 25, NYPL-GL. DECEMBER: 1, Martin; diary, NYPL-GL; memo, Metcalf

1885 JANUARY: *City of Dreadful Night*, HCL-M; 7, NYPL-GL; 15, NYPL-GL; 19, diary, NYPL-GL; 22, Martin. APRIL: 8, NYPL-GL. MAY: 5, NYPL-GL; 14, NYPL-GL; *Quiver of Love*, NYPL-O. JUNE: 29, NYPL-GL; *Hawthorne and His Wife*, Metcalf. JULY: 7, NYPL-GL; 14, list in diary, NYPL-GL; 27, letterpress copy, NYPL-GL; 29, NYPL-GL. AUGUST: 1, *Balzac*, NYPL-O; 21, NYPL-GL. SEPTEMBER: 5, Martin; 9, letterpress copy, NYPL-GL; *Eagle* clipping, HCL-M. OCTOBER: 5, YUL-B; Thomson *Essays*, HCL-M. NOVEMBER: diary, NYPL-GL; 30, NYPL-GL. DECEMBER: 20, Martin; memoir, Metcalf; 31, NA-T.

1886 JANUARY: 10, NYPL-GL; 25, draft (in "Daniel Orme" ms), HCL-M. FEBRUARY: fragment, Metcalf; 14, power of attorney, NYPL-GL; *Voice from the Nile*, described by J. H. Birss in *Notes and Queries*, 5 March 1938; 24, NYPL-GL. MARCH: 16, NYPL-GL. APRIL: 2, Martin; water-colors, Metcalf; draft (in "Daniel Orme" ms), HCL-M. MAY: 5, NYPL-GL; transcript in Madigan, *Word-Shadows of the Great* (New York, 1930). JUNE: 7, NYPL-GL; 13, satires, HCL-M; 22, Bennett; NYPL-GL. JULY: 15, NYPL-GL; 21, HCL-M. AUGUST: 1, HCL-M; 7, Metcalf; Metcalf; 19, letterpress copy, NYPL-GL. SEPTEMBER: 28, letterpress copy, NYPL-GL. OCTOBER: 12, NYPL-GL; 15, letterpress copy, NYPL-GL. NOVEMBER: *Tea Leaves*, HCL-M; *Na Motu*, NYPL-O. DECEMBER: 25, *Childhood* & *Gems*, HCL-M

1887 MARCH: accounts, HCL-M; diary, NYPL-GL. MAY: *Gems*, HCL-M. JUNE: clipping, HCL-M. JULY: 16, NYPL-GL. SUMMER: information from Ferris Greenslet. OCTOBER: inscribed engraving, Metcalf

1888 JANUARY: 20, HCL-M; 24, HCL-M; 27, Vietor; 29, ms [facsimile], AAS. FEBRUARY: 1, HCL-M. MARCH: 15, book-rack, Metcalf; 26, passenger-list, NA-T; memo, Metcalf; 29, Martin. APRIL: 7, Martin; 10, HCL-M. MAY: diary, MHS-S. JUNE: 11, will, NY-HR; *Omoo* to Stevenson, HCL. JULY: 12, NYPL-GL; engraving from letter-head of the Surf Hotel. AUGUST: 13, Margaret Stevenson's letters, *From Saranac to the Marquesas* (New York, 1903). SEPTEMBER: diary, NYPL-GL; 6, *The Letters of Robert Louis Stevenson*, ed., Sir Sidney Colvin (New York, 1925); 7, [facsimile] ms of *John Marr*, HCL-M; deposit, HCL-M; 18, HCL-M. OCTOBER: 20, transcript in COL-S; *Life of Nelson*, HCL-M. NOVEMBER: *John Marr* to Elizabeth Melville, NYPL-O; *John Marr* to Stoddard, YUL-VV; 16, ms, HCL-M; clipping, HCL-M. DECEMBER: 4, *Shelley*, unlocated; 13, postmarked envelope, Morewood; diary, MHS-S; 31, Martin; annotated *White-Jacket*, Metcalf; clipping, HCL-M

1889 JANUARY: 4, YUL-B. FEBRUARY: 10, HCL-M. MARCH: 2, ms, HCL-M; 14-15, letterpress copies, NYPL-GL; 16, NYPL-GL; HCL-M. JUNE: 19, HCL-M; 30, NYPL-GL. AUGUST: Balzac *Correspondence*, NYPL-O; 8, clipping, HCL-M. SEPTEMBER: 8?, clipping, HCL-M; 23, will, MHS-S; 25, HCL-M. OCTOBER: 8, YUL-B. NOVEMBER: 20, NYSoL; 21, HCL-M. DECEMBER: 5, Willets; AAS; 23, HCL-M

1890 JANUARY: 5, HCL-M; 9, HCL-M; 12, Rosenbach; Murray V; 13, HCL-M; [Oct 24, 1892, YUL-V]. FEBRUARY: Thomson *Life*, HCL-M; 13, ms, HCL-M; YUL-A; *Letters of Robert Louis Stevenson*; 25, unlocated; 28, MHS-S. MARCH: 5, YUL-B; 23, HCL-M; 30, telegram, NYPL-GL. APRIL: 1, charge, NYSoL; 9, letterpress copy, COL-S; 18, charge, NYSoL; memoir, Metcalf. MAY: 23, Morewood; 31, charge, NYSoL. JUNE: 13, charge, NYSoL. JULY: 19, HCL-M. AUGUST: 10, Barrett. SEPTEMBER: clipping, NYPL-O. OCTOBER: 2, in La Farge, *Reminiscences of the South Seas* (Garden City, 1912); 14, letter-book, HCL; 20, HCL; 22, letter-book, HCL. DECEMBER: 14, diary, MHS-S; 17, NYPL-GL; Balzac's works, NYPL-O; draft & ms "Timoleon," HCL-M

1891 JANUARY: 8, NYPL-GL; 10-19, charges, NYSoL; La Farge *Reminiscences*. FEBRUARY: 5, charge, NYSoL; 6, *Letters of Henry Adams*, ed., W. C. Ford (Boston, 1930); 12, charge, NYSoL; Schopenhauer volumes, HCL-M; 13?, La Farge

Reminiscences; diary, NYPL-GL; 24, *Landseer's Dogs,* Metcalf. MARCH: La Farge *Reminiscences.* APRIL: 19, ms, HCL-M. MAY: ms, HCL-M; deposit, HCL-M; 28, NYPL-GL. JUNE: 13, transcript [by Elizabeth Melville], Metcalf; 16, deposit, LC-RB. AUGUST: ms, HCL-M. SEPTEMBER: 28, death certificate, NY-HR (copy, Murray); telegrams, NYPL-GL; NYPL-GL; diary, NYPL-GL

PLATES

Front: harpoon, engraving from Scammon, *The Marine Mammals of the North-western Coast of North America* (San Francisco, 1874) / Melville's Customs Inspector's badge, Metcalf

I: Allan Melvill portrait, HL

II: Maria Melvill portrait, Murray (photograph by Frick Art Reference Library)

III: Gansevoort Melville miniature, NYPL-GL / R. T. Greene daguerreotype, Metcalf

IV: Henry Johnson journal, Loring

V: Lemuel Shaw daguerreotype, Metropolitan / Elizabeth & Malcolm Melville daguerreotype, Binnian

VI: Twitchell portrait of Melville, Metcalf

VII: Allan & Sophia Melville daguerreotypes, Morewood

VIII: photographs of Helen Maria, Augusta, & Frances Priscilla Melville, NYPL-GL / photograph of Catherine Hoadley, Morewood

IX: Arrowhead drawing unlocated; reproduced from photograph, Weaver / Arrowhead photograph, Morewood

X: Hawthorne engraving, Metcalf / Hoadley photograph, Morewood

XI: Maria Melville photograph, Morewood / Herman & Thomas Melville ambrotype, HCL-M / Melville children photograph, Metcalf

XII: Gansevoort photographs, NYPL-GL

XIII: Melville photographs, Metcalf

XIV: Melville portrait & photographs, Metcalf

XV: Elizabeth & Herman Melville photographs, NYPL-GL / Frances Melville & Henry Thomas photograph, Metcalf (copy by Bachrach) / Bessie Melville photograph, Metcalf / Stanwix Melville photograph, Morewood

The Endless Study

When brought together, the bibliography intended for this book added too many pages to an already cumbersome work. I must be content to say that, to the best of my knowledge, all materials in print relevant to Melville were consulted, though my reading of criticisms printed since his death may have been less thorough. Printed materials quoted in the text are identified there, with further information, when necessary, given in the locations of textual sources.

It seemed better to use this space for a listing of my sins of omission, numerous though they be. These are the things I am conscious of having left undone — the errands I should have run, the unfollowed hints, the pursuits still waiting for a hunter. Although the Log offers a maximum number of clues for further investigation, there are certainly important clues and materials left behind, unnoticed by me, in every collection searched, whether public (such as the bottomless riches of the Gansevoort-Lansing Collection) or such concentrated private collections as the whaling libraries of Paul C. Nicholson and M. M. Armstrong. Here are some of the waiting jobs:

There is more to be learned about the childhood through the papers of early family friends, doctors, ministers, teachers, and business associates of Allan Melvill, so it would have been very worthwhile to look for the descendants of Caroline Yates Taylor, Daniel P. Parker, Joseph Greenleaf, and others mentioned in those years. (Though the family of the Revd Robert Swan does not now live in Pittenweem, it should be somewhere in Scotland.)

Whole branches of the family were left untraced, merely through my discouragement with the known destruction of family papers. Where are the papers of the Peebles? Van Schaicks? Of the D'Wolfs? And some relatives have been left total mysteries — for example, cousin Doolittle, the Lenox expressman. A main hope in outlining the family trees of the Melvills, Gansevoorts, and Shaws (among the biographical sketches) is that this may lead to other relevant archives.

The newspapers of each port touched by one of M's ships should have been examined for the period while the *Acushnet*, the *United States*, the *Cortes*, etc., were in port. A knowledge of Spanish would have encouraged this, perhaps.

Despite his many names and peculiar talents, the career of John B. Troy before and after Tahiti should be traceable.

No real search was made for Franklin D. Roosevelt's trunk of ships' logs — reported missing on 30 July 1947 by the Director of the Franklin D. Roosevelt Library at Hyde Park.

Luther Fox of Rensselaerville, N. Y., was too close to a Melville neighborhood to be ignored either before or after Honolulu. If Fox is found to have worked on an Erie Canal boat, Steelkilt will have been located.

Where are the papers and journals of M's messmates and traveling companions – of Hubbard, Cunningham, Mr & Miss Rousse? Where are the descendants of Herman Melville Greene and Herman Melville Russ?

I left two places of prime importance unvisited and unsearched: Galena and Gansevoort. And I did not go to England. And the promises of East Hampton, Long Island, were never tested.

Certain newspapers were not carefully examined, even such promising ones as Cramer's *Daily Wisconsin;* and vital years of the *Berkshire Eagle,* now missing from the office file, remain unfound and uninspected.

There is more published work by M than has been identified – there is surely more in *The Albany Microscope,* and there are too many later suggestions (essays of the *Mardi* period, the excursion to West Point, perhaps even "Agatha") to ignore this probability.

The papers of those supporters of M (outside the Duyckinck circle), such as Willis and Curtis, should have been more persistently sought, along with the papers of friends on the edge of literature, such as Doctors Lockwood and Gardner. And it seems unthinkable that no more remains to be discovered about the life and ideas of E. J. M. Fly, E. C. Hine, Col. Rankin, Alexander Bradford, William E. Cramer, Dr Oscar De Wolf.

More hard work should have gone into the identification of M's reviewers, both friendly and unfriendly, to see what lies behind their anonymity, and the personal papers of identified reviewers (such as Briggs, Bourne, Ripley, Jones) should have been located and examined for further information.

With the voyages of Thomas Melville occurring during M's first creative years, all his ships & experiences should be more fully investigated, as a source possibly drawn on by his brother.

It is merely another symptom of incompleteness that the only foreign language comments on M should be from France, a country that did not (as far as is known) publish his works during the author's lifetime, while the reviews in those countries that did publish translations have not been located – though they certainly exist. Many contemporary translations may remain to be discovered.

I have left the "Powell Papers" as much a mystery as I found them; the second volume of his *Living Authors of America,* announced by Stringer & Townsend for publication in 1850, with a chapter on Melville, could not have vanished so totally. Newspaper serial publication is a probability.

The trickle through the autograph market of M's letters to his American publishers and editors indicates the chance that a fuller picture of his relations with Wiley & Putnam, Harper's, etc., is yet to be uncovered.

Despite the almost accidental finds of reprintings (as far scattered as Buffalo and Salem) of M's anonymous periodical writing, no systematic search of all American newspapers of the '50s was made.

I did not employ a maximum effort to examine the Special Collections of Columbia University for Melville references.

With the number of Melville's friends and relatives whose lives ended at the Bloomingdale and other asylums, the archives of these institutions should have been examined – correspondence, visitor records, case histories – if any of this material has been preserved.

A conspicuous failure: my inability to trace the originals of those Melville letters to Hawthorne that we are still obliged to use through the published transcripts by Hawthorne's children.

Who wrote and syndicated "The Career of Mocha Dick" (copyright 1892)? Is it a fake?

The movements of Stanwix Melville, especially in California, were not too secret to be traced; the archives of the hospital in which he died were *not* destroyed in the San Francisco fire of 1906.

Hudson, Loti, Conrad — they were certainly touched off by a spark of Herman Melville, but when and how, exactly?

Perhaps this book should have been more rightly named — *Melville: The Endless Study*.

J. L.

*

INDEX

*

Index

Index

Index

Index

Index

C

Index

Campbell, Alexander, *Sketches of Life and Character*, 620

Campbell, Robert, 634

Campbell, 811

Campbell's lecture room, 60

Canada, packet ship, 332

Canoll, J. W. Henry, 796-797

Canterbury Cathedral, 325-326

Capelle, Mme, 340-341, 343, 366

Capitol, clipper ship, 457

"Career of Mocha Dick," 106-108, 118, 154-155, 607

Carleton, J. W., *The Natural History of the "Hawk" Tribe*, 800

Carlyle, Thomas, 299, 303, 312-313, 371, 437
German Romance, 376, 396

Carolus, Italian brig, 759-760

Carpenter, George W., 45

Carr, 201

Carson's "Old Red Mill," 403

Cary, Alice, 676

Cary, Rev Henry Francis, 278

Cary, Phoebe, 676

Carysfort, British, 170

Casco, yacht, 807

Cass, 184

Casserly, 204

Cassidy, William, 61

Caswell, John M., 79

Caxton Press, 834

Cayuga Tocsin, The, 186

Center, Capt, 9

Center, Rev Samuel, 64

Century Club, New York, 717

Century Magazine, 385

Cervantes, Miguel, *Don Quixote*, 173, 490, 508, 532, 549

Chace, *see* Chase

Chalmers, Alexander, ed., *The British Essayists*, 616

Chalmers, Thomas, 352

Chamberlain, Levi, 169

Chambers, Ephraim, *Cyclopædia: or, An Universal Dictionary of Arts and Sciences*, 231

Chambers, Sir William, 330

Chambers's Edinburgh Journal, 212-214, 225, 228, 246

Chamier, Frederic, 338

Chancellor Livingston, Hudson River steamer, 9, 15, 18, 34

Chandlen, William E., 683

Channing, William Ellery, jr, 268, 436, 465

Channing, 254

Chapman, Frederic, 337-338

Chapman, George, 332, 595-596, 626-627

Chapman, John, 517

Chapman & Hall, 337

Charlemagne, 339, 344

Charles I, 523

Charles II, 336

Charles and Henry, whaleship, xxiv, xxxiii, 65, 110, 152-156, 158-159, 162-165, 198

Charles Carroll, whaleship, 125, 128

Chase, Frederic Hathaway, *Lemuel Shaw*, 639

Chase, John, 172-174, 182, 377, 578

Chase, Joseph, 111

Chase, Owen, 107, 114, 119, 125-126, 128
Narrative, 119, 407, 409

Chase, William Henry, 119, 128

Chasles, Victor Euphémion Philarète, 219, 300-301, 303-304, 307, 310-311

Chateaubriand, François Auguste René, Vicomte de, *Atala*, 210
Memoirs, 294

Chatham Theatre, 311

Chatterton, Thomas, 350, 363-364, 483

Chaucer, Geoffrey, 714, 753, 756, 765

Cheever, Rev George B., 210

Chenery, Cyrus, 25

Cheney, Theseus Apoleon, 706

Chester Cathedral, 530

Chesterfield, Philip Dormer Stanhope, 4th Earl of, 19, 83

Chicago Magazine, 578

Chicago Tribune, The, 259

Child, Francis James, 608

Childs, W. L., 690

Childs Albany Directory, 54, 59, 64-65

Childs Paper, 602

Chorley, Henry Fothergill, 204, 365

Christian Examiner, The, 276

Christian Observatory, The, 246

Christian Parlor Magazine, The, 224

Christian Union and Religious Memorial, 355

Church, 672

Church, Nathan, 91

Church of the Sepulchre, 544-545

Churchill, Charles, 650

Cibber, Colley, *She Would, and She Would Not*, 332

Cicero, 577

Ciceronian Debating Society, Albany, 79

Cincinnati Daily Gazette, 591

Cincinnati Enquirer, 591

Index

Index

Index

Index

Index

Index

Index

Index

Index

Index

Index

Index

Index

Index

Index

Index

Index

Index

Springer, John S., *Forest Life and Forest Trees*, 447

Squier, Ephraim George (*pseud.* Samuel A. Bard), *Waikna*, 506

Staël-Holstein, Anne Louise Germaine (Necker), Baronne de, 651
Corinne; or, Italy, 323, 351
Germany, 647, 651

Stanley, Arthur Penrhyn, *Sinai and Palestine*, 710

Stanly, Joseph, 171

Stanly, 506

Stanton, Edwin M., 659, 666, 673

Stanwix Hall, Albany, 74-76, 79, 644, 753

Star, schooner, 165

Starr, Dr Alfred, 690, 732, 742

Starr, George, 689, 742

Steadman, J. Warren, 400

Stearns, Norman W., 599

Stedman, Arthur, xxxiii, 445, 451, 583, 753, 804-805, 821, 836-837

Stedman, Edmund Clarence, xxxiii, 620, 750, 787, 804-806, 810, 823, 831
A Library of American Literature, 805, 819
Poets of America, 804

Stephens, Ann Sophia, 580

Stephens, John Lloyd, 248

Sterne, Lawrence, 295, 303
Tristram Shandy, 348

Stetson, Charles, 122

Stetson, John, 119, 130, 165-167

"Stetson," 330

Stevens, 338-339, 349

Stevenson, James, 31, 50, 286, 408

Stevenson, Mrs Margaret, 808

Stevenson, Robert Louis, 807-809, 822
The South Seas, 833
The Wrecker, 808

Stewart, Charles S., *A Visit to the South Seas*, 48, 261

Stewart, Judge, 480

Stibbs, Edward Cambridge, 332-333, 350, 365

Stoddard, Charles Warren, 693, 800, 807-808, 833
Summer Cruising in the South Seas, 736, 800, 831

Stoddard, Richard Henry, xxxiii, 445, 684, 710, 735, 750, 810-811
The Lion's Cub, 831

Stoddard, Mrs R. H. [Elizabeth Drew Barstow], 710

Stokes, Mrs J. H., 318

Stone, Henry D., 76

Stone, William Leete, *Life of Joseph Brant*, 432

Stone, 351

Storer, Capt, 247

Storer, 247

Story, Judge, 280

Stowe, Harriet Beecher, 523
Uncle Tom's Cabin, 465

Strangford, Lord Viscount, 686

Strasbourgh Cathedral, 574

Strauss, 551

Street, Alfred Billings, 459-461, 477, 756, 764
Frontenac, 683

Stribling, C. K., 172, 180-181, 184

Stringer & Townsend, 370

Stuart, Lord Dudley, 468

Stuart-Wortley, Lady Emmeline Charlotte Elizabeth [Manners], 334

Sturgis, Russell, 334

Sullivan, Mrs, 297, 301

Sully, Thomas, 262

Sumner, Charles, 254, 312, 372, 454-455, 634-639, 666

Sun, Baltimore, 432

Sun, London, 208

Surr, Thomas Skinner, *A Winter in London*, 60

Surrey Theatre, London, 350, 352

Swain, William, 453

Swan, Rev Robert, 6, 745

Swedenborg, 319, 559

Sweeney, Daniel, 96, 110

Sweet, Dr, 62

Swift, Jonathan, 530, 563
Gulliver's Travels, 293, 295, 299, 304
Tale of a Tub, 339

Swift, Capt, 113

Swiftsure, Hudson River steamer, 45

Sylva, Amado, 139, 143, 153

Symmons, Dr, 289

Symonds, A., *At John Murray's*, 200

T

Taber, John, 267

Tairapa, 141

Taithorn, R. J., 318

Tait's Edinburgh Magazine, 212

Talfourd, Thomas Noon, *Final Memorials of Charles Lamb*, 336, 363

Tammany Hall, 132-133, 188, 270, 290

Tappan, Lewis[?], 393-394, 418

Tasso, Torquato, 558, 563, 646-647

Index

Index

Index